The Constant and Changing Faces of the Goddess

The Constant and Changing Faces of the Goddess: Goddess Traditions of Asia

Edited by

Deepak Shimkhada and Phyllis K. Herman

The Constant and Changing Faces of the Goddess: Goddess Traditions of Asia,
Edited by Deepak Shimkhada and Phyllis K. Herman

This book first published 2007. The present binding first published 2009.

Cambridge Scholars Publishing

12 Back Chapman Street, Newcastle upon Tyne, NE6 2XX, UK

British Library Cataloguing in Publication Data
A catalogue record for this book is available from the British Library

Cover design by Sushil Ranjit, Colorado, USA, sushilranjit@gmail.com

ISBN (10): 1-4438-1134-3, ISBN (13): 978-1-4438-1134-7

TABLE OF CONTENTS

ACKNOWLEDGMENTS

The editors would like to thank all the contributors to this volume for their time, energy and research to make the volume come together as a nicely woven tapestry of thoughts. The editors would also like to express their gratitude to the Foundation for Indic Philosophy and Culture, affiliated with the School of Religion at Claremont Graduate University, and the Gould Center for Humanistic Studies of Claremont McKenna College for grants in support of the volume. To Dr. Marilee Scaff and Mary Hicks for their meticulous editorial hands in shaping the volume in its present condition the editors owe their gratitude. For her many valuable comments on the manuscript the editors are indebted to Prof. Cynthia Humes. Finally, the editors would like to thank the editorial staff at CSP for putting up with them while the volume was in production.

—The editors

PREFACE

The rise of the American women's movement in the 1970s opened the way for a cultural engagement with the goddess traditions of Asian religions. This cultural engagement, however intellectually challenging or experientially transforming, was nonetheless framed by the ideological and social system of western monotheism. In the harsh light of a newly awakening feminist consciousness western monotheism appeared as thoroughly masculinized. Visual representations of the Christian deity and the savior who appeared in the world were male. Further, the notion of the incarnation of the deity in the form of a son only intensified the experience of the divine as masculine. Finally the powers and benefits of the divine were mediated exclusively through a male hierarchy of priests and clergy. These mediators, popes, bishops and priests are richly represented in Christian iconography.

In terms of social organization western patriarchy had much in common with patriarchal social orders in the rest of the world. Political power was exercised primarily, if not exclusively, by males in the social order and male dominance was the norm in the family. However, in monotheistic patriarchal societies the fact that the symbolic order was masculine meant that male dominance in the social order was difficult to dislodge. The interest, then, of American feminists in Asian goddess traditions arose out the need to imagine an alternative symbolic order where the cosmic powers of the divine were not thoroughly masculinized. The Asian context provided them with an unimaginable wealth of resources. Their encounter with Asian goddesses was mediated by monographs on particular goddesses and anthologies of goddess traditions from a region that provided an introduction to the myths, character, and exploits of the goddesses. American feminists saw in these resources the possibility of imagining a different symbolic order and appropriated them as a "theology," an alternative to the system of ideas and symbols of Christian theology.

Much was missing in this first encounter. The goddess traditions of Asia are richer and more complex than the narratives and iconographies of their goddesses. They are essential elements of a vast diversity of cultures, integrated and integrating factors in social, familial, agricultural, economic, and political life. A fuller encounter with Asian goddess traditions will require meeting the goddesses as they participate in the cultural worlds of their devotees. To study goddess traditions will also require studying the cultures in which they play important roles.

Specific cultural contexts are complex, with ethnic, racial, class and religious diversity within them, and the figure of the goddess becomes increasingly complex when read in terms of such a cultural microcosm. Piya Chatterjee in "Towards a Ritual Political Economy of the Goddess" provides an excellent example. The plantation economic of Northern Bengal with its feudal, colonial and post-colonial social orders creates an economic and social matrix within which the goddess appears differently. In the lavish celebrations organized by the plantocracy her powers are mediated by patrons and priests, in the domestic space of a Nepali woman her powers are mediated by the possession trances of a Nepali woman. Power—political, economic and religious power—is mediated differently in each of these contexts. The modes of mediation are multiple, through festivals, temples, ritual, propitiations, dance, discipleship, trance, and dreams; each of these intersect with gender, ethnicity, caste and class in different ways. Some modes of mediation stabilize existing economic and political relationships, others challenge or subvert them. Although the goddess is integral to multiple contexts, her roles simply mirror the complexities of the social world she inhabits.

In fact the political and social contexts generate ever new incarnations of the goddess and configurations of her power as Mary-Ann Milford-Lutzker shows in her "Politicization of an Icon." The nationalist movement in India called forth a new manifestation of the goddess as Bharat Mata, Mother India, who was at the same time a symbol of the nation and an embodiment of the land itself, invoked even as a secular symbol to make her appeal universal. During the bloody struggle with the British her iconography drew on the fearless warrior goddess Durga and the ferocious bloody Kali. The revolutionary freedom fighters called on their followers to imitate her. After independence Bharat Mata was invoked as a purely Hindu goddess, an icon for the emerging Nationalist Party.

This collection of articles gathered under the title, *The Constant and Changing Faces of the Goddess: Goddess Traditions of Asia*, offers the possibility of a genuine cross-cultural encounter with manifestations of the goddess in Asia, for most of these articles are interested in the goddesses at work in their cultural contexts. This collection goes beyond questions of who is the goddess? what are her manifestations? what are her characteristics? to the larger question of what work does the goddess do in her cultural context?

This collection is further enriched by the inclusion of articles that deepen the conversation between eastern and western perspectives on the feminine divine. Gang Song's article explores the influence of the Virgin Mary brought to China by the Jesuits on the figure of Gunayin, the beloved Chinese goddess of mercy. The most fascinating of these east/west conversations is Janet Hoskins's sketch of Caodaism, a new religion that emerged in the 1920s as a Vietnamese synthesis of Asia religions resulting from the domination of China and French Catholic Christianity imposed during the colonial period into a nationalist religion with a universal message. The addition of Joan of Arc to the pantheon of nine female immortals responds both to the women's movement and the need to make the French colonial legacy decidedly Vietnamese. Through these articles we see the goddess traditions operate also as a form of international currency that passes between cultures and is transformed in the process.

Goddess traditions are dynamic, continuously evolving, shaped by the local dramas of politics, the tensions between ethnic groups, the struggles over economic resources, and the needs to claim, subvert or defend class identities. Goddess figures are also fluid, they are capable of multiple manifestations; they borrow from each other's stories, and absorb each other's characteristics. This collection documents both the constant and the changing face of the goddess.

—Karen Jo Torjesen
Dean, School of Religion and Director, Women's Studies
Claremont Graduate University

INTRODUCTION

THE EDITORS

The genesis of this volume originated when Shimkhada was asked to host the 2005 Asian Studies on the Pacific Coast (ASPAC) conference in Claremont, California.[1] The conference presentations focused on the multiplicity of Asian goddesses: their continuities, discontinuities, and importance as symbols of wisdom, power, transformation, compassion, destruction, and creation. The title of the volume, *Constant and Changing Faces of the Goddess: Goddess Traditions of Asia,* reflects the inherent complexity and paradoxical nature of the goddess. Although the nucleus of this volume resulted from the 2005 ASPAC conference, the editors wanted the book to be more than a "conference proceedings." To that end, additional scholars were invited in order to provide a more varied representation of the goddess tradition of Asia, culminating in our selections drawing from research on Indian, Nepali, Chinese, Japanese, and Vietnamese traditions.

The essays contained herein demonstrate that while treatments of the goddess may vary regionally, culturally, and historically, it is possible to note some consistencies in the overall picture of the goddess in Asia. She can be, among others, lover, wife, mother, destroyer, transformer, agent of salvation, and ecological archetype.

This book provides a comprehensive treatment of subjects that we hope will be useful for students in religious studies, gender studies, and women's studies. With the intent of making the volume truly broad in scope, an effort has been made to include works written by art historians, sociologists, anthropologists, and religious studies scholars.[2] Culture

---

[1] It was the thirty-ninth conference of the Asian Studies on the Pacific Coast since it began organizing conferences annually. Although other universities on the Pacific Coast had previously hosted the conference, Claremont Graduate University was honored to host the conference for the first time in 2005.

[2] For example, the essay about the Bharat Mata is written by an art historian using art historical methodology, such as iconography, to study the evolution of the ontological concept of the goddess, whereas "Meeting the Goddess: Religion, Morality, and Medicine in a Fishing Community in Hong Kong Forty Years Ago,"

cannot be separated from religion; they are intertwined as an organic whole, and variations manifest themselves in the rituals and daily lives of the people. In this sense, all the essays are interconnected: the goddess manifests in many forms and appeals to differing aspects of a particular culture as a paradigm of the divine feminine, yet we recognize the unique nature of each of the Asian goddess traditions.

For the sake of thematic convenience the volume has been divided into five sections: 1) In the Beginning, 2) The Malleable Goddess: Historical Transformations of the Goddess, 3) Meeting the Goddess: Economics and Politics of the Goddess, 4) One and Many: Multiplicity and Manifestations of the Goddess, and 5) Myth Making and Serving the Goddess Today.

In her essay, Helen Hye-Sook Hwang reconstructs the ancient Korean religion devoted to Mago, the Great Goddess from East Asia. Magoism, as she terms it, was the primary tradition of Korea up until the seventeenth century. Hwang argues that because of its fierce adherence to female principles, the ancient roots have been erased and distorted by official historiographers and East Asian patriarchal ideologues. She shows how nationalism, ethnocentrism, and colonialism contributed to an effort to perpetuate male domination over women and nature.

In the section "The Malleable Goddess: Historical Transformations of the Goddess," our contributors focus on how the identity of a goddess can shift through history. David Gray shows how Dākinīs and Yoginīs are incorporated into the ostensibly "nontheistic" Buddhist religion. They appear to have been originally considered by Buddhists to be demonic entities, but have eventually become important but sometimes dangerous, not completely "rehabilitated" Buddhist goddesses, who inspired Tibetan female practitioners.

Phyllis K. Herman's "Sita Masala: From the Vedas to the Kitchen" reveals how the Valmiki heroine, Sita, the "embodied furrow," encompasses and integrates many of the pre-historic and historic functions of an agricultural great goddess figure. Through morphologies of gold, fire, agricultural prosperity, and purity, Sita proves herself to be the embodiment of the wealth of the earth: a furrow made fertile by fire, and always a gold, luminescent being. Ancient goddess worship associated with agriculture and especially the production of plentiful food may have combined in the history of Hinduism to situate Sita in the most suitable site for her worship in the modern age—the kitchen.

---

and "Lakshmi and Alakshmi: The Kojagari Lakshmi Vrata Katha of Bengal" are written by anthropologists. Similarly, other essays are written by experts in the religious studies field.

Kenneth D. Lee introduces the Bodhisattva of Compassion, Avalokiteśvara, who has gone through various transformations for the sake of helping sentient beings in different cultures and time periods. Technically speaking, he explains, a bodhisattva does not have any gender characteristics because ultimate reality is emptiness (*śūnyatā*). Through multicultural engineering, however, the East Asians envisioned Avalokiteśvara in the forms of Kuan-yin in China, Kwanse'um in Korea, Kannon in Japan, and Quan-um in Vietnam, graceful and powerful feminine symbols that illustrate the quintessence of the Bodhisattva of Compassion. Lee demonstrates how these multiple images have been inspired and popularized by many legends, folklore, and artistic work, revealing historic trends and cultural differences throughout Asia.

Janet Hoskins describes Caodaism, a new religion born in 1926 in Saigon. Known officially as Dao Dao Tam Ky Pho Do, "The Great Way of the Third Revelation," Caodaism celebrates new revelations through spirit messages that affirm the common origin of all world traditions. Accordingly, Caodaism presents an Asian synthesis of the three great East Asian traditions; includes Judeo-Christian figures such as Jesus Christ and Moses; and even integrates the veneration of spirits of nature and great heroes, such as Victor Hugo, the Chinese poet Li Bai, and Joan of Arc. Veneration of the Mother Goddess and of female saints and deities such as Quan Am (also Kuan Yin, Kannon, Guanyin), Joan of Arc, and the Virgin Mary appeal to followers of feminist spirituality, but rules pertaining to marriage, divorce and the family seem to reassert traditional sex roles rather than displacing them. Still, Hoskins notes the ideological gender parity of Caodaism, and further documents the historical "feminization" of the religion in both its leadership and membership.

Using both visual and textual sources, Gang Song explores the competitive relationship between the Virgin Mary and Guanyin in late Ming China. Gong first draws a comprehensive picture of religious life in early seventeenth-century China. Next, Gong shows how both Guanyin and Mary were depicted as intercessors between two worlds: humanity and divinity, male and female, good and evil, and body and spirit. The Virgin Mary arrived at a time when Guanyin had gained great popularity as savioress of the world and rekindled the goddess tradition in China, setting up a favorable environment for the introduction of the Holy Mother who shared many similarities in iconography, miraculous life, and worship patterns. These deities were meaningful to worshippers in different periods and places in a process of continual negotiation as religious rivals.

In the third section, "Meeting the Goddess: Economics and Politics of the Goddess," our authors examine the various forces of the goddess propelled by distinct economic and political factors in society. E. N. Anderson, for example, reevaluates in light of recent scholarship his meeting the goddess Tin Hau as she possessed a spirit medium in a Hong Kong fishing community decades ago. Tin Hau was merciful, familial, and gentle—dutiful daughter and sister to her father and brothers, and then dutiful mother-figure to her seafaring worshipers. Just as Tin Hau acted dramatically and bravely to save her male kin, as a divine savioress she was a powerful defender and protector, combating other supernaturals to care for her charges on the water. As we have seen in the case of other deities studied in this book, Tin Hau could take on the iconography and features of Kun Yam (Guanyin), the most popular female deity in China, to such a degree that in some areas the two are equated. In her mode of possession, the goddess interacted with humans as one of their community, a living, breathing, vocal person, one they knew and understood.

Piya Chatterjee offers an ethnographic case study of divine embodiment, women, and labor in the tea plantations of North Bengal. She shows how gender and power affect the "labors of spiritual action" for her subject, Durga Mata. Durga Mata is believed to have direct access to the sacred; in "becoming" the goddess, she allows us to see some of the gendered complexities inhered with heterodox and folk traditions of religious belief—and the politics of literacy and faith. When the goddess' manifestations are situated within the terms of "political economy," it troubles the Durkheimian binary between the "sacred" and the "profane."

Mary-Ann Milford-Lutzker describes how the once-gentle, docile figure of Bharat Mata—Mother India, initially secular in nature and universal in its inclusiveness, was transformed into the patron deity of the Indian Independence movement *Swaraj*. *Bande Mataram* (Hail to the Mother) became the rallying cry for the revolutionaries. Over a period of decades, Mother India absorbed the iconography and mythical powers of various deities. Yet the author shows that Mother India is portrayed variously by new artists even today, demonstrating the power and variability of this goddess.

In her essay June McDaniel offers multiple glimpses of Kali in some of her temples in West Bengal. She demonstrates that in the Bengali tradition of *Shaktism*, the worship of *Shakti* or feminine divine power, there are three major outlooks or types: folk, *tantric/yogic,* and *bhakti*. Each of these types understands the goddess in different ways. Further, Kali manifests herself in various forms. She may be seen in visionary experiences or *darshan*, she may be ritually placed in statues, she may spontaneously appear in rocks and springs, and she may pervade the atmosphere of sacred sites. She may also enter the minds of human beings, and fully or partially take them over.

Bidyut Mohanty focuses on the linkages between Orissa's agrarian economy, the role of women, and the Oriya language scripture called the *Laksmi Vrat-katha*. Since the sixteenth century, the *Vrat-katha* or vow story of Lakshmi, has been annually recited in each and every household of rural Orissa on the occasion of *Laksmi puja* in the months of late October and early November. The *Laksmi Vrat- katha* was consciously developed by a social reformer to help make people aware of the contributions of women in the agrarian economy. It has been a continuous legitimizing force in Orissan society. Mohanty's textual analysis of the Oriya *Vrat-katha* shows the ways in which the text acknowledges the contributions of women, as well as how it reflects and informs images of women in their own eyes as well as in the eyes of society.

In the section on "One and Many: Multiplicity and Manifestations of the Goddess," the goddess manifests in many forms—*bhudevi* (as mother earth), *goma* (as mother cow), and of course, as the beautiful Saraswati, the goddess of learning, among others. Here lies the ability of the goddess to appear in as many forms as the situation demands.

Christopher Key Chapple explores historical references with import for modern Hindu views of ecology. According to traditional Indian philosophy and cosmology, the world is a gendered, feminine place. Throughout the Indian story tradition, women have embodied the power symbolized by numerous goddesses. By giving honor to the earth, women give honor to the goddess and recognize the power of the goddess who resides within them. Chapple shows that women in all corners of India and beyond draw on the imagery of the goddess to communicate a modern message. He asserts that devotion to the goddess in both traditional and contemporary forms can stir the world to an increased sense of urgency in regard to the plight of Mother Earth. He closes with a brief survey of contemporary work by women scholars and activists in creating dance, dramas, artwork, and rituals that honor the earth. Through this connection between the earth goddess and the current state of the world, these women have publicized the contemporary issue of environmental degradation.

Shimkhada writes of Goma, an embodiment of the goddess who serves as the protagonist of the Sanskrit text *Swasthani Brata Katha*. Although Goma is portrayed as an ordinary woman in the story, the extraordinary circumstances in which she was born and the challenges she faced clearly place her in the category of a goddess. Goma is depicted as a goddess in mortal form who, like her counterparts Sati and Parvati, overcomes multiple obstacles hurled at her by the Lord Shiva in an attempt to force her surrender. Born of cow dung, Goma the mortal girl transforms herself into a goddess incarnate in her later life.

Drawing from her position as a feminist and non-Indian goddess devotee, and therefore not obliged to fulfill what is still perceived to be the ultimate role for every woman in India, Małgorzata (Margaret) Kruszewska reconsiders the myths and iconography of Sarasvati. She proposes that by acknowledging Sarasvati as "She who has no husband, no child," followers can begin to redefine for themselves the female principle in goddesses. Rather than the traditional role models of female *shakti* powers that are tied to domesticity and motherhood, Kruszewska suggests revisioning and reclaiming Sarasvati as another aspect of the sacred feminine, thus becoming a viable alternative to goddesses defined mainly in their duties as mothers and wives. Kruszewska demonstrates Sarasvati's ability to serve as a potent resource for modern feminist Devi adherents.

Chia-Lan Chang discusses the appearance of vegetarian nuns serving as abbesses in convents and temples in the late nineteenth century. Chang explains that these vegetarian nuns are not *bhiksunis* (fully ordained Buddhist nuns), because they receive neither *bhiksuni* precepts nor tonsure, according to Vinaya Pitaka (Buddhist discipline). Similar to the unshaven laywoman image of Bodhisattva Avalokitesvara in the legend of Miaoshan, an indigenous manifestation of the Bodhisattva Avalokitesvara or Guanyin in China, vegetarian nuns do not express their religious piety in the form of receiving tonsure or Buddhist ordination rites, but rather in their religious consciousness and daily practice. Vegetarian nuns leave their families, practice *pancasila* (Five Precepts) or Bodhisattva-samvara (Bodhisattva Precepts), and live in convents under a vow of celibacy. They subjectively identify themselves as orthodox Buddhist nuns and obtain recognition as such from both Buddhists and the public in Quanzhou. Vegetarian nuns thus embody the legend of Miaoshan and constitute an alternative female *sangha* (monastic order) between fully ordained Buddhist nuns and *upasikas* (female lay devotees). The goals of vegetarian nuns are to seek purity and assurance of a favorable reincarnation through celibacy. Resistance to marriage and influence of family members are the most common motives for vegetarian nuns' participation in the monastic order.

Like Chang, Sthaneshwar Timalsina sees an opportunity for goddess imagery to support newly important sensibilities. Timalsina explores select Hindu myths of the goddess that reverberate in romantic literature to support an embodied cosmology and enlightened ecological vision. He puts forth a non dual argument that plants and humans coexist in partnership, and should remain free from the complex of domination. This new rationale redefines what is perceived as right action. If one adopts the rationale that a human being does not own the land or control property but is a caretaker and steward, the human being is thus not removed from the land but is part and parcel of the dust from which he comes and to which he returns. Timalsina illustrates this sentiment through various myths, and thereby provides an Indian model of ecological awareness.

Like the goddess with her multiple personae, this volume brings together multifaceted papers that place the goddesses of Asia in proper perspectives. Although most of the primary sources on Asian goddesses began to appear in English translations in the 1960s and 1970s, the study of the South, East, and Southeast Asian goddess as a subject of academics has been somewhat lacking. These works tended to focus primarily on iconography or history. Interpreting the goddess within the context of cultural, religious, social, economic, and even political contexts is a recent development. We will consider this volume a contribution to this current trend of study if it enables readers to trace the varied threads in which the tapestry of the Asian goddess is woven.

PART I

IN THE BEGINNING

CHAPTER ONE

ISSUES IN STUDYING MAGO, THE GREAT GODDESS OF EAST ASIA: PRIMARY SOURCES, GYNOCENTRIC HISTORY, AND NATIONALISM

HELEN HYE-SOOK HWANG

Mago麻姑[1] is the Great Goddess from East Asia whose tradition has been forgotten in the course of history but nonetheless survives to this day. Although the subject of Mago remains largely unexplored, I have documented a wealth of primary sources from Korea, China, and Japan. In analyzing and theorizing these sources, I have unveiled a complex and systemic tradition that is derived from the veneration of Mago as supreme divinity and named it Magoism. While the term Magoism is my neologism, its concept proves to be ancient in origin. Magoism is explicitly and implicitly referred to as "the State of Mago," "the Principle of Mago," and "the Affair of Mago" in various literature from Korea.[2] Magoism connotes

---

[1] Pronounce Ma as in Mama.

[2] The *Budoji (Epic of the Emblem City)* records that most people forgot "the Affair of Mago" and that "the Principle of Mago" became vain, when the reign of Dangun, more commonly known as Old Choson (ca. 2333 BCE-ca. 232 BCE), ancient state of Korea, which I call the third oldest Magoist confederacy, underwent the process of disintegration caused by the invasion of neighboring Chinese regimes (See the *Budoji*, Chapter 25, 90-91). Also, as I will quote later, the *Goryoesa (Chronicle of the Goryoe Dynasty)* records that people sang, "Ah, ah, if the State of Mago leaves us now, when will it return?" during the late period of the Goryoe (918-1392) Dynasty. As I will also cite below, one Chinese example stands out: Ta'ao T'ang (Tang poet) of the mid 8th century sang, "Once Miss Hemp [Magu] has gone away, none knows when she will come again." Ta'ao T'ang's nostalgia for the lost history of Magoism remains unrecognized among the Chinese and the Daoist until today. People's longing for the return of the State of Mago

the trans-patriarchal cultural matrix of East Asia in which East Asian women have held religious and political authority. Revivifying Magoism restores East Asian female agency, which has been underrepresented and misrepresented within East Asian, patriarchal, and/or Euro-American ethnocentric discourses.

This article introduces a gamut of Magoist primary sources widely interspersed throughout Korea, China, and Japan, and explores the mytho-historical implications of Magoism. The pan-East Asian existence of the Magoist literature comes across as surprising if not anomalous, because the official historiography does not hint a transnational gynocentric unity in ancient times of East Asia.[3] Appropriating C. W. Sydow's theory of oicotyfication (the same folktale type that is found in different regions), which explains the mechanism of folktale transference from one region to another,[4] I postulate that East Asian peoples thrived under the political and cultural banner of Magoism in ancient times. In explicating ancient Magoism I find nationalist and/or ethnocentric perspectives fundamentally inadequate. Magoism as pre-patriarchal in origin is also pre-nationalist and pre-ethnocentric. It shows nationalism as a by-product of patriarchal political establishments.

Characteristically, primary sources suggest the primacy of Korean Magoism not only in quantity but also in quality: Magoist sources from Korea outnumber her counterparts. Also, Korean sources witness Mago's supreme divinity and a coherent history of Magoism. The *Budoji (Epic of the Emblem City),* the primary text of Magoism, asserts Magoism as the

---

appears in many folk literature pieces as well as written records of Korea, China, and Japan. For further discussion, see Helen Hye-Sook Hwang, "The Female Principle in the Magoist Cosmogony" in *Ochre Journal of Women's Spirituality* (Fall 2007), 5-6.

[3] I limit my reference of East Asia to Korea, China, and Japan from which the corpus of Magoism has been documented.

[4] I explicated in detail C. W. Sydow's theory of oicotypification in my dissertation. To summarize, the pan-East Asian existence of Mago folktales supports two speculations: First, the active story-tellers of Magoism migrated across the subcontinent of East Asia. Second, East Asian peoples were once under the cultural influence of Magoism and then were later subdivided into different nation states. In the case of Mago oicotype, both scenarios are relevant. See C. W. Sydow. *Selected Papers on Folklore* (New York: Arno Press, 1977), 11-59 cited in Helen Hye-Sook Hwang, *Seeking Mago, the Great Goddess: A Mytho-Historic-Thealogical Reconstruction of Magoism, an Archaically Originated Gynocentric Tradition of East Asia* (Claremont Graduate University, Claremont: CA, 2005), 6-9.

primal tradition of ARCHAIC KOREA.[5] The Korean corpus systematically portrays Mago as progenitor, creator, and sovereign, while its Chinese and Japanese counterparts are fragmentary and partial. Magoism remains invisible in the latter two sources. Consequently, neither Mago's provenance nor the history of Magoism is explicitly stated in the latter two sources. Why do Korean sources attest to Magoism, whereas Chinese and Japanese counterparts vaguely adumbrate it?[6] This question is not only crucial but also potentially controversial because its answer requires a reconstruction of the pre-Chinese Magoist history that is primarily identified as Korean.

This study argues that archaic Magoists later known as ancient Koreans were not only the creators of pre- and proto-Chinese [read patriarchal] magoractic [read Magoist theocratic] civilizations but also the bearers of Magoist sovereignty to different peoples. This is nothing less than what the mythology of Magoism from Korea conveys. Of course, such history is unthinkable within the realm of official [read patriarchal and nationalist] historiography. In the foreground, the mytho-history of Magoism remains hypothetical subjected to further studies. Nonetheless, its implications are ground-breaking and far-reaching. The mytho-history of Magoism offers an alternative paradigm by way of mapping out a supra-nationalist consciousness with which ancient Magoist Koreans resisted patriarchal ideologies of nationalism and ethnocentrism. I posit that, because of its fierce adherence to female principles, the ancient history of Magoist Korea has been subjected to erasure and truncation in the official historiography of East Asia.[7] Both Magoism and the history of ancient Koreans, inextricably predicated on the gynocentric world, have

---

[5] By ARCHAIC KOREA, I mean the Magoist peoples of East Asia who were pre- and supra-nationalist and multi-ethnic. Linguistically speaking, the root "*han*" in Hanguk (State of Han, Korea) adumbrates this Magoist origin, as its meaning includes "one," "big," "great," "same," "full," "middle," "right," or "outward." See YongSu Bak, *GyoeRyeMal YongRye Sajeon (the Dictionary of Korean Spoken Language)*, 2166-2167. Also "Hanguk" refers to the first confederacy of Magoism to be mentioned in a later section of this article.

[6] I do not suggest that Chinese and Japanese sources are similar in any way. From the limited amount of data from Japan, I infer that Japanese Magoism is more closely tied to Korean Magoism than is Chinese Magoism.

[7] The discussion of how the ancient history of Magoist Korea has been made occult is beyond the scope of this article. I explained in my dissertation three major historical processes brought by patriarchal ideologues of China, Korea, and Japan respectively. See Hwang, *Seeking Mago,* 86-8.

been subverted by East Asian patriarchal ideologues.

Primary Sources of Magoism

The *Budoji (Epic of the Emblem City)* and the *Handan Gogi (Archaic Histories of Han and Dan)*, which I deem as two major texts of Magoism, reemerged in the mid 1980s. My first acquaintance with the *Budoji,* an extraordinary text allegedly written in the late 4th or early 5th century, opened my eyes to the unusual tradition of Magoism.[8] Along with its complex and sophisticated language, the overt gynocentric principle that runs through this mythic epic immediately caught my attention. My fascination with the *Budoji* increased as I learned that the *Budoji* was the first and only "extant" volume of fifteen books entitled the *JingSimRok (Literature of Illuminating Mind/Heart),* all possibly written by the same author(s).[9] The titles of the *JingSimRock*'s fifteen books include a broad range of topics such as musicology, astronomy, mathematics, calendar, history, geography, rituals, healing and medicine, agriculture and silk production, pottery making, and others. The *Budoji* itself occupies a unique place as it presents a universal origin story followed by the history of the oldest magocratic states.

Intrigued by the *Budoji,* I began to seek out a larger corpus of Mago texts around 2002. The results were beyond expectation.[10] I soon learned that Mago literature exist not only in Korea but also in China and Japan. An abundance of Magoist texts was soon discovered in such various genres as myths, toponyms, folktales, sagas, poetry, and paintings. Even more revealing was the evidence of Magoism within the historical and

---

[8] I have studied Magoism independently. I embarked my study on Magoism as I sought my own cultural roots as a self-motivated Korean feminist. I first encountered the *Budoji* in 2000 in an unexpected way. For detailed discussions, see Hwang, "The Female Principle in the Magoist Cosmogony," 4-5.

[9] I suggest that Bak JeSang, the alleged author, and his wife Kim, along with their familial members, be the co-authors of the *Budoji.* See Hwang, *Seeking Mago,* 109-114. Nonetheless, the authorship of the *Budoji* remains to be an area of further study.

[10] Mago was already, albeit limitedly, familiar to the Korean populace in the late 1990s. Various cultural and literary events associated with Mago included a storybook, film, festival, and village ritual by 2002. Numerous folktales of Mago were readily available on, besides academic sources, websites operated by various organizations such as province and city information sites, tourist sites, and general interest sites.

religious texts from these countries. With that, it was not difficult to find a link to another unusual text, the *Handan Gogi,* a complex text that, to say the least, chronologically records the pre- and proto-Chinese history of Korea.[11] The *Handan Gogi* not only accords with the mytho-history of Magoism recounted in the *Budoji* but also complements it with rich chronological, cultural, theological, and mythic materials.

The aforementioned primary sources can be classified into the following five categories:

(1) The *Budoji (Epic of the Emblem City)* and the *Handan Gogi (Archaic Histories of Han and Dan),* both of which were translated and published in modern Korean in 1986;[12]
(2) Folktales and toponyms from Korea, China, and Japan;
(3) Mythic accounts from the *Samguk Sagi (History of Three Kingdoms)* and the *Samguk Yusa (Memorabilia of Three Kingdoms),* the alleged oldest books of Korea;
(4) Folklore including sagas, poems, paintings, and miscellanies from Korea; and
(5) Daoist texts, toponyms, and folklore including legends, paintings, and miscellanies from China.

A serious reading of the *Budoji* and the *Handan Gogi* necessarily exposes the lost mythology and history of Magoist Korea. In other words, both the *Budoji* and the *Handan Gogi* attest to Korean Magoism, which have been largely forgotten by modern Koreans. The *Budoji,* written in the late 4th or early 5th century of Silla Korea, recounts the mythic beginning of Mago followed by the ethno-genesis of East Asians. It discloses a yet-to-be known magnificent epic that illumines, in an unbroken stroke, the female-centered narrative of cosmogony, ethno-genesis, and pre- and proto-Chinese history of magocratic Korea. Its thirty-three chapters envisage a panoramic history of the gynocentric world, its beginning, flowering, and declining of archaic Magoist Korea. While mainstream

---

[11] The authorship of the five texts compiled in the *Handan Gogi* varies from the mid 7th century Silla through the 16th century. See Hwang, Seeking Mago, 118-119.

[12] Bak, JeSang. *Budoji (Epic of the Emblem City),* EunSu Kim tr. (Seoul: Hanmuhwa Press, 2002, c1986). There are three translations of the *Handan Gogi 桓檀古記 (Archaic Histories of Han and Dan*). The *Handan Gogi* was first translated in Japanese and published in Japan in 1982. See the *Kandan Koki (Archaic Histories of Han and Dan),* Kashima Noboru, tr. (Pusan: Minjok Munhwasa, 1986; Tokyo: Rekishi to Gendaisha, c1982).

academics remain silent about these books, independent scholars and amateur historians have taken them seriously.[13] A commentary of the *Budoji* has been recently published by Thomas Yoon in English as well as Korean.[14] Commentaries, which support the archaic history and culture of Korea recounted in the *Handan Gogi,* have mushroomed since its publication. Among them, I find IlBong Yi's resourceful for my study as it corroborates the *Handan Gogi* within the context of Chinese historical and mythological writings.[15]

Over three hundred folktales and toponyms are found from Korea.[16] These orally transmitted stories, with the exception of a small number of them documented in the *Hanguk Gubi Munhak Daegye (A Survey of Korean Oral Literature),* have not been systematically complied by scholars.[17] Magoist toponyms include Mago-san (mountain of Mago), Mago-am (rock of Mago), Mago-seong (Walled City of Mago), Mago-dong (village or cave of Mago), and many others.[18] Sources from Japan mark only four entries.[19] While more comprehensive documentation is required from Japan, Japanese sources are no less pivotal in piecing together seemingly isolated Magoist data across time and vast geography. The Chinese corpus, despite its fragmentary and derivative nature, is by no

---

[13] Both the *Budoji* and the *Handan Gogi* continue to be dismissed by academic Koreanists. I discussed the authenticity issues of these books in my dissertation. See Hwang, *Seeking Mago*, 98-101.

[14] Thomas Yoon, *The Budozhi: The Genesis of MaGo (Mother Earth) and the History of the City of Heaven's Ordinance* (Notre Dame, IN: Cross Cultural Publications, Inc., 2003).

[15] IlBong Yi, *SilZeung Handan Gogi (Verified Handan Gogi)* (Seoul: Jeongsin Segyesa, 2003).

[16] When I completed my dissertation in 2004, I documented over two hundred folktales and toponyms. The number continues to grow, as I further research.

[17] See Hwang, *Seeking Mago*, 250-253.

[18] Place-names take up about thirty percentages of folktales that number around 300.

[19] Japanese sources of Mako (as is pronounced in Japanese) are: Mt. Mako occurs in Miyako, Okinawa; Mako-iwa (rock of Mago) occurs in Yamanashi山梨縣; and Mt. Mako麻姑射 (Hakoya no Yama) is mentioned in *The Tale of the Heike*, tr. by Hiroshi Kitagawa and Bruce T. Tsuchida, (Tokyo: University of Tokyo Press, 1975), 226. Two entries are stated to connote Mako in the *Nihon Kokugo Daijiten* 日本國語大辭典 *(Japanese Language Dictionary)* (Tokyo: Japan, 1976). First, it refers to the passage from the *Chuang Tzu*. Second, it indicates the Palace of former-emperor.

means small or insignificant. My documentation of the literature of Magu, as it is pronounced in Chinese, includes Daoist texts as well as hitherto unknown folklore and landscapes including numerous toponyms. Magu, as the goddess of longevity, appears as a minor deity in the Daoist pantheon. However, these various sources prove to be pre-Daoist. Along with Japanese sources, Chinese sources provide integral information to the overall feature of Magoism in East Asia.

Last but not least, the fact that Mago is mentioned in the *Samguk Sagi* and the *Samguk Yusa*, the two allegedly oldest texts from Korea, is indicative of the very archaic nature of Magoism.[20] Once we are able to recognize that Mago is referred to as Nogo 姑 or Nogu (Crone or Ancient Goddess), a common name for Mago, Magoism is no longer invisible in these texts. Besides, Magoist literature appears in the 17th and 18th century renowned Korean literature (sagas) including the *SukHyangJeon (Tale of SukHyang)* and the *SimCheongJeon (Tale of SimCheong)*; poetry of Kim Sagot; an anonymous poem engraved on the rock of Nakhwa (Fallen Flowers); a painting of Kim HongDo, and miscellanies.[21] These folkloric fragments are crucial in valorizing the survival of Magoism throughout the dark period whose historical scheme I will explain at a later section. They demonstrate the transitory process in which Magoism has become demythologized and trivialized among Koreans.

---

[20] By pointing out the extensive records of Nogu in these texts in association with the imperial or heroic myths of Silla, Baekje, and Goguryoe, ancient States of Korea, GwangSik Choe, Korean historian, discloses the divine status of Nogu as Samsin (Triad Deity). Choe reports that the records of Nogu disappear from these texts around the fourth and fifth century CE. In the case of Goguryoe, it does not appear after the reign of Sovereign Micheon (r. 300-331), in the case of Silla the reign of Sovereign SoJi (r. 479-500), and in the case of Baekje the reign of DongSeongWang (r. 479-501). *Samguk Sagi* and *Samguk Yusa* cited in GwangSik Choe, *Uri Godaesa-ui Seongmuneul Yoelda (Opening of Our Ancient History)* (Seoul: Hangilsa, 2004), 141-8. According to Choe's research, it appears that Korean historiographers began to dismiss the archaic tradition of Magoism from the early 4th century (Goguryoe) through the end of the 5th century (Silla and Goguryoe).

[21] Among these, the *SukHyangJeon (Tale of SukHyang)* thematically centralizes the providence of Mago who is portrayed as "crone," grandmother and the divine for SukHyang, the main female character. Among miscellanies, included are the *Baridegi*, a Shamanic lyric, and the *PyoHaeRok (Logbook of Shipwreck)* by Hancheol Jang in the 1770s.

The Mytho-History of Magoism

Some archaeologists have advocated an urgent need of using myths and folktales in interpreting "prehistoric" archaeological discoveries where written records are simply absent. According to Fumiko Ikawa-Smith, archaeologist from Japan, the study of folklore began to be developed as a new method in an effort to pursue "scholarly inquiry" about women in Japanese ancient history in the first half of the 20th century.[22] This, alongside the method of archeomythology, which Marija Gimbutas advocates in her pioneering work, *the Language of the Goddess*, lends credence to my effort to study Magoist folktales as historical data.[23] Unlike the studies by Ikawa-Smith and Gimbutas, however, this study faces a much more fundamental difficulty. Due to the prevalence of Sinocentric views, the pre-Chinese Korean history has been utterly "unthinkable." There exists no "hypothesized history" of ancient Korea that the pre-patriarchal mythology of Magoism testifies. When history is absent, it is implausible to study archaeology of the time. In the case of Magoism, archaeological artifacts remain meaningless if not anomalous, while myths and folktales are abandoned as non-data.

This study is an effort to reconstruct an ancient history of Korea from a Magoist perspective. While the *Budoji* and the *Handan Gogi* provide systematic accounts on the diachronic developments of Magoist Korea from the mythic beginning of Mago until the onset of the Choson Dynasty (1392-1919), mythic tales and popular literature of Magoism from both Korea and China offer a folk history of Magoism. This study's historical assessment not only gives an overview to the vicissitudes of Magoism but also pieces together particular records on women and Goddesses from East Asia, which may otherwise be viewed as isolated or irrelevant data. Based on my feminist hermeneutics of the *Budoji* and the *Handan Gogi*, I posit that women were the primary agents of Mago's sovereignty. I postulate that the political/religious leaders of early Magoist polities—from HwangGung to YuIn, HanIn, HanUng, and Dangun—were predominantly women. Based on the *Budoj*i's account of the Magoist cosmogony and its cultural implications in numerous data, I deem that these women leaders

---

[22] Fumiko Ikawa-Smith, "Gender in Japanese Prehistory" in *In Pursuit of Gender: Worldwide Archaeological Approaches*, Sarah M. Nelson and Myriam Rosen-Ayalon, eds. (Lanham, MD: Altamira Press, 2002), 324-5.

[23] Marija Gimbutas, *The Language of the Goddess: Unearthing the Hidden Symbols of Western Civilization* (San Francisco: Harper &Row, 1989), xviii.

operated political regimes that are substantially different from patriarchal monarchical rules. I name ancient Magoist political leadership as magocracy where the female principle is venerated as religious and political authority for everyone including men. Magocracy connotes the archaic gynocentric political system of East Asia, which represented Mago's sovereignty. Accordingly, I recognize the three oldest confederacies of Magoist Korea, Hanguk (ca. 7199 BCE-ca. 3898 BCE), Danguk (ca. 3898 BCE-ca. 2333 BCE), and Budo Choson (ca. 2333 BCE-ca. 232 BCE), otherwise known as Old Choson as historical embodiments of magocracy. Dating of the archaic states of Hanguk, Danguk, and Old Choson follows the *Handan Gogi*. These dates are subject to debate and modification based upon further study.

Periods	Heroines and/or states	Major Events
Mythic	-Mago SamSin (Triad Deity) -HwangGung -YuIn	-The Paradise of Mago -The First Diaspora northward, northeastward, and farther migration
Archaic or Golden	-Hanguk (HanIn) ca. 7199 BCE-ca. 3898 BCE -Danguk (HanUng) ca. 3898 BCE-ca. 2333 BCE	-First Magocratic Confederacy -Second Magocratic Confederacy
Budo	-Old Choson (DanGun) ca. 2333 BCE-ca. 232 BCE	-Third Magocratic Confederacy -The Second Diaspora
Post-Budo	- Silla (57 BCE-935), Goguryoe (37 BCE-668), Baekje (18 BCE-660), Gaya, and other states -Goryoe (918-1392)	-The Third Diaspora -Korean States gradually lost the confederated system; Magocracy lost hegemony
Dark	-Choson (1392-1910) -Korea -South Korea and North Korea	-The Fourth Diaspora -Magoism underwent a political and cultural suppression in Korea; Choson lost the major territory of East Asian subcontinent
Revival	-After 1986	-Magoism partially revives in Korea

As is shown in the table above, the history of Magoism and the history of ancient Korea are inseparable. The fact that Magoism and Korea are inextricably tied in archaic times is hidden from modern Koreans themselves. By "ancient Magoist Korea," I mean the religious and political conglomeration of Magoist East Asian peoples. Magoism gave rise to ancient Koreans, while the latter embodied the former. Thus, a historical development of Magoism indispensably entails a reconstruction of the archaic history of Korea. Since Magoism in Korea appears to have undergone a process of rampant suppression during the modern Choson Dynasty (1392-1919), the dark period, most modern Koreans do not have a conscious recognition of Magoism. Not many are aware that Korean traditional culture, art, custom, language, religions, and archeology are the extant reservoir of Magoism. Korean Magoist sources prove reliable that Magoism was the dominant belief-system for Koreans from the cosmogonic beginning of Mago until the end of the Goryoe Dynasty (918-1392). The 17th century marked a watershed, when Magoism was, to an unprecedented massive scale, subject to erasure and distortion by Neo-Confucian political and cultural ideologues. In other words, Magoism *was* the primary tradition of Korea more or less up until the 17th century in Korea.

The history of Magoism can be viewed in six periods: Mythic, Archaic, Budo, Post-Budo, Dark, and Revival Periods.

1. Mythic Period: In this time of the mythic origin and ethno-genesis of the four primeval races, history and consciousness exist undifferentiated. The Magoist cosmogony is characterized by the parthenogenesis of Mago.[24] The mythology of Magoism underscores not only that the primordial history of humans maintained a cultural and political unity through the veneration of Mago, the Great Goddess, but also that all peoples are kindred as progeny of Mago Samsin (Triad Deity, Mago and her two daughters).

According to the mytho-history of Magoism, primal Koreans/East Asians from the Paradise of Mago known as Magoseong (Citadel of Mago) migrated northward and subsequently northeastward.[25] Scholars speculate that the Paradise of Mago, the epicenter of the world, was

---

[24] See Hwang, "The Female Principle in the Magoist Cosmogony" in *Ochre Journal of Women's Spirituality* (Fall 2007), 1-21.

[25] According to the *Budoji*, the four primal human races left for four corners of the world. See Hwang, *Seeking Mago*, 164-169.

located in the Pamirs, present Tajikistan (see [Map]), Central Asia, bordered with the western tip of the Xinjiang Autonomous Region, China.[26] According to the *Budoji*, early East Asians led by HwangGung (Yellow Vault), granddaughter of Mago, settled in Cheonsan天山 (Tianshan in Chinese, Heavenly Mountain), north of the Pamirs. To consider both the *Budoji* and the *Handan Gogi,* they migrated further north to Siberia, the vast territory of East Asia, and spread out farther. It remains to be studied as to their migratory routes into the vast land. The *Handan Gogi* attributes the geographical locus of the first magocratic confederacy, Hanguk, to the region of Lake Baikal, eastern Siberia. Interestingly, various mythological and archaeological studies account for the Paleolithic Culture in Mal'ta adjacent to Lake Baikal as one of the most pivotal Paleolithic Sites of the world. Indeed, the migratory theory of early peoples from Mal'ta culture into the Americas and elsewhere corroborates the mythic narrative of the *Budoji* and the *Handan Gogi*. Archaeological data postulates that Mal'ta culture, Siberia, was one of the early communities of Magoist East Asians. This hypothesis ties the mythic period of Magoism to the culture of Mal'ta dated to 18000-13000 BCE.[27]

2. Archaic or Golden Period: This period is represented by the two archaic magocratic confederacies, Hanguk (ca. 7199 BCE-ca. 3989 BCE) and Danguk (ca. 3989 BCE-ca. 2333 BCE).[28] Projecting the mythic period within the periodic scheme as the Paleolithic, this period may correspond to the Neolithic and the early Bronze Age.[29] According to the *Handan Gogi,* Hanguk comprised twelve states whose names are extant.[30] Danguk was composed nine states. HanIn and HanUng as well as DanGun in the next period indicate both titles of leadership, that is, Sovereign of Hanguk, Danguk, and Budo Choson, and the names of founders. The *Handan Gogi*

---

[26] These scholars include EunSu Kim, translator of the *Budoji*, and Thomas Yoon, commentator of the *Budoji* among others.

[27] For more discussions, see Hwang, *Seeking Mago*, Chapter 6.

[28] I disagree with the exponents of the *Handan Gogi* on naming of the second archaic polity of Korea. While the majority of (male) interpreters congruently name it Baedalguk or Cheongguguk, I call it Danguk . See Hwang, Seeking *Mago*, 197-202.

[29] This needs to be studied further. When the large part of Korean "prehistory" remains uncharted, it is difficult to characterize periodic demarcations.

[30] The territories of these twelve states appear to cover in North, East, and part of central Asia. Some names of these twelve states are phonetically akin to Sumer and Ur. See Hwang, *Seeking Mago*, 194.

provides chronologies and names of seven HanIns for Hanguk and eighteen HanUngs for Danguk.[31]

According to the *Budoji,* during this period as well as an earlier one, cross-cultural unity was promoted and maintained by the effort of magocratic envoys dispatched by Magoist sovereigns. The Magocratic tradition of dispatching envoys whose mission was to consolidate Magoist political and religious unity as well as transmit technologies of the time among the peoples of the world originates in the mythic period. Pre-patriarchal Magoism appears to have reached its pinnacle during the period of Danguk.[32] Danguk (ca. 3898 -2333 BCE) is characterized by the civilization of Sinsi神市 (Divine Market/City), a gynocentric civilization enabled by the leadership of the founder HanUng herself. The civilization of Sinsi appears in no way as "primitive." According to the *Budoji* and the *Handan Gogi*, it produced not only the invention of such technologies as constructing palaces/temples, ships, and vehicles that displayed unprecedented nautical prowess with which HanUng herself took itinerary visits to daughter-states. Also the foundation of East Asian civilizations including calenderics, linguistics, intellectual discourse, celebrations, social institutions, rituals, domestic and inter-political administrations were developed in this period. I am not saying that the people of Sinsi are technically and intellectually advanced. The female principle on which it is based convinces us to think this civilization as one of the most ideal historical developments with the high quality of life itself.

3. Budo Period: Budo (the Emblem City) is a colloquial name for Old Choson, otherwise known as Dangun Choson (ca. 2333 BCE-ca. 232 BCE). Budo Choson is interchangeably used with Dangun Choson in this study. Although the civilization of Budo is in nature a replica of the previous civilization of Sinsi, according to the *Budoji*, it is distinguished in some unique ways. Dangun, the founding sovereign of Budo Choson, envisioned a Mecca of Magoism, that is Budo, in East Asia. This utopian vision, based on the mythic knowledge of the Paradise of Mago, the primordial home of humanity, was to realize the mandate of Magoism, that is, to inform all peoples of their common origin from Mago. Budo was a multi-centered polity comprising many city-states located in the "four

---

[31] *Handan Gogi,* 27; 44.

[32] It needs to be studied further that these envoys (Magoist priestesses/shamans, predominantly female) are known as "goddesses" in other cultures. For the discussion of Tiamat in the Sumerian myth, see Hwang, *Seeking Mago*, 214-218.

directions" of continental East Asia in order to invite peoples of the world. The administration of Budo expediently enabled intercultural exchanges and co-habitations by holding periodic conventions. However, history proves that Budo's magocracy was phasing out to its eventual disintegration. The nine-state-confederacy of Danguk was reduced to the three-state-confederacy known as three Hans, which was later changed to three Chosons. The simplification of sub-states suggests a gradual weakening of magocracy over the period of several millennia from the twelve-state-confederacy to the nine-state-confederacy, and finally the three-state-confederacy.

An archaic confrontation between Chinese patriarchal powers and Korean magocratic powers sheds new light on "official" prehistory of East Asia. From its inception, the magocratic leadership of Budo Choson faced invasions by the early Chinese polities led by Yao, Shun, and Yu, the allegedly ancient Chinese kings whose lineage succeeded Fuxi, Shennong, and Huangti from an earlier time.[33] Inevitable was the confrontation between the newly formed Chinese patriarchal powers and the traditional Korean magocratic powers as the former sought out hegemony. The *Budoji* describe the rise of Chinese political powers as pseudo-Magoist inflicting military attacks upon archaic Korean sovereignty. It denounces the rise of Yao's regime as the second most horrible disaster that yielded irreversible consequences of chaos and violence in the history of Magoism. Beginning as a dissident force that interrupted the confederacy of magocratic city-states, the Chinese powers eventually brought the demise of Budo Choson over the period of two tens of centuries. As the federal administration of Budo was greatly hindered, the sovereignty of Budo collapsed circa 232 BCE. The decline of Budo Choson meant the defeat of Magoism as political authority. Consequently, this opened a new era to see the establishment of the first Chinese Dynasty of Qin (221-207 BCE). Post-Budo Korean states arose in an attempt to regain the glorious history of their predecessors but the Chinese regime had grown too formidable to restore the confederacy of archaic Korea. Magocracy is gone to the background of pre-Chinese history soon to be obliterated by the Chinese historiographers.

[33] The *Handan Gogi* mentions the early heroes of China such as Fuxi, Shennong, and Huangti as consanguineous descendents of the royal lineage of Magoist Korea in the fourth millennium BCE. See Hwang, *Seeking Mago*, 237-239.

4. Post-Budo Period: This period corresponds to another two millennia from "proto-history" to the end 14th century CE. Post-Budo states mushroomed but federal protection from magocracy was no longer available. From the early centuries CE on, as history proves, the expansion of Chinese monarchical regimes successfully impaired the reuniting effort of the proto-historic Korean States represented by Goguryoe, Baekje, Gaya, and Silla. Magoist Koreans were dispersed once again not so much more geographically but politically. The fact that the *Budoji* is an epic narrative by early Sillans who called their state, SoBudo (Little Budo), suggests the magocratic political orientation of early Sillans. Early Sillans, perhaps together with other post-Budo Korean States, faced a challenge: Outwardly they strove to establish political alliances from the post-Budo states and at the same time domestically they adopted the system of monarchy. Sillans were moving from magocracy to proto-patriarchy. Post-Budo Koreans struggled between the traditional and the new.[34] While partially importing Chinese institutions, they retained magocratic legacies. Nonetheless, as history proves, patriarchal powers among Koreans gradually gained hegemony.

This is the period of nostalgia for the bygone rule of magocracy, Budo. The loss of magocracy appears to have been recognized by the Chinese as well as Koreans until the end of 14th century. The following two accounts, one from a 9th century Tang Chinese poet and the other from a 13th century Korean folklore, are particularly telling:

> Once Miss Hemp [Magu] has gone away, none knows when she will come again.[35]

> [I]f the State of Mago leaves us now, when will it return?[36]

---

[34] Political leadership of early Silla faced two opposite positions between the adherents to Magoist tradition and the followers of Chinese political models. Nonetheless, the traditionalists appear to have held strong influence until the end of the 7th century in Silla, when two female sovereigns were consecutively enthroned. See Hwang, *Seeking Mago*, Chapter 7, for more discussions.

[35] Ta'ao T'ang (Tang poet) cited in Edward. H. Schafer, *Mirages on the Sea of Time: The Taoist Poetry of Ts'ao T'ang* (Berkeley: University of California Press, 1985), 98.

[36] It is reported that this folk lyric was widely sung during the late period of Goryoe. See the *Goryoesa (Chronicle of the Goryoe Dynasty),* vol. 36, Sega, King Chunghye, cited in *GoChoson-ui Jonggyo Hyoekmyoeng (The Religious Revolution of Old Choson),* JungPyoeng Noh. (Seoul: Daehan, 2003), 130.

In expressing nostalgia, the above two accounts show a conspicuous difference. The first addresses the disappearance of Mago as she is known as a goddess of mysterious origin among the Chinese, whereas the second refers to "the State of Mago," the rule of Mago.

5. Dark Period: This period marks from the modern Choson Dynasty (1392-1919) during which Magoism was subjected to an overt oppression until mid 1980s. Anti-traditional and anti-women policies were taken in favor of Neo-Confucianism by pro-Chinese administrators of Choson. Magoism disappeared from official discourse. The word "Mago" became occult in official domains. The mythic literature of Mago was demythologized and also demonized. Mago folktales were despised as meaningless if not ridiculous. The remnants of ancient historical records were further obliterated. Korea was transformed into a full-fledged patriarchal nation-state.[37] Even today Korean culture still staggers from the stranglehold of rampantly sexist Neo-Confucianism.

6. Revival Period (from 1986 on): The publication of the *Budoji* in modern Korean marks the watershed for a new era in which Magoism begins to resurface. A small number of Korean folklorists began to value Mago folktales. Cultural events, literary writings, as well as village rituals were created and revived for the last two decades. The year 2002 saw the production of the film *Mago*, which nonetheless failed in mobilizing viewers, to say the least.[38] Independent scholars began to publish their exegeses of the *Budoji* and the *Handan Gogi* in various ways including

---

[37] The anti-traditional Neo-Confucian transformation of the Choson Dynasty at the end of the 14th century is explicated in Martina Deuchler's work, *The Confucian Transformation of Korea: A Study of Society and Ideology* (Cambridge, Mass.: Council on East Asian Studies, Harvard University; Distributed by Harvard University Press, 1992). See also Hye Sook Hwang, "Seong-ui Gwanjeom-eseo Bon Hanguk Yoeksa-wa Jonggyo (1): Goryoe-wa Choson Chogi-ui Hanguk Yoeseongdl: (Korean History and Religion Viewed from a Gender Perspective (Part I): Korean Women during the Goryoe and early Choson periods)," in *Segye-ui Sinhak (Theology of the World)* Vol. 52 (Fall 2001), 175-208.

[38] See *Mago* directed by Hyoen-il Kang and written by Kyung-ki Jang. Contrary to its advertisement, this film proves to be an utter loss at multiple levels. Its ambitious patriarchal takes take pride in making pornographic cinematography of women. My critique of Mr. Jang's portrayal of Mago was publicized in Korea through two major women's newspapers, *Women's Newspaper* and *Woman Times* as well as *Dong-A Weekly* in May 2002.

websites and public lectures.[39]

Beyond Nationalism and Ethnocentrism

The mytho-history of Magoism illumines not only the common ancestry of all peoples to Mago followed by the ethno-genesis of East Asians but also the formation of nation states. In this study, I view the establishment of nationalist/ethnocentric regimes in ancient times as an onset of nationalism and ethnocentrism. Furthermore, this study exposes that the nationalist/ethnocentric perspective is a hallmark of patriarchal rules. My reconstruction of the Magoist historical scheme combines two working chronologies: One is the mythic pedigree of Mago recounted in the *Budoji* and the other the chronology of archaic Korea as well as China and Japan based on the *Handan Gogi*. I have conjoined them in a coherent chronology (see [Figure]). This is only a working model, which is subject to modification upon further study.

Magoist populations from the mythic period throughout the archaic period belong to an era that is pre-nationalist and pre-ethnocentric. This is the era of Mago, the gynocentric rule. The period of Budo witnesses the rise of the Chinese as a monarchical political force that gives a way to nationalist and ethnocentric establishments. Coping with the expansion of patriarchal rules, "gynocentric archaic Koreans" continues to uphold moral authority by advocating supra-nationalism, an ancient form of feminism. In the course of the post-Budo and the dark periods, Koreans have fully joined the current of nationalist world order.

According to my interpretation of the *Handan Gogi*, archaic Koreans are referred to the people of "Han" and "Dan," which also indicate the two oldest confederacies of Magoist States, Hanguk (State of Han) and Danguk (State of Dan). They are sometimes referred to as "the people of the Giant State" in Chinese records. However, they are more often obliterated than remembered in Sino-centric East Asian history. Neither the history of Han and Dan nor the cosmogony of Mago has survived in Sino-Centric history of East Asia. Nonetheless, Chinese records could not completely remove the trace of archaic Koreans. From the perspective of Magoism, I posit that DongI東夷 (Eastern Peoples of Archery) and GuI九夷 (Nine Peoples

[39] For further information, see Hye Sook Hwang, "Hanguk-jeok Yoeseongjuui Sasang-eul Yoengseong-euro Kotpiugi: Mago Yoesinhak: (Flowering a Korean Feminist Thought: The Study of Mago, the Great Goddess," in *Yoe/Seong IRon/ (Theory of Women and Gender)* Vol. 7 (2003), 7-22.

of Archery), whose meanings later changed to the "non-Han-Chinese barbarians,"[40] are the colloquial references to archaic Koreans by the Chinese. These terms, DongI and GuI, suggest an ancient enforcement of Chinese nationalist/ethnocentric [read patriarchal] ideologies.[41]

The Magoist chronology of East Asian polities exposes the derivative nature of East Asian nation-states from archaic Korean Magoism. It is the history that is told by ancient Koreans. For this, one may label this study as a nationalist endeavor. Such a label is inadequate for two related reasons. First of all, nationalist perspectives are inherently flawed in accessing Magoism. This study show that not only national identities but also national geographic territories are differently configured in archaic times of East Asia. Viewed from nationalist and androcentric perspectives, the pan-East Asian corpus of Magoism appears as non-data. In short, a patriarchal/nationalist view is misleading in investigating the pre-patriarchally originated tradition of Magoism.[42]

Secondly and more importantly, archaic Magoism, as testified by ancient Korean Magoists, contests an establishment of nationalist/ethnocentric regimes. The *Budoji* is poignant in denouncing the establishment of the

---

[40] DongI is generally recognized as proto-Chinese East Asian peoples including ancient Koreans. See Sara M. Nelson, *The Archaeology of Korea* (Cambridge; New York: Cambridge University Press, 1993), 151. The Magoist history of early East Asia reinstates DongIs and GuIs as proto-Chinese Magoist Koreans. The character I夷 in DongI (Eastern Is) or GuI (Nine Is) is, as some Korean scholars state, composed of great大 and archery弓, and thus DongI is etymologically a term of honor meaning the Eastern Peoples of Archery. IlBong Yi states that GuI (Nine States of Archers) refers to Baedalguk, which I name Danguk, the second oldest magocratic confederacy of nine-states. It is also known that Confucius himself addresses DongI and GuI as the Land of the Great Man君子 to which he himself wished to return. See IlBong Yi, *SilZeung Handan Gogi (Verified Handan Gogi),* 45-7.

[41] Early China is known as patriarchal and patrilineal. K. C. Chang mentions that if China had a matrilineal and matriarchal historical stage, "it must have occurred long before the Three Dynasties [Xia, Shang, and Chou]." K. C. Chang, *Art, Myth, and Ritual: The Path to Political Authority in Ancient China* (Harvard University Press, 1983), footnote 1, 9.

[42] Sarah M. Nelson has pointed out the irrelevance of national boundaries in approaching Korean prehistory and writes, "At this stage [the Neolithic] the present national boundaries were wholly irrelevant, and networks of trade and other interaction probably characterized the entire region [of East Asia]" See Sarah M. Nelson, *The Archaeology of Korea*, 109.

Yao's rule [read the Chinese rule], a precursor of the nationalist/ethnocentric state calling it the second greatest disaster in history. The formation of the Yao's regime is nailed as private and arbitrary (read nationalist or ethnocentric) and therefore it is morally and politically wrong. In this sense, I regard ancient Magoism as fundamentally feminist as well as gynocentric.[43] Ancient Magoism advocates a radical form of feminism that opposes the aggression of patriarchal/nationalist regimes. The *Budoji* does not describe early Sillan Magoists as hopeless idealists who insisted on the return of the lost magocracy. On the contrary, they accepted *national* identities in coping with nationalist ideologies.[44] In the case of early Sillans, supra-nationalism is not a mere rejection of nationalism but a nation-based mechanism that impairs nationalism. By "ancient Magoist Koreans," I mean a religious and political community of East Asian peoples, that is, pre-and proto-Chinese East Asian peoples who maintained supra-nationalist principles derived from the ancient knowledge of Magoism. Likewise, ancient Koreans were anti-ethnocentric, the Magoist legacy often misunderstood by modern Koreans. Ultimately, a feminist Magoist perspective exposes the origin of nationalism as a byproduct, an instrument of patriarchal powers, which rose to disrupt magocratic social order.

---

[43] Scholars have used such words as "gynocentric" (Adrienne Rich and others), "matristic" (Marija Gimbutas), and matriarchal (Heide Goettner-Abendroth) to provide better conceptions in their studies of prehistoric female-centered societies. In my explication of Magoism, I distinguish gynocentrism from feminism. While gynocentrism implies pre-patriarchally originated culture/consciousness characterized by female agency, feminism indicates an anti-patriarchal culture/consciousness, which counter-balances the malfunction of patriarchalism. Feminism by definition presupposes a patriarchal development. It is an idea that women must resist patriarchal binds. Gynocentrism is an original (read pre-patriarchal) idea of women and by women but for everyone that promulgates the way of the Female. It is a matrix that transcends patriarchal histories and cultures. Magoism promulgates both gynocentrism and feminism.

[44] I agree with Matilda Joslyn Gage who sees the formation of nationality in prehistoric gynocentric societies. In other words, national identities are pre-patriarchal in origin. See Matilda Joslyn Gage, *Woman, Church and the State: A Historical Account of the Status of Woman through the Christian Ages with Reminiscences of Matriarchate* (Chicago: Charles H. Kerr & Company, 1893), 32. In Magoism, it is of importance to distinguish national identities from nationalist identities. While the former refers to a diversity of peoples in different political communities within the principle of unity, the latter proves to be a patriarchal ethos coupled with ethnocentrism and colonialism.

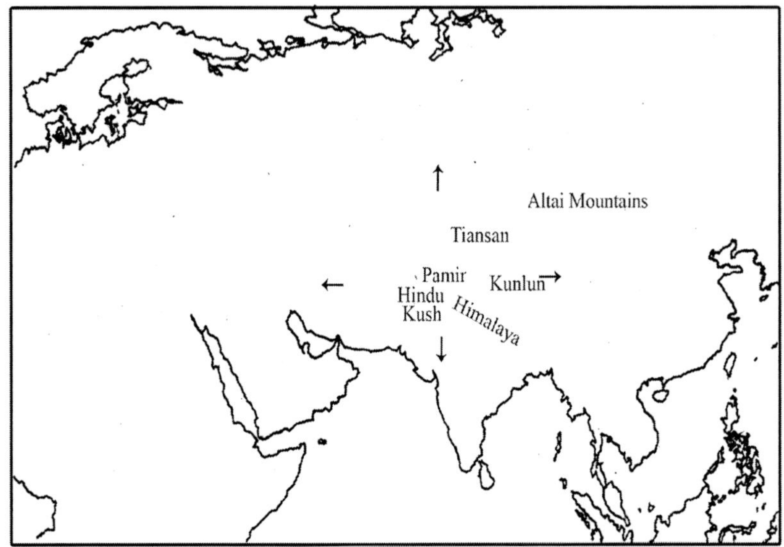

Map: Migration of Four Primal Races

This study of Magoism necessarily exposes nationalism that is operating in East Asian Studies. With a few exceptions, many scholars are uncritical of the work of Sinocentrism. Among others, its impact on Korean Studies is huge and detrimental. I find international scholarly discussions on Korean nationalism misleading and doubly oppressive. Koreanists, let alone Sinologists and Japanologists, lacking in an effort to view Korean materials in their own right, often begin their analyses with the presupposition that the history of Korea began under the colonial influence of China and Japan from ancient times. While blindly endorsing Chinese and Japanese nationalisms backed by Euro-American cultural imperialist assumptions, they toss out new studies on ancient Korean history and culture labeling them as "nationalist" and therefore unreliable and unauthentic. This practice among Koreanists has made Korean Studies a larger tomb of non-data.

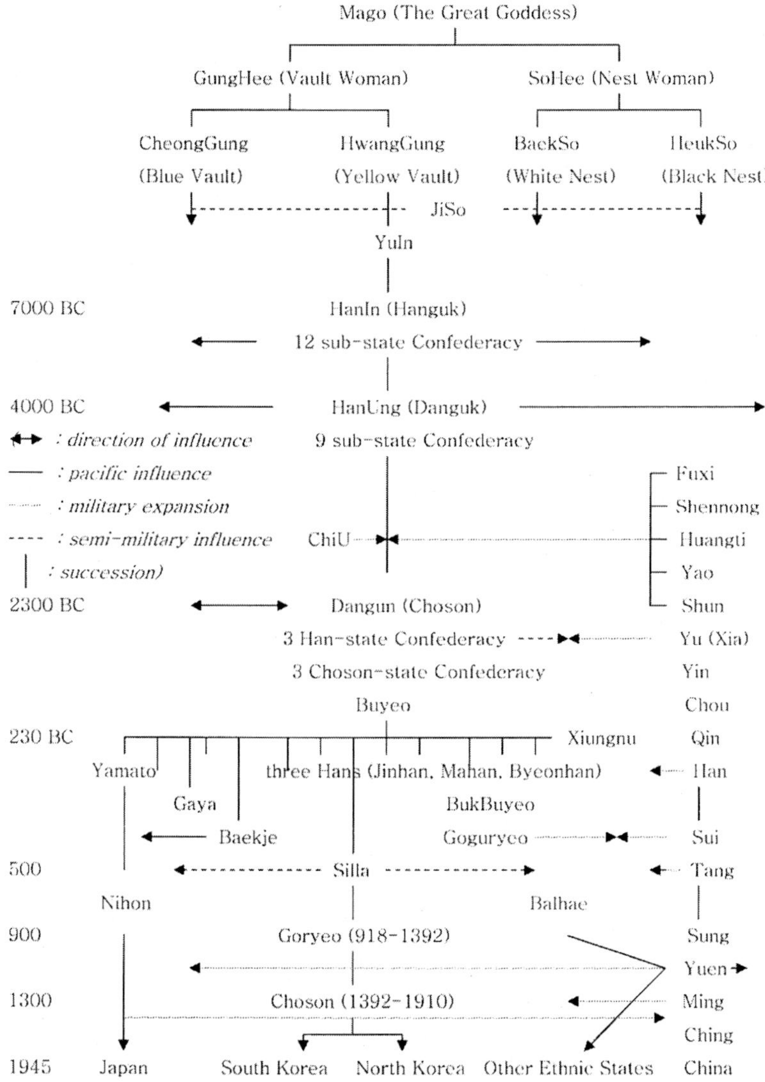

Figure: History of Magoism and East Asian States

Conclusion

In documenting and analyzing a wealth of primary sources including myths, toponyms, folklore, and historical/religious/literary texts transnationally interspersed throughout Korea, China, and Japan, I have reconstructed Magoism. In this effort, indispensable are the *Buodji* and the *Handan Gogi,* which recount that Magoism prevailed among East Asian peoples in pre- and proto-patriarchal times. Reconstructing the mytho-history of Magoism necessarily reveals the ancient gynocentric history of Magoist Korea, which has been erased and distorted by patriarchal ideologues. Accordingly, the mytho-history of Magoism sketches the territorial landscape of ancient East Asian Magoists from Central Asia to North and East Asia. "Archaic Magoist Korea" indicates the pre- and proto-Chinese Korean confederacies, which embodied Magoism as a religious and political ethos. It is characterized by *magocracy* in which women represented religious and political authority of Mago, the Great Goddess. The defeat of the confederated political system of magocratic city-states by patriarchal forces historically known as the Chinese presaged the erasure and fabrication of the history of Magoist Korea. Even after the disintegration of magocracy, Magoism as a cultural and national ethos continued to flourish among Koreans up until the 17th century. Koreans have gone the dark period of Magoism when the Choson Dynasty (1392-1919) transformed itself into a full-fledged patriarchal nationalist state until the re-emergence of old texts the *Budoji* and the *Handan Gogi* in mid 1980s.

How can we define and affirm national and ethnic diversities of peoples in non-hierarchical and non-colonialist ways? This is a crucial question for contemporary feminists to answer. Archaic Magoist Koreans (read East Asians) asked this question in their efforts to maintain and defend Magoism against the formation and expansion of patriarchal political powers. The history documented by the *Budoji* and the *Handan Gogi* tells us that archaic Magoist Koreans were quite successful at keeping nationalist and ethnocentric ideologies at bay for a long time. This supra-nationalist principle runs through the mythology of Magoism. It is predicated on the common origin of all peoples from Mago and the Magoist mandate of restoring original unity among the peoples of the world. Archaic Magoist confederacies of Hanguk, Danguk, and Budo Choson freshly offer a new paradigm to us to overcome a nationalist and ethnocentric ethos and realize non-colonialist world order. Nationalism (and also ethnocentrism and colonialism) is nothing less than a historical by-product brought by patriarchal rulers in their effort to perpetuate their domination over women and the rest of the universe. Magoism suggests that the feminist endeavor of resisting nationalism by supra-nationalism is not only necessary but also historically-rooted. Magoist Korean ancestors were quite successful in this task for several millennia. This is a curial piece of historical materials.

References

Chang, K. C. Art, Myth, and Ritual: The Path to Political Authority in Ancient China (Harvard University Press, 1983).

Deuchler, Martina. *The Confucian Transformation of Korea: A Study of Society and Ideology* (Cambridge, Mass.: Council on East Asian Studies, Harvard University; Distributed by Harvard University Press, 1992).

Gage, Matilda Joslyn. *Woman, Church and the State: A Historical Account of the Status of Woman through the Christian Ages with Reminiscences of Matriarchate* (Chicago: Charles H. Kerr & Company, 1893).

Gimbutas, Marija. *The Language of the Goddess: Unearthing the Hidden Symbols of Western Civilization (*San Francisco: Harper & Row, 1989).

Hwang, Helen Hye-Sook. "The Female Principle in the Magoist Cosmogony" in *Ochre Journal of Women's Spirituality* (Fall 2007).

—. *Seeking Mago, the Great Goddess: A Mytho-Historic-Thealogical Reconstruction of Magoism, an Archaically Originated Gynocentric Tradition of East Asia,* Ph.D. dissertation (Claremont Graduate University, Claremont: CA, 2005).

Ikawa-Smith, Fumiko. "Gender in Japanese Prehistory" in *In Pursuit of Gender: Worldwide Archaeological Approaches*, Sarah M. Nelson and Myriam Rosen-Ayalon, eds. (Lanham, MD: Altamira Press, 2002).

Nelson, Sarah M. *The archaeology of Korea* (Cambridge; New York: Cambridge University Press, 1993).

Schafer, Edward. H. *Mirages on the Sea of Time: The Taoist Poetry of Ta'ao T'ang* (Berkeley: University of California Press, 1985).

Yoon, Thomas. *The Budozhi: The Genesis of MaGo (Mother Earth) and the History of the City of Heaven's Ordinance* (Notre Dame, IN: Cross Cultural Publications, Inc., 2003).

Korean, Chinese, Japanese Languages

YongSu Bak, *GyoeRyeMal YongRye Sajeon (the Dictionary of Korean Spoken Language)* (Seoul: Seoul National University Press 2006).

Choe, GwangSik. *Uri Godaesa-ui Seongmuneul Yoelda (Opening of Our Ancient History)* (Seoul: Hangilsa, 2004).

Hwang, Hye Sook. "Hanguk-jeok Yoeseongjuui Sasang-eul Yoengseong-euro Kotpiugi: Mago Yoesinhak: (Flowering a Korean Feminist Thought: The Study of Mago, the Great Goddess," in *Yoe/Seong IRon/ (Theory of Women and Gender)* Vol. 7 (2003), 7-22.

—. "Seong-ui Gwanjeom-eseo Bon Hanguk Yoeksa-wa Jonggyo (1): Goryoe-wa Choson Chogi-ui Hanguk Yoeseongdl: (Korean History and Religion Viewed from a Gender Perspective (Part I): Korean Women during the Goryoe and early Choson periods)," in *Segye-ui Sinhak (Theology of the World)* Vol. 52 (Fall 2001), 175-208.

Noh, JungPyoeng. *GoChoson-ui Jonggyo Hyoekmyoeng (The Religious Revolution of Old Choson)* (Seoul: Daehan, 2003).

Yi, IlBong. *SilZeung Handan Gogi (Verified Handan Gogi)* (Seoul: Jeongsin Segyesa, 2003).

Historical Sources

Bak, JeSang. *Budoji (Epic of the Emblem City)*, EunSu Kim tr. (Seoul: Hanmuhwa Press, 2002, c1986).

Gye, YoenSu ed. *Handan Gogi (Archaic Histories of Han and Dan),* EunSu Kim tr. *(Seoul: Girinwon, 1985).*

—. *Handan Gogi (Archaic Histories of Han and Dan),* Minsu Yi tr. (Seoul: Hanppuri, 1985).

—. *Handan Gogi (Archaic Histories of Han and Dan),* SeungGuk Im tr. (Seoul: Jeongsin Segyesa, 1986).

—. *Kandan Koki 桓檀古記 (Archaic Histories of Han and Dan),* Kashima Noboru tr. (Pusan: Minjok Munhwasa, 1986); (Tokyo: Rekishi to Gendaisha, c1982).

PART II

THE MALLEABLE GODDESS: HISTORICAL TRANSFORMATIONS OF THE GODDESS

CHAPTER TWO

ḌĀKINĪS AND YOGINĪS: ON THE ORIGIN AND DEVELOPMENT OF AN EARLY MEDIEVAL INDIAN BUDDHIST GODDESS TRADITION

DAVID GRAY

At first glance, Buddhism is not a religious tradition that one would expect to have a rich goddess tradition. On the one hand, Buddhism has often been characterized as a non-theistic tradition, a characterization that would seem to preclude goddess worship. Moreover, the rich Buddhist traditions of iconography do not, again at first glance, seem to highlight female figures. Most of the best-known works of Buddhist art focus on male figures, such as the historical Śākyamuni Buddha, cosmic buddhas such as Amitābha and Vairocana, or the great bodhisattvas such as Avalokiteśvara and Mañjuśrī. When one examines the history of Buddhism more deeply, one discovers a rich goddess tradition just below the surface. Goddesses appear in the records of Buddhist architecture and literature within a few centuries after the religion's founding; indeed, they are present in the earliest strata of Buddhist art and architecture, and their presence increases as Buddhism develops in South Asia. One of the richest Buddhist goddess traditions, centering upon the figures of the *ḍākinī*s and *yoginī*s, appears in the latest phase of South Asian Buddhism, the Tantric phase, which began in seventh century. This tradition flourished in South Asia until Buddhism disappeared from most of the subcontinent around the thirteenth century. However, Buddhist goddess traditions survived in Nepal and the surrounding Himalayan areas. They were also disseminated to Tibet, where they thrived, and whence they spread throughout Central and East Asia.

Before discussing this tradition, however, it is important to clarify the status of "goddesses" in Buddhism. It is true that Buddhism, doctrinally at least, is "non-theistic," provided that we understand this term in a somewhat narrow sense. Buddhist philosophical traditions rejected the notion that there is a supreme deity who created the world, and upon whom living beings are dependent for their existence or salvation.[1] Buddhists, however, generally accepted the complex South Asian cosmology that included a large number of divine beings, including the "gods" (*deva*) of the Vedic Hindu tradition. They simply denied that any of these deities had a privileged status as creator deities, and argued instead that they, like humans and animals, were "creatures." Buddhists held that all beings, from the loftiest god to the lowliest worm, are conditioned entities, created not by a creator deity, but existing in forms commensurate with their past actions or *karma.* Gods, on account of their excellent *karma,* exist in superior forms and enjoy very long lives, but they too were subject to decay and death, and hence did not enjoy any sort of ultimate status.

Since the gods of Vedic Hinduism were seen as devoid of ultimate status, Buddhists instead tended to emphasize the figures of buddhas, awakened beings, who were thought to be humans who had achieved the ultimate state of complete awakening. By the early centuries of the first millennium C.E., Mahāyāna Buddhism developed an increasingly elaborate pantheon consisting of cosmic buddhas and bodhisattvas, such as Amitābha and Avalokiteśvara, who were believed to be accessible to the faithful via prayer and meditation.[2] While not rejecting the pan-South Asian belief in gods and spirits of various types, Buddhists created a new pantheon of enlightened beings who were thought to transcend the "worldly deities" of popular South Asian religion.

---

[1] For an excellent discussion of Buddhist non-theism see Asanga Tilakaratna, "Buddhist Non-theism: Theory and Application," in *Approaching the Dharma: Buddhist Texts and Practices in South and Southeast Asia,* ed. Anne M. Blackburn and Jeffrey Samuels, Seattle: BPS Pariyatti Editions, 2003, 125-149. See also the discussions in *Buddhist Theology: Critical Reflections by Contemporary Buddhist Scholars,* ed. Roger R. Jackson and John J. Makransky, London: RutledgeCurzon, 2000.

[2] Amitābha Buddha is particularly well known due to the popularity of his cult is East Asia. Regarding him, see Luis O. Gómez, *The Land of Bliss: The Paradise of the Buddha of Measureless Light,* Honolulu: University of Hawaii Press, 1996, and *Approaching the Land of Bliss: Religious Praxis in the Cult of Amitabha*, ed. Richard K. Payne and Kenneth K. Tanaka, Honolulu: University of Hawaii Press, 2003.

There were several ways in which "goddesses"[3] entered the Buddhist pantheon. A relatively small number of female deities entered the "front door" of the Buddhist pantheon, meaning that they were recognized as "enlightened" deities, buddhas or bodhisattvas, in the Buddhist pantheon. These include the great bodhisattva Tārā, a goddess who became increasingly popular in South Asian Mahāyāna Buddhism from the mid-first millennium C.E. onward, and who continues to be very popular in Tibetan and Himalayan forms of Buddhism.[4] The great bodhisattva Avalokiteśvara, while understood to be a male figure in South Asia, was gradually transformed into a female deity in China, becoming ultimately the best-known and most beloved goddess in East Asian Buddhist traditions.[5]

However, the "new" Buddhist pantheon of enlightened deities contained a paucity of female figures. This was largely due to the widespread belief in Buddhist circles that only men could become buddhas, and that women needed to attain male bodies if they wished to become completely awakened.[6] Hence, although women, like all other beings, had the latent capacity to become awakened, they needed to first attain a male human body to actualize this potential. The door to the official pantheon, then, was almost but not completely shut to female figures.

There was, however, a "back door" through which female figures often entered the Buddhist pantheon. This was the door of popular religiosity. Buddhism has never existed in a vacuum, and has always been impacted

---

[3] Here I do not use the term "goddess" in the narrow South Asian sense of female members of the old Vedic class of deities (*deva, devī*). Rather, I use this term to refer to any female object of worship in the Buddhist pantheon. These include both deities thought to be awakened or nearly awakened, such as buddhas and bodhisattvas, as well as "unawakened" divine figures, whose status in the Buddhist tradition will be discussed below.

[4] Regarding the goddess Tārā, see Stephan Beyer, *The Cult of Tārā: Magic and Ritual in Tibet*, Los Angeles: University of California Press, 1973, and Martin Wilson, *In Praise of Tara: Songs to the Savioress*, London: Wisdom Publications, 1986.

[5] Regarding the Chinese transformation of Avalokiteśvara, see Chün-fang Yü, *Kuan-yin,* New York: Columbia University Press, 2000.

[6] Regarding the androcentricity of Buddhist traditions, see Diana Y. Paul, *Women and Buddhism: Images of the Feminine in the Mahāyāna Tradition*, Los Angeles: University of California Press, 1979, Liz Wilson, *Charming Cadavers: Horrific Figurations of the Feminine in Indian Buddhist Hagiographic Literature,* Chicago: University of Chicago Press, 1996, and also Bernard Faure, *The Power of Denial: Buddhism, Purity, and Gender.* Princeton: Princeton University Press, 2003.

by the beliefs and practices popular in the social contexts in which it is present. Despite its official insistence that awakened buddhas and bodhisattvas are the only soteriologically efficacious deities, many other types of divine entities have been popular objects of worship in Buddhist contexts.

The encroachment of popular divinities upon Buddhist cult settings is evident in the earliest strata of architecture and literature. During the early centuries of Buddhism in South Asia, there was widespread belief that the natural world was pervaded by spirits who had great power to impact human life, for good or ill, if pleased or displeased, respectfully. These figures, known as *yakṣa* when male, *yakṣī* when female, were important in popular religious practice, and Buddhists accordingly adopted them into their pantheons. Early Buddhist architecture is replete with depictions of these deities, and they also frequently turn up in early Buddhist literature as interlocutors of the Buddha.[7] Unlike the "awakened" deities, these popular deities were often considered to be bloodthirsty, and were worshipped via animal sacrifices. Buddhists, who resisted the practice of animal sacrifice, usually insisted that these deities had been "converted" by the Buddha or one of his disciples. As a part of the conversion process, they are typically forced to forgo meat-eating, and to adopt a vegetarian diet. They thus achieve the status of a "protector of the [Buddhist] doctrine" (*dharmapāla*). While not yet enlightened, they are portrayed as devoted to the Buddhist tradition, and are thought to direct their latent aggressive tendencies toward those who are hostile to Buddhism.

This conversion process had been underway since the early period and was a highly effective Buddhist strategy for the dissemination of the religion. As Bernard Faure noted, Buddhists have "felt compelled to convert or subdue the local deities, to erase the memory of the places, to reconvert or desacralize spaces, to decode and re-encode legends."[8] Despite their lesser status within the Buddhist pantheon, these "convert"

---

[7] For a fascinating discussion of this phenomenon (with ample depictions of the *yakṣa* and *yakṣī* in Buddhist architecture) see Robert Decaroli, *Haunting the Buddha: Indian Popular Religions and the Formation of Buddhism,* London: Oxford University Press, 2004. For an example of the *yakṣa* in early Buddhist literature see the *yakkhasayutta,* trans. in Bhikkhu Bodhi, *The Connected Discourses of the Buddha: A New Translation of the Samyutta Nikāya,* Boston: Wisdom Publication, 2000, vol. 1, pp. 305-316.

[8] See Bernard Faure, "Space and Place in Chinese Religious Traditions," *History of Religions* 26.4 (1987): 341. See also his discussion of this phenomenon in an East Asian context in his *The Rhetoric of Immediacy: A Cultural Critique of Chan/Zen Buddhism,* Princeton: Princeton University Press, 1991, 258-261.

protector deities have often been objects of considerable devotion. This, in part, is a reflection of their popularity prior to being admitted into the Buddhist pantheon.[9] In addition, they are often thought to be particularly efficacious in addressing the needs of their devotees.[10]

One of the most important early Buddhist goddesses, Hāritī, evidently entered the Buddhist pantheon in this fashion. According to Buddhist legend, she was originally a *yakṣī* demoness associated with smallpox, who was notorious for her tendency to devour small children, despite the fact that she herself was a mother of five hundred children. She was cured of this habit by Śākyamuni Buddha, who hid her youngest child in his begging bowl in order to vividly demonstrate to her the sorrow mothers feel when they lose a child. In addition, he pragmatically promised her that, should she renounce eating children, the monks would make food offerings to her, in order to satisfy the insatiable appetite of her and her children. She thus renounced her practice of anthropophagy, and instead became famed as a goddess who bestows fertility and protects small children.[11] Her images became common at Buddhist sites during the early centuries C.E., reflecting her popularity as an object of worship.[12] The first Buddhist goddess well attested in the South Asian archeological record is thus a "convert," a demonic *yakṣī* transformed into a protective goddess.

We find this pattern repeated many centuries later with the development of Tantric Buddhism. During the early medieval period,[13] Buddhists in South Asia began composing ritual texts focusing on the cult

---

[9] Indeed, such popularity is probably a requirement for such admission.

[10] For an interesting analysis of a contemporary South Asian Buddhist pantheon, particularly with regard to the hierarchy and dialectical opposition between the buddhas and the demonic entities subjugated by them, see Bruce Kapferer, *A Celebration of Demons: Exorcism and the Aesthetics of Healing in Sri Lanka,* 2nd ed., Washington: Smithsonian Institution Press, 1991, 172-78. As Kapferer demonstrates, the deities who occupy the lower positions in the hierarchy receive greater attention in ritual than the more otiose figures at the top of the hierarchy.

[11] For a discussion of Hāritī and her cult see Serinity Young, *Courtesans and Tantric Consorts: Sexualities in Buddhist Narrative, Iconography, and Ritual,* New York: Routledge, 2004, 39-41.

[12] See A. D. H. Bivar, "Hāritī and the Chronology of the Kuṣāṇas," *Bulletin of the School of Oriental and African Studies* 33 (1970): 10-21.

[13] Here I follow Ronald Inden's definition of "early medieval India" as a period bounded by "the collapse of the kingdom of the Cālukyas around AD 750 and the establishment of the Delhi Sultanate early in the thirteenth century." See his "Hierarchies of Kings in Medieval India," in *Contributions to Indian Sociology* 15.1-2 (1981): 99. This, incidentally, was the period during which Tantric forms of Buddhism thrived in India.

of a class of goddesses variously known as *ḍākinī*s or *yoginī*s. These texts, which were known as Yoginī Tantras, were notable for their focus on female deities, which appears to be an almost unprecedented development in the history of Buddhism. They were also well known, even infamous, for their advocacy of transgressive behavior. Their composition began by the late seventh century or early eighth century. The Yoginī Tantras appear to have developed outside of the mainstream Buddhist community, and to have received heavy influence from non-Buddhist traditions, particularly from Śaiva traditions of Hinduism,[14] as well as from local folk religious traditions.

By the ninth century,[15] important Yoginī Tantras such as the *Hevajra*[16] and *Cakrasamvara*[17] tantras became key scriptures of the Tantric Buddhist tradition that was institutionally based in North India, studied and practiced at important Buddhist centers such as Nālandā[18] and Vikramaśīla.[19] From this institutional basis, they were rapidly transmitted

---

[14] This has been argued by Alexis Sanderson in several essays over that past twenty years. See particularly his "Vajrayāna: Origin and Function," in *Buddhism into the Year 2000: International Conference Proceedings*, no editor, Los Angeles: Dhammakaya Foundation, 1994, 87-102.

[15] For example, the earliest commentary on the *Cakrasamvara Tantra,* composed by Jayabhadra, an abbot of the Vikramaśīla monastery complex in Bengal, appears to date to the early- to mid-ninth century. For a discussion of this issue see my *The Cakrasamvara Tantra: A Study and Translation of The Discourse of Śrī Heruka,* New York: American Institute of Buddhist Studies/Columbia University Press, 2007.

[16] For a study and translation of this text, which was composed by the late eighth or early ninth century, see David L. Snellgrove, *The Hevajra Tantra: A Critical Study,* London: Oxford University Press, 1959.

[17] For a study and translation of this late eighth century Buddhist text see my forthcoming book.

[18] Nālandā was an important Buddhist monastic center located in what is currently the state of Bihar in Northeastern India. It eventually became an important center for the study and practice of the Buddhist Tantras, including the Yoginī Tantras. Important figures in the dissemination of the Yoginī Tantras, such as Nāropa, were associated with Nālandā. See Herbert V. Guenther, trans. *The Life and Teaching of Nāropa*, 1963, repr., Boston: Shambhala Publications, 1986. On Nālandā in general see Sukumar Dutt, *Buddhist Monks and Monasteries of India*, London: George Allen and Unwin Ltd., 1962.

[19] Vikramaśīla, which was located along the Gaṅgā River in what is now the province of West Bengal, appears to have been an important early center for the study and practice of the Yoginī Tantras from the early ninth century onward, as indicated by the large numbers of commentaries on these texts composed by the

to the Kathmandu valley of Nepal and were disseminated to Tibet and China,[20] beginning during the tenth century. As they became very popular in Tibet, these traditions, and the goddesses advocated by them, survived the downfall of Buddhism in India. The worship of these goddesses continues to thrive in Nepal and Tibet, as well as other regions influenced by Tibetan Buddhism, such as Mongolia and China. Since the Chinese occupation of Tibet in the mid-twentieth century, these traditions have been disseminated throughout the world by exiled Tibetan lamas.

One of the most notable features of the Yoginī Tantras is, as the name suggests, the central prominence given to a class of female figures, the Yoginīs or Ḍākinīs.[21] Like Hāritī, these goddesses do not appear to have been originally Buddhist, but rather appear to have been "converted" or appropriated from popular strata of South Asian religious practice. They also appear to have been originally considered by Buddhists to be demonic entities, prior to their rehabilitation as Buddhist goddesses.

The term *yoginī* in Sanskrit is a feminine noun, literally meaning "she who possesses *yoga.*" However, this term does *not* typically designate female *yogī*s or yoga practitioners. Instead, in pre-modern South Asia the term typically evoked visions of dangerous and magical non-human beings. Indeed, the definitions listed in a popular Sanskrit dictionary begin with the following: "Female demon or any being endowed with magical power, a fairy, witch, sorceress."[22] The yoginīs tend to have fearsome

---

abbots of this institution. For a discussion of this phenomenon see the introduction of my forthcoming book.

[20] There were several attempts at disseminating the Yoginī Tantras in China. Several of these works were translated during the Northern Song dynasty. While these works were accepted into Chinese Buddhist canons, their practice traditions do not appear to have been successfully transmitted to China. Regarding this see C. Willemen, *The Chinese Hevajratantra: The Scriptural Text of the Ritual of the Great King of the Teaching, the Adamantine One with Great Compassion and Knowledge of the Void.* Leuven, Belgium: Uitgeverij Peeters, 1983. Yoginī Tantra practice traditions were transmitted to China during the Yuan dynasty, when a number of associated ritual and meditation manuals were translated into Chinese from Tibetan. These works were excluded from the official Chinese Buddhist canon, but a number of them were preserved as extra-canonical mss. collections, a number of which have been published in Taiwan over the past forty years.

[21] In Buddhist Yoginī Tantras such as the *Cakrasamvara* and the *Abhidhānottara,* the terms *yoginī* and *ḍākinī* are used interchangeably to refer to the same category of goddesses. However, the terms have distinct derivations and histories, which will be discussed below.

[22] Sir Monier Monier-Williams, *A Sanskrit-English Dictionary* (1899, corr. ed., Delhi: Motilal Banarsidass, 2002), 858.1.

appearances that corroborate these negative associations.[23] They are often theriomorphic, and appear to derive from older strata popular goddesses such as the *yakṣī* nature spirits and the ferocious "mothers" (*mātṛ*), who were perennial objects of local cults in South Asia. As a class of deities, the yoginīs are first found in Hindu traditions, usually as subordinate attendants to deities such as Śiva and Durgā.[24]

The term *ḍākinī* likewise originally had negative connotations. This term originally does not appear to derive from Sanskrit.[25] They appear in Buddhist sources during the mid-first millennium of the common era, and they are initially portrayed as a non-human class of ferocious, man-eating demonesses, much akin to the *yakṣī* and *rākṣasī* demonesses of earlier Buddhist lore. One of the earliest appearances of the ḍākinī in Buddhist literature occurs in the *Laṅkāvatāra Sūtra,* in a chapter advocating vegetarianism. In it carnivores are threatened with the following fate:

> The [carnivore] is born again and again as one who is ill-smelling, contemptuous, and insane among the families of the Caṇḍāla, the Pukkasa, and among the Ḍomba. From the womb of a ḍākinī he will be born into a carnivorous family, and then into the womb of a Rākṣasī and a cat; he belongs to the lowest class of men.[26]

---

[23] For an intriguing study of the early medieval cult of the Yoginīs in India see Vidya Dehejia, *Yoginī Cult and Temples: A Tantric Tradition* (New Delhi: National Museum, 1986). In this work, Dehejia documents the fearsome appearances of the Yoginīs, who are often theriomorphic. She also notes how the local population fear the Yoginī temples, which are typically open circular structures located in desolate spots such as hilltops.

[24] For a fascinating study of the yoginīs as they appear in early Hindu Tantric texts as well as their early history in Indian mythology see David G. White*, Kiss of the Yoginī: "Tantric Sex" in South Asian Contexts*, Chicago: University of Chicago Press, 2003.

[25] Manfred Mayrhofer has hypothesized that the term *ḍākinī* originally derives from an Austronesian language such as Muñḍa. See his *Kurzgefasstes etymologisches Wörterbuch des Altindischen* (1953; Heidelberg: C. Winter, 1986), vol. 1, 461. See also the discussion in Adelheid Herrmann-Pfandt, *Ḍākinīs: Zur Stellung und Symbolik des Weiblichen im Tantrischen Buddhismus* (Bonn: Indica et Tibetica Verlag, 1992), 115 n. 1.

[26] My trans. of *Laṅkāvatāra Sūtra* 8.14-15, from the Sanskrit in P. L. Vaidya, ed. *Saddharmalaṅkāvatārasūtram* (Darbhanga: The Mithila Institute, 1963), 105.

This passage, which dates no earlier than the seventh century,[27] depicts the *ḍākinī* in a negative light, and in particular associates them with meat-eating, a behavior which, in India, was largely associated with outcaste groups such as the Ḍomba, Caṇḍāla, and Pukkasa, with wild animals, and with fiendish demonesses such as the *rākṣasī*. This association is also found in other texts composed during this period. The Buddhist author Śāntideva associated the ḍākinī with carnivorous animals and demons as follows: "Tigers, lions, elephants, bears, serpents, all enemies, and likewise all hell guardians, ḍākinīs, and *rākṣasa* demons are all restrained by restraining the mind alone. By subduing the mind alone, they all become subdued."[28] Given the danger presented by these creatures, texts such as the *Lañkāvatāra Sūtra* included magical spells that a monk could recite to protect himself from being attacked by them.[29]

Like the yoginīs, the ḍākinīs appear to have been originally Hindu deities, associated with Śiva as well as other Śaiva deities, such as Mahākāla.[30] The Buddhist philosopher Dharmakīrti, who was active during the late sixth and early seventh century,[31] referred to a now lost

---

[27] The *Laṇkāvatāra Sūtra* was probably composed during the fourth century, as Florin Sutton has argued. See his *Existence and Enlightenment in the Laṇkāvatāra-sūtra* (Albany: State University of New York Press, 1991), 13-19. However, the extant Sanskrit of this scripture is from a late rendition of this text. The term *ḍākinī* does not appear in Bodhiruci's sixth century Chinese translation of this passage, or in a similar passage that precedes it. In both cases, the term *rākṣasī* (羅殺女) stands in the place of *ḍākinī* (T.16.671.564b18-19, 563a24-25). This clearly indicates that, as the *ḍākinī* came to the attention of Buddhist writers, they were initially assimilated with the flesh-eating *rākṣasī* demonesses. I am grateful to Nobumi Iyanaga for bringing Bodhiruci's trans. to my attention.

[28] My trans. of *Bodhicaryāvatāra* 5.4-5, from the Sanskrit ed. in P. L. Vaidya, *Bodhicaryāvatāra with Commentary* (Darbhanga: The Mithila Institute, 1960), 51. This text was most likely composed during the eighth century; Śāntideva has been tentatively dated to 685-763 C.E. See Kate Crosby and Andrew Skilton, *Śāntideva: The Bodhicaryāvatāra* (New York: Oxford UP, 1995), viii.

[29] For an example of this see the *dhāraṇī* chapter of the *Lakāvatāra Sūtra,* translated in D. T. Suzuki, *The Lankavatara Sutra: A Mahayana Text,* 1932, Delhi: Motilal Banarsidass, 1999, 223-225.

[30] For a discussion of the ḍākinīs in Hinduism see Adelheid Herrmann-Pfandt, "The Good Woman's Shadow: Some Aspects of the Dark Nature of Ḍākinīs and Śākinīs in Hinduism," in *Wild Goddesses of India and Nepal,* ed. Axel Michaels, Cornelia Vogelsanger and Annette Wilke, New York: Peter Lang, 1996, 39-70.

[31] Toshihiko Kimura has argued that Dharmakīrti lived c. 550-620 C.E. See his "A New Chronology of Dharmakırti" in *Dharmakīrti's Thought and its Impact on Indian and Tibetan Philosophy,* ed. Katsura Shoryu (Wien: Verlag der Österreichischen Akademie der Wissenschaften, 1999), 209-214.

genre of Śaiva Hindu texts known as Ḍākinī Tantras that were infamous for their advocacy of violent ritual.[32]

In order for these "demonic," non-Buddhist goddesses to enter the Buddhist pantheon, it was first necessary to account for their conversion. According to a mythic account related by the Indian Tantric Buddhist master Śubhakarasimha,[33] the *ḍākinī* were originally goddesses associated with the fierce Śaiva deity Mahākāla. They were notorious for their nasty habit of killing and devouring men. They did this in order to attain a magical substance hidden within their bodies that bestowed the power of flight as well as other magical powers. In order to convert them, the Buddha Mahāvairocana assumed the fierce garb of Mahākāla, and proceeded to devour the *ḍākinī.* They begged that he spare them, and he agreed to do so, provided that they forgo killing people, and feed on corpses instead.

This myth merely presents them as non-Buddhist evildoers who are coerced into refraining from preying on humans, and to engage instead in the obnoxious but innocuous practice of necrophagy. But the fact that Buddhists in the late seventh century were composing such myths is a sign that the *ḍākinī* were undergoing a transformation during this period. While previously portrayed by Buddhists as dangerous non-Buddhist goddesses, it was precisely during this period that they began to be portrayed positively as powerful Buddhist goddesses.

This new portrayal first appears in the earliest Yoginī Tantra, a text usually known as the *Samvara Tantra,*[34] which was composed by the late seventh or early eighth century.[35] This text opens with the following remarkable passage:

---

[32] See Alexis Sanderson, "History through Textual Criticism in the Study of Śaivism, the Pañcarātra and the Buddhist Yoginītantras," in *Les Source et le temps,* ed. François Grimal, Pondicherry: École française d'Extrême Orient, 2001, 11-12, n. 10.

[33] This account occurs in the commentary on the *Mahāvairocana-abhisambodhi Sūtra* composed by Śubhakarasimha and his Chinese disciple Yi-xing, composed in Chang-an, China, during the early eighth century. The myth occurs in the Chinese canon at T.1796.39.687.b17-c11. For a translation and study of this text see my article "Eating the Heart of the Brahmin: Representations of Alterity and the Formation of Identity in Tantric Buddhist Discourse," *History of Religions* 45.1 (2005): 45-69.

[34] Its full name is the *Sarvabuddhasamayoga-ḍākinījālasamvara Tantra.* While the Sanskrit original is lost, the text is preserved in translation in the Tibetan canon.

[35] While the date of composition of the *Samvara Tantra* is not known, it clearly was composed prior to Amoghavajra's journey from China to South Asia in the early eighth century, as it is described in his *Index of the Vajraśekhara Sutra Yoga*

> The seal[36] of the magic (*māyā*) of all women lacks passion and is not passionless, and is also not dependent on the mean [between these extremes]. This is the supreme path of nonduality. The magic of all women is particularly greater than all [other] magic. It is achieved naturally through the powers of reality itself. [So long as] one is respectful toward women in this world, she will be attained with all goods, bliss, and joy, even if one has done evil. If one returns to one's own nature, [these] will be attained with the magic of all women. This seal of amazing magic is symbolically indicated as *ḍākinī*. *Ḍā* means sky travel, and she who is directly realized in the elements (*dhātu*), that is, who has achieved [the ability] to range all throughout the sky, is called the *ḍākinī.* She who is united with all buddhas by means of the union (*samvara*) of all seals without exception is known as the *ḍākinī.* She who is the *ḍākinī* is composed of the Buddha elements. The *ḍākinī* who is the nature of all buddhas has achieved [the ability to] go everywhere.[37]

This text is remarkable for several reasons. It demonstrates continuity with the earlier lore concerning the ḍākinī, particularly with regard to their power of flight,[38] which is also a feature of the myth related by Śubhakarasimha. The power of flight is likewise attributed to the yoginī in Hindu Tantric literature.[39] Yet, here their association with evildoing or with Śaiva deities has disappeared. Instead, we are told that the the ḍākinī "is composed of the Buddha elements" and has "the nature of all buddhas." In other words, for the authors of this text the ḍākinīs have clearly successfully made the transition into the Buddhist pantheon, and have apparently achieved a quite high status within it, as enlightened beings.

---

in Eighteen Sections (T. 869), which was composed c. 746 C.E. For a detailed, annotated English translation of this important text, see Rolf W. Giebel, "The *Chin-kang-ting ching yü-ch'ieh shih-pa-hui chih-kuei:* An Annotated Translation." *Journal of Naritasan Institute for Buddhist Studies.* 18 (1995): 107-201.

36 This literally translated the term *mudrā, phyag rgya.* In addition to indicating a seal, this term can also designate the female consort of a male deity. In Tantric Buddhist contexts, it also designates the four "seals" employed in meditation and ritual. For a discussion of this term as used in Buddhist literature see E. Dale Saunders, *Mudrā: A Study of Symbolic Gestures in Japanese Buddhist Sculpture*, Princeton: Princeton University Press, 1960.

37 My translation of the text preserved at To. 366, sDe-dge rgyud 'bum vol. ka, 151b.

38 Indeed, this appears to be the first Buddhist text to seek to derive the term *ḍākinī* from the Sanskrit verbal roots √*dī* or √*dā,* "to fly."

39 For a detailed exploration of this see David White's *Kiss of the Yoginī.*

It is probably not coincidental that this transition seems to be marked by a reevaluation of the status of women. This text appears to extol women, and calls for their respectful treatment by the male adept. This is markedly distinct from the misogyny common in a great deal of Buddhist literature. While it is not clear to what extent this reflects an actual improvement of the status of women in Buddhism, the Yoginī Tantras, generally speaking, have a focus on women and female deities to an degree that far exceeds that of any other class of Buddhist literature.[40]

To get a better sense of the status of the *ḍākinī* and *yoginī* in the Buddhist Yoginī Tantras, it would probably be helpful to look more closely at one of the Tantras. In the remainder of this paper, we will look closely at a very influential Tantra that focuses upon them, the *Cakrasaṃvara Tantra.* A Buddhist text most likely composed during the

---

[40] The question of the extent to which the Yoginī Tantras reflects an empowered status of women in early medieval South Asian Buddhism is an open question that has been much debated. Miranda Shaw has argued that women actively participated in the construction of traditions that gave rise to the Yoginī Tantras, and that this participation was later erased once these traditions were transferred into the male-dominated environment of the Buddhist monastery. See her book *Passionate Enlightenment: Women in Tantric Buddhism,* Princeton: Princeton University Press, 1994. Her conclusions have been strongly criticized, most notably by Ronald Davidson in his recent book *Indian Esoteric Buddhism: A Social History of the Tantric Movement,* New York: Columbia University Press, 2002. Davidson argues that there is no evidence for such participation either in the textual or archeological record, and that this evidence suggests a decline of active female participation in Buddhist institutions at this time, as follows: "Our sources suggest that, even while individual women exercised power and authority in political and economic affairs in specific regions during the medieval period, they did not extend that involvement into Buddhist institutions. We have many ways of determining the approximate percentages of women participating in Buddhist activities; particularly important are epigraphic, ethnographic, and textual sources. These sources show a remarkable convergence: women probably constituted between 1 percent and 20 percent of individuals acting in most religious capacities from the medieval period to the present. The data are sketchy, but they indicate that women's numbers precipitously declined during the period of esoteric Buddhism, particularly in high status and authoritative religious positions. Far from being supportive of women's participation, the Mantrayāna was decidedly deleterious to the religious aspirations of those women desiring participation as independent and equal persons." (2002:92,93) Davidson is likely correct about this, but it is curious that works extolling women and female deities arises during a period of decline in the active participation of women in Buddhist institutions.

late eighth century,[41] the *Cakrasaṃvara Tantra* quickly became one of the most popular Buddhist Tantric traditions in India[42] and was disseminated to Tibet and the Himalayan regions, where it remains an important tradition to this day.

In the *Cakrasaṃvara Tantra*, like the *Saṃvara Tantra* discussed above, the terms *ḍākinī* and *yoginī* designate a class of goddesses who play a significant role in the traditions of iconography and meditation associated with this scripture. The *Cakrasaṃvara Tantra,* like most Buddhist Tantras, focuses on a maṇḍala, series of concentric circles illustrating the deities that are to be visualized by adepts of this tradition.[43] The Cakrasaṃvara maṇḍala is goddess oriented, as a majority of the deities contained within it are female. It centers upon the divine couple, Śrī Heruka and Vajravārāhī. They are surrounded by a circle of four goddesses known as the "essence yoginīs," who collectively constitute the "gnosis wheel" (*jñānacakra*) of the maṇḍala. They, in turn, are surrounded by three wheels known as the "mind," "speech," and "body" wheels. Eight deity couples inhabit each of these wheels, for a total of twenty male "heroes" (*vīra*) and twenty-four female yoginīs. Lastly, the maṇḍala is guarded by eight fierce goddesses who guard the cardinal and ordinal directions.

The Cakrasaṃvara tradition holds that this maṇḍala came into existence via an act of conversion similar to that described by Śubhakarasiṃha. According to the Indian commentator Indrabhūti, in the distant past the Hindu deities Bhairava and Kālarātri, along with a host of followers, occupied a series of twenty-four pilgrimage sites scattered throughout South Asia, and engaged in violence and wanton sexuality in these places. Distressed by this behavior, the Buddha Mahāvajradhara along with a host of his followers, assumed their appearance, and subjugated them, occupying their sacred sites.[44]

---

[41] For a discussion of the dating of this text see the introduction of my forthcoming study and translation of this scripture.

[42] Judging by the dozen commentaries and many more ritual manuals connected with this text that are preserved in the Tibetan canon, it appears to have been one of the most popular traditions at the time the Tibetan translators visited North India, from the tenth through fourteenth centuries.

[43] For examples of the maṇḍalas of the *Cakrasamvara* and related tantras see *The Circle of Bliss,* ed. John C. Huntington and Dina Bangdel, Chicago: Art Media Resources, Ltd, 2003, 51-54.

[44] Indrabhūti's account occurs in his Cakrasaṃvara commentary at To. 1413, D rgyud 'grel vol. tsa, 49b-52a. For a translation and analysis of this myth see my forthcoming book. Indrabhūti's dates are unknown, but he probably lived no earlier than the tenth century. Regarding this myth, see also Ronald Davidson,

This act of conversion gave rise to the maṇḍala, which is centered upon the figures of Śrī Heruka and Vajravārāhī, ensconced atop Mt. Kailash at the center of the world. They are surrounded by the twenty-four yoginīs and their consorts, who occupy the sacred sites scattered across South Asia. This myth serves several purposes, one of which is justifying the Buddhist adoption of Śaiva Hindu deities. It also creates for practitioners the powerful sense that the deities of the mandala pervade the universe. As the *Cakrasaṃvara Tantra* informs the reader at the beginning of chapter forty-one, the chapter that lists the twenty-four sacred sites: "The ḍākinīs are all-pervasive, in all of the superior seats (*pīṭha*) and so forth. They are born in land after land, endowed with gnosis in their own places of birth. They are the ḍākinīs known as the mistresses of the adamantine maṇḍala."[45]

There were several ways to engage with this maṇḍala. One was to seek to engage with it externally via the practice of pilgrimage, a practice that has always been popular for Buddhists.[46] However, the maṇḍala was also thought to pervade one's body, linking the macrocosm of the universe with the microcosm of the practitioner's body. In this tradition, this link was forged through the practice of "body maṇḍala" meditation, in which the adept visualizes the maṇḍala, with all of its deity couples, existing within his or her body.[47] In a very real sense then, one views one's self as "made of ḍākinīs," just as the ḍākinīs are "composed of the Buddha elements."[48] In other words, seeing oneself as pervaded by these

"Reflections on the Maheśvara Subjugation Myth: Indic Materials, Sa-skya-pa Apologetics, and the Birth of Heruka," *Journal of the International Association of Buddhist Studies* 14.2 (1991): 197-235.

[45] This and all other passages from the *Cakrasaṃvara Tantra* are my translations from my forthcoming translation and edition of this text.

[46] Even after Buddhism died out in most of South Asia, the Cakrasaṃvara pilgrimage tradition lived on. It was, for example, repeatedly transplanted to the landscape of Tibet. For a study of a Tibetan pilgrimage circuit associated with the Cakrasaṃvara see Toni Huber, *The Cult of Pure Crystal Mountain: Popular Pilgrimage and Visionary Landscape in Southeast Tibet*, London: Oxford University Press, 1999.

[47] For a study of this practice see my forthcoming article "Mandala of the Self: Embodiment, Practice and Identity Construction in the Cakrasaṃvara Tradition," *Journal of Religious History*.

[48] For this tradition, the connection between buddhas and ḍākinīs goes both ways. Chapter one of the *Cakrasaṃvara Tantra* informs the reader that the great Buddha Vajrasattva is "the hero made of all ḍākinīs." This expression is understood to refer to the "network of ḍākinīs" (*ḍākinījāla*) that is thought to pervade both the universe as well as the body of the adept.

enlightened goddesses is, for this tradition, an essential step toward the achievement of the ultimate goal of awakening.

The passage quoted above from the *Cakrasaṃvara Tantra* is also interesting as it highlights another important aspect of ḍākinī lore, namely, the belief that these goddesses can manifest as human females. "They are born in land after land," found at the sacred sites such as those listed in the Tantra. This is very important, for, according to this tradition, a male adept cannot gain awakening unless he finds one of these human ḍākinīs, and wins her over as a consort. Hence the chapter ends with the following passage:

> However many there may be at other additional [places], they are Śrī Heruka's yoginīs. They are the ladies of the maṇḍala for him, the Great Churner Śrī Heruka. These twenty-four ḍākinīs pervade everything, the animate and inanimate. This commitment of the ḍākinīs is indeed the transformative meditation. Meditative states, and so forth-anything whatsoever-should be brought to completion on the surface of the earth. [If] one is always heteropraxical, naked and equipoised at night, all heroes, yoginīs and those which are born from the Hero are delighted. The self-emergent worship should be performed with offerings of gesture and dance. Everything is achieved without exception by means of the worship of the left.

This passage highlights a great concern of the *Cakrasaṃvara Tantra*. One of the central aims of this text appears to be helping male adepts to identify and win over the yoginīs, whose assistance is thought to be requisite for the completion of the "transformative meditation" that leads to enlightenment. Hence the text contains a series of chapters, fifteen through twenty-four, that focus on these figures. These chapter describe the various classes of yoginīs, so that the adept can recognize them when he meets them. For examples, the ḍākinīs, who are members of the clan of the deity Padmanarteśvara, are described as follows:

> The woman who is reddish golden is redolent with the scent of lotus. Although her look is naturally placid, it is accompanied by an impassioned appearance. The woman whose fingernails are reddened and likewise her eyes, and who has drawn lotuses in her house, is one who is born into the clan of Padmanarteśvara.[49]

[49] This passage occurs in chapter eighteen of the *Cakrasaṃvara Tantra.*

The male adept first needs to identify a human woman who is a ḍākinī of the same clan as he.[50] Having identified her, he then needs to win her over. This is achieved via knowledge of the ḍākinīs' secret language, which consists of coded syllables and sign language. He also has to observe a proper protocol with her. In the case of the *Cakrasaṃvara Tantra,* this involves observing "heteropraxy" or *vāmācāra.* Literally meaning the "conduct of the left," this involves privileging the left side of the body in social interactions, as well as engaging in conduct that would normally be forbidden under the rule of the caste system, such as enjoying food with a women of a different caste, eating with her from the same bowl. Such conduct is, in the South Asian context, counterintuitive and transgressive, since the left side is considered inauspicious, and shunned in ordinary social intercourse.

Should the adept succeed in winning over the ḍākinī, she will conduct him to the Tantric feast, where the yoginīs consort with their male counterparts, and engage in feasting, song, and sexual union. According to the commentators, this union is for the purpose of the practice of yogic arts that result in the transformation of the subtle bodies of both the male and female practitioners, which is essential for the attainment of awakening.[51]

Despite the central importance of the ḍākinīs and yoginīs in this Tantra, they paradoxically retain elements of their earlier demonic nature in this text. Although it is essential that the male adept gain their companionship, failing to successfully win them over can, apparently, have disastrous consequences. Chapter thirty-eight threatens the yogī who has broken his Tantric commitments[52] with the terrible fate of being devoured by the ḍākinīs and yoginīs, invoking their old portrayal as nefarious cannibal demonesses:

> Have no doubt that this bad natured one, who is a commitment killer, an evil doer, and a Brahman slayer, will be eaten by many thousands of ḍākinīs. This deceived, bad natured one, a fool of wicked conduct: I will not rescue him when he is being devoured by the yoginīs. Amidst the

---

[50] In this tradition, one is assigned to a clan when one undergoes initiation into the tradition's mandala.

[51] For a detailed study of these practices see Miranda Shaw's *Passionate Enlightenment,* as well as Gray, *The Cakrasamvara Tantra,* 103-131. For a study of the Hindu Tantric practices that appear to have been important influences on this Buddhist tradition, see David White's *Kiss of the Yoginī.*

[52] The "commitments" (*samaya*) are vows that the adept takes during his or her initiation into the mandala of the tradition.

secret ones the sacrificial victim is indeed this very adept who has fallen from the world of the Buddha, and who harms the guru and the commitments.

Indeed, this passage evokes the demonic *yakṣī,* who appear to be a precursor of the *ḍākinī.*[53]

In spite of the remarkable elevation of the ḍākinīs and yoginīs from dangerous non-Buddhist demonesses to enlightened goddesses, they retained elements of their earlier fearsome natures. This is most notable in their iconography; they tend to be portrayed with fierce demeanors, and their appearance is sometimes terrible. It also appears that their conversion was not final. Buddhist hagiographical literature is filled with references to dangerous non-Buddhist ḍākinīs who can be encountered in fearsome places such as charnel grounds.[54] Moreover, when the Indian Buddhist saint Padmasambhava traveled to Tibet, Tibetan accounts inform us that he encountered and subjugated numerous hostile female spirits that are designated as "ḍākinīs." One such encounter is described as follows:

> And then while he was coming into Kharag, a white snow ḍākinī prepared to strike him with lightning. She cast down upon him nine bolts of lightning at one time. He entwined them about his finger and cast them into the water. She, Modeh Palmo, then fled into Lake Paltso. But as the Master placed his vajra onto the surface of the water, it flew into a roiling boil. In this manner her flesh was separated from her bones and her white skeleton cleansed. Then she said, "A door has opened in this black lake of regret." Having so spoken, she escaped to the surface and arose from the lake.
>
> The Master then threw the vajra at her and blinded her in one eye. He said, "If you make obstacles, I will kill you on the spot."
>
> Since he so spoke, she spoke before the Master, "Oh the face of the Teacher! Vajra Skull Garland Skill! I will not make obstacles; I am comforted by the very thought of this vow. Since I did not nourish the inclinations of this mind of fruition, it degenerated. I take refuge in the master and will obediently do whatever he asks." Having offered her life

---

[53] The term "secret one," *guhyakā,* is an old term for the *yakṣī,* which occurs several times in this text in reference to the ḍākinīs and yoginīs.

[54] For example, the Tibetan biography of the Indian mahāsiddha Kāṇha portrays him as engaged in struggles with Śaiva Ḍākinīs for the control of sacred sites such as Devīkoṭa. See David Templeman, *Tāranātha's Life of Kṛṣṇācārya/Kāṇha,* Dharamsala: Library of Tibetan Works and Archives, 1989, 37-39.

> force, she was bound under oath. He gave her the secret name Fleshless Vajra Turquoise Lamp. She was appointed the guardian of a treasury.[55]

For Tibetans, the conversion of the *ḍākinīs* and the other deities of Tibet to Buddhism marks a turning point in the dissemination of Buddhism there. According to the legends, it was their conversion that permitted the establishment of Buddhism in Tibet. These *ḍākinīs,* whom Padmasambhava would appoint as guardians of hidden "treasuries" of Buddhist texts and images, would later teach, encourage, and protect the Tibetan "treasure finders," who were destined to reveal their treasures.[56]

While the *ḍākinīs* retained their fierce demeanor and may never have been completely converted to enlightened Buddhist goddesses, they became extremely important figures wherever the Yoginī Tantras were disseminated. This is particularly the case in Tibet, where they are treasured as spiritual guides, who enlighten and inspire serious Buddhist practitioners.[57] They served this role, naturally, in the lives of many important male Buddhist masters.[58] But they also inspired Tibetan female practitioners as well. For example, in the early eighteenth century the Tibetan nun Orgyan Chokyi, one of the few Tibetan women to compose an autobiography, reported that she decided to write this work due to the prompting of a ḍākinī.[59] As such, these goddesses continue to be important figures in a thriving Buddhist tradition.

---

[55] My translation of a story related in Orgyan Lingpa's fourteenth century *lha 'dre bka' thang,* one of the text collections in his *bka' thang sde lnga.* See *bka' thang sde lnga,* N.p., mi rigs dpe skrun khang, 1986, 39-40.

[56] Regarding the "treasure" tradition of Tibetan Buddhism, see Tulku Thondup, *Hidden Teachings of Tibet: An Explanation of the Terma Tradition of Tibetan Buddhism,* repr. ed., Boston: Wisdom Publications, 1997, and also Janet Gyatso, *Apparitions of the Self,* Princeton: Princeton University Press, 1999.

[57] For a study of the *ḍākinī* in the Tibetan tradition see Judith Simmer-Brown, *Dakini's Warm Breath: The Feminine Principle in Tibetan Buddhism*, Boston: Shambhala Publications, 2001.

[58] See, for example, Richard Barron*, The Autobiography of Jamgön Kongtrul: A Gem of Many Colors*, Ithaca, NY: Snow Lion Publications, 2003.

[59] Fortunately for the English-speaking reader, her autobiography has been translated. See Kurtis R. Schaeffer, *Himalayan Hermitess: The Life of a Tibetan Buddhist Nun,* London: Oxford University Press, 2004.

References

Davidson, Ronald M. *Indian Esoteric Buddhism: A Social History of the Tantric Movement.* New York: Columbia University Press, 2002.

Decaroli, Robert. *Haunting the Buddha: Indian Popular Religions and the Formation of Buddhism.* London: Oxford University Press, 2004.

Gray, David B. *The Cakrasamvara Tantra: A Study and Translation of The Discourse of Śrī Heruka.* New York: American Institute of Buddhist Studies/Columbia University Press, 2007.

Shaw, Miranda. *Passionate Enlightenment: Women in Tantric Buddhism.* Princeton: Princeton University Press, 1994.

Simmer-Brown, Judith. *Ḍākini's Warm Breath: The Feminine Principle in Tibetan Buddhism*. Boston: Shambhala Publications, 2001.

White, David G. *Kiss of the Yoginī: "Tantric Sex" in South Asian Contexts*. Chicago: University of Chicago Press, 2003.

Title: Śrī Ākāśa Yoginī Mañḍala.
Contemporary Newari Artist: Ratna Vajrācārya
Date: 1118 N. S. (1998 C.E.), Private Collection

CHAPTER THREE

SITA MASALA: FROM THE VEDAS TO THE KITCHEN

PHYLLIS K. HERMAN

For the past few years, I have concentrated my fieldwork and most of my publications on the *Sita Rasoi* shrines extant in some form all over modern India. My previous work on these popular kitchen shrines has dealt mainly with the Valmiki Sita as the epic embodiment of certain orthodox Vedic mythic and ritual concepts regarding the close connections between a wealth of foodstuff and utopian kingship. As I have demonstrated elsewhere,[1] there are orthodox mythic and ritual connections between the Valmiki heroine, various Vedic goddesses and feminine powers, wealth, prosperity, and food. Here, however, I wish to address Sita's curious enshrinement as a reflection of a more ancient—or at least different mode—of worship, one particularly of and associated with goddesses.

The ideal and idealistic figure of the Valmiki Sita makes visible an inchoate tradition of popular and devotional influences of goddesses before and after the Valmiki *Ramayana* that reverberate in later literature and in the religious landscape of Hinduism. Working backward or forward historically with regard to the Valmiki *Ramayana* is a precarious proposition, not only because the text is so referentially dense but also because the evidence about its creation and early reception is circumstantial. In fact, Robert Goldman is of the opinion that the understanding of the Valmiki epic can be divided into only two real stages of apprehension: the aesthetic and didactic in the earliest use of the poem, and the devotional and nationalistic in the later. He goes on to note that

[1] Phyllis K. Herman, "Relocating Ramarajya: Perspectives on Sita's Kitchen in Ayodhya," *International Journal of Hindu Studies,* 2, no. 2 (1998) "Sita in the Kitchen: The Pativrata and Ramarajya," *Chakra,* 1 (2004).

"The devotional element never permeated the Sanskrit epic and has left the bulk of it untouched."[2]

I, too, will leave the bulk of the story untouched. However, I am going to consider a few of the episodes, particular characterizations, and descriptions of Sita in the Valmiki *Ramayana* that do seem to reflect devotional notions distinct from and predating the Vedic tradition. Moreover, as I hope to point out, the popular and/or *devotional* paradigms and descriptions that appear in the Valmiki *Ramayana* with regard to Sita are fundamental to her modern role as a *chef de cuisine.* The Valmiki heroine, Sita, the "embodied furrow," could encompass and integrate many of the pre-historic and historic functions of an agricultural Great Goddess figure.

The most basic ingredient going into the epic characterization of Sita is her association with the furrow and the wealth of the earth. This connection is a well-known association found within the Vedic texts in their association of *sita* (the furrow) with Viraj, Shri-Laksmi, and other Great Goddesses. But, in all likelihood, the relationship between the sacred feminine and agriculture existed in the undocumented Indian tradition as well, and I wish to review here what evidence we might have of this. If one wants to argue a theory about popular tradition in India, there is no more slippery slope on which to begin than the Indus Valley. The precise nature of the religious orientation of the Indus Valley culture has not been established conclusively. Even though scholars have long noted the primacy of goddess symbolisms, the worship of "local" deities, and the role of *le paysage sacre* in early or archaic agrarian milieus, one can only speculate that these links existed in the Indus Valley. However, as Kathleen Erndl points out, "It has become a truism among scholars of Hinduism that worship of goddesses has its basis in the Indus Valley civilization…or another indigenous Indian culture."[3]

The people of the *Vedas* were not only pastoral but also semi-pastoral and semi-agricultural. They maintained elements in their religious life that acknowledged the worship of goddesses and agricultural cults. Goddesses or divine female powers are venerated in the *Rig, Sama*, and *Yajur* Vedic traditions. An early example of the importance of the divine feminine is reflected in some of the Rig Vedic creation myths: for example, the *Purusha Sukta* has its enigmatic reference to a supreme feminine power,

---

[2] Robert P. Goldman and Sally J. Sutherland Goldman,, *The Ramayana of Valmiki: An Epic of Ancient India*, Vol. I (Princeton, NJ: Princeton University Press, 1995), 45.

[3] Kathleen Erndl, *Victory to the Mother: The Hindu Goddesses of Northwest India in Myth, Ritual, and Symbol* (USA: Oxford University Press, 1992), 20.

Viraj. There is much more emphasis on Great Goddess figures in the later *Atharva Veda*. The *Atharva Veda* may provide a "historical–religious link between the earliest Vedic period and the later emergence of the more popular-oriented epics…such as the Mahabharata and the *Ramayana*."[4] As well as exhibiting greater interest in the divine feminine than the other Vedas, the *Atharva Veda* generally contains material and descriptions that may indicate the ongoing process of historical amalgamation, demonstrating the incorporation of an earlier or contemporary popular tradition that had to be assigned a place in Vedic tradition.

I have dealt elsewhere with Atharva Vedic description of the goddess/cow of abundance, Viraj, and her connection to ideal sovereignty. In this *Veda,* she is accorded the status of Great Goddess, taking several forms and providing all that is necessary for life. Yet, Viraj does not appear in the *Brahmanas* and *Samhitas* as a living or animate goddess. She does not lose her power in ritual descriptions, especially with regard to kingship, but she becomes a much less personalized form of the divine feminine. In fact, in the royal ritual descriptions, the Goddess or divine feminine power functions primarily in the form of Shri, who is identified consistently with or as Viraj. Later, in the epic texts, especially with regard to ideal kingship, the functions of Viraj will be connected to the functions of Draupadi and Sita. I have suggested that one clue to this assimilation might lie in this early association of Viraj with Shri that is found in the Brahmanical texts.

However, in assessing the later historical ascension of Shri-Lakshmi and her identification with Sita, we may see something of early Indian notions concerning the Goddess that, as a *subtext* within the Vedic tradition, found expression and acceptance within that tradition and later within the epics. The power of the Great Goddess, Shri-Lakshmi is clearly recognized in the *Shri Sukta*, a text appended to the Rig Veda and contemporaneous with the *Brahmanas* (1000–500 BCE).[5] Notions of the connections between the feminine power and food, prosperity, wealth, royalty, gold, and more meet in the composite figure of this goddess, just as they will in the characterization of the Valmiki Sita. In the *Sukta*, Shri-Laksmi presents herself as more closely akin to what, in all likelihood, were pre-Vedic agricultural deities.[6] Descriptions of her in the *Sukta*

---

[4] Wendell Charles Beane, *Myth, Cult and Symbols in Shakta Hinduism* (Leiden: E.J. Brill, 1977) 101-102.

[5] S.K. Ramachandra Rao, *Sri Sukta: Text With Translation and Explanation,* (Bangalore: Kalpatharu Research Academy, 1985).

[6] See Ananda K. Coomaraswamy, *Yakshas: Essays in the Water Cosmology,* ed. Paul Schroeder (New York: Oxford University Press, 1993) 36.

suggest a great goddess figure—the text states that "she is unending nourishment and one who is the mistress of all creatures" (Sh.S.:9)—yet she also expresses a "local" imagery that may antedate but remain contemporary with and influential on the Vedic tradition. She is associated with the Bilva tree. She lives in the lotus pool and sits on a lotus. Shri is connected to the waters (*apah*), and she is called the moist one, her progeny being the mud.[7]

Reinforcing this "local" imagery is her description in terms that might be characterized as devotional. The *Shri Sukta* may be expressing an early form of devotion to the goddess: the worshipper seeks refuge in her (*saranam prapadye,* Sh.S.:5) and she is identified as the one who satisfies and is satisfied (*tripta tarpayanti,* Sh.S.:4). The text has several *shlokas* that ask her to directly grant her abundance, an excellent example being: "May I attain the pleasures of mind, wishes, and truth in speaking; and may wealth of cattle, abundant food, wealth, and good name (Sh.S.:10).

As Alf Hiltebeitel suggests, this *shloka* may be a devotionalized form of the Vedic myth and ritual description wherein Shri confers or bestows virtues and wealth on the gods and on the king.[8] In the *Shri Sukta*, she is asked as a transcendent goddess to give these things directly to her admirers. As the "mistress of all creatures," she bestows all that is necessary for life and sustenance directly upon the supplicant, suggesting the possibility that Shri-Lakshmi, while having been assimilated into Vedic ritualism, at the same time openly retained an intimate tie to a more concrete and personal sort of religious experience.

There is another aspect of the *Shri Sukta*'s depiction of Shri-Lakshmi that I would like to note here. The *Sukta* continually extols the beauty and attributes of Shri; she is honey-like, moon-faced, and radiant as the sun. In the Brahmanical scriptures, the terms *shri* and *lakshmi* are often identified with precious metal gold and in the *Sukta*, this identification is embodied, incarnated in the goddess Shri-Lakshmi. The text consistently and especially identifies her with and as gold. The first *shloka* makes mention of this twice: "[she] is gold-colored (*hiranya-varnam*)…[and] golden (*hiranyamayim*, Sh.S.:1). This identification of the goddess and gold may also suggest the commonality in symbolism for the fruits of the earth—food and precious metals—that would have preceded the *Vedas*.

The descriptions of Shri in the Vedic *Sukta* most probably demonstrate the continuing process of an intermixture of the religious ideas that were

[7] Passim.

[8] Alf Hiltebeitel, *The Ritual of Battle: Krishna in the Mahabharata* (Ithaca: Cornell University Press, 1976), 153 (see note 37).

part of what has been termed the "Two Traditions." Spoken of as the "Great Tradition" (Brahmanical) and the "Little Tradition" (popular strata) of Indian religious history, the terms are misleading in several ways: one being that it is essentially impossible to delineate clearly or at all times what is to be labeled Vedic or popular. Still, scholars must take into account the *presence* of an orientation developing under the influence of ritualism and continuing distinct from it. By the time of the epics, Shri-Lakshmi provides the poets with the paradigm of a "down to earth" figure: a localized and personified golden deity who can bestow or grant through the medium of sacrifice and by direct appeal.

The epic form should also be given its due: recognition of referents to the Vedic tradition could never constitute a complete exegesis of an epic paradigm. In the delineation of the Sanskrit epic figure of Sita, the simultaneous influence of Vedic mythic and ritual concepts concerning the Goddess and of certain popular notions of the Goddess and of *bhakti*-like descriptions and features appear within the epic narrative. Sita is a prime instance of Erndl's observation that "The period of the epics is one of transition in the integration of goddesses into the Hindu pantheon."[9]

In the Valmiki *Ramayana*, Sita is likened to Shri and Lakshmi throughout the text, but "the divine furrow," Sita, has her own distinct personality. It is reasonably certain that the identification of fertile woman and furrow found or preserved in many civilizations would have been a feature of an agricultural, pre-Vedic and Vedic India. Thus, the miraculous ascension of Sita from the plowed earth could reflect a popular religious apprehension not necessarily in conflict with the ritual procedure, both concerned with the fertility of the earth and the attainment of its wealth. The birth of the Valmiki Sita from the earth *during a ritual* is a description that would have had wide appeal and could be correlated to all sorts of general ideas concerning and worshipping goddesses. Sita is eminently desirable precisely as the embodiment of a wealth that is vital to humanity. She can and must be appropriated.

In the critical edition of the Valmiki *Ramayana*, Sita is introduced in the *Bala Kanda*, the first of seven books. This book—a later interpolation—details Sita's birth, her "bride price" (*virya*), her putative *svayamvara*, and her wedding with Rama. Sita herself, in other another and probably older section of the epic, narrates these events, but the *Bala Kanda* introduces us to her roles in the epic. Janaka states:

> Now at one time, as I was plowing a field, a girl sprang up behind my plow. I found her as I was clearing the field, and she is thus known by the

[9] Erndl, *ibid.*

name Sita, furrow.

Sprung from the earth, she has been raised as my daughter, and since she was not born from the womb, my daughter has been set apart as one for whom the only bride price is great strength (*virya*)." (1.65.14–17)

Sita's account of this event appears in the Ayodhya *Kanda*, where she notes that "the lord of men [Janaka] had obtained vast wealth, he felt, in obtaining me" (2.110.31). The great majority of later Hindu works have adopted these substantially similar versions of her birth. The Valmiki *Ramayana* does not specify the ritual Janaka was performing when Sita appeared, but it takes for granted the audience's awareness that a king, plowing within the "circle of the fields," must be participating in rites associated with fertility.

As Heidi Pauwels and others have pointed out, the *svayamvara* of Sita is not a "self-choice" marriage by any means.[10] She neither appears physically nor is described in the *Bala* and *Ayodhya Kandas*' depictions of the marriage contest. It is *the story of her birth* that is consistently emphasized in both books' descriptions. Born of no-womb, *ayonija* (an epithet used to describe her throughout the epic), but embodying the fertility of the earth itself, Sita is a divine commodity nonpareil! In the *Ayodhya Kanda* description, Sita notes that it is precisely her miraculous birth that makes it hard for Janaka to find a suitable husband for her (2.110.33–36). While the stress on contest has its referents in Vedic royal myths and rituals, the *svayamvara* theme in the *Bala* and in the *Ayodhya Kandas* of the *Ramayana* provides the narrator opportunities to showcase the desirability of the divine feminine and define the qualities, attitude, and behavior that must be demonstrated to possess her—all of which are embodied in Rama's paradigmatic *virya,* heroism or manly courage.

Attainment of this heroine can never be a matter of mere appropriation, and the *svayamvara* theme serves as a suitable device for winnowing out those unfit for Sita. The Valmiki *Ramayana* provides two versions of inappropriate behavior by the kings and princes who come to Mithila expressly to vie for Sita. In the *Bala Kanda*, having lost their bids, the suitors attack the city but are vanquished and described as of *viryam alpam*, "too little heroism" (1.65.20). In the *Ayodhya Kanda*, the suitors take one look at the bow and leave (2.110.42). By contrast, Rama comes to Mithila with no royal pomp and in humble attire, for the purpose of seeing the great bow and attending a sacrifice (2.110.43). Having consistently

---

[10] Heidi Pauwels, "'Only You': The Wedding of Rama and Sita, Past and Present," in *The Ramayana Revisited,* ed. Mandrakanta Bose (Oxford: Oxford University Press, 2004) 168.

been described as one possessed of and demonstrating *mahavirya*, Rama attains Sita where the other royal personages, lacking the proper attitudes and attributes of their *varna* have failed.

The epic use of the contrast and contest of *kshatriyas* as an illustration of proper attainment of the heroine does not preclude a broader interpretation of the event in terms of society in general. Rama, the ideal warrior, is identified early in the *Bala Kanda* as of divine origin, even though, as Goldman suggests, this may be evidence of a later accretion.[11] In the Valmiki *Ramayana*, the persona of Rama, sometimes supernatural, can at other times and situations be described as more human than divine. As the divinity born into this world, he can function as the ultimate paradigm of the perfect human: his actions could have references for all *varna*s who listen to his tale. As both the ideal *kshatriya* and the ideal *man*, Rama can correctly appropriate the wealth of the earth.

The wedding ceremony in the *Bala Kanda* of the *Ramayana* first introduces Sita as an active (if still silent) character in the text. The marriage of Rama and Sita is noteworthy on many levels, one of which being that it is from the Valmiki text that Sita first attains her widest fame in Indian tradition: she becomes the quintessential ideal wife or *pativrata*. The body of the Valmiki *Ramayana* will go on to extol Sita as being always intent upon Rama; she thinks only of him even in separation. With her entrance into the drama at the wedding, her role in the epic develops as one defined by her situation as the wife of Rama. In many passages throughout the text, Sita directs constant devotion toward her husband and receives his devotion in return. Indeed, Rama speaks of his love for Sita in terms of sexual longing and the ecstasy of union, as well as the great pain of separation from the beloved.

The themes of contest, correct approach, proper appropriation, and the devotion inherent in the semi-divine ideal marriage are implicit throughout character relationships and plotline of the *Ramayana* story. Within the body of the epic though, descriptions of Sita and the events of her life underscore the theme that she is infinitely desirable, the "goddess/heroine" whose favor must be attained in the right manner. And, of course, she carries with her the continual reminder of her extraordinary birth, her famous name, Sita.

Sita's obvious desirability is but one of the ways in which Valmiki associates her with the goddess and goddess worship. Whenever those who wish to approach her for favor, she is specifically and suitably situated in recognizably "local" terms and circumstances. In Pancavati,

---

[11] Goldman, Vol. I, pp. 43-47; 69.

described in the *Aranya Kanda*, she is living in the idyllic woodlands, complete with beautiful water, trees, and hills. It is there that Ravana finds Sita, using deceit in order to come near her. His opening speech to Sita is significant: "Who are you, golden woman dressed in garments of yellow silk, wearing a lovely lotus garland, and like a lotus pond yourself (3. 46.15). He tenders a list of the numerous goddesses she might be, including—as one might expect given the imagery in the *Shri Sukta*—Shri and Lakshmi (3.44:16-26). What follows is pretty explicit sexual description of why Ravana wants her. Sita's "golden appearance," augmented by clothes and jewels, is precisely why she is so attractive to Ravana.[12]

After successfully abducting Sita, the *rakshasa* king places her within an Ashoka grove and visits her there, imploring her to grant her favors. But his inappropriate approach has not only guaranteed that he will never attain her but also precipitated his eventual ruin. Hanuman describes this Ashoka grove in the *Sundara Kanda* as extremely beautiful and lush, containing a mountain peak, trees, and a stream (5.12.*passim*). Hanuman looks for Sita in this grove and notes the incredible beauty, though barely discernable, of a maiden seated in utter dejection. He concludes, given her loveliness, golden hue, moonlike qualities, wealth of jewels, and so forth, that she is Sita. In *Sarga* 14, he tells us that she is "young and golden and as beloved by all the people as Shri, goddess of fortune" (5.14.6). He also remarks on Sita's miraculous birth and the yearning that Rama feels for his beloved wife. In this description, as in Pancavati, we are reminded of the *Shri Sukta* and the goddess surrounded by allusions to the wealth that she is and guarantees.

This and the following episodes of the *Sundara Kanda* reinforce Sita's goddess-like nature and recall her history. Once again, the text uses the poetic device of contrast to illustrate inappropriate and appropriate ways to approach her. Hanuman overhears the inappropriate (to say the least) advances of Ravana, who employs many guises and expends many wily words in his attempts to win her favor. Sita refuses him over and over, eventually placing a straw between herself and Ravana (a *sitarekha?*) that the demon cannot cross. He explodes in a rage, but she responds with the observation that she herself could destroy him with her own "brilliance" or "brilliant energy" (*tejas*)—a particular mention of the power of Sita's own golden power (5.20:20).

---

[12] Sally Sutherland Goldman, "Anklets Away: The Symbolism of Jewellery and Ornamentation in Valmkik's Ramayana," in *The Ramayana Culture: Text, Performance and Iconography,* ed. Mandrakanta Bose (New Delhi: D.K. Printworld (P) Ltd., 2003) 157.

After Ravana has left, one of the *rakshasa* women speaks of a dream she has had, wherein Rama vanquishes Ravana and destroys Lanka. This premonition addresses the divine strength of Sita as well: in the dream, the demonness sees Sita's own power—Sita rises from her husband's lap and strokes the sun and moon with her hands. The *rakshasa* tells her companions that, based on this dream, "Now only Maithili, the daughter of Janaka—and only if she is propitiated by our falling at her feet—can save the *rakshasa* women from this grave danger" (5.25.31).

In contrast to Ravana, Hanuman ponders long on the most effective and proper way to approach Sita—after all, he is a monkey, a creature considered inauspicious by *shastras.* Moreover, she might simply dismiss him as Ravana in yet another disguise. He begins by reciting her own history to her, but Sita is still suspicious. Finally, Hanuman is able to convince her of his good intent with his words and by showing her Rama's signet ring. He then falls at her feet and addresses her with cupped hands. Hanuman successfully accomplishes his mission, crossing the "Sitarekha" and offering Rama's ring in exchange for Sita's jewel.

One of the most famous of the episodes centering on Sita as a figure both as part of ritual tradition and as belonging to a tradition that would come to treat her as an independent goddess is the ordeal by fire, the *Agnipariksha.* This episode may be a later interpolation, but it remains a crucial part of the Valmiki *Yuddha Kanda* (6.103 104). Although we all know, having been with her in the Lanka, that Sita has been faithful to Rama, he finds it necessary to test his wife. She enters the flames much like an oblation in the sacrifice (6.104.24-26). The confluence of the Vedic tradition especially concerned with the sacrifice and what might be popular tradition, both of which deal with the morphologies of fire, gold, agricultural prosperity, purity, and the goddess may be impossible to untangle in the *Agniparikhsha*. Sita proves herself yet again to be the embodiment of the precious wealth of the earth: an allusion to both gold and agriculture.

The association between Sita and gold is unexpectedly made explicit in the last book of the Valmiki *Ramayana*. In the *Uttara Kanda,* Rama decides that the time is ripe to perform an *Asvamedha*, even though his wife, whose presence is prerequisite, has been banished and lives in exile at Valmiki's hermitage. To take her place in the ritual, Rama calls for a golden figure *(kancanim*) of her to be consecrated (7.82.19). Gold and objects of gold were used the performance of Vedic rituals, and particularly associated with the royal *Ashvamedha* within the early Vedic texts.[13] As Stephanie Jamison notes though, when discussing these much earlier treatises on sacrifice, "This problem [the wife of the *yajamana* not being in attendance] is dealt with in a *novel* way in a famous makeshift in the *Ramayana*, in which Rama makes a golden image of the absent Sita to substitute for the required patni and allow him to perform ritual."[14]

Is it possible that the Valmiki *Ramayana* implemented this innovation because the golden likeness had referents not only to the seeking of ends by means of the sacrifice but the attempt to evoke the localized deity by the representation of the heroine, one who is repeatedly likened to Shri and Lakshmi? This iconization of Sita may point to an essential "underground" amalgamation in the history of Hinduism: There are the Vedic orthodox as well as popular devotional aspects to the golden imagery associated with the goddess. While this icon of Sita is invested with power, there is no mention of literal worship of that image, only its continuing presence. We do know, of course, that images become essential to Hinduism, but we cannot accurately trace or correctly impute to any particular tradition the exact history of icon worship. Still, there is the possibility that Sita's historical alliance with agriculture, food, wealth, and the golden goddess, Shri-Lakshmi, might be continued and reinforced in the *kancanim* and that the wealth of the earth is signified in and attainable from the presence of this image. Only if the earth continues to produce can people be prosperous and properly nourished.

As part of the description of the *Ashvamedha* in the *Ramayana,* the "return to origins" of Sita certainly participates in the regenerative aspects of the sacrifice. Sita, by re-entering the earth, regains the fertile potentiality that was hers at birth. The parallel between the events of the first and last *Kandas* is evident: Born during a royal sacrifice as the wealth of the earth, she returns during a royal sacrifice to this original state. No less than the earth goddess herself, Dharani, seated on an elegant throne, places Sita on her lap (7.88.10-15) and returns her to her birthplace below. Rama's devotion to Sita is never diluted or lessened: Bereaved, he remains "married" solely to her. Rama does not choose another wife after Sita, and "In sacrifice after sacrifice, he continues to use a golden (image of) Janaki to serve as the *patni*" (7.89.4). As such, Sita figuratively and literally remains in a primal form (something of a "motherlode") to ensure wealth and prosperity both below and above the ground.

The Valmiki Sita does not emerge from that epic an independent

---

[13] See Jan Gonda, *The Functions and Significance of God in the Ved,* (Leiden: E.J. Brill, 1991) passim.

[14] Stephanie W. Jamison, *Sacrificed Wife, Sacrificer's Wife: Women, Ritual, and Hospitality in Ancient India* (New York: Oxford University Press, 1996) 35.

goddess; this development comes much later, after the Rama *kathas* themselves undergo innumerable iterations and reiterations. Still, the Sita figure, as specifically described in the Valmiki *katha*, is imbued with enough of Shri-Laksmi's popular history, functions, and associations to contribute to her later identification with that goddess in many of the Shri-Vaishnavaite devotional texts. The Valmiki Sita is not, by far, fully identified as Shri-Lakshmi however, nor will it be Shri-Lakshmi who presides over the modern *Sita Rasoi* shrines. The Valmiki Sita's relation to Vedic mythic and ritual notions of ideal kingship is certainly a factor in putting her in the kitchen, as I have discussed elsewhere. But the Valmiki text also contains numerous allusions that suggest that the "devotional element" of the so-called Little Tradition played a part as well. As such, one may think of the Sita of the *Rasoi* shrines as signifying that very definition of complex mixtures in Indian cooking, *masala.*

A great deal of time passes between the composition of the Valmiki *Ramayana* and the appearance of *Sita Rasoi*s as places of worship. To separate out what is "orthodox" and what is "popular" in the establishment of the *Sita Rasoi* shrines may be impossible; yet we must note when and where the earliest mention of such a shrine appears. The first written record of a *Sita Rasoi* shrine is in the text that praises the birthplace of Ram, Ayodhya. The *Ayodhya Mahatmya* appears during the great Ramaite bhakti movement of the fifteenth to eighteenth centuries in Northern India. Precisely as Rama becomes a focus of devotion, so do other important figures of the *Ramakatha.* With Sita in particular, ancient goddess worship associated with agriculture and especially the production of plentiful foodstuffs, may have combined in the history of Hinduism to land her in the most suitable site for specific worship of her in the modern age—the one place where food must be plentiful and nourishment distributed—the kitchen.

CHAPTER FOUR

KANNON: THE GODDESS OF COMPASSION IN JAPAN

KENNETH D. LEE

Kannon (Regarder of the Cries of the World) is the name of the Japanese goddess who is known as Avalokiteśvara, the Bodhisattva of Compassion, who originated from Indian Buddhism and has been worshiped throughout the Buddhist world. Revered and adored by followers of the Mahāyāna Buddhist tradition, Avalokiteśvara is a unique deity in the Buddhist pantheon and has been venerated as equally as the Buddha, and sometimes more, especially by art lovers. Earlier iconographic representations portray Avalokiteśvara as a male figure. For instance, in the second to third century C.E., a typical image of Avalokiteśvara in Gandhara, a region of northwest India, had a pronounced jaw, long wavy hair adorned with jewelry, and a moustache. However, in East Asia, Avalokiteśvara, who is known as Kuan-yin in China, Kwanse'um in Korea, Kannon in Japan, and Quan-am in Vietnam, was portrayed in the female form. For example, in T'ang China, the white-robed Kuan-yin appeared to be decidedly feminine, with a face that was round with layered chins, body that was supple in a natural sway, eyebrows curved, lips red, rosy cheeks, and overall beautiful and effeminate look. Although this transformation remains a mystery, a closer examination of the cultural traditions, scriptural sources, and indigenous iconographies of local cults may provide helpful clues to better understand the fluid and changing form of the Goddess of Compassion. This study traces the evolution of the worship of Avalokiteśvara from India to Japan, and discusses the sexual transformation of Avalokiteśvara in East Asia.

The sexual transformation from the masculine Avalokiteśvara to the feminine Kannon has fascinated many scholars. Some scholars have supposed that this change occurred with the influence of Taoist yin-yang reinterpretations, which may have arbitrarily assigned wisdom, the more rational character of Buddhist virtues, as yang with male characteristics, and compassion, the more emotional character, as yin with female characteristics.[1] The French Sinologist H. Maspero has suggested an explanation for the transformation of Avalokiteśvara into a female form: "Mahāyāna Buddhism had always considered enlightenment as the conjunction of wisdom and compassion. Symbolically, in Tantric Buddhism, wisdom is considered to be male and compassion female. With the introduction of Tantric Buddhism in the eighth century made popular by many Tantric masters who were active at that time, all the Buddhas and Bodhisattvas were provided with female consorts."[2]

In Mahāyāna Buddhism, a bodhisattva (Jpn. *bosatsu*), literally meaning "enlightened existence," is a compassionate being who has voluntarily chosen not to enter *nirvāna* (the state of enlightenment) in order to remain in this world, the realm of *samsāra* (transmigration or rebirth), to help others who are still suffering. According to Mahāyāna teaching, a bodhisattva's path will last for three, seven, or thirty-three eons, during which time he/she collects an inexhaustible amount of merit through the continuous practice of six perfections (*pāramitās*): generosity, morality, patience, energy, meditation, and wisdom. These perfections indicate the primary qualities that a bodhisattva seeks to unify compassion (*karuṇā*), skillful means (*upāya*), and wisdom (*prajñā*); of these, compassion is considered to be the most important, because it provides the whole motivation for entering the bodhisattva path. Beyond these six *pāramitās*, as the bodhisattva progresses to four final stages of the path, he/she will be able to manifest various supernatural powers. Then when the bodhisattva completes the tenth stage, or "ground," he/she will realize supreme enlightenment and become a Buddha.

In India, the bodhisattva Avalokiteśvara, which means "the Lord who sees (from on high)"—indicating that Avalokiteśvara looks down from the realm of Amitābha (Jpn. Amida; "the Buddha of Boundless Light"), the name of the central Buddha in Pure Land or Shin Buddhism, with love and compassion, ready to respond to the needs of sentient beings—is probably the most important bodhisattva in Mahāyāna Buddhism and is featured prominently in the *Lotus Sūtra.* In the *Karaṇdavyūha Sūtra,* it is said that Avalokiteśvara originally appeared as a ray of white light emanating from the right eye of Amitābha, who was engaged in deep-seated meditation.[3]

[1] Chün-fang Yü, *Kuan-yin: The Chinese Transformation of Avalokiteśvara* (New York: Columbia University Press, 2001), 20.

[2] Kenneth Ch'en, *Buddhism in China: A Historical Survey* (Princeton: Princeton University Press, 1964), 341-342.

[3] John Clifford Holt, *Buddha in the Crown: Avalokiteśvara in the Buddhist Traditions of Śri Lanka* (New York: Oxford University Press, 1991), 47-48.

The Bodhisattva then chanted the "six-character" dhāranī (magical spell), *Om maṇi padme hūm* (O the Jewel in the Lotus!), a *nembutsu* (lit. "mindfulness of the Buddha"; a meditational practice) that was adopted and recited repeatedly by followers of Nichiren Buddhism as the central practice to realize enlightenment. The popularity of Avalokiteśvara is due to the personification and embodiment of *karuṇā* (compassion) and is thus called *Mahākaruṇā*; the other necessary component of a Buddha being wisdom, *prajñā*, which is embodied in *Manjuśri*. Strictly speaking, like all great bodhisattvas in Mahāyāna Buddhism, Avalokiteśvara cannot be said to possess any gender characteristics, although in India the deity is usually portrayed as a handsome and princely young man. Iconographically, Avalokiteśvara is often depicted with a thousand arms and a thousand eyes to convey his compassionate nature expressed in all directions. He is also eleven-headed (in the form of *ekādasa*), because when he looked at suffering humanity, his head split open from pain. The earliest eleven-headed Avalokiteśvara that is dated to the late fifth to early sixth century C.E. can be seen in Cave 41, Kanheri, Maharastra, India.[4]

In China, Avalokiteśvara is known as Kuan-yin (Perceiver of Sounds). According to Chinese legends, Kuan-yin is regarded as the spiritual son of Amitābha, although she always appears iconographically as a female figure. Surviving examples of Kuan-yin portrayed as a female figure can be seen at the Buddhist sculptural sites located in Tun-huang in Kansu, Hangshow in Chekiang, Ta-tsu in Szechwan, and Ta-li in Yünnan, which are dated in the late T'ang and early Sung (late ninth to early tenth century); The British Museum currently houses several colorful banners from the Tun-huang, which portray Kuan-yin as a fashionably dressed woman, carrying a censer in one hand and a banner in the other, guiding a soul to paradise. Two Ch'ing scholars, Chao I (1727–1814) and Yü Cheng-hseih (1775–1850), found several references to either Kuan-yin appearing as a woman to save someone, as in the case from Fa-yüan chu-lin of Kuan-yin appearing as a woman in 479 to P'eng Tzu-chiao in prison and loosening him from his shackles, or to real women being addressed as Kuan-yin, as in the case of the last empress of the Ch'en, née Shen, who became a Buddhist nun and received the religious name "Kuan-yin" in 617.[5] In her book, *Kuan-yin*, Yü explains that sexual transformation of Avalokiteśvara occurred sometime between the T'ang and Sung dynasty.

---

[4] Susan L. Huntington, with contributions by John C. Huntington, *The Art of Ancient India: Buddhist, Hindu, Jain* (New York: Weatherhill, 1985), 265.

[5] *Taishōshinshū daizōkyō* (The Buddhist Canon Newly Compiled during the Taishō Era), ed. by Takakusu Junjirō and Watanabe Kaigyoku (Tokyo: Taishō issaikyō kankōkai, 1924-1935), vol. 53, 484c.

In the Sung period, the feminine incarnation of Kuan-yin was known as the Fish-basket Kuan-yin (Yu-lan Kuan-yin) or the Wife of Mr. Ma (Ma-lang-fu), discussed in the well-known folk tale of Princess Miao-shan.[6] According to legend, Kuan-yin was actually the daughter of the King of the Chou Dynasty, the Princess Miao-shan (Wonderful Goodness), who was sentenced to death by her father for refusing to marry a suitor of her father's choice. The story goes like this:

> Miao-shan was the third daughter of King Miao-chuang (Wonderful Adornment). She was by nature drawn to Buddhism, keeping a vegetarian diet, reading scriptures by day, and meditating at night from an early age. The king had no sons and hoped to choose an heir from among his sons-in-law. When Miao-shan reached the marriageable age, however, she refused to get married, unlike her two elder sisters, who had both obediently married the men chosen by their father. The king was greatly angered by her refusal and punished her harshly in different ways. She was first confined to the back garden and subjected to hard labor. When, with the aid of gods, she completed the tasks, she was allowed to go the White Sparrow Nunnery to undergo further trials in the hope of discouraging her from pursuing the religious path. She persevered, and the king burned down the nunnery, killed the five hundred nuns, and had Miao-shan executed for her unfilial behavior. While her body was safeguarded by a mountain spirit, Miao-shan's soul toured hell and saved beings there by preaching to them. She returned to the world, went to Hsiang-shan, meditated for nine years, and achieved enlightenment. By that time, the king had become seriously ill with a mysterious disease that resisted all medical treatment. Miao-shan, disguised as a mendicant monk, came to the palace and told the dying king that there was only one remedy that could save him: a medicine concocted with the eyes and hands of someone who had never felt anger. She further told the astonished king where to find such a person. When the king's messengers arrived, Miao-shan willingly offered her eyes and hands. The father recovered after taking the medicine and came to Hsiang-shan with the royal party on a pilgrimage to offer thanks to his savior. He recognized the eyeless and handless ascetic as no other than his own daughter. Overwhelmed with remorse, he and the rest of the royal family all converted to Buddhism. Miao-shan was transformed into her true form, that of the Thousand-eyed and Thousand-armed Kuan-yin. After the apotheosis, Miao-shan passed away and a pagoda was erected to house her relics.[7]

Interwoven with Buddhist scriptural references, the legend of Miao-shan existed in various forms and could be recited by many villagers, even

---

[6] Yü, *Kuan-yin,* 407-448.

[7] Ibid., 293-294.

today. Many women undoubtedly resonated with the sympathetic themes found in the story, such as the importance of an independent female spirit, family, filial piety, and sacrifice.[8] The climax of the story is clearly Miao-shan's willing sacrifice of her eyes and hands to save her father from dying from an incurable illness. This supreme act of sacrifice explains why Miao-shan was transformed into the Thousand-eyed and Thousand-handed Kuan-yin. Other Chinese tales say that when Miao-shan's soul toured hell, her radiance turned hell into paradise, so the god of hell sent her back to earth again, now transformed as Kuan-yin, riding on a lotus flower, holding a lotus in her hands, and wearing a flowing white robe.[9] Consequently, the presence of the white garment has led many scholars to trace the origin of the iconography to Tantric sources, connection made to the female consort of Avalokiteśvara in Tibetan Buddhism, the White Tārā (in Sanskrit, Pāndaravāsinī, meaning "clad in white"[10]).

In Korea, Avaloṭeśvara is known as Kwanse'um (also Kwanum). In the southern province of Kyongju in south Korea, located in Mt. T'oham from Bulguksa, in Sokkuram or "stone cave hermitage," the eminent Korean monk, Eisang (625–702), promoted Hwaom (Chinese "Huayen"), centering on the worship of Kwanum Posal worship during the United Shilla Kingdom in 680 CE. In Sokkuram, there are several prominent cave carvings of Kwanum Posal, which represented compassion, and was among the Buddha triad—the other two being Taeil Yorae (Skt.

---

[8] Kwan Yin as comforter, healer, and female exemplar has been adopted as a personal deity by a growing number of Western women, whether Buddhists or not. Sandy Boucher, *Discovering Kwan Yin: The Buddhist Goddess of Compassion* (Boston: Beacon Press, 1999).

[9] Ibid., 248.

[10] In his book, *Bodhisattva of Compassion*, John Blofeld relates the evolution of Kuan-yin to the Tibetan deity, Tara. Tara is regarded as "a beautiful female divinity able to manifest herself in twenty-one different forms to help sentient beings." Blofeld believes that Kuan-yin shares Tara's two main functions: to rescue people from suffering and to help them to overcome their binding delusions. He explains that Kuan-yin is the Chinese version of portraying compassion through a beautiful and friendly deity in idealized human form, much like the way Tara was viewed in Tibet. Blofeld adds that there are many paintings that show Kuan-yin's posture and mudras to be akin to Tara's. In his book, *Hinduism and Buddhism*, Sir Charles Eliot offers a similar analysis that the creation of the female Kuan-yin was probably "facilitated by the worship of Tara, frequently represented as caressing a child." Eliot explains that the Chinese religious sentiment required a Madonna-like deity who gives sons to those who were childless. (John Blofeld, *Bodhisattva of Compassion: The Mystical Tradition of Kuan Yin* (Boston: Shambhala, 1988), 124-130.

Mahāvairocana), which sat in the center as the symbol of the sun and light, and Munsu Posal (Skt. *Manjuśri* Bodhisattva), which sat on the left, as the symbol of wisdom—that represented the blessed Hwaom ideal of a "Buddha land." Due to Eisang's teachings, all of Korea came to be thought of as a Buddha land, and various areas came to be thought of as sacred places in which Kwanum or Munsu Posal resided. Directly behind the main statue, there is a finely carved statuette of Kwanum, depicted as a woman, which stands 2.2 meters tall. Kwanum's clothing is draped with exquisite detail, with her right hand holding a garment cord between her thumb and forefinger, and her left hand holding a vase with flowers in it. The most striking feature, however, is Kwanum's headdress, which has eleven heads arranged symmetrically in rows of seven, three, and one, symbolizing wisdom.

In Japan, Avalokiteśvara is known as Kannon (Regarder of the Cries of the World; also Kanzeon and Kwannon). The Pure Land scriptures present Kannon as one of the two attendants—the other being Seishi, who embodies wisdom—of the Amida Buddha (Skt. Amitābha). An excellent example of a wooden sculpture from the Asuka period is the figure in the Hōryūji, a large temple founded by Prince Shōtoku in the southern Nara prefecture, of the bodhisattva Kannon, known as the Kudara Kannon (Kudara in Japanese means Baekje, the seventh century kingdom in Korea). In popular religion Kannon was frequently portrayed in feminine form, possibly stemming from the *Lotus Sūtra*'s statement that the Bodhisattva will take on the guise of a woman or any other figure in order to lead sentient beings to salvation, and perhaps to suggest the feminine representation as more expressive of compassion. In the *Lotus Sūtra*, Kannon is the compassionate bodhisattva who responds to the suffering of all sentient beings and helps them toward salvation. According to Chapter 25 in the *Kannonkyō Sūtra*, Kannon appears in this world in various forms to save those who called out her name. In the iconographical portrayal of Kannon in the *Sūtra*, the artist conveys her spirit of compassion by drawing a hand of Kannon in the act of catching and saving someone who has fallen off a mountain. The *Lotus Sūtra* confirms this sentiment as it says: "If from the peak of (Mt.) Sumeru, people would hurl him down, let him think of the Cry-Regarder's [Kannon] power, and like the sun he will stand firm in the sky."

In the Japanese idealization of the Bodhisattva of Compassion, Kannon appears in many different forms to save people according to their time and place. This idea is actually consistent with the *Avalokiteśvara Sūtra*, which mentions thirty-three specific forms or incarnations (*keshin*)[11] of the Goddess of Compassion, who comes in many forms to save those who are suffering. Iconographically, Kannon is often depicted with eleven heads (Juichimen-Kannon), symbolic of spreading compassion in all directions, and she is also often shown with a thousand hands (Senju-Kannon), symbolic of her ability to embrace earth and alleviate the suffering of all people in the earthly realm. Since she is one of the principal attendants of Amida, the Buddha of the Western Paradise, there is a figure of the Amida among her eleven heads. As for other manifested images of Kannon, mostly reproduced from various types from China, statuettes of Kannon date back as far as to 606 C.E. For instance, there is the Kannon with eight arms (Fuku-kenjaku-Kannon), with a thousand hands (Senju-Kannon) or eleven heads (Juichimen-Kannon), and a Yumechigai-Kannon ("who changes dreams" into happy dreams), dated to 660, which are preserved in Nara at the Hōryūji, the oldest Buddhist temple in the country. The Kondō (main hall) of the Hōryūji also houses a series of paintings—the Amida triad, consisting of Amida Buddha flanked by his two attendants, Kannon and Seishi, and other various Kannons—which were in existence around 710. At the center of the rotunda in Hōryūji, there is a statue of Kannon, which is attributed to the work of Prince Shōtoku, who is regarded to be the father of Japanese Buddhism. At the Tōdaiji, the great official temple of Nara, inside the Sangatsudō chapel, there is dry lacquer-work of an early eighth century sculpture of Kannon with eight arms and three eyes (the third in his joined hands), flanked by the Gods Bonten (Brahma) and Taishakuten (Indra). In Kōfukuji, another central temple of the Nara period, another image of Kannon is placed between two great embroideries, one of which represents the Potalaka Mountain (Kannon's heaven) and the other, Amida's Paradise. In Japan, the most widely known pilgrimage sites—about one hundred—are devoted to Kannon, attracting many worshipers to visit each one of the sites in proper order, which is believed to save the believer from Hell and to open the gates to Paradise.

Kannon occupies a major place in the liturgy of the Pure Land School, which is the most popular form of Buddhism in Japan today. In the liturgical works by Shinran (1173–1262), the founder of the True Pure Land School (*Jōdo shinshū*), the Goddess of Compassion is referred to as "*guze* Kannon" (world-saving bodhisattva of compassion). In the *Kōtaishi Shōtoku hōsan*, Shinran described Shōtoku Taishi, the renowned prince regent who is regarded as the father of Japanese Buddhism for his

[11] In traditional Japanese Buddhist art and sculpture, the "Sho Kannon" represents the unchangeable form of the deity—the "pure and sacred form"—while her other manifestations are commonly referred to as the thirty-three *keshin* (incarnations).

monumental role in officially promoting Buddhism in Japan in the Seventeen-Article Constitution (*Jushichijō kenpō*) in 604 C.E., as the reincarnation of *guze* Kannon. What is particularly important to note is Shinran's use of the adjective *guze* (world-saving), in describing both Kannon and Prince Shōtoku. Shinran's use of the adjective *guze* refers to his significant role as the founder of Buddhism and also as a manifestation of the bodhisattva Kannon.

In order to better understand Shinran's profound worship of Kannon as the savior of the world, we must consider the historical and spiritual context of Shinran's time in the Kamakura period (1185–1333). In Shinran's time, the emergence of an exclusive form of practice in Kamakura Buddhism was closely connected with the development of *mappō* consciousness. Integrated into the Pure Land tradition by Tao-ch'o (562–645), the idea of *mappō* refers to a qualitative view of time that is envisioned in relation to the lifetime of Śākyamuni.[12] *Mappō* refers to the degenerating age of Buddhism—lasting 10,000 years—when people are no longer able to realize enlightenment because they are far removed from historical Buddha's teachings and practices. In other words, the spiritual, moral, and physical conditions on earth are seen to progressively deteriorate in direct proportion to the time that has elapsed since the Buddha's *parinirvana* (complete realization of enlightenment; "death"). During the Heian period, 949 B.C.E. came to be accepted as the date of the Buddha's death, and Buddhist circles adopted the explanation that the period of True Dharma and Counterfeit Dharma each lasted for 1,000 years, placing the commencement of *mappō* in 1052 C.E.13. The *mappō* doctrine provided a way to account for the desperate situation in Japan, and instilled a new fear with its implication of an age when the dharma

---

[12] *Shinshū shōgyō zensho*, 1: 378-379; see also Jan Nattier's *Once Upon a Future Time: Studies in a Buddhist Prophecy of Decline* (Berkeley: Asian Humanities Press, 1991).

[13] Buddhist tradition maintains that as the world moves farther and farther away from the time of the historical Buddha, understanding of his teachings grows increasingly distorted, and the people's capacity to practice and benefit from those teachings accordingly declines, until eventually Buddhism is lost. In the age of True Dharma (*shōbō*), lasting 500 (some say 1,000) years, the Buddha's teaching is properly practiced and enlightenment can be attained; in the age of Counterfeit Dharma (*zōbō*), lasting 1,000 (some say 500) years, the teaching is practiced but enlightenment is no longer possible; and in the age of degenerating Dharma (*mappō*), lasting 10,000 years, only teaching remains; one finds neither practice nor proof. Edward Kamens, *The Three Jewels: A Study and Translation of Minamoto Tamenori's Sanbōe* (Ann Arbor, MI: Center for Japanese Studies, 1988), 44-46.

would be lost. As the foundation of the central government began to collapse, the focus of Buddhism shifted from protection of the State to personal salvation.[14] The *mappō* doctrine influenced Shinran, who believed that Shōtoku Taishi was the incarnation of Kannon who compassionately appeared in Japan during *mappō*. This is the main reason why Shinran referred to Shōtoku Taishi as *guze* Kannon in his hymns.

In the Appendix of *Kōsō wasan* (Hymns of the Pure Land Masters, 1248) Shinran found special significance in the timing of Prince Shōtoku's birth: "Born on the first day of the first month in the first year of Emperor Bidatsu, 1521 years after the passing of the Buddha."[15] According to a widely accepted belief, the world entered the last dharma-age (*mappō*—the final period in the decline of the dharma in the world) 1500 years after Shakyamuni's death. Thus, Prince Shōtoku's life corresponded to the onset of the last age, and Shinran regarded him as a manifestation of the bodhisattva Kannon, who appeared in Japan precisely at this time to guide beings to the Pure Land path.[16]

> Entrusting ourselves to the vow of the inconceivable wisdom of the Buddha through the kindness of Prince Shōtoku, we have entered the true stage of the settled mind and have become like Maitreya (Jpn. Miroku), the Buddha-to-come.
>
> The world-saving bodhisattva of compassion, *guze* Kannon, who appeared and announced himself as Prince Shōtoku is like a father, never deserting us, and like a mother, always looking after us.
>
> From the beginningless past to the world of present, Prince Shōtoku has compassionately looked after us like a father and stayed close to us like a mother.
>
> Prince Shōtoku has compassionately recommended and led us to believe in the vow of inconceivable wisdom of the Buddha, so that we are now able to enter the true stage of the settled mind.
>
> May all those who entrust themselves in *tariki* (Other-power) to fulfill the benevolence of the Buddha, spread the two aspects of the *nyorai* (Tathāgata) Buddha's virtue throughout the ten quarters.
>
> The world-saving Prince Shōtoku of great love stays in our heart like he is our father; the world-saving bodhisattva of compassion, *guze* Kannon, stays in our heart like she is our mother.

---

[14] Salvation here was often conceived of in a worldly rather than a religious sense. Many nobles in the late Heian period seem to have looked upon rebirth in the Pure Land as an extension of their elegant lifestyle into the next world, without any fundamental questioning of the values that lifestyle presupposed.

[15] *Kōsō wasan* (Hymns of the Pure Land Masters), 1248, *Teihon Shinran Shōnin zenshū*, vol. 2 (Kyoto: Hōzōkan, 1969).

[16] Ibid.

> From the incalculable aeons of the past to this present world, out of Prince Shōtoku's great compassion, we have now entered the inconceivable wisdom of the Buddha, which is beyond the notion of good and evil, pure and impure.
>
> Prince Shōtoku, the religious founder of Japan: we are profoundly indebted and grateful to him. Trust him wholeheartedly and praise him always.
>
> Out of deep concern for the people of Japan, Prince Shōtoku came to enlighten people by proclaiming the compassionate vow of *nyorai*. Let us rejoice and praise him always!
>
> Through countless lives and incalculable eons of the past to this present world, every one of us has received his profound compassion. Trust him wholeheartedly and praise him always.
>
> With his compassionate care, Prince Shōtoku always provides for us and protects us and encourages us to receive the two aspects of *nyorai* Buddha's virtue.[17]

We can clearly see from these *wasan* (hymns) that Shinran worshiped Prince Shotoku as the incarnation of Kannon and the manifestation of the Buddha's virtue of love and compassion.

In his *Kōtaishi Shōtoku hōsan* (Hymns in Praise of Prince Shōtoku), Shinran describes Prince Shōtoku, with his significant achievements and contributions to the promotion of Buddhism in Japan, as the incarnation of Bodhisattva Kannon who appeared in Japan during *mappō*. In support of his belief that Shōtoku was an incarnation of Bodhisattva Kannon, Shinran traces Shōtoku's karmic connections to previous dharma masters in India and China:

> In India, Prince Shōtoku was known as queen Śrīmālā and in China, he appeared as master Hui-ssu.
>
> In China, in order to help sentient beings, Prince Shōtoku was reborn five hundred times both as a man and a woman.
>
> In order to spread the Buddhist teachings, Prince Shōtoku appeared at the Hunan province on Mount Heng in the form of various incarnations in order to spread the *nyorai*'s teaching.
>
> In order to help sentient beings toward enlightenment, Prince Shōtoku appeared as Master Hui-ssu in the temple at Mount Heng, and he was known as the Master of the Southern Mountain.[18]

---

[17] *Shōzōmatsu wasan* (Hymns of the Dharma-Ages), 1257, *Teihon Shinran Shōnin zenshū*, vol. 2 (Kyoto: Hōzōkan, 1969); signed Gutoku Zenshin.

[18] *Kōtaishi Shōtoku hōsan* (Hymns in Praise of Prince Shōtoku), *Shinshū shōgyō zensho*, vol. 2, Hymns 11-14.

According to Shinran, in this hymn Prince Shōtoku was born as Queen Śrīmālā, who renounced her imperial duties in order to become a devoted nun and a disciple of Buddha. In other words, Shinran is essentially claiming that Prince Shōtoku received the dharma directly from Śākyamuni Buddha. Consequently, Shinran's vision of Shōtoku incarnated as a woman has special significance. Because Kannon was understood to be feminine, Shinran obviously had a positive view of femininity. Shinran's explanation of Shōtoku's incarnation as Queen Śrīmālā in India confirms that Shinran identified with Shōtoku's idea of salvation for all sentient beings, including and especially women, who were considered by older and traditional schools of Buddhism to be inferior.

A perfect example of Kannon's manifestation in the feminine form to save sentient beings is found in a dream account of Shinran. After twenty years of Buddhist study at the Tendai center at Mount Hiei since he first became a monk at the age of nine, Shinran took a hundred-day retreat at Rokkakudō, a temple dedicated to Kannon in Kyoto city, where the bodhisattva manifested herself as Shōtoku Taishi, told Shinran that she would incarnate herself as a woman. This revelation became significant for Shinran's religious and personal development, because soon after the dream account he broke his vow of celibacy when he married Eshinni and had several children. Through the dream and the truth of the prophecies, according to Eshinni, Shinran came to believe that Shōtoku was his personal savior. After receiving divine inspiration at Rokkakudō, Shinran soon met Hōnen by way of fate, according to the dream account, and set out on an active campaign to spread the Buddhist message of salvation in the name of the Amida Buddha among the countryside masses.

The account of Shinran's dream at Rokkakudō is found in several places: in his *Kyōgyōshinshō* (Teaching, Practice, Faith and Enlightenment), Eshinni's letters, Kakunyo's *Honganji no Shōnin Shinran denne* (Illustrated biography of the Master Shinran of the Honganji temple), and in the *Shinran muki* (Shinran's Dreams).[19] A copy of the

[19] *Kyōgyōshinshō*, *Shinshū shōgyō zensho,* 2: 202; *Eshinni shōsoku*, *Shinshū shōgyō zensho*, 5: 104-105; and *Honganji no Shōnin Shinran denne*, *Shinshū shōgyō zensho*, 3: 640. There are two versions of the *Shinran muki*. The first, listing a total of three dreams, is reproduced in Furuta Takehiko, *Shinran shisō: Sono shiryō hihan* (Tokyo: Fuzanbō, 1975), 3-5. The second version, reproduced in *Shinran Shōnin senshū kankokai*, ed., *Teihon Shinran Shōnin zenshū*, 9 vols. (Kyoto: Hōzōkan, 1969-70), vol. 4, pt. 2, 201-2, mentions only one dream. It contains a more detailed account of the third dream than the other *Shinran muki* does.) One version of this last work describes three dreams that made a lasting impression on Shinran: one occurring in 1191, the second in 1200, and the third in

Shinran muki by Shinran's disciple Shinbutsu (1209-1261)[20] and another version recently discovered by Hiramatsu Reizo, which has been authenticated to be in Shinran's handwriting, provide evidence of the profound impact that Shinran's dream encounter with Kannon had on his life:[21]

> *Guze* Kannon appeared as a righteous monk at Rokkakudō. Dressed in simple white robes and seated on a large white lotus, he said to Shinran: "If a practitioner is driven by sexual desire because of his past karma, then I shall take on the body of a holy woman (*gyokunyo*) to be ravished by him. Throughout his entire life I will adorn him, and at death I will lead him to birth in Pure Land." After saying these words, *guze* Kannon proclaimed to Zenshin [Shinran]: "This is my vow. Expound it to all people." Based on this proclamation, I realized that I needed to tell this message to millions of people, and then I awoke from my dream.[22]

The following is Kakunyo's account of the appearance of Kannon in Shinran's dream, taken from the *Honganji shōnin Shinran denne* (An Illustrated Biography of Shinran):

> On the fifth day of the fourth month in the third year of Kennin (1203), Shōnin had a vision at night in the hour of the Tiger. According to records, the world-saving bodhisattva of compassion [*guze* Kannon] of the Rokkakudō manifested himself in the form of a holy monk of dignified appearance, wearing a white robe and sitting in a proper posture on the pedestal of a huge lotus flower. He said to Zenshin: "If you are obliged to have sexual contact with a woman through some past karma, I will transform myself into a beautiful woman and become your partner. I will

---

1201; there are two copies of Shinran's dream, one written by Shinran himself and the other by a disciple (dates of these texts unknown). Found in the Senjuji collection, Mie prefecture, and in *Shinran-Shōnin zenshū*, vol. 4, 201-202.

[20] *Shinran muki* (Shinran's Dreams) was discovered in *Senshū*-ji, the head temple of the Takada Branch of Shin Buddhism, and when the author was determined to be Shinbutsu, a leading disciple of Shinran, the contents of his vision of Prince Shōtoku as a manifestation of Bodhisattva Kannon was verified.

[21] Reizō Hiramatsu, "Takada hoko shin hakken shiryō ni yoru shiron" in *Takada gakudō*, no. 46 (1959), 14-24.

[22] *Shinran muki* ["Record of Shinran's Deram"], *Shinran Shōnin zenshū*, vol. 4, 201; *Honganji Shōnin Shinran denne*, *Shinshū shōgyō zensho* 3, 640; *Shinran yume no ki, in Shinran Shōnin zenshū kankōkai*, ed., *Teihon Shinran Shōnin zenshū* (Kyoto: Hōzōkan 1969-70), vol., 3, 640. Interestingly, supporting the legend that Shinran was married to Princess Tamahi, the daughter of the then Prime Minister, Kujō Kanezane, the expression "holy woman" (*gyokunyo*) is the basis for the name Tamahi (*gyoku* and *tama* in Japanese are identical characters read differently).

adorn you with virtues throughout your life, and at your death I will guide you to the Land of Utmost Bliss.[23]

Particularly interesting in this passage is the sexual transformation of Bodhisattva Kannon, who has been traditionally worshiped as a male figure in Buddhism. Scholars remain uncertain about the beginning of female worship of Kannon in Japan, but this account provides one logical rationale for its origin and development. Many writers have interpreted this part of Shinran's dream in modern terms, suggesting that Shinran left Mount Hiei because he desired to have sexual relations—Shinran's subsequent marriage to Eshinni and birth of his children are consistent with this interpretation. Although monks typically took vows not to eat meat and to abstain from sexual relations, during Shinran's time it was widely known that many monks lived with women who bore them children; they simply pretended to remain celibate by not legally marrying the women they lived with. Unwilling to be hypocritical like his peers, Shinran was the first monk who openly and legally married a woman. Moreover, according to *Jōdo Shinshū* scholar, Hattori Shisō, Shinran had at least two, perhaps three wives, and a total of seven children.[24] In any

[23] *Honganji Shōnin Shinran denne*, *Shinshū shōgyō zensho* 3, 640.

[24] Hattori Shisō, *Shinran nōto*, 1948; rpt. (Tokyo: Fukumura Shugppan, 1972). There is, however, some inconclusive discussions about the timing and number of the marriage(s). Legend says that Shinran married Lord Kujō Kanezane's daughter, Tamahime, in Kyoto, but there is no conclusive proof of this, especially since there is no such name found in the Kujō family geneology; Recent studies have shown that this legend originated from the Kantō community of Shinran's followers, and first appeared in *The Secret Transmission of the Biography of Shinran* during the Muromachi Period (1338-1573). There seems to be some shreds of evidence indicating that Shinran's marriage took place in Echigo, presumably with Eshinni. Compare, for instance, in the postscript of the *Kyōgyōshinshō*, the phrase "I am therefore neither monk nor layman" (*sō ni arazu zoku ni arazu*), written about the fact of his exile, has the feeling of having been written by a married person. It also implies that Shinran was not "neither monk nor layman" when he was training with Hōnen in Kyoto, which means that he continued to follow all the Buddhist precepts, including celibacy; The phrase "neither monk nor layman" also supports the theory that Shinran entered the married life after he was exiled as a common criminal and returned to lay status, no longer having to observe the precepts, especially celibacy. On the other hand, Kasahara believes that Shinran's marriage to Eshinni took place in Echigo, and that this was his second marriage; During the Kamakura period, it was a common practice for people to have several wives. Kasahara Kazuo, *Shinran to tōgoku nōmin* (Tokyo: Yamakawa Shuppansha, 1957). In any case, there is no conclusive evidence. Regarding an extensive study on

case, in view of his master Hōnen's teaching of complete reliance on the Other-power, Shinran's decision to publicly break the Buddhist precept of celibacy was based on his belief that marriage did not hinder one's birth in the Pure Land.[25]

We have examined the unique and fluid nature of the Bodhisattva of Compassion, Avalokiteśvara, who for the sake of helping sentient beings in different cultures and time periods, has gone through various transformations, particularly as a woman in East Asia to symbolize the feminine expression of compassion, like that of a loving mother. Technically speaking, however, a bodhisattva does not have any gender characteristics because ultimate reality is emptiness (śūnyatā). However, just as the Tathāgata Buddha taught the Dharma using expedient means (*upāya*), there is nothing peculiar about the feminization of the Goddess of Compassion by communities or persons that call upon the bodhisattva for help in times of suffering. In fact, the *Śurangama Sūtra* explains that the Bodhisattva of Compassion appears in thirty-three forms, of which six are feminine: nun, laywoman, queen, princess, noble lady, and virgin maiden.[26] Thus, Avalokiteśvara, the Bodhisattva of Compassion, can surely appear as Tārā in Tibet, Kuan-yin in China, Kwanse'um in Korea, Kannon in Japan, or Quan-um in Vietnam, for the sake of sentient beings needing her compassionate aid. In some cases, in order to help seafarers, the Bodhisattva of Compassion may appear as Yu-lan Kuan-yin with fish baskets to help the common people who yearned for children and worshiped her as the "giver of children." It follows then that our study of the evolution of the worship of the Bodhisattva of Compassion should not

---

Eshinni's background, see Hattori Shisō's *Zoku Shinran nōto*, 1950; rpt. (Tokyo: Fukumura Shuppan, 1970).

[25] Although his teacher, Hōnen, never married, he advised: "People should always live by creating the proper condition for being able to say the nembutsu. If you cannot say the nembutsu as a celibate, say it by getting married. If you cannot say it by being married, say it as a celibate. If you cannot say it while remaining at one place, say it as you wander on your travels. If you cannot say it on your travels, say it at home. If you cannot say it while securing your daily necessities, say it by having others obtain them for you. If you cannot say it by others obtaining the necessities for you, say it by securing them yourself. If you cannot say it by yourself, say it with together with friends and comrades. If you cannot say it with other people, say it by yourself confined at home. Food, clothing, and shelter are necessary only in so far as they create the proper condition for people to say the nembutsu." Hōnen, 1133-1212, *Senjakushū : gendaigoyaku* / Hattori Eijun yakuchū (Tokyo: Daitō Shuppansha, 1980), 102.

[26] Lu K'uan Yü (Charles Luk), translator. *The Śūrangama Sūtra* (London: Rider, 1966), 137-38.

be so focused on the gender issue. Rather, our study may be more insightful if we tried to understand the origins of the various titles attributed to the Bodhisattva of Compassion, which are often proliferated through folklore, in order to better understand the communities' needs and the salvific role that Avalokiteśvara, Kuan-yin, Kwanse'um, Kannon, or Quan-um played in those respective societies. Consequently, such transformations were not restricted to Kuan-yin alone. For instance, the future Buddha, Maitreya, was transformed into a totally new form of a "laughing Buddha," a practice that is still prevalent in China and Southeast Asia. Such transformations may have evolved perhaps to reflect certain prevailing ideals, which are valued by the Chinese people, such as having an offspring, prosperity, and so on.

In conclusion, in East Asia, it appears that Avalokiteśvara was gradually transformed into a female deity beginning in China roughly around the time of the late T'ang and early Sung period as a result of a combination of esoteric influences from India and Tibet, Southeast Asian themes of feminine consorts for deities, and Tibetan esoteric rituals that explored feminine themes. Another factor that may have contributed to the sexual transformation of Avalokiteśvara in East Asia is the influence of Taoism, which may have assigned the loving and compassionate nature of Avalokiteśvara as idealized in the female, mother-goddess-like qualities, which were proliferated iconographically and through popular folk tales. By the time Buddhism entered Japan in the mid-sixth century, the Japanese adopted a highly sophisticated version of Avalokiteśvara who had the ability to manifest itself as either male or female, as exemplified in Shinran's dream where Kannon appears as Prince Shōtoku and also promises Shinran that Kannon would become his future wife. In the end, Kannon, as well as Kuan-yin, Kwanse'um, and Quan-um, expresses the same quality of the Buddhist *ethos* of love and compassion that is idealized in the bodhisattva Avalokiteśvara. With its chameleon-like nature and expedient ability to manifest itself in different forms for the sake of those who are suffering, the Bodhisattva of Compassion is in its essence, faceless, genderless, and formless, yet plays an important role in promoting the Buddhist *ethos* and sustaining ecumenical and universal sangha. Thus, the multiple images of Avalokiteśvara should be understood as the multi-religious and cross-cultural symbol, which was idealized as a goddess with many desirable attributes, which was popularized by many legends, folklore, and artistic work. Through multi-cultural engineering, the East Asians envisioned Avalokiteśvara in the forms of Kuan-yin in China, Kwanse'um in Korea, Kannon in Japan, and Quan-um in Vietnam as graceful and powerful feminine symbols to illustrate the quintessence of the Bodhisattva of Compassion.

CHAPTER FIVE

FROM KUAN YIN TO JOAN OF ARC: FEMALE DIVINITIES IN THE CAODAI PANTHEON

JANET HOSKINS

Abstract

Scholars of Vietnamese religion have described two parallel traditions, one identified with goddesses, spirit mediums, and indigenous forms of worship, and another identified with Buddhism, Confucianism, and Taoism, literate religions brought to Vietnam during the thousand year period of Chinese domination. Caodaism is a new religion, born in 1926 in Saigon, which presents an Asian synthesis of the three great East Asian traditions, and includes Judeo-Christian figures such as Jesus Christ and Moses, as well as Victor Hugo and the Chinese poet Li Bai. Joan of Arc takes her place in the pantheon as an assistant divinity to the Mother Goddess, who is the Creator of humanity, and Kuan Yin (Quan Am in Vietnamese) who embodies Buddhist values of mercy and compassion. The relationship between female divinities and the Supreme Being, called Caodai and represented as the Left Eye of God, is explored in this paper.

Images

At end of paper: Fig.1) The Mother Goddess is depicted surrounded by nine female immortals and many handmaidens at the Mother Goddess temple in Tay Ninh. Fig. 2) The Left Eye of God on the globe in the Tay Ninh temple. Fig. 3) The Caodai pantheon as represented above the altar in the new Garden Grove temple in California. Fig. 4) Chants to the Mother Goddess and the nine female immortals at the festival held for the mid autumn harvest moon at the Court of Heavenly Reason temple near San Jose, California.

Scholars of Vietnamese religion have often described two parallel traditions, one identified with goddesses, spirit mediums, and indigenous forms of worship, and another identified with Confucianism and Taoism, literate religions brought to Vietnam during the thousand year period of Chinese domination. Buddhism, which was introduced to Vietnam in the fourth century B.C.E., is practiced primarily in its Mahayana forms, better known to Americans as the Zen tradition. Because of its longer history, it has tended to be less identified with Chinese domination, although most forms of Vietnamese Buddhism are heavily influenced by Chinese culture.

Caodaism is a new religion, born in 1926 C.E. in Saigon, which presents an Asian synthesis of Confucianism, Buddhism, and Taoism, but also includes Judeo-Christian figures such as Jesus Christ and Moses, and integrates the veneration of spirits of nature and great heroes. Although in Western languages this syncretic faith is known by the name given to the Supreme Being ("Cao Dai" = the highest tower), its official name is *Dao Dao Tam Ky Pho Do*, "The Great Way of the Third Revelation," signaling the new revelations of spirit messages received in the early twentieth century showing the common origin of all world traditions. With about six million followers worldwide, Caodaism is now the third religion of Vietnam and is expanding its presence in overseas communities in the United States, Australia, France, Canada, and Germany. Caodai temples have the external form of Gothic cathedrals, with a nave, high towers, and carved pulpits, but inside they are filled with the colorful animals and images of Asian mythology: dragons, giant naga snakes, cranes, turtles, phoenixes, and unicorns. The central symbol of the divine light is a naturalistic left eye, the Eye of God (*thien nhan*), surrounded by the rays of the sun.

The Mother Goddess of Caodaism, whose symbol is the lotus flower, is addressed with the name Dieu Tri Kim Mau, the Golden Mother of the Jasper Pond, and her lineage is in many ways recognizably Chinese, since she represents the forces of yin or female energy in opposition to those of yang. But the Mother Goddess is also a figure who draws on indigenous traditions, who works to save human beings not through the administrative hierarchy of the church but through acts of compassion and mercy. She calls many of her followers to her directly, and her festival falls in the mid-autumn harvest season, in a splendid carnival with dragon dances and colorful costumes similar in many ways to the American Halloween.

What is the relationship between the goddess and the left eye of God? How does a Holy Mother who incarnates fleshy suffering and a warm heart relate to the occult mysteries represented by Taoist spiritist techniques and Confucian hierarchies? Are the blendings of Caodai cosmology an instance of what Clifford Geertz has called "*un syncretisme a l'outrance*"—an excessive, even transgressive mixture of East and West, the traditional and the modern—or is the relationship between the female goddess and the male god a model of gendered duality and cosmological balance that we would do well to learn from?

This paper explores the representation of feminine spirituality in a new religious movement, which has gathered several million followers in the first few decades of its emergence, and is now spread through a vast diaspora that runs from Saigon and Phnom Penh to Paris and Montreal, including a splendid new temple in Sydney, Australia and another under construction in "Little Saigon" (in Los Angeles), California, which has the largest Caodaist overseas community. It makes what are, in effect, two separate arguments about goddesses in Caodaism:

(1) The first is that the Caodai concept of a female co-Creator of the universe draws on indigenous traditions of *Dao Mau*, a goddess-centered faith which is often represented as the oldest and original faith of the Vietnamese, before domination by China. Goddesses like the Holy Mother and Quan Am are popular for being close to individuals with the least social power and interceding for them to the highest level of Heaven. They serve a function similar to that of the Virgin Mary in Catholicism, and Caodaist churches in the United States have also received spirit messages from the Virgin Mary herself.

(2) The second is that the introduction of French heroines into Caodaism, specifically Joan of Arc, is part of a gesture of encompassment and inclusion that builds on elements of Vietnamese heritage and their Western analogues. The veneration of women warriors like the first century C.E. Trung sisters and the third century C.E. Lady Trieu, who fought to drive back Chinese, laid the groundwork for Caodaist recognition of a French saint who was inspired by spirit messages to defend her homeland. Other great figures from French history—such as the nineteenth century literary giant Victor Hugo, a spiritist with a strong interest in Asian religions, have also been incorporated as saints in the Caodai pantheon. The spirit of Victor Hugo is the head of the overseas mission for Tay Ninh, the largest denomination, and he is joined by Louis Pasteur, La Fontaine, Aristide Briand, and Vladimir Lenin. But Asian figures like by Li Bái, the Chinese Taoist poet, remain more important than any European spirit. Li Bái serves as the Invisible "Pope" of Caodaism, and most of his spiritual advisors are associated with Buddhism and Taoism, not Western humanism.

Introduction to Caodai History

Caodaism's highly developed literary sensibility emerged in the context of a spiritual crisis in the largest French colony in Asia, where teachings about democratic ideals clashed with the experience of colonial authority. The first disciple of Caodai was Ngo Minh Chieu, an official of the French colonial administration, who combined interest in meditation, asceticism, and Chinese Taoist classics with readings in European spiritism. Chieu had a vision of the left eye of God, circled in light and rising up over the stars, moon, and rising sun, which became the sign of God worshipped on Caodaist altars. Soon he met other spiritists in Saigon who had made contact with a supreme spirit, identified with the first letters of the new romanised Vietnamese alphabet, and they combined forces when they realized they were receiving messages from the same Supreme Being.

On November 18, 1926, the religion declared its official birth in a dramatic ceremony that drew some fifty thousand people. Though resisted by Buddhists, Catholics, and French officials, who feared the political potential of a "Vietnamese national religion," the faith was soon a phenomenal mass movement. By 1930, it numbered a half million by conservative estimate, and soon had garnered several million followers, embracing at least one-eighth of the population in what was to become South Vietnam. Its eclectic mixture of "the gods of Europe" and "the gods of Asia" drew the support of French-educated intellectuals, peasants, and landlords, who yearned for an immediate contact with spirituality, presented as hybrid of indigenous traditions and modern democratic ideals. Caodaism filled a spiritual void for a people for whom Catholicism was identified with alien colonizers, Buddhism was idealistic but passively amorphous, and Confucianism was tied to an older hierarchy already eclipsed by colonial dislocations.

Later spirit messages described an elaborate religious organization, which featured a system of ranks similar to that of the Vatican (a Pope, female and male Cardinals, Bishops, and Priests) and mandated the construction of a "Holy See" with the Gothic towers of a Catholic cathedral and a colorful interior filled with dragons, phoenixes, nagas, and unicorns. Led first by Pope Le Van Trung and then by the charismatic spirit medium Pham Cong Tac, the religion established its headquarters in Tay Ninh and built 1300 temples throughout the south and central region of the nation. Caodaists pray four times a day to altars in the home, usually featuring photographs of ancestors as well as the image of the Eye of God, and meet on the new moon and full moon for more elaborate ceremonies at the temple. Rituals involve prayer, chanting, and offerings of fruits and flowers, incense, tea, and wine presented in an intricately stylized ceremony accompanied by sacred music. Séances are held separately, usually at midnight, and may be restricted to mediums who are part of the official hierarchy (especially at Tay Ninh).

A dozen other denominations of Caodaism developed in the years 1934–1964, spreading its influence throughout the Mekong Delta and up into the area around Danang and Hue. While the Tay Ninh Church was involved in political struggle against French colonialism and massive ritual ceremonies, the smaller groups stressed meditation, mysticism, and intimate spirit séances. New religious innovations, often inspired by séance communications from other mediums, produced a constantly expanding body of spirit messages, creating a theology which grew with the times until 1975, when the communist take-over of South Vietnam closed most of its temples for about twenty years. In 1997, as part of a policy of renovation and opening up to the rest of the world, the Socialist Republic of Vietnam recognized Caodaism and re-opened many of its temples, although they must now operate under stringent government supervision. Spirit séances are strictly forbidden, and the divinely mandated religious organization has been modified. Although Caodaism is deliberately universal and tolerant of other beliefs, it has suffered a history of political persecution and repression by both the French colonial administration and the communist government of Vietnam. With many thousands of Caodaists now living overseas in immigrant communities in the United States, Australia, France, and Canada, it is now expanding its presence in exile, turning the Caodaists who were forced to leave their country into the teachers of a new generation of religious leaders and dignitaries of all nationalities.

The Goddess and the Left Eye of God

The image of the Mother Goddess represented at her temple in Tay Ninh is based on the story of her apparition to the Han Emperor Han Vu De (141 B.C.E.–87 C.E.) of China, who prayed for her to appear on the fifteenth day of the eighth lunar month, the autumn equinox. The goddess blessed his sincerity by appearing and granting him holy peaches of immortality. Since that miracle, many other people have prayed to her, and she has shown them love and compassion whatever their social position.

The left eye does not represent, as Americans might believe, the female side of divinity but the male side. The left is the side that looks towards the rising sun, and it is the side of positive, male energy, and of growth, forcefulness, and passion. The right, by a similar oppositional logic, is the side of the setting sun, and it is passive, female energy, and of darkness, weakness, and softness. In East Asian cosmologies, the Supreme Being is associated with yang (Vietnamese *duong*) in contrast with yin (Vietnamese *am*), and it is the interaction of these opposing forces that brought the universe into being.

The origin of humanity comes from the Goddess Dieu Tri Kim Mau, who is the source of the first sexual fluid or *tinh*, which is also the name for the sexual fluids produced in men's bodies as semen (*ngon tinh*) and in women's bodies as the ovum (*am tinh*). When an individual receives a spark of the divine light, that individual's spirit is incarnated and the body comes to life. The divine light or spirit comes from the Supreme Being, but the Mother Goddess provides the perispirit or soul, the part of the spirit which can travel out of the body, and the human mother and father provide the flesh of the material body.

Human beings, unlike plants and animals, have intelligence, souls, and spirits, so they can aspire to unite the three treasures and achieve unification with God. These three elements have their origin in the primordial unity of the world before the division of heaven and earth, a state of being described as the "world before heaven." But since we live in the world after heaven, our spirits have been contaminated by worldly desires and sufferings, and we need to purify them through spiritual discipline to reach a higher state of enlightenment and eventual transcendence.

Caodai altars, in each temple and indeed even in each home, represent these three treasures with flowers (for the regenerative, sexual energy of *tinh*), alcohol (for the breath or vital energy of *khi*), and tea (for the spiritual energy of *than*). One glass represents the sky with its sun, moon, and stars; another the earth with its waters, fire, and wind; and the last represents the human being, with his/her sexual fluids, breath, and spirit. Spiritual discipline signifies the third glass, the crucible of forces at work within the body of each human being. The Great Mother is also called Duc Me, the Holy Mother, since she is the Mother of all living creatures. When she makes contact with her disciples in séances, she calls them children (*cac con*) and can help to heal them or relieve their misery.

Quan Am is a female Boddhisattva, an enlightened being who assumes the form of a gentle goddess to help the living. Her counterpart is Quan Cong, a monstrous-looking male general, who is a fierce controller of homeless demons. The peaceful, white clad Quan Am is balanced by the ferocious red-faced Quan Cong, so that her power to rescue those in suffering or peril is accompanied by his power to repel danger and protect his followers. In Caodai temples, an image of Quan Am is often found on the right side of the Eye of God, facing the door where female disciples enter, while an image of Quan Cong is found on the left side of the eye of God, facing the door where the male disciples enter.

Many Vietnamese ethnologists and folklorists have argued that goddess worship is a survival of a primitive or matriarchal period in Vietnam's history (Ngo Duc Thinh 1996, 1999, 2004). Consistent with the evolutionary scheme described by Engels, they see the mother goddess as a form of popular religion which has outlasted foreign and elite traditions such as Confucianism. The cult of spirits (*dao tho than*) and especially goddesses was considered to be "authentic Vietnamese religion," with the goddesses resident in the Sam mountain (the Lady of the Realm) and Ba Den, the Black Lady of Tay Ninh, as among the most important entities venerated in Vietnam's traditional culture. Festivals devoted to mother goddesses, and particularly the Mid-Autumn festival when the Mother goddess is worshipped and celebrated all over Vietnam, were sometimes seen as opportunities for young people to meet and for the sanctioned breaking of taboos (Taylor 2004: 50). These festivals were seen as forces to integrate Vietnamese culture, uniting disparate sectors of society and preserving a communal spirit through time.

The Mother Goddess in Caodaism combines the attributes of these indigenous goddesses with a universal, multi-racial pantheon that includes European writers, philosophers, and humanists as well as Asian ones. Through séances, the Mother Goddess has personally called many people who might have strayed from their own heritage with the reminder that they should return to her as the primordial mother of all the Vietnamese. In the first spirit séances held in Saigon in 1925, the three men who would become the first Caodai spirit mediums made contact with the spirit of a deceased relative, then a young girl (who was later revealed to be a female immortal), and then, through this young girl's spirit, finally the Mother Goddess herself, who asked them to hold a special feast for her on the day of the mid-Autumn festival. It was only four months after the Mother Goddess had made her appearance that these young mediums were told that they could also converse with the Supreme Being.

The story of the founding of the religion is repeated in many smaller stories of individuals who are called to the faith. Do Van Ly, the former Vietnamese ambassador to the United States during the Kennedy presidency, was called personally by the Mother Goddess upon his return to Vietnam in 1963. After spending more than twenty years overseas, her voice was the first spiritual contact he had with his homeland, and she was the spirit he first venerated when he decided to devote himself to building up Caodaism as a Vietnamese national religion (*quoc dao*), which could also be a means for the salvation of the rest of the world. The Mother Goddess often calls women in the guise of Quan Am, the merciful one, who is prayed to by people seeking healing or at least a relief from suffering.

These female divinities represent the values of compassion and empathy, which transcend the administrative structure of the religion and can be extended to persons who are not members of the faith. While Confucian values teach the importance of right conduct (Vietnamese *nghia*) and respectful, harmonious social relations, a feminine sensitivity is needed to understand why someone might deviate from right conduct. The Mother Goddess is able to go beyond rules and conventions to be charitable and sympathetic, at times exceeding the requirements of law or morality to save individual souls in distress. She commands the "ship of salvation" *(thuyen bat nha)* that brings these lost souls back to unite with God, and her mission is defined in this prayer:

> The Mother Goddess saves humanity from the ocean of sufferings,
> Liberating them from their karmic obligations,
> Guiding their spirits up to heaven.
> With the assistance of the nine female immortals
> The goddess rules over yin energy…
>
> Creating the path for all spirits to be redeemed
> For all spirits, regardless of their level, heavy and dark
> Venerated ancestors, saints, immortals, or Buddhas
> To return to their home in heaven
> Whether or not they followed all the laws or achieved illumination
> The Mother Goddess works to eliminate punishment and hell.
> The Supreme Being has revealed a universal salvation,
> An amnesty for all souls, so that they can now unify with Him.
> The gentle Mother Goddess received the order to lift young and old
> From all directions South, North, East, and West.
> Establishing the amnesty, abolishing the evils,
> To teach and guide humanity to the universal life[1].

When Caodaism was established, hell was closed down, allowing the compassion of the Mother Goddess to reach out to every person and offer them the prospect of salvation.

---

[1] This prayer is translated from the Vietnamese by Dr. Hum Dac Bui, from an undated spirit message received in Phnom Penh. It is chanted on the day of the festival of the Mother Goddess to describe her functions on this earth.

The main feast of the Mother Goddess is celebrated on the fifteenth day (full moon) of the eighth lunar month, at the same time as other Chinese and Vietnamese mid-autumn harvest festivals. A special banquet is prepared with cooked foods, flowers, and fruit of many kinds, and chairs are provided for the Mother Goddess and each of the nine female immortals, who are served tea and wine. Although all other major ceremonies require the clergy to enter in a fixed, hierarchical order and dress male dignitaries in yellow, turquoise, and red (the colors of Buddhism, Taoism, and Confucianism/Catholicism), none of these divisions and colors is appropriate for worshipping the Mother Goddess. All of her disciples dress in simple white tunics, as "we all stand equal before the divine mother," and female dignitaries lead the offerings. At the Great Temple in Tay Ninh, the feast of the Mother Goddess is preceded by a parade with dragon dances and floats celebrating the achievements of female heroines like the Trung sisters and female protective deities like the handmaidens of the Mother Goddess. Many stalls are set up from different parts of Vietnam, celebrating the contributions that women have made to religious, cultural, and social life.

The Background to the Veneration of Joan of Arc

Joan of Arc came into the Caodai pantheon as part of a spiritual campaign to heal the wounds of colonialism and absorb European spirits into an Asian pantheon. French colonial authorities imposed a series of official holidays that celebrated France and the Catholic Church. These included the July 14, Bastille Day; May 11, for Saint Joan of Arc; Easter Monday; Ascension; Pentecost; All Saints' Day; Christmas; and New Year's. There was not a single holiday associated with Buddhism, Confucianism, or Taoism, although the Vietnamese did get two days off for the Tet New Year festivities. In 1929, a special celebration was held to commemorate the five hundredth anniversary of the triumph of Joan of Arc at Orléans, who vividly reminded the Vietnamese of the Trung sisters, their own female military heroines. On May 5, 1930, one student newspaper urged people to boycott the Joan of Arc festivities: "The French nationalists suck our blood; they shoot us to death; they bend our head down; they strangle us; they steal our money to celebrate the memory of Joan of Arc while forbidding us to commemorate our own ancestors. That's really cruel, uncivilized. That's a real shame for us. We must unite our efforts. We must stand up to protest against the irrational prodigality of the French imperialists. We must demand our liberties, our freedom to form associations, the liberty to commemorate those who have served well our poor and miserable people…We should definitely not participate in the festivities of 11 May, showing plainly that we can no longer tolerate our shame" (Lam 2000: 65).

Controversies about whether the people of Indochina should join the French in the cult of Saint Joan or reject it in the spirit of nationalism filled the headlines of the Vietnamese language papers in the early 1930s. A resolution to these debates appeared within Caodaism through the intervention of Saint Joan's spirit in a séance. Noting that she, like them, was once a young girl whose spirit messages were misunderstood, Joan of Arc came to join the new religion and support its efforts to achieve national recognition.

"The deliverance of France by an ignorant peasant girl would have been impossible without God, but it was considered in its time as a horrible heresy, isn't that so? And yet, the English invaders were driven out of France. Do you think it is possible to defeat brutal force by moral force alone? If so, how should we answer this question?

"When a people achieves consciousness of itself and finds its own force in this self consciousness, this is already a weapon that no one can defeat. Millennial Annam under foreign domination, China in the past and France now, has become wiser because of its sufferings and its oppression, already building up a national consciousness which can be put into action to respond to any reactionary movements." (message received Feb 24, 1934 in Tay Ninh, cf. *Les Messages Spirites*)

At this point in the séance, Mr. Truyen, who had come to ask about the difference between materialism and spiritism, spoke, "Isn't that true of any form of social agitation?" The spirit of Joan of Arc answered him:

"You must work first to consolidate and fortify this consciousness, so that deliverance will be possible. Be patient, since there is a great force latent in the soul of your people. You need to know how to use it. Do not expect anything from foreign countries. Communism is only a bluff. It is a great exploitation of the credulity of oppressed people. It is an ointment that calms their pain but does not cure it. And as for the Internationalist An? What advantage comes to nationalist politics from internationalism? Is Wilson satisfied? The creation of the League of Nations comes from internationalism, but what results can it give us? If not, then internationalism is just a holding line for the capitalist armies. It is all bluff." (message received Feb 24, 1934 in Tay Ninh, cf. *Les Messages Spirites*).

The spirit of Saint Joan not only offered advice on politics, but also on personal matters. Latapie, a Frenchman who was appointed a Caodaist bishop (*Giao Su*), came to a séance to resolve his ambivalent feelings about a woman named Sau, who was unfaithful to him. (It is unclear whether this was a sexual betrayal or a political one). Saint Joan counseled him to forgive, and promised to help her to heal from what seems to have been a serious illness:

J'y suis en effet, cher frère Latapie	I am here now dear brother Latapie
A qui puis-je donner une nouvelle vie.	To whom I would give a new life
Assoifé de toute trendresse	Thirsting for all tenderness
Vous vous trouvez dans une réelle faiblesse	You find yourself feeling great weakness
Avec votre infidèle Sau	With Sau who has betrayed you
Vous l'encouragiez à vous trahir	You encouraged her to betray you
Elle est maintenant condamné avec sévérité	Now she has been severely condemned
A des souffrances morales parmi les pires.	To moral sufferings among the worst
Elle n'obtiendra son salut que par vous.	Only you can save her now
Aidez-moi donc dans vos prières et je pourrai tout.	Help me now with your your prayers and I can be capable of anything
Soyez fidèle à notre Maître Divin	Be faithful to our Divine Master
Faites avec dévouement votre devoir de Saint	Carry out your duties as a Saint
Nous sommes là pour vous aider	We are here to help you out
Et faciliter votre tache, il faut y penser	And make your job easier, if you think
Un corps d'Esprits européens est à ce jour constitué	A group of European spirits is assembled on this day
Ils travailleront avec vous en communauté	They will work with you as a community
Soyez donc vaillant	So be brave now
La grandeur d'âme française en dépend.	The greatness of the French soul depends on it.
Au revoir.	See you later.

(Phnom-Penh, on February 17 1933 at 2:15 in the morning)

In all of these instances, the French heroine helps to define a form of salvation that should speak to both Asians and Europeans, that is global and cosmopolitan rather than narrow and exclusive. As Caodaism emerged at the same time as the women's suffrage movement, its gender politics were also articulated in terms of the struggle for female emancipation. Speaking to a Frenchwoman, Mme. Perreux, as well as various dignitaries, Saint Joan explicitly highlighted the gender parity of Caodaism: "Yes, this is the only religion which grants to women a spiritual power which is virtually equal to that of men. This will show a kind of justice that Christianity has for a long time denied women." (Séance at Tay Ninh on September 22, 1934). Women in Caodaism can hold the ranks of cardinals and archbishops, and the first female cardinal, Lam Huong Thanh, is represented on the front of the Tay Ninh Holy See, above the door entered by female disciples, while the first Caodaist temporal Pope, Le Van Trung, is above the door entered by male disciples.

There are no representations of Joan of Arc inside the Holy See at Tay Ninh, but Caodai festivals have featured floats and displays that have celebrated her at the Mother Goddess festival. These images were published in the 1940s by Marguerite Gobron, who collected them in a book after the death of her husband, Gabriel Gobron, the first French disciple of Caodai and a chronicler of its history and philosophy (M. Gobron 1949, G. Gobron 1948). The photograph shows Saint Joan on a white horse wearing white armor, dressed more or less like a Caodaist herself, leading both Vietnamese and French people to self-determination.

Spiritists in France, like the famous medium Léon Denis, had reclaimed Joan of Arc in a number of publications. They argued that her voices had been neglected by many historians, who also failed to see the ways in which she fused the Celtic spirituality of Brittany with French nationalism (Denis 1923: 171-188). In 1898, a spirit identifying herself as Joan dictated a message by automatic writing in Paris that seemed to prophesy the devastation of World War I (Denis 1923: 173), and various other messages were also reported in *La Revue Spirite*, the journal founded by Allan Kardec to codify and regulate spirit messages received in France and evaluate their validity (Monroe 1999: 239-246). Caodaists corresponded with many French spiritists and reprinted "messages from the great spirits of France" translated into Vietnamese (Nguyen Ngoc Tho, 1928). Caodaists argued, like their French counterparts, that expert opinion played a crucial role in the legitimation of knowledge, so spirit specialists were needed to decide which messages would be added to the corpus of fact, and which rejected. In this way, the authorship of spirit communications was displaced from subjective products of terrestrial minds into raw scientific data about the beyond.

Caodaists give Joan of Arc a place as the sixth female goddess among the nine goddesses (or immortals, *tien*) who are responsible for helping the Mother Goddess in saving humanity. There are nine spiritual dimensions (nine heavens) that are governed by the nine female goddesses. Therefore there are nine sessions of requiem (nine *cuu*), one every nine days after death for praying for the soul to transcend the nine heavens in order to reach unification with God. Each female goddess helps the soul to go through her dimension into the next one. These goddesses or female immortals are also often called archangels (*tien*). In the Caodaist hierarchy of spiritual achievement, the highest rank is attained by those—such as Kuan Yin—who become living Buddhas. The second rank is attained by immortals or archangels (*tien*), the third by saints (*thanh*), the fourth by venerated ancestral spirits (*than*), and the fifth by sages or humanists (*nhon*). Joan of Arc is a saint in the Catholic system, but in Caodaism she has been given a promotion to occupy the rank of a female immortal or archangel (*tien*).

From Iconography to Belief and Practice

Although Caodaists have become famous for innovating the practice of having female Cardinals and religious dignitaries, the emphasis on liberation has been more focused on national and religious goals than on sexual equality. The tensions between hierarchy and egalitarianism were evident from the syncretistic beginnings of this religious movement. Its Confucian elements celebrated the literary achievements of an elite, its Taoist occult practices focused more on the relation of man to nature rather than to society, and its esoteric tradition was primarily Buddhist in inspiration. What was novel about Caodaism, however, was that in contrast to all three of Vietnam's "great teachings," it fostered a more personal and direct contact with God.

While Confucianism can be described as an ethical system, Taoism as a metaphysical one, and Buddhism as a philosophy of self-realization, what Caodai added to the mix was a more personal form of both monotheism and polytheism. Caodai spirit mediums could have direct conversations with God and the various saints, and the goal of Caodai meditation exercises was to study directly from the spiritual entities themselves. Caodai, as the Supreme Being, spoke directly to his disciples, and encouraged them also to communicate with the other great spiritual leaders of history. In this way, the "personal relationship with Jesus," which is advocated by some Protestant groups, was expanded to include a much wider Asian pantheon of spirits, and a more cosmopolitan spirituality was born.

This more personal, direct, and activist form of religious communication influenced the new religion's orientation to the world and to sexual politics. Both men and women have served as spirit mediums, and one particular method—the *am/duong* or yin/yang method—involves a male and female spirit medium relating the same message in turns. Caodai prophecies contain millenarian elements that challenge the powers that exist today, while, at the same time, they show respect for many forms of occult knowledge that go back centuries. The *Tan Luan* or New Code of Conduct is Confucian in its prescriptions for women to honor their fathers, husbands, and sons, and also in its tolerance for divorce or a husband's taking a second wife if his wife has not produced a male descendant. But

Caodai is unusual in world religions in seeking parity—equal numbers of male and female dignitaries—and in allowing women to hold high-ranking positions.

Because the Socialist Republic of Vietnam has not allowed spirit séances to ordain new religious officers in Tay Ninh, the leadership of Caodaism's largest denomination is "decapitated"—an aging group of dignitaries who are forced to administer their religion not according to its own constitution but according to the rules of a communist-appointed management committee. Women's greater longevity and many years of service in the religion (uninterrupted by military service or prison camp) have often made them the only guardians of Caodai temples during stressful times. Membership in many denominations has been "feminized," with many more women attending ceremonies than men, perhaps because they are less likely to suffer the social censure that being religious may bring to professionals and civil servants in Vietnam today. This reverses certain hierarchical relationships between the Holy Sees in Vietnam and the diasporic communities in the United States and elsewhere, and creates a series of new problems of religious inspiration and invention.

In the overseas community, deference to the holy centers in Vietnam has also prevented the emergence of a separate official hierarchy, although there is a new generation of leaders who have proven themselves quite dynamic and effective as web masters, religious teachers, and writers, even if they do not formally hold high religious office. The highest ranking Caodai dignitary at a 2004 retreat in San Martin, California was a female archbishop, Ngoc Tuyet Tien, and the temple, Thien Ly Buu Toa, was founded by her and the female spirit medium Bach Dien Hoa as one of the earliest Caodai temples in the United States. It has been the only one to receive and distribute spirit messages since 1977.

The Confucian elements of Caodaism's "Code of Conduct," or *Tan Luat,* have been particularly challenged in California. Veneration of the Mother Goddess and of female saints and deities like Quan Am, Joan of Arc, and the Virgin Mary appeal to followers of feminist spirituality, but rules pertaining to marriage, divorce, and the family have seemed to re-assert traditional sex roles rather than displacing them. Divorce can be requested by a woman only in cases of desertion, offending the in-laws, or infertility, but in practice many allowances have been made for different cultural contexts and standards. Women are active in California temples in fundraising, organizing youth groups, hosting religious ceremonies with good food, and attending international conferences. Caodai's innovation in defining a new way to "live a religious life" (*song tu*) not only in the monastery but also in the family home has certainly opened doorways to greater female participation in religious leadership than is the norm in Buddhism or Roman Catholicism.

Conclusions

Because of the ways in which the Mother Goddess and other female divinities subvert hierarchy and preach compassion, Caodaist cosmology is divided between one branch which asserts the importance of rank, order and regulation, and another which offers sympathy to those of simple origins who do not achieve worldly recognition. The "men of stature" who predominate in formal theology—heroes, poets, and scholars—are balanced by the spirits of simpler "women of compassion," who love all their children equally and do not care about worldly divisions. Joan of Arc, as a female soldier, seems to straddle these divisions, but she is ultimately grouped with other female divinities and worshipped as a gentle guardian rather than as a martial figure. In this way, Caodaism brings together opposing themes in Asian and even Occidental religious life and presents the example of a modern religion which synthesizes gender division in a unifying practice premised on the possibility of universal redemption.

References

Blagov, Sergei 2001. *Caodaism: Vietnamese Traditionalism and its Leap into Modernity.* New York: Nova.

Bui, Hum Dac, with Ngasha Beck 2000 *CaoDai: Faith of Unity*. Fayetteville, AR: Emerald Wave Press.

Denis. Léon 1923 *Jeanne D'Arc, Médium*. Reprinted in 2001 in Editions Trans-atlantiques, Imprimerie Lienhart, Aubenas d'Ardèche.

Fjelstad, Karen 1995 *Tu Phu Gong Dong: Vietnamese Women and Spirit Possession in the San Francisco Bay Area*. PhD dissertation in Anthropology, University of Hawaii.

Gobron, Gabriel 1948 *Histoire et Philosophie du Caodaisme*. Paris: Dervy.

Gobron, Marguerite 1949 *Le Caodaisme en Images*. Paris: Dervy

Lam, Truong Buu 2000 *Colonialism Experienced: Vietnamese Writings on Colonialism, 1*900-1931. Ann Arbor: University of Michigan Press.

Monroe, John 1999 Making the Séance "Serious": *Tables Tournantes* and Second Empire Bourgeois Culture, 1853-1861. History of Religions, v. 43: 219-246.

Ngo Duc Thinh 1999 "The Pantheon for the Cult of Holy Mothers", *Vietnamese Studies* 131: 20-35.

Ngo Duc Thinh, ed. 1996 *Dao Mau o Viet Nam* The mother goddess religion in Vietnam Ha Noi: Nha Xuat Ban Van Hoa Thong Tin.

Ngo Duc Thinh 2004 Paper for "Mother Goddess Religion in Vietnam" conference at UCLA.

Nguyen Ngoc 1928 *Tho Thanh Ngon Than Tien Dai Phap* (Messages des Grands Espirits de France: A. Kardec, Léon Denis, Rayon). Saigon: Cao Dai Thu Vien.

Oliver, Victor L. 1976. *Caodai Spiritism: A Study of Religion in Vietnamese Society.* Leiden: E.J. Brill.

Taylor, Phillip 2004 *Goddess on the Rise; Pilgrimage and popular Religion in Vietnam*. Honolulu: University of Hawaii Press.

Tran Quang Vinh. ed. *Les Messages Spirites de la 3ième Amnistie de Dieu en Orient.* 1962: Tay Ninh: Saint-Siège du Caodaisme.

Werner, Jayne Susan 1981. *Peasant Politics and Religious Sectarianism: Peasant and Priest in the Cao Dai in Viet Nam.* New Haven: Yale University Press.

Illustrations

Fig.1. The Mother Goddess is depicted surrounded by nine female immortals and many handmaidens at the Mother Goddess temple in Tay Ninh. Photograph by author.

Fig. 2. The Left Eye of God on the globe in the Tay Ninh temple. Photograph by author.

Fig. 3. The Caodai pantheon as represented above the altar in the new Garden Grove temple in California. Photograph by author.

Fig. 4. Chants to the Mother Goddess and the nine female immortals at the festival held for the mid autumn harvest moon at the Court of Heavenly Reason temple near San Jose, California. Photograph by author.

CHAPTER SIX

BETWEEN BODHISATTVA AND CHRISTIAN DEITY: GUANYIN AND THE VIRGIN MARY IN LATE MING CHINA

GANG SONG

In his apologetic work *Daiyi pian* (In Place of Doubts, 1621), the late Ming scholar-convert Yang Tingyun (1557–1627) attempts to clarify the doubts regarding the Virgin Mary, the Mother of God, according to the Roman Catholic Church. He specifically points out three symbolic identities—the virgin, the mother, and the savior—when he discusses a picture of Madonna and the Child that had been recently introduced by the Jesuits. Yang then makes a cautious conclusion: "As soon as Christ was born, he obtained his perfect body and perfect power. One should not look at him in terms of the difference of small and big, how dare one say that he is an infant? As to a match of the Holy Mother and so-called Guanshiyin in popular terms, the latter is surely not equivalent to the former."[1]

Yang's conscious distinction between the Virgin Mary and Guanyin revealed his worry at the inter-religious confusion of his contemporaries, since he himself once experienced a hard time as a devout lay Buddhist. On one hand, although the two figures originated from two different religions, they were often blended with each other in the late Ming period (1590s–1640s), largely due to similar iconography and characteristics such as compassion, purity, and child-giving power.[2] On the other hand, since the Jesuits, according to their missionary strategy in China, mainly targeted Chinese scholars and officials, to equate devotion to Virgin Mary among the elite with the worship of Guanyin in popular culture would

---

[1] Yang Tingyun. *Daiyi pian*, in *Tianzhujiao dongchuan wenxian*, ed. Wu Xiangxiang. Taipei: Xuesheng shuju, 1979. 592.

[2] Standaert, Nicolas. *Yang Tingyun, Confucian and Christian in Late Ming China*. Leiden: Brill, 1988. 123-124.

become a serious breach between the upper and the lower classes in late Ming society. The Jesuits were aware of this confusion, but their missionary strategy fostered this misunderstanding, and their clarifications were not strong or consistent. As long as the confusion did not lead to "dangerous idol-worship," they would tolerate "friendly" misunderstandings of the Chinese commoners. It served the cause of a broader conversion to Christianity, and in one way reflected the conflict and negotiation between Catholicism and native religions.

However, this inconsistency did not affect the rapid growth of the Marian cult in China. As it turned out, the Virgin Mary in the late Ming religious arena was represented as a mild competitor, cloaking the aggressive substitution for Guanyin, whose identity by that time had gone through a complicated history of indigenization. These two religious icons, though having sharply different foundations in Europe and China, were paired for a striking appropriation during their late Ming encounter.

Using both visual and textual sources, this presentation uncovers the paradoxical relationship between Virgin Mary and Guanyin. A series of important questions emerge: what roles did the Virgin Mary and Guanyin play in their respective religious and cultural traditions? How did the Jesuits represent Mary by utilizing the popular Chinese belief in Guanyin? Did certain external factors—changing social psyche, political vacuum, or religious syncretism—affect the complex process of Mary–Guanyin exchange and competition? By concentrating on these factors, we will be able to take a closer look at the religious life in early seventeenth-century China.

Adaptive Iconographies

Avalokiteśvara by the late Ming period has been transformed from a noble, male-looking bodhisattva (though originally supposed to be asexual) in Mahayana Buddhism to a feminine deity for all Buddhist believers, monks, nuns, and laymen alike.[3] The Chinese name Guanshiyin, more widely called Guanyin, means "the one who listens to the sounds of the world." It clearly points to her unconditional compassion to save all sentient beings that call upon her help in time of disease or misfortune.[4]

---

[3] Yü Chünfang. *Kuan-yin: the Chinese Transformation of Avalokiteïvara*. New York: Columbia University Press, 2001. 294.

[4] Sun Changwu. *Zhongguo wenxue zhongde Weimo yu Guanyin*. Beijing: Gaodeng jiaoyu chubanshe, 1996. 70-73; Reis-Habito, Maria. "The Bodhisattva Guanyin and the Virgin Mary," *Buddhist-Christian Studies* 13 (1993): 62.

One of her most popular images during the late Ming period was that of the White-robed Guanyin.[5] In a print collection titled *Guanyin sanshi'er xiang* (Thirty-two Forms of Guanyin, 1622), all thirty-two images have a decidedly feminine look, shape, and gesture. They wear white robes, the color white being a symbol of enlightenment, only a few of them decorated with flower designs. An exemplary image from this collection shows that this White-robed goddess is standing on a lotus leaf above the wavy sea. Her affectionate face suggests a feeling of peace and calmness. Her firm standing on the lotus leaf indicates her power to help people safely sail through the "bitter sea of suffering," which divides the mortal world and the Pure Land. The visual representation is so compelling that a viewer may forget the distinctions between divine and human, temporal and eternal, and the finite and infinite.[6] It is not surprising that Gu Yanwu (1613–1682), a Confucian scholar who lived through the Ming–Qing transition, particularly noted, "Among the deities who enjoy the offerings of incense in the temples and monasteries under heaven, none can compete with Guanyin. The Great Being has many forms of transformation. But people in the world mostly worship that of the White-robed One."[7]

The popularity of the White-robed Guanyin was also found through her child-giving power that in fact had scriptural basis, for example, in the *Lotus Sutra*:

> The Bodhisattva Perceiver of the World's Sounds possesses great authority and supernatural powers … For this reason, living beings should constantly keep the thought of her in mind. If a woman wishes to give birth to a male child, she should offer obeisance and alms to Bodhisattva Perceiver of the World's Sounds and then she will bear a son blessed with merit, virtue, and wisdom. And if she wishes to bear a daughter, she will bear one with all

---

[5] Kenneth Ch'en proposed that the Chinese White-robed Guanyin originated from Tantric tradition of White Tārā. However, Yü Chünfang argued that the "white robe" and sexual transformation of Guanyin could have been a Chinese creation mainly influenced by indigenous scriptures, miracle stories, and arts. See Yü, *Kuan-yin*, 248-253.

[6] This image is no. 19 form of Guanyin. See *Mingdai muke Guanyin huapu* (Model Collection of Woodcut Guanyin in the Ming Dynasty). Shanghai: Shanghai guji chubanshe, 1997. 129. The original woodcut is held in Anhui Provincial Museum, China.

[7] Gu Yanwu. *Guzhong suibi* (Random Notes Taken Amid the Reeds), in *Hanshan xianguan congshu*, Vol. 61. Here I use part of Yü Chünfang's translation in *Kuan-yin*, 253.

> the marks of comeliness, one who in the past planted the roots of virtue and is loved and respected by many persons.[8]

Deeply influenced by the Confucian patrilineal mentality, the Chinese supplicants would have without doubt chosen boys rather than girls when they called upon Guanyin. The White-robed Guanyin, also regarded as the Child-giving Guanyin, was therefore frequently represented holding a boy in her arms.[9] During the late imperial period, the overlapping iconography continued to exist and gained great popularity in Chinese daily life, as can be seen in a Qing print used for sacrificial offering.[10] The worship of Guanyin became a shared practice not only among the elite but also among the commoners in late imperial Chinese society.

The feminized image of Guanyin absorbed various elements from Chinese culture. It meanwhile showed a capability to adapt non-Chinese representations, for Buddhist scriptural traditions indeed provided a basis for the goddess to take different forms and save different types of people, who could be either Chinese or non-Chinese. This dynamic nature enabled her to even assume certain Western forms. In a painting attributed to the famous Yuan literati Zhao Mengfu (1254-1322), Guanyin is represented in a very uncommon style. Not only does she wear a black garment, but also her hair-dress and deep eye sockets reveal a non-Chinese feature. The artist also seems conscious of the light effect on the figure, a technique scarcely seen in traditional Chinese paintings. Though the child held in her arms and the other child standing next to her have noticeable Chinese features, the exchanging glances between them and the mother are not a normal Chinese composition. It seems that in this painting only the white bird and the jade vase with a willow branch suggest that the female figure is Guanyin.[11] If one considers the fact that the Franciscan missionaries came to the Yuan court at the end of the thirteenth century, while Zhao

---

[8] Watson, Burton, trans. *The Lotus Sutra*. New York: Columbia University Press, 1993. 300. To keep the same female gender of Guanyin, I change "him" to "her" in Watson's translation.

[9] See, for example, Chen Lianqi, ed. *Lidai Guanyin baoxiang* (The Sacred Images of Guanyin through Various Dynasties). Beijing: Zhongguo shudian, 1998. No. 25. The painting is said to be drawn during the Ming, but the artist is unknown.

[10] Wang Shucun, ed. *Guanyin baitu* (A Hundred Images of Guanyin). Guangzhou: Lingnan meishu chubanshe, 1997. 22. The title is "Baiyi Songzi Guangyin" (White-robed Child-giving Guangyin). This leaflet is categorized as a *zhima* (paper horse), a term used in funeral ceremony for paper figurines and paper money to be burned on behalf of the deceased.

[11] See Chen Lianqi, ed. *Lidai Guanyin baoxiang*, No. 20.

Mengfu was serving Kublai Khan, one will tend to connect this unusual image of Guanyin with the Franciscan iconography for the Virgin Mary.[12]

Art historians are now attempting to establish an iconographic link between Guanyin and Virgin Mary that pre-dates the Ming dynasty. Lauren Arnold's recent research suggests that the Franciscan Madonna of Humility may have inspired the Chinese depiction of the Child-giving Guanyin.[13] If one compares a mid-fourteenth century gothic painting of Madonna of Humility to the aforementioned Ming painting of Child-giving Guanyin, one will certainly see similar symbolic renderings between the two.[14] By sharing the identity of a compassionate, maternal intercessor between two worlds, the Chinese goddess Guanyin might have started an inter-religious adaptation of Christian iconography for Virgin Mary even before the arrival of Jesuit arts in the late sixteenth century.

Besides Marian iconography, an increasing number of Westerners coming to China during the late Ming also became models for mimicry. No other form of Guanyin possesses a more sensational visual effect than the one depicted in a Ming print collection titled *Cirong wushisan xian* (Fifty-three Manifestations of the Compassionate Face [of Guanyin]). In this particular image, Guanyin takes the appearance of a European man. Although the exact source is not traceable, the image definitely originates from Western models.[15] It is a perfect example of cultural hybridization. The oval frame is decorated with lotus flower designs, but the mustached man in it has a high nose, deep eye sockets, long hair, wearing a tight, black medieval style suit, and holding a wand in his right hand. His sight boldly meets a viewer's attention, another technique scarcely seen in traditional Chinese portraits. However, the child holding the palms to his

---

[12] The most successful Franciscan missionary to China at that time was Giovanni di Montecorvino (1247–1328), who won the trust of Mongol rulers in China and secured a foothold in Beijing. See *Yuanshi*, Beijing: Zhongguo dabaike quanshu chubanshe, 1985. 68, 128.

[13] Arnold, Lauren. "Folk Goddess or Madonna? Early Missionary Encounters with the Image of Guanyin," in *Encounters and Dialogues: Changing Perspectives on Chinese-Western Exchanges from the Sixteenth to Eighteenth Centuries*, ed. Xiaoxin Wu. Nettetal: Sankt Augustin, 2005. 227-238.

[14] An exemplary image of Madonna of Humility is the one painted around 1350 by Guariento di Arpo (ca. 1310 -1370), now held in the Getty Center Museum.

[15] Gao Ruizhe suggests that this particular image of Guanyin looks very similar to a portrait of King Louis XIII (1601-1643) painted by Philippe de Champaigne (1602-1674). It is now held in the Prado Museum in Madrid, Spain. See Gao Ruizhe, *Qingchu Guanyin huapu Cirong wushisan xian banhua yanjiu* (A Study of the Early Qing Collection *Fifty-three Manifestations of the Compassionate Face [of Guanyin]*). M.A. Thesis. National Taiwan Normal University, 2005.

right, the vase with a willow branch, and the half-shown bird along the frame, all indicate his identity as "Guanyin."[16] The dramatic representation demonstrates how the Buddhist goddess, "miraculously" transformed, could adopt new cultural elements for a religious end.

Unlike Guanyin, the Virgin Mary did not have any scriptural basis that could allow the adaptation of her iconography in different cultures. However, the spread of Marian cult in Europe since the Middle Ages resulted in a process of localization in which the Virgin likewise assumed a variety of forms depending on different religious, cultural, and artistic tastes. A quick comparison of one European illustrated book and its Chinese reproductions reveals how the Virgin Mary icon was adapted for the intended audience. The source of imagery is a book entitled *Evangelicae Historiae Imagines* (1593), containing 153 copper engravings and contemplative texts for each picture in the companion volume.[17] The selected picture "annunciation" is the first plate among others, and it is the highlight of Virgin Mary's life which connects the trinity of Father, Son, and Spirit. In the picture, Angel Gabriel is depicted descending in the midst of shining clouds, where God announces Christ's birth in the human world, and approaching Mary's house to deliver the divine message. Mary stands in prayer and obediently accepts God's will.[18]

Around 1619, the Portuguese Jesuit João da Rocha (1583–1623) published in Nanjing his *Song nianzhu guicheng* (Rules for Reciting the Rosary), in which fifteen woodblock illustrations based on those originals in the *Evangelicae Historiae Imagines* were made to accompany the fifteen prayers in the translated *Rosary*. The "annunciation" also appears in the beginning, but its composition and artistic style are changed dramatically to satisfy a typical Chinese taste. The multi-scenery layout in the original is reduced to one scene in the Chinese reproduction. Gabriel descending from heaven is changed to a small bird. The same figure approaching Mary, once a male in Christian tradition, now takes a feminine look and shape. Mary in turn looks more like a Chinese woman (or Guanyin?), wearing a long, white robe and kneeling down before a

---

[16] The image is No. 51 manifestation of Guanyin. See *Mingdai muke Guanyin huapu*, 101.

[17] The texts were written by Jerónimo Nadal (1507–1580), one of the founders of the Society of Jesus, and the illustrations were engraved by the "Wierx brothers" of Antwerp. See Nicolas Standaert, ed. *Handbook of Christianity in China, Volume One: 635-1800*. Leiden: Brill, 2001. 812.

[18] A detailed account of this episode can be found in Mathieu Orsini, *The Life of the Blessed Virgin Mary* (New York: Peter F. Collier, Catholic Publisher, 1880), 78-85.

Chinese style stool. The bed and screen with a landscape painting behind her, the windows and roof of the house, as well as the *bajiao* (banana) tree and rockery outside, all contribute to a typical Chinese setting. In this sense, da Rocha and the Chinese artist virtually transformed the icon of Virgin Mary from a European one to a Chinese one.[19]

The Jesuits' conscious effort to blend into Chinese culture extended to the image of Madonna and Child, one of the major icons of Catholic arts. As was mentioned before, the image probably already started to appropriate the iconography and rituals of Guanyin during the Yuan time. Reliable evidence can definitely be found in the late Ming, when Matteo Ricci (1552–1610) and his fellows came to China and presented to the Chinese audience Marian iconography along with other fantastic objects. In his journal later published by Nicolas Trigault (1577–1628) and his letters to European correspondents, Ricci recorded that some Chinese converts had visions of Virgin Mary, wearing a white robe and holding a child, who miraculously saved them from serious diseases.[20] These accounts did not seem to fit well the dominant icon of black-robed Madonna. Different from some print books like da Rocha's *Rosary*, most Jesuits' paintings of Madonna and Child retain European medieval conventions, as can be demonstrated in one faithful reproduction collected in a late Ming "ink cake" album titled *Chengshi moyuan* (The Ink Garden of Mr. Cheng, 1605).[21] Thus one possible explanation for this white-robed Mary directs to the popular iconography of the White-robed Guanyin in the same period. Ricci did not clarify that the Holy Mother often dressed black instead of white, nor did he forbid the converts from circulating miracles and dreams of this type.

Responses of Chinese scholars to Marian iconography differed from that of the converts. In his *Kezuo zhuiyu* (Idle Words of a Guest), Gu Qiyuan (1576–1628) records his first impression of Virgin Mary's image,

---

[19] The image used here is from a copy of the *Song nianzhu guicheng* currently held at the Getty Research Institute, Los Angeles.

[20] Ricci, Matteo. *China in the Sixteenth Century: The Journals of Matthew Ricci, 1583-1610*, trans. Louis J. Ggllagher. New York, Random House, 1953. 473; Liu Junyu, Wang Yuchuan, and Luo Yu, trans. *Li Madou quji* (Complete Works of Fr. Matteo Ricci, S.J.), Vol. 4, "Letters (II)." Taipei: Guangqi chubanshe, 1986. 283.

[21] The inscription at the bottom reads "In Sem[inario] Jap[onico] 1597," which indicates its connection with a certain Japanese artist influenced by Western painting. See Standaert, *Handbook of Christianity in China*, 811; Lin Li-chiang, *Proliferation of Images: the Ink-stick Designs and the Printing of the Fang-shih Mo-p'u and the Ch'eng-shih Mo-yuan*, Ph.D. Dissertation. Princeton University, 1998. 215-223.

"The Heavenly Lord is presented in Ricci's painting as a little child held in the arms of a woman called the Heavenly Mother. The picture is painted in five colors on a copper plate. The facial feature is lifelike. Her body, arm, and hands seem to protrude tangibly above the surface. The higher and lower parts of her face, if seen directly, are no different from a living person."[22] The European-style portrait, of course, aroused the feeling of exoticism among Gu and other audiences.[23] Ricci's explanation for the live visual effect of Mary's appearance implied the excellence of European art, which in a subtle way highlighted her superior authority over native Chinese deities, including Guanyin.

Comparable Narratives I: Life

The Jesuits faced a great challenge to promote Marian worship when they found that many Chinese firmly believed in the goddess Guanyin. It seemed impossible to remove this "idol" without erecting a rival, more powerful icon of the Virgin Mary for the Chinese, especially female devotees. Narratives on Mary's life were translated and published during the late Ming in addition to adaptive iconography, thus forming another level of inter-religious competition and superimposition. As shall be seen in the following comparison of two biographical narratives, one on Guanyin and the other on Virgin Mary, there is a striking resemblance. On the surface level, these life stories deliver religious "truths" in a similar way by which an exemplary feminine role is justified. On a deeper level, both narratives followed a similar pattern—pure quality versus inferior nature—in the attempt to overcome the actual circumstances governing women in medieval European and Chinese society.

The *Nanhai Guanyin quanzhuan* (Complete biography of Guanyin of the South Sea) was a Ming rewritten version of the legend of Princess Miaoshan, who turned out to be a metamorphosis of the compassionate bodhisattva Guanyin.[24] In this story, Miaoshan, the third daughter of King

---

[22] Gu Qiyuan. *Kezuo zhuiyu*, in *Baibu congshu jicheng*, Ser. 100, Vol. 6, 18b-19a. Here I use Lin Li-chiang's translation with a few changes. See Lin, *Proliferation of Images*, 222-223.

[23] See Standaert, *Handbook of Christianity in China*, 817.

[24] The date and life of the author Zhu Dingchen are unclear, but the work itself is connected with another late Ming religious narrative called *Xiangshan baojuan* (Precious Scroll of Xiangshan), which in turn originates from certain stele version made in the Song time. See Yü, *Kuan-yin*, 298-301, 438-441; Dudbridge, Glen. *The Legend of Miaoshan*. London: Ithaca Press for the Board of the Faculty of Oriental Studies, Oxford University, 1978. 10-20; 51-58.

Miaozhuang in the *Xinglin* Kingdom, at her young age devotes herself to a Buddhist life of vegetarianism, chanting and meditating, and celibacy. She denounces an arranged marriage and angers her father, who has only three daughters and no male heir. The subsequent persuasions of her parents and sisters are in vain. Nor could the nuns from the White Sparrow Temple change her mind. Though Miaoshan out of compassion miraculously saves the temple from being burned, she has to face the death penalty ordered by her own furious father. She travels in hell, but transforms it into a paradise by chanting Buddhist sutras. She comes back to the human world and achieves enlightenment under the help of Buddha. At this time the king's sins generate a mysterious disease, but out of filial piety Miaoshan (now identified as Guanyin) transforms into a monk physician and offers the only effective remedy: her own eyes and hands to the ill father. The father is thus converted to Buddhism. Finally, after pacifying the chaos caused by some demons, Miaoshan helps recover the kingdom and realizes a happy family reunion.[25]

Compared to the earlier versions of Miaoshan's legend, this late Ming narrative has a striking hybrid feature by blending various religious, moral, and literary traditions into one Buddhist exemplum. However, the basic image of Miaoshan as an exemplary model for all women remains unchanged. While still in the human world, she chooses to live a lay Buddhist life in the royal court. Her piety is incomparable, even the nuns are put to shame for their worldly attachments. While in hell, Miaoshan shows her supreme power of compassion, thus saving all sinful beings out of the hell. When she becomes Guanyin, Miaoshan again demonstrates her exemplary role in her extreme act of bodily mutilation. It is both a filial act in human terms and a testimony of universal love from the enlightened goddess. With this model-creation Miaoshan–Guanyin indeed embodies the Buddhist truth of nirvana.

Miaoshan's transcendence from a human to a bodhisattva points to another aspect regarding womanhood in reality. At the very beginning we are told that the king wants to have a male heir. The Jade Emperor instead delivers him three sinful souls who are able to reincarnate in the human world but must change their sex from male to female. This episode reveals the inferior status of women both in Chinese family system and Buddhist institution. As a family member, a woman has to obey patrilineal conventions on such issues as arranged marriage and giving birth to a son. As a Buddhist devotee, she has to abide by the rule in the hierarchical system of reincarnation and accept that only through a much longer,

[25] A full text of the story is available online at http://1bird.net/502x.exe.

harsher life than that of a man can she achieve enlightenment. Amazingly, all of these disadvantages are overcome in Miaoshan's legend through her pure body and mind. Her vow of celibacy underpins the ideal of virginity. Her simple faith helps her go through many hardships. Her purity further empowers her to fulfill the duty of filial piety and protect the kingdom. As a result, human norms for womanhood can no longer define her as an inferior being, or a source of pollution and chaos. Her virtuous life breaks gender distinction that confines Chinese women. Indeed, Miaoshan–Guanyin became so popular during the late Ming time that the Spanish Augustinian friar Martín de Rada (1533–1578) noted that, among the "saints" whom the Chinese revered, "a woman called Quanyin (i.e. Guanyin)" was honored the most.[26]

The Jesuits could find many reasons to regard this popularized goddess as an "idol" from their Christian standpoint. Nonetheless, when creating a Chinese version of the life story of the Virgin Mary, they had to share a similar model-making process, which, however, was directed to the Christian faith rather than the Buddhist one. More importantly, in popular narratives, it seemed better to challenge the "idol" for its own sake but not the moral implications along with it.

Just like Guanyin in China, the Virgin Mary also represented the epitome of womanhood in Europe throughout the Middle Ages.[27] When the Italian Jesuit Alfonso Vagnone (1566–1640) compiled the *Shengmu xingshi* (Authentic Biography of the Holy Mother, 1631), his concern was the transfer of Mary's defining characters from a European setting to a Chinese one. The work consists of three volumes: the first is a brief life story of Mary; the second is a theological elaboration of certain key points in her life; and the third focuses on miracle tales of Mary as a universal savior. Among Ming biographies of Christian saints, *Shengmu xingshi* was unique for its comprehensive representation of the Mother of God.

However, Mary's role likewise faced paradoxical womanhood in reality. Even in the European context, her role was problematic to many believers based on fundamental Christian doctrines such as the inferior status of human body/flesh and women's inherited character as forbidden-fruit-eaters.[28] This could be one reason that Vagnone uses several topics in the second volume to explain the divine prophecy, moral perfection, marvelous signs about the birth of Mary. He further makes specific explanations on the concept of Immaculate Conception, which was barely

[26] See Dudbridge, *The Legend of Miaoshan*, 7.

[27] Reed, Teresa. *Shadows of Mary: Reading the Virgin Mary in Medieval Text*. Cardiff: University of Wales Press, 2003. 1-15.

[28] See Reed, *Shadows of Mary*, 41-44.

considered a settled argument under the Holy See in the seventeenth century.[29] The transfer of Mary's story to China may have presented some theological or practical troubles in Europe, and conventional Chinese attitudes toward womanhood paralleled those found in Europe. The challenge for the Jesuits was to adjust their narration of Mary's life according to the Chinese preference.

In response to the diminished role of womanhood in late Ming society, Vagnone in his biography clearly emphasizes the pure virtues of Mary. From the beginning, Mary assumes an innocent, pure body inside her mother's womb. As soon as she devotes herself to God, she makes a vow to maintain virginity. Though she has to be a wife by God's intervention, the vow remains unbreakable, for it is also God's will. The most amazing part comes when Mary gives birth to Christ with her virginity intact. The Holy Mother thus in a different way overcomes the risk of an impure body or fallen flesh of women in reality. Moreover, Mary's spiritual and moral purity helps her conquer the gender-based prejudice. Vagnone mentions twice the cherished Confucian virtue of filial piety—one on her burying the diseased parents and the other on her rejection of marriage with the excuse of her parents' will. Compared with Miaoshan–Guanyin's extreme filial act in the *Nanhai Guanyin quanzhuan*, Mary does not seem to build up enough credit for this virtue. Nonetheless, in Vagnone's account, a series of virtues, including faith, hope, love, wisdom, rightness, endurance, and honesty, are elaborated in detail.[30] They overlap with key Confucian moral codes, effectively allowing the Jesuits to define femininity according to the Ming society's cultural tastes, and to hold the respect of Confucian scholars at the same time. Not surprisingly, the incomparable virtues embodied by the Holy Mother were frequently quoted and discussed by Chinese scholar-converts.[31]

---

[29] Orsini, *The Life of the Blessed Virgin Mary*, 23-32.

[30] Vagnone, Alfonso *Shengmu xingshi* (Life of the Holy Mother), in *Tianzhujiao dongchuan wenxian sanbian*, Vol. 3, ed. Wu Xiangxiang. Taipei: Xuesheng shuju, 1998. 1365-1375.

[31] In addition to Yang Tingyun's aforementioned comments on Mary, Giulio Aleni (1582-1649)'s discussions with Fujian converts on Mary's virtuous life can serve as supportive evidence. See Li Jiubiao. *Kouduo richao* (Daily Record of Oral Instructions), in *Yesuhui Luoma danganguan Ming-Qing Tianzhujiao wenxian* (Chinese Christian Texts from Roman Archives of the Society of Jesus), Vol. 7, ed Nicolas Standaert. Taipei: Taipei Ricci Institute, 2002. 443-445; 470-473; 587-594.

Comparable Narratives II: Salvation

When comparing the narratives on the miraculous and virtuous lives of Guanyin and Mary, one may recognize that the two adopt a similar pattern in terms of model-creation, truth-making, and adjustment to womanhood in reality. However, the mechanism for this late Ming inter-religious competition went far beyond a straightforward process of action and reaction. Not only did the Buddhist goddess and the Christian deity compete with each other in the Jesuits' search of a broader iconographic and biographical recognition, but the Jesuits also extended this challenge to their salvific powers.

First of all, Guanyin and Mary were said to be able to save individuals from various disasters. The fundamental truth of suffering human life—birth, old age, sickness, and death—in Mahayana Buddhism determined that compassion of Buddha and bodhisattvas be reached to all sentient beings. As one of the most popular texts in the late Ming time, the *Lotus Sutra* listed twelve kinds of perils from which Guanyin saved specific individuals, such as those falling into fire, being imprisoned, and coming across *luosha* (i.e., *rākṣasa*, hungry ghosts who eat human beings alive). Along with the popular Guanyin belief, the list of perils was further expanded by various cults, getting closer to daily emergencies such as difficult childbirths and suicides.[32] The Mother of God, on the other hand, did not have an equivalent biblical authorization, but her grace definitely came from Jewish origin and apostolic tradition. The veneration of the Blessed Virgin, also called *hyperdulia*, gained increasing popularity in late medieval Europe among the veneration of other Christian saints. Therefore, it was not difficult for Vagnone to compile a separate volume to record miracles in Mary's life, showing her incomparable love to people in need, whether elders or children, criminals or saints, rich men or poor people, and men or women.

Virgins and widows in late Ming society made up a special category of individuals for whom Guanyin and Virgin Mary would offer protection in time of emergency, since they themselves served as models of virginity and chastity. The exemplary roles crossed religion and morality, so in a competing manner they reinforced moral authority of Neo-Confucian doctrines which could barely control radical ideas from within the school and materialist life in urbanized and commercialized late Ming society from without.[33] In *Shenmu xingshi*, there is a special part titled "The Holy

---

[32] See Yü, *Kuan-yin*, 471-472.

[33] Peterson, Willard. "Confucian Learning in late Ming Thought," in *The Cambridge History of China: Volume 8, The Ming Dynasty, 1368-1644, Part 2*, ed.

Mother Saves Chastity from Dangers," in which Vagnone not only describes miraculous deeds of Mary among virgins, but he also gives examples about her protecting male chastity. The latter type of stories seemed to be absent in late Ming accounts of Guanyin. The extended meaning of *zhen*, or chastity, on the one hand, could be traced back to a Christian belief in soul-flesh conflict both for men and women. On the other hand, the Jesuits could take advantages of this re-defined term to win over more converts, female or male.[34]

As was mentioned above, the Chinese bodhisattva and the Christian deity competed in another field, child-giving, which was crucial to all Chinese abiding by the established tradition of ancestor worship. In his postscript for the *Zhiyue lu* (Record of Pointing at the Moon), the Confucian scholar Qu Ruji (1548-1610) records his personal story about having a son with the power of Guanyin. Although he constantly chants various names of Guanyin, Qu does not get a son like his two friends did. After a strange dream followed by an accidental visit to a temple, Qu finds a sutra showing two unusual names for Guanyin which he did not know to chant before. The sudden enlightenment draws attention of Guanyin and a son is born.[35] Qu's experience can be taken as one example for popularity of Guanyin cult in the late Ming. It reaffirms the bodhisattva's child-giving power found in canonical writings, for example, the *Lotus Sutra*.

Nonetheless, when the Jesuits circulated the miracles of Mary, the monopoly of the Child-giving Guanyin was seriously challenged. In his journal, Ricci recorded a live story on how the Mother of God substituted the role of Guanyin in childbirth. He wrote,

> "Another convert one day told the Father how he threw away all idols in his house, except one saved by his wife because of her reluctance. It was a statue of Guanyin. It was said that Guanyin was the daughter of a Chinese king. She would not get married in her entire life. Chinese women at time of childbirth often pray for Guanyin's protection. Since his wife was about to labor soon and yet she had dystocia in the past, she would not discard the statue. The convert asked the Father for an advice. The Father said, 'Since Guanyin did not help your wife in her past childbirth, you should teach your wife to venerate another virgin, the true Holy Mother. She experienced no pain when giving birth to Jesus.' The Father thus gave him

---

Twitchett, Denis and Frederick W. Mote. Cambridge: Cambridge University Press, 1998. 708-839.

[34] Menegon, Eugenio. *Ancestors, Virgins, and Friars: The Localization of Christianity in Late Imperial Mindong (Fujian, China), 1632-1863*. Ph.D. Dissertation, University of California, Berkeley, 2002. Chap. VI.

[35] See Yü, *Kuan-yin*, 138-141.

> a portrait of the Holy Mother to replace the Guanyin statue. He also asked him to teach his wife to chant seven times Our Father and Hail Mary. The convert did what the Father said and persuaded his wife to concede. Upon the time of delivery she had no difficulty and gave birth to a son. The day was exactly a holiday for the Holy Mother. Therefore, the whole family became converted."[36]

Ricci's description clearly indicates the Jesuits' knowledge of Guanyin's popularity among the Chinese. They grasped this chance to promote Mary as a virgin rivaling Miaoshan–Guanyin, and as the true Mother of God at the same time. In one letter written in 1586, Ricci reported that the portrait of Madonna and Child was believed to help the birth of a son in a local official's family, and thereafter many women who did not have a son ran into the house of a Chinese convert, for he happened to keep a portrait of the Holy Mother.[37] In Vagnone's biography of Mary, there are also several tales describing how the Mother of God responds to requests of childless parents. Her power is so amazing that she could even resurrect a baby who died soon after his birth. Although the Jesuits were cautious not to encourage the converts' intentional blending of Mary's icon with that of Guanyin, practically they had to put the two in a battle-of-faith and demonstrate the Holy Mother's superior power. By cursing Guanyin as an "idol," the Jesuits ironically erected a similar "idol" which appropriated the divine authority from the former.

In addition to the above individual miracles, Guanyin and Mary were also depicted as protectors of religious institutions or countries in general. Miaoshan's recovering of the *Xinglin* Kingdom from the hands of demons was just one version among many others in late Ming religious literature. The compassionate, responsive, and mighty bodhisattva often appeared in popular novels, including *Xiyou ji* (Journal to the West) by Wu Cheng'en (ca. 1500–1582), *Tianfei jishi chushen zhuan* (Biography of the Heavenly Consort Who Saves the World) by Wu Qian, and *Fengshen yanyi* (Investiture of Gods) by Lu Xixing (1520–1601). The Lord of Heaven and the Holy Mother, on the other hand, were not only told by the Jesuits that they had saved a number of European countries from the invasions of "barbarians", but they in reality were also firmly believed by the imperial family of the Southern Ming, who wished to defeat the evil, "barbarian"

---

[36] See Liu Junyu, Wang Yuchuan, and Luo Yu, trans. *Li Madou quji*, Vol. 2. 382-383. In Gallagher's translation, however, Miaoshan-Guanyin and her life story are not mentioned. See *China in the Sixteenth Century*, 409.

[37] Guan Zhenhu, trans. *Li Madou pingzhuan* (from Henri Bernard's *Le Pere Mathieu Ricci et La Societe Chinoise de son Temps (1522-1610)*, 1937). Beijing: Shangwu yinshuguan, 1993. 110-111.

nicely the fifteen illustrations. The ritual in each part starts by reciting "Ave" ten times and "In Heaven" one time, followed by a meditation of that episode. Then comes the "offering" section, in which the devotee addresses the Holy Mother, and talks of one specific joy, suffering, or grace that she has experienced. The third, also the final section, is a short prayer, concluded by chanting "Ave" once. This work emphasizes a private worship of Mary, much like the common use of *Rosary* in medieval Europe.[42] Another similar text written by Jean Froes (1590–1638), titled *Song Shengmu nianzhu moxiang guitiao* (Rules to Recite and Meditate the Holy Mother's Rosary), bears the same feature, except that the ritual has sixty-three short meditations by counting a total of sixty-three beads.

While Guanyin cults were simplifying canonical Buddhist rituals, the Society of the Holy Mother and other lay associations also negotiated with the missionaries for a less elaborate system of Catholic liturgies and formalities. In both situations, certain indigenous elements could be seen blending into the orthodoxy of worship. The flourishing Christian and Buddhist communities in the late Ming formed a tangled network through continuous appropriation and competition. Their rival relation was vividly reflected in a contemporary collection of rules for a Christian association, in which it says, "When some outsider gets sick, he invites monks and Taoists. If he invites our members to recite scriptures, it means that he regards the Lord of Heaven no different from a bodhisattva. Surely we should not go. Be careful! Be careful!"[43]

Conclusion

In the late Ming intercultural context, we discover several modes of religious representations—iconography, narrative, and ritual behavior—which played a part respectively in a culture's process of making varied truth-claims for itself. In each mode, Guanyin and Mary were depicted as the intercessors between two worlds: humanity and divinity, male and female, good and evil, and body and spirit. Moreover, the bodhisattva and the Christian deity engaged often invisible yet realistic competitions. Mary arrived at a time when Guanyin gained increasing popularity as savior of the world and reinforced the goddess tradition in China. Prevalent worship

[42] Winston-Allen, Anne. *Stories of the Rose: The Making of the Rosary in the Middle Ages*. University Park: Pennsylvania State University Press, 1997.
[43] *Huigui zongyao* (Summary of Rules for Christian Societies), in Standaert, *Roman Archives*, Vol. 12, 484-485.

of this feminized, localized deity set a favorable environment for the introduction of the Holy Mother, who shared many similarities with her in iconography, miraculous life, as well as worship patterns. Marian devotion in competing with Guanyin belief offered an additional method to convert the Chinese to Christianity. The presentation of Christian dogma through the Mother of God hence fused into the transformation of native religious icons and narratives.

The late Ming parallel between Marian devotion and Guanyin worship was not a haphazard episode. In fact, Marian cult survived an underground existence during the mid-Qing and became active again in a new inter-religious and intercultural context. It reappeared, for example, during the Boxer Rebellion (1898–1901), in which the "White-robed" Mary was said to show up miraculously in front of her devotees and protect them from the fatal attack of violent boxers.[44] The lasting interactions of these two traveling goddesses thus testify that such representative religious icons continue to be meaningful to cultural encounters in time and space.

References

Primary Sources

Huigui zongyao (Summary of Rules for Christian Societies), in *Yesuhui Luoma danganguan Ming-Qing Tianzhujiao wenxian* (Chinese Christian Texts from Roman Archives of the Society of Jesus), ed. Nicolas Standaert. Taipei: Taipei Ricci Institute, 2002, Vol. 12.

Mingdai muke Guanyin huapu (Model Collections of Woodcut Guanyin in the Ming Dynasty). Shanghai: Shanghai guji chubanshe, 1997.

Couplet, Philippe. *Histoire d'une dame chrétienne de la Chine* (Paris: Michallet, 1688), trans. Xu Yunxi. *Yiwei Zhongguo fengjiao Taitai.* Taipei: Guangqi chubanshe, 1965.

Gu Qiyuan. *Kezuo zhuiyu*, in *Baibu congshu jicheng*, Ser. 100, Vol. 6.

Gu Yanwu. *Guzhong suibi* (Random Notes Taken amid the Reeds), in *Hanshan xianguan congshu*, Vol. 61.

Li Jiubiao. *Kouduo richao* (Daily Record of Oral Instructions), in *Yesuhui Luoma danganguan Ming-Qing Tianzhujiao wenxian*, Vol. 7.

Liu Junyu, Wang Yuchuan, and Luo Yu, trans. *Li Madou quji* (Complete Works of Fr. Matteo Ricci, S.J.). Taipei: Guangqi chubanshe, 1986.

---

44 Chen Xiao and Tan Huosheng, "Linghun yu routi: 1900 nian jiduan qingkuang xia xiangtu jiaomin de xinyang zhuangtai (Spirit and Flesh: Faith of the Rural Christians in the Extreme Situation in 1900)," *Wenshizhe* (Literature, History, and Philosophy) 1 (2003).

Ricci, Matteo. *China in the Sixteenth Century: The Journals of Matthew Ricci, 1583-1610*, trans. Louis J. Ggllagher. New York, Random House, 1953.

Vagnone, Alphonso. *Shengmu xingshi* (Life of the Holy Mother), in *Tianzhujiao dongchuan wenxian sanbian*, Vol. 3, ed. Wu Xiangxiang. Taipei: Xuesheng shuju, 1998.

Watson, Burton, trans. *The Lotus Sutra*. New York: Columbia University Press, 1993.

Yang Tingyun, *Daiyi pian*, in *Tianzhujiao dongchuan wenxian*, ed. Wu Xiangxiang. Taipei: Xuesheng shuju, 1979.

Secondary Sources

Yuanshi (Yuan History). Beijing: Zhongguo dabaike quanshu chubanshe, 1985.

Arnold, Lauren. "Folk Goddess or Madonna? Early Missionary Encounters with the Image of Guanyin," in *Encounters and Dialogues: Changing Perspectives on Chinese-Western Exchanges from the Sixteenth to Eighteenth Centuries*, ed. Xiaoxin Wu. Nettetal: Sankt Augustin, 2005. 227-238.

Chen Lianqi, ed. *Lidai Guanyin baoxiang* (The Sacred Images of Guanyin through Various Dynasties). Beijing: Zhongguo shudian, 1998.

Chen Xiao and Tan Huosheng, "Linghun yu routi: 1900 nian jiduan qingkuang xia xiangtu jiaomin de xinyang zhuangtai (Spirit and Flesh: Faith of the Rural Christians in the Extreme Situation in 1900)," *Wenshizhe* (Literature, History, and Philosophy) 1 (2003).

Dudbridge, Glen. *The Legend of Miaoshan*. London: Ithaca Press for the Board of the Faculty of Oriental Studies, Oxford University, 1978.

Gao Ruizhe. *Qingchu Guanyin huapu Cirong wushisan xian banhua yanjiu* (A Study of the Early Qing Collection *Fifty-three Manifestations of the Compassionate Face [of Guanyin]*). M.A. Thesis. National Taiwan Normal University, 2005.

Guan Zhenhu, trans. *Li Madou pingzhuan* [from Henri Bernard's Le Pere Mathieu Ricci et La Societe Chinoise de son Temps (1522-1610), 1937]. Beijing: Shangwu yinshuguan, 1993.

Lin Li-chiang. *Proliferation of Images: the Ink-stick Designs and the Printing of the Fang-shih Mo-p'u and the Ch'eng-shih Mo-yuan*. Ph.D Dissertation. Princeton University, 1998.

Menegon, Eugenio. *Ancestors, Virgins, and Friars: The Localization of Christianity in Late Imperial Mindong (Fujian, China), 1632-1863*. Ph.D. Dissertation, University of California, Berkeley, 2002.

Orsini, Mathieu. *The Life of the Blessed Virgin Mary*. New York: Peter F. Collier, Catholic Publisher, 1880.

Peterson, Willard. "Confucian Learning in late Ming Thought," in *The Cambridge History of China: Volume 8, The Ming Dynasty, 1368-1644, Part 2*, ed. Twitchett, Denis and Frederick W. Mote. Cambridge: Cambridge University Press, 1998.

Reed, Teresa. *Shadows of Mary: Reading the Virgin Mary in Medieval Text*. Cardiff: University of Wales Press, 2003.

Reis-Habito, Maria. "The Bodhisattva Guanyin and the Virgin Mary," *Buddhist-Christian Studies* 13 (1993): 61-69.

Standaert, Nicolas, ed. *Handbook of Christianity in China, Volume One: 635-1800*. Leiden: Brill, 2001.

—. *Yang Tingyun, Confucian and Christian in Late Ming China*. Leiden: Brill, 1988.

Sun Changwu. *Zhongguo wenxue zhongde Weimo yu Guanyin*. Beijing: Gaodeng jiaoyu chubanshe, 1996.

Wang Shucun, ed. *Guanyin baitu* (A Hundred Images of Guanyin). Guangzhou: Lingnan meishu chubanshe, 1997.

Winston-Allen, Anne. *Stories of the Rose: The Making of the Rosary in the Middle Ages*. University Park: Pennsylvania State University Press, 1997.

Yü Chünfang. *Kuan-yin: the Chinese Transformation of Avalokiteïvara*. New York: Columbia University Press, 2001.

Online sources

Nanhai Guanyin quanzhuan (Complete biography of Guanyin of the South Sea). http://1bird.net/502x.exe.

PART III

MEETING THE GODDESS: ECONOMICS AND POLITICS OF THE GODDESS

CHAPTER SEVEN

MEETING THE GODDESS: RELIGION, MORALITY, AND MEDICINE IN A FISHING COMMUNITY IN HONG KONG FORTY YEARS AGO

E. N. ANDERSON

When I met the goddess Tin Hau, the Empress of Heaven, she was in the body of a burly fisherman about sixty years old. He was speaking with a high, rather girlish voice, though his movements remained those of a powerful older man. Every year, on her festival day—the 23rd day of the 3rd lunar month—she possessed him. This had gone on for many decades; no one remembered how long. It was a part of life at Castle Peak Bay in the western New Territories of Hong Kong.

The year was 1966. No one thought it at all strange that gods and goddesses possessed mortals, or that the gender and physical attributes of the possessing deity had no relation to those of the spirit medium. Possession trances were part of daily life.

I had gone there to do research on fishing and on the fishing community.[1] Several thousand fishing families lived on the bay. The active fishers lived on their boats and rarely came ashore. Others, former fishers moving into the shore world, lived in pile houses built over the tidewater. Today, 40 years later, the bay is filled, and a new city built on it. The boat people have disappeared—they have moved ashore and assimilated to shore life. I am recalling a truly vanished world.

These fishermen were members of a distinctive ethnic group who called themselves "People on the Water" (*seui seung yan* in standard Cantonese, *soi song yan* in boat dialect, *shui shang ren* in Putonghua). They were called "Tanka" by the land people (*taan ka* C, *dan jia* P), but

---

[1] I spent over a year there in 1965-66 and another in 1974-75.

this term they found intensely offensive. They spoke a dialect of Cantonese and were culturally Cantonese. Various claims about their distinct culture and "tribal" origins were made by land people and by some of the literature, but these are myths. The boat people comprised an occupational subculture, as fishermen do in most of East and Southeast Asia, and indeed in most of the world—not a separate cultural group. (This, and all that follows, is fully discussed, with references, in Anderson 1970, 2005.) Their patron deity was Tin Hau (*Tianhou* in Putonghua). Elsewhere, notably in Taiwan, Tin Hau is familiarly known as Mazu (a familiar title for a respected woman, "something like 'Granny'" in the words of Nyitray 2000:165), and this is the source of the name Macau (*A ma kau*, Ma [zu] Temple). Few were so casual about her name in Hong Kong.

Tin Hau feast day in 1966 began at 11 p.m. the previous night, with spectacular explosions of long chains of firecrackers. These chains hung from boat masts as well as from shoreline roofs and poles. Boats began to move in from everywhere in the western New Territories: tiny hook-and-liners that held nuclear families, medium-sized slender shrimp trawlers and gill netters run by large extended families, and the huge, archaic, spectacularly photogenic hand-trawlers, still often moved by sail, and managed by crews of up to 60 or 70 persons. Through the darkness of the bay, under the vast sharp-tipped mass of Castle Peak, the boats arrived one by one or in small fleets. Dawn revealed a solid sheet of boats covering the whole bay.

In the center lay one huge old sail-powered hand-trawler. Boats clustered densely round it. Sampans shuttled back and forth, carrying people to it or to the fringing boats. This boat had just come from mainland China, from up the river near Guangzhou. Its captain and his family had managed to steal the ancient, venerable image of Ma Tsu from a particularly holy temple there, just before Mao's Red Guards swooped down to desecrate and destroy. The boat family fled in their boat to the religious freedom of Hong Kong, just in time for the image to serve as the focus of the festival day. (It later found home in a small new temple on the shore overlooking the bay.)

Early in the morning, great commotion attracted me to this boat. Another boat maneuvered through the pack of smaller craft, carrying the living Tin Hau to the sculptured one. The living Tin Hau had the needle-sharp tip of the handle of a huge magic (*ling*, numinous) iron pitchfork stuck through his cheek. When he moved, several fishermen had to carry this heavy iron. The tip entered his mouth and protruded about half an inch from his cheek. He purportedly felt no pain, but in fact flinched visibly when footsteps or waves shook the iron.

This man was a *mou si* (*wu shi* P), "shaman master." (*Wu* originally meant a shaman, but today it means a spirit medium; the technical distinction is that a shaman in trance sends his or her soul to the other world to explore and act, while a spirit medium in trance receives another soul, temporarily suspending his or her own personhood. There are also various technical aspects of trance and cosmology that distinguish the shaman.) The mou si was the highest class of spirit medium on the waterfront. Lesser mediums, such as "chanting men," "star dukes" and "worship women," could go into trance and receive souls, but they could not receive such powerful beings as Tin Hau, and they could not do much with their powers. A mou si could heal or kill, give luck or give ruin, predict the future or reveal hidden things. The few mou si of the area were feared and respected.

The mou si established himself on the huge old boat, by the venerable Tin Hau image. A steady stream of sick people then came to him from all the boats around; the line was many hundreds long, and he must have seen nearly or quite a thousand patients that day. He spent the day writing charms on yellow paper. Often he cut his tongue and wrote the charm with the blood, using his tongue as a brush. These charms were to be burned, and the ash drunk with herbal tea. I noted that the herbs indicated were often ones that actually would treat the condition involved—at least in Chinese herbalist belief.

In midafternoon, the mou si moved (with much help from strong young fishermen) down the gangplank and over to the regular Tin Hau temple on the west side of the bay. Here, on an isolated spit of land, a small gray-brick temple fit into the side of a small hill. Within it was a Tin Hau image—much larger, but much less ancient and venerable, than the one on the boat. In front of it, on the bayshore flats, rose a huge pole-and-mat building, several stories high. In this, Cantonese operas and music went on for much of the day. The temple image had to be able to see these through the temple door. People told me of a Tin Hau festival, some years before and in another village, at which the opera had been invisible to the temple image. Several village elders died in the following year. Obviously, Tin Hau was most upset. So, at Castle Peak, the community elders were careful to give Tin Hau a clear view.

The mou si took up residence in the Tin Hau temple for the rest of the day, while the strongest and toughest fishermen leaped for rockets in the courtyard. Small rockets soared up from a rickety bamboo platform. Whoever caught a falling rocket obtained a large construction of metal foil, colored paper, and bamboo, ornamented with rings, jade bits, and the like. These constructions brought good luck, especially sons and wealth. Whoever got a jade ring from one of them would have a son in the coming year. The first rocket gave its catcher the luckiest construction, and so on through over 60; even the last was still a lucky break.

The leaping men represented religious clubs that had organized during the year to provide funds for Tin Hau's festival day. A group of people would get together and pledge, say, $10 apiece every month, for this purpose. Such a group was a *ui* (P *hui* "society"), specifically a *paai san ui* (*bai shen hui*, "worshiping-gods society"). These groups were vitally important in the society of the waterfront, for they were the only formal social channel for uniting boat people and land people. Otherwise, boat and land dwellers distrusted and avoided each other. Religion brought them together. Castle Peak Bay was a Durkheimian community (Durkheim 1995); the people of the bay thought of religion as pre-eminently a way of integrating the community. They were aware that religion is a way of representing human society. Their small wooden images mirrored human society—usually that of the Qing Dynasty (1644-1911), but not always. The Chinese pantheon is so self-consciously a representation of this world's society that one mou si had an image of a Heavenly Police Commissioner, a British colonial in full blue uniform with shorts and pith helmet!

After the main opera and the leaps for rockets, dusk began to fall, and Tin Hau left the body of her mou si. He became an ordinary fisherman again, dazed and exhausted, and apparently with no memory at all of the day. Suddenly ignored, he wandered off to recover.

Then came the feasting. The main events were the ui feasts. Each ui repaired to a local restaurant or hall, there to eat mightily. The land people reveled in sea food; the boat people, who ate fish every day, took the opportunity to eat pork, chicken, and duck, foods they could rarely afford. The beautiful paper constructions were broken up and the parts auctioned off—one of those jade ornaments that gave a son could bring hundreds of dollars. This went into the ui treasury for next year's festival.

Meanwhile, all day long, many other activities went on. Firecrackers and music sounded. Feasts took place on every boat and in every home. People in vast streams swarmed around the Tin Hau temple. Boats jammed the harbor, constantly coming and going. Cars and vans jammed the highway to the city. The scene was the ultimate in "heat and noise," the rather revealing Chinese phrase for a really good time.

The Tin Hau fair was the major festival at Castle Peak Bay. That year, it even eclipsed New Year, because of the newly arrived venerable image and the dramatic performance of the mou si. (When I returned in 1974-75, Tin Hau day was tamer; the mou si was gone, the venerable image was installed in a temple on shore, and the day was just an ordinary religious occasion. Even so, tens of thousands of people went to the temples to pray, burn incense, and offer food.) The day brought clearly into focus many of the themes of life on the waterfront.

One point raised by the encounter with Tin Hau was that religious and empirical medicine were not separated at Castle Peak. Tin Hau was not alone in prescribing empirically effective herbal medicines. (The effectiveness of many Chinese herbal medicines has been established by modern biomedical research, though most still await trial.) All the spirit mediums of the bay area did the same. I was once present when a grandmother came with her sick grandson to seek help through a spirit medium. The spirit medium called up the grandmother's own long-deceased grandmother, who provided (via the medium's voice, suddenly become that of an elderly lady) a perfectly ordinary and thoroughly effective cold remedy. Other mediums, consulting on matters of fright or neurotic behavior, gave good psychotherapeutic advice. By contrast, the various schools of Daoist priests who worked in the area mainly carried out exorcism rites, driving away devils that caused sickness and misfortune; no use treating such cases with mere herbs!

The vast majority of medical activity at Castle Peak was purely empirical and secular. Of this, most, including all initial treatment of anything wrong, was through household manipulation of regimen, especially diet. Healthy eating graded into medicinal foods, and these into outright herbal cures; the boundary was impossible to draw (a point familiar to all students of Chinese everyday health practice). In general, illness was natural, and naturalistic theories accounted for it. Most often, these were based on maintaining a balance of hot, cold, wet, and dry. (Historically, these were a fusion of yin-yang theories with Hippocratic-Galenic and Indian ideas seeping across Asia in medieval centuries).

Naturalistic medicine thus wins out in ordinary life, and its triumph seems to explain the combination of naturalistic and divine healing. A local proverb held that "even the gods are subject to fate," and apparently the gods have to give place to natural, empirical medicine, too.

Historically, Tin Hau was a young fisherwoman of the Song Dynasty, who saved her father and brothers from storms. Along the waterfront, several versions of the story were current. Some said she saved her father and brother by magic or by shamanistic vision-travel. Most, however, said she actually sailed herself, and rescued her male kin by sheer raw courage and physical strength—a decidedly non-canonical story that shows the boat people's liberal attitude toward women very clearly indeed. Most agreed that she died young (sometimes in a boat accident at sea) and went to Heaven (Tin, *tian*), where she gained appointment as the patron deity of fishermen along the South China coast.

The canonical story in Chinese texts is that she was a girl, Lin Moniang, who was born on the 23rd day of the 3rd month in 960 A.D. in southern Fujian. She saved her relatives magically, in a dream or vision, and later refused to marry. She brought rain and otherwise worked miracles (Nyitray 1996, 2000). The texts give long histories of her divine promotion through bureaucratic ranks (Nyitray 2000; Watson 1985), but this was of no interest to the fishermen.

The boat people are not the only ones to change this story to suit their own sentiments. Other versions of the tale hold that she killed herself rather than marry a man she did not want (Watson 1985)—a variant of the story that yields some insight into Chinese attitudes to women and marriage; Chinese hold that women should marry, but Tin Hau is far from the only heroine-goddess who gained respect partly through marriage refusal. Nyitray rightly points out that the varied accounts of her life "are evidence of the efforts of local populations to mold the life of the future goddess in their likeness, that is, to claim Mazu as one of their own" (Nyitray 2000:168.)

She had two spirit helpers, Hearing-the-Wind Ears and Thousand-mile Eyes, who listen and watch for the troubles and sufferings of her worshipers—and, secondarily but importantly, for the sins of those who deserve condign punishment. In her temples, she was always represented with these at her side. In some shrines, including the little Hong-Kong-made one that watches me while I write these lines, these helpers have morphed into two young girl attendants.

In addition to being the patroness of fishermen in general, Tin Hau was the particular patroness of Castle Peak Bay and the fishermen and shore-dwellers there, though the land people had their own temple (the Three Sages temple on a hill above the bay pier). As such, she watched over all aspects of their lives, from childbirth and fertility to weather and wealth. Her role as a local deity for the whole bay community made the land people unite with the boat people in the religious organizations and committees. She thus became the major promoter of community harmony.

One must distinguish between the god of a particular *community* of people and the god of the *locality* inhabited by it. Tin Hau was the community god. The locality gods were various local representatives of the T'ou Tei Kung [*tudigong*], the Locality Duke or "earth god." These local *t'ou tei* were often worshiped in the form of phallic stones.

She was a living presence, constantly helping out people, though her role was hard to separate out from the roles of other protective deities. One distinctive feature of her cult was that the boat people (unlike the land-dwellers) made small images of deceased children of the family—the boys riding tigers, the girls riding white cranes—and placed these by or in the Tin Hau shrine in the central cabin of the boat. Tin Hau was a protectress of children in her life, according to many of the stories, and she so remains. Tin Hau could give good fortune; when one fisherman made an amazing haul and earned $30,000 Hong Kong in one day, he promptly went to her temple to offer thanks and a significant sacrifice. He knew who had helped him.

The boat people tried hard to stay on the good side of many deities, and to avoid offending them. An accident at sea could occasionally be from vengeance by Tin Hau for neglect of her cult, but was more apt to be due to the Sky God, the Sea Surface God, or the dragons of the sea and cloudy sky. It could possibly be the result of actions by any of the many other supernatural beings that populated the marine cosmos.

Tin Hau had one clear role: she had to protect a fisherman who accidentally caught a sacred fish (*san yu*, P *shen yu*). These were fish that appeared bizarre, immensely strong, and apparently derived from two separate and normally incompatible orders of being. One was the sturgeon, a very rare, large fish that appeared to be both a fish and a dragon. (Like a Chinese dragon, it looks bizarre and powerful and has tendrils around its mouth.) Sea turtles appeared to be both fish and turtle. Whales and porpoises appeared to be both fish and mammal; their mammalian behavior and internal structure were well known. Sawfish were not uncanny, but were immensely strong and truly strange in appearance, so they were sacred fish. Any of these fish, when caught, had to be immediately released. If they died, they had to be taken to Tin Hau's temple and hung there; they dried and remained there indefinitely. Ancient, dust-covered mummies of sturgeons or sawfish, or at least the saw-like toothed beaks of the sawfish, hung from the walls of all local Tin Hau temples.

Tin Hau thus had two direct moral functions: she promoted community, and she managed what little conservation ethic existed in the Hong Kong fishery. In general, the fishermen of the region had no concept of conservation or fisheries management, but the importance of saving sacred fish carried over into a general sense that fish were not mere foodstuffs, and that they had to be treated with some minimal degree of consideration.

More generally, Tin Hau was one of a vast interlocked heavenly bureaucracy, whose charge was to promote, enforce, and sacralize human communal life. Morality was social; it was a regulation of the ordinary affairs of human interaction. It was also very strongly based on the teachings of Confucius and Mencius. All educated people took their ethical training from the works of these two sages, and all uneducated people knew at least the outlines and commoner phrases. The language of ethical discourse reflected Mencian positions; a rascally lowlife was considered ignorant (*mou man*, P *wu wen*), from Mencius' position that education was necessary to develop our inner goodness, and anyone without culture (*wu wen*) would lapse into curmudgeonry. Virtue, then, was human nature, but its specifics had to be trained in. In practice, it was the behavior that makes human interaction most enjoyable, satisfying, and long-lasting: trustworthiness, forbearance, mutual aid and support, and thoughtful civility. The gods modeled all this by their own harmonious social life and just, fair dealings with each other and with humans. Disaster was the result of neglecting social obligations. Failing to let Tin Hau see her opera was an unpardonably selfish, thoughtless, inconsiderate act—truly *mou man*—and thus punished as such, not merely Tin Hau selfishly wanted to see the show.

The role of goddesses in the heavenly bureaucracy is well illustrated by Tin Hau. She was merciful, familial, and gentle—dutiful daughter and sister to her father and brothers, and then dutiful mother-figure to her worshipers. She was, however, no weak figure. She acted dramatically and bravely to save her male kin; recall that most of the stories at Castle Peak had her actually sail out onto the stormy sea to rescue them or search for them. She was a powerful defender and protector, combating other supernaturals to care for her boat-based charges (see Nyitray 2000 for a general view, based on Taiwan research, that closely parallels Hong Kong beliefs; and Nyitray 2005 for a full bibliography on Tin Hau).

As a strong and courageous woman, Tin Hau became an unofficial patron of Taiwanese rights, and her festival turned into a way the people of Taiwan could assert these against the repressive regimes of the early Nationalist government (Nyitray 1996, 2000; Nyitray also reports that Tin Hau in the Philippines merged with the Virgin Mary, in the cult of the Virgin of Casasay; Nyitray 2000:176, 205; see also Sangren 1988, 1993).

Iconographically, Tin Hau appeared like a less splendid version of Kun Yam (Guanyin), the most popular female deity in China. Tin Hau's relationship with Guanyin is so close that in other areas the two are equated (Nyitray 2005; Watson 1985). The boat people of Castle Peak

Bay kept the two goddesses sharply distinct. Tin Hau was the patron of the whole community.

According to Vivian-Lee Nyitray, the leading Western authority on the Tin Hau cult, Tin Hau "ranks second only to the Buddhist bodhisattva Guanyin as a female object of popular devotion" in China as a whole (Nyitray 2000:165). She was related not only icongraphically but also hagiologically to Guanyin; like Guanyin, Tin Hau was a merciful activist, watching out for her followers. Guanyin herself was very popular at Castle Peak, especially with women, who saw her as their personal protector and helper—a goddess for the great dispersed community of women more or less as Guanyin—Tin Hau was the goddess for the dispersed community of fisherfolk. was the goddess to whom women appealed first and foremost; she understood them, knew their needs, and was preeminent in caring for children, households, women themselves, and related issues of health, fertility, and survival.

Other female deities had only minor roles in the area. Female figures related to medicine, childbirth, and household had their importance to at least some individuals, but occupied much less significant places in the community.

Rosemary Ruether, in her recent book on goddesses in the western world (Ruether 2005), provides an account of goddesses in the western world's religions. These religions she finds to be male-dominated, and the personae of the goddesses involve assertions of male power alternating with mystical and sexual fantasies. Ruether explains them as creations and projections of males interested primarily in maintaining power.

Many Western goddesses were fertility goddesses. The concern with fertility is understandable in a male-dominated religion. However, other goddesses were virginal, even puritanical. One wonders what men saw in goddesses like Diana/Artemis. Artemis was so militantly anti-sex that, when Actaeon accidentally saw her bathing, she turned him into a stag and set her hounds to tear him to pieces. The final resolution of Western goddess-worship has been the cult of the Virgin Mary, a virgin who yet bore children.

East Asian goddesses seem a more powerful and complex set, less narrowly concerned with fertility or its opposite. China has nothing quite like India's Parvati/Durga/Kali (feminine aspects of Shiva) or Lakshmi (Vishnu's feminine side) or Sarasvati (Brahma's), but Chinese goddesses are still an exciting group. To be sure, Guanyin has Indian roots (being a feminization of the Indian Buddhist deity Avalokiteshvara), but she has been thoroughly sinicized (Yü 2001). She has taken traits of the Queen Mother of the West and the visionary cloud-ladies (Schafer 1973) of ancient Chinese myth, as well as the attributes of a self-sacrificing, dutiful Confucian daughter (Yü 2001).

Tin Hau is thoroughly Chinese, and a former living person. She was concerned with fertility in that she can help give sons (note the sex preference), but she is not a fertility goddess. Her nonmarriage and presumptive virginity were not points of significance at Castle Peak Bay. Nyitray (2005) has thoroughly explored the many ambiguous and transgressive aspects of the Tin Hau cult in China as a whole; the boat people would have understood little of the subtleties, but they had less ambiguity to deal with, since they saw no basic conflict between femininity and power. Presumably Tin Hau got her start as a deity of fishermen, and only later, as her cult spread to the land-dwelling majority, did problems arise with her power, refusal to marry, and triumphant femininity.

If, with Durkheim, we see a religious system as representing the society that invokes it, we will naturally look for Tin Hau in the Chinese social system. Tin Hau was a strong woman: rescuing her menfolk, curing the sick, saving her animals, actively guarding communities, giving wealth and luck to her favored ones, and possessing strong men to provide active, direct, personal leadership to her community. She did all this without fanfare; she was no Homeric Athena, badgering her worshipers and constantly demanding more from them. On the other hand, she was not averse to making her will known in no uncertain terms, as the village that failed to put their opera in her line-of-sight attested.

In short, she was far from the western stereotypes of patriarchal China. She was certainly not the abjectly downtrodden and abused woman familiar in western stereotypes of China (e.g. Eastman 1988).

Did she have a Durkheimian reality? In a word, yes, and it was not far to seek. She was the typical boat woman.

The Cantonese boat people of south China were famous throughout their homeland for their open, forthright behavior and rough-and-ready egalitarianism. This extended to the women. Boat women were far from being liberated in the modern American sense. They had to defer to husbands and often to grown sons. They feared going on shore, because of sexual and physical harassment by land people. They had to be modest and careful in behavior. They had to pray for sons, and rejoice more in sons than in daughters (though this was far less true of boat women than among the land-dwellers next door). Ideologically, they were second-class citizens, if rather less so than women in much of China.

However, they had tremendous social power. They also had very appreciable physical power; rowing boats and hauling nets develops impressive muscles. They participated in all decisions, and made many of the key ones. They—not their husbands—usually determined whom their sons and daughters married. Indeed, many boat girls made their own choices and *then* went to their *mothers* for approval; fathers were often confronted with a *fait accompli* (so much for Confucian theory). Moreover, the girls had considerable sexual freedom. Many of them worked as "singing girls" for years before marriage; no stigma attached to this.

Boat women participated as full partners in running and managing boats. The senior woman on board was second only to the senior man (her husband or—after his death—her son) in authority. Boat life was normally egalitarian and consultative, but life at sea often demands fast decision-making and clear chains of command, so the senior woman's power was real and vital. In fact, a strong woman could, and often did, exert more than trivial control over the senior man, especially if it was her son. Wifebeating or other abusive behavior was almost unknown. (Having a wife who can fight back with the full strength of a sailing-boat crew member is definitely a factor to consider.)

Also, women often bonded with their sons' wives, in contrast to the frequent Chinese case of bitter rivalry. The natural structural tensions were mollifed by the lack of patrilineages among boat people and of landed property. Conversely, boat women had to work together, cook together, and raise children together, and thus they had maximal opportunity for bonding and maximal reason to do so. A solidary group of wives on the boat would generally get its way.

Tin Hau was a sailor girl turned goddess. It is no wonder that, in the minds of her worshipers, she continued to act as such: strong, independent, and authoritative, but also nurturant, gentle, and calm. She could reward her supporters or be condignly fierce to those who slighted her. Rather than being a projection of male fantasies or power hunger, she was a divinization of everyday reality—a vision of what an actual boat woman would do if she could.

Significantly, she was the most important divine figure among the boat people. The Jade Emperor, ruler of all the gods, was far away (like the earthly ones of the past). The most important local male gods, Guan Gong and the locality gods, were land-dwellers' deities. The Sky God and Sea Surface God were impersonal natural forces, vaguely "male" but really nonhuman and nongendered. Several minor male figures were of concern to the boat people, but none matched Tin Hau.

Tin Hau's model and superior in the heavenly hierarchy, Guanyin, was probably the most widely worshiped single divinity in the region (as she is in many Chinese communities). Guanyin was primarily worshiped by women, who saw her as one of themselves, attentive to their concerns. Guanyin too was no meek or limited figure. Both Tin Hau and Guan Yin had a role in balancing out the patricentered aspects of Chinese culture (see Yü 2001).

Thus, the boat people of Castle Peak Bay had a female deity—once a living woman—as leader and representative. She could express the ideals, dreams, and realities of the lives of women, and of men too, on the water. She had a freedom and authority of which the women could only dream, and she had the comforts of heaven, but she came from their own background and was one of their people.

When she possessed a spirit medium—significantly, a senior male of community-level status—everyone could meet her in person, talk to her, and get her help in sickness and in luck. She interacted with them as one of their community. She was not an abstract and remote being; she was a living, breathing, vocal person, one they knew and understood.

Acknowledgements

I am grateful to Vivian-Lee Nyitray for help with this paper.
I am grateful to the many people who helped me at Castle Peak Bay.

References

Anderson, E. N. 1970. *The floating world of Castle Peak Bay.* Washington, DC: American Anthropological Association.

—. 2005. *Floating world lost.* In press, University Press of the South

Durkheim, Emile. 1995. *The elementary forms of the religious life.* Tr. Karen Fields (Fr. orig. 1912). New York: Free Press.

Eastman, Lloyd. 1988. *Family, fields and ancestors.* Oxford: Oxford University Press.

Nyitray, Vivian-Lee. 1996. "The Sea Goddess and the Goddess of Democracy." In *The annual review of women and religion*, edited by Arvid K. Sharma. Albany: SUNY Press. Pp. 164-177.

—. 2000. "Becoming the Queen of Heaven: The Life and Career of Mazu." In *Goddesses who rule*, edited by Elisabeth Benard and Beverly Moon. New York: Oxford University Press. Pp. 165-180.

—. 2005. "Questions of Gender in Tianhou/Mazu Scholarship." Ms.

Ruether, Rosemary Radford. 2005. *Goddesses and the divine feminine: A western religious history.* Berkeley: University of California Press.

Sangren, P. Steven. 1988. "History and the Rhetoric of Legitimacy: The Ma Tsu Cult of Taiwan." *Comparative studies of society and history* 30:674-697.
—. 1993. "Power and Transcendence in the Ma Tsu Pilgrimages of Taiwan." *American ethnologist* 20:564-582.
Schafer, Edward. 1973. *The divine woman: Dragon ladies and rain maidens in T'ang literature*. Berkeley: University of California Press.
Watson, James L. 1985. "Standardizing the Gods: The Promotion of T'ien Hou ("Empress of Heaven") along the South China Coast, 960-1960." In *Popular culture in late imperial China,* edited by David Johnson, Andrew J. Nathan, and Evelyn S. Rawski. Berkeley: University of California Press. Pp. 292-324.
Yü Chün-fang. 2001. *Kuan-yin: The Chinese transformation of Avalokiteśvara*. New York: Columbia University Press.

Select Additional Bibliography

Davis, Edward L. 2001. *Society and the supernatural in Song China*. Honolulu: University of Hawaii Press.
Dean, Kenneth. 1993. *Taoist ritual and popular cults of southeast China*. Princeton, NJ: Princeton University Press.
Mote, Frederick. 1999. *Imperial China, 960-1800*. Cambridge, MA: Harvard University Press.
Thompson, Laurence. 1979. *Chinese religion*. Belmont, CA: Wadsworth.
Weller, Robert. 1987. *Unities and diversities in Chinese religion*. Seattle: University of Washington Press.
Wolf, Arthur (ed.). 1974. *Religion and ritual in Chinese society*. Stanford, CA: Stanford University Press.

CHAPTER EIGHT

SHE DANCES MADLY: TOWARDS A RITUAL POLITICAL ECONOMY OF THE GODDESS

PIYA CHATTERJEE

Fourteen years ago, I met a Goddess. I was told of witches, too, but I was never introduced to one. But I might have met a couple here and there, masked by their ordinariness, and the necessary secrecies of their dangerous power. I was not expecting to meet either a Goddess or a Witch as I began my ethnographic and historical study of women and labor in the tea plantations of North Bengal.[1] However, I was pleased to encounter them, because what their stories taught me were important lessons about the ways in which embodiment, affect, and political economy come together to teach us something important about the sacred: the ineffable mix of the mundane with the mysterious, and the ways in which gender and power are always implicated within the labors of spiritual action.

Landscapes of Tea

The tea plantations of North Bengal are the home-base of these particular goddesses and witches. Started by the British in the 1850s, this plantation economy stretches from North Bengal across Assam. The plantation enclave dominated the colonial economy of this region, and tea's importance to the postcolonial Indian exchequer cannot be underestimated. Because local villagers refused to work in the harsh

[1] I began ethnographic work in North Bengal plantations in 1992. Much of this essay is built on material collected at that time. However, my longer project on women, labor, and colonial history involved both historical and ethnographic analysis. I continue to be involved with tea plantation communities and am involved in new research and organizing projects there.

regime of plantation labor, most workers were brought in from the Chotanagpur plateau, the Nepal hills, and from southern India.

In North Bengal, the ethno-racial composition of the plantation working-class is constituted of a mix of lower-caste Nepali and *adivasi*[2] communities, who are highly diverse: Gond, Santhal, Oraon, Munda, among others. It is a highly plural ethno-racial landscape, which was quickly marked in the familiar dichotomous politics of "divide and rule" by British planters—between Nepali (*paharia*) and so-called "tribal" (*madesia*)[3] communities. The postcolonial plantocracy, of both staff and managers, is dominated by North Indian and Bengali upper-castes. In the Darjeeling hills, more upper-caste Nepali planters (in the manager class) can be found, but on the whole, a Bengali and Punjabi upper-caste plantocracy is the norm.

Missionary activity in the region is as old as the plantations and the ethnic pluralities intersect with a variety of religious traditions: Christian, Muslim, Hindu, Buddhist—and religious practices not claimed as "Hindu," though they are familiar to what Milton Singer and others have called the "Little Traditions" of Hinduism.[4] However, as a mark of respect to various *adivasi* practices (some of which are shrouded in secrecy from outsiders in the plantation), I don't place these within the dominant ambit of caste-Hindu practices.[5]

---

[2] The term adivasi is used here to indicate autochtonous status. However, I recognize its homogenizing move as problematic. It is used self-referentially by both the Oraon and Munda in the plantations, as well as by others marked as "lower caste" and originally from the Chotanagpur Plateau.

[3] Interestingly, this dichotomy between paharia ("of the hills") and madesia ("of the middle country") is used in various British ethnological texts such as Herbert Risley's magisterial *The Tribes and Castes of Bengal.* What is important to note, though, is that the binary "congealed" the diversities within these communities into an evolutionary dichotomy. Thus, Nepalis were seen as a "thriving" agrarian caste while the madesia or "tribals" were viewed as *jungles* or "of the jungle"—primitive and savage. These articulated a now familiar topos of differential civilization upon plural communities and were used in various ways towards plantation management.

[4] For the classic anthropological discussions of this, see Marriot, McKim.1955 Little Communities in an Indigenous Civilization. In *Village India: Studies in the Little Community*.pp. 171-222. McKim Marriot, ed. Chicago: University of Chicago Press and Singer, Milton.1972 *When a Great Tradition Modernizes: An Anthropological Approach to Indian Civilization.* Chicago: University of Chicago Press.

[5] There were many instances, for example, in which I could not attend Santhali and Oraon rituals because of the ways in which my own upper-caste/class privilege

Indeed, the Santhali term, *diku* (or outsider) is usually reserved for non-Santhali and specifically caste-Hindus who are viewed as oppressors. Given the catastrophic historical impact of pre-colonial feudal systems of caste-privilege, and the overlay of British colonial settlement policies upon their communities, this is a counterstance[6]—a conscious alterity in the community's refusal to be "gazed at"—which gestures to thinking beyond the "continuum" model when addressing religious interactions at the "folk" level. In contrast, Nepali lower-caste communities claim a Hindu-ness quite explicitly. While it is beyond the scope of this particular essay to demonstrate the fine calibrations in lower-caste Nepali Hindu practices, I want to underscore the ways in which these gradations (and claims) of Hindu-ness and non-Hindu-ness mark not only the pluralities from which the Goddess emerges—it also marks the dominant terms of social power and history against which we must understand her manifestations.

Apart from these ethno-racial and religious separations across diverse working communities, the plantation labor hierarchy is also deeply gendered. Indeed, approximately 70 percent of the labor force in the fields is female. Women workers, both Nepali and *adivasi,* occupy the lowest rung of wage-labor in the plantation labor system. This is a labor that is necessary, but de-valued, in terms of actual wages received, yet paradoxically, the feminization of labor creates the terms of an enduring fetishism around women's bodies. Women's labor is also vitally necessary across the global commodity chain as tea circulates in the historical economy of the world market.[7] It is women's so-called "nimble plucking"

---

was read as both intrusion, perhaps even a threat to the sacred-ness of those very practices. My sense of "plurarity" in these highly diverse ethno-racial and religious interactions is always mediated through the issues of power and historical dominance.

[6] In this phrase, I borrow from Gloria Anzaldúa as she formulates an understanding of Chicano/a consciousness/resistance as a historical position. See her "La conciencia de la mestiza: Towards a New Consciousness." In *Making Face, Making Soul—Haciendo Caras—Creative and Critical Perspectives by Feminists of Color*, ed. Gloria Anzaldúa. San Francisco: Aunt Lute Books, 1990. pp. 377-389.

[7] Cynthia Enloe provides a cogent feminist analysis of commodification and labor in international political economy. See her now classic *Bananas, Beaches and Bases: Making Feminist Sense of International Politics*, University of California Press, 1990. pp. 124-150.

that helps to create the fetishism of the commodity: tea as the quintessential drink of femininity and empire.[8]

Alterities and Patriarchies of the Sacred

The feudal patronage system of the plantation is thus marked by complex ethno-racial, religious, and gendered cleavages. In actual social practice, there is a great deal of blurring between these analytic divisions—especially in the Labor Lines. However, because of the abiding historicized inscriptions about "civilization" (both British white and Hindu upper-caste) which mark some plantation bodies as "primitive" (out-caste, "tribal"), it is important to mark those zones of cultural action where the Goddess is also not claimed—where she might, indeed, not be welcome.

In this essay, I will use "thick description" of a few ethnographic vignettes to suggest the affective-political economies of the Goddess: of alterities, memory, and the manner in which embodied social action creates another moral economy of legitimacy and power. The argument will be based on the following conceptual presumptions and approach.

The **first** rests on the notion of "intersecting otherness."[9] As I have noted earlier, the intersections of ethno-racial, religious gendered and class difference create the terms of "otherness" in the politico-historical economy of the plantation. Otherness is an intersectional and collectivist process, and it is upon this presumption that the analysis proceeds. I will suggest, through this formulation, that "intersecting otherness" traffics across a constitution of "alterity" which is multiple. It breaks open the self—other dialectic. It is beyond the binary. Otherness, in this regard, is tracked on simultaneous axes of alterity: planter, mazdoor, women, men, Hindu, non-Hindu, Nepali, adivasi, priests, goddesses, and witches.

The **second** conceptual underpinning in the essay is the use of "labor" as a principal metaphor and tool of analysis. When the Goddess'

---

[8] For this particular argument, see my book, *A Time for Tea: Women, Labor and Post/Colonial Politics on an Indian Plantation*. Durham: Duke University Press, 2001.

[9] While this specific phrasing is mine, I draw from Kimberle Crenshaw's theoretical framing of "intersectionality" as a way to conceptualize the ways in which categories of identity/power actually work in social practice. Taking her own suggestion of "intersectionality" as a transitional concept, I use it to think about religion, class, and gender simultaneously. See her Kimberlé Williams Crenshaw, *Mapping the Margins: Intersectionality, Identity Politics, and Violence Against Women of Color*, 43 Stan. L. Rev. 1241 (1991).

manifestations are situated within the terms of "political economy," it troubles the Durkheimian binary between the "sacred" and the "profane." From the beginning, I understood that any conventional analysis of labor (bodily work for production) had to be parsed against this analytic binary. Even within the actual landscape of tea bushes, constituted as a strange bonsai forest by the most arduous of bodily toil, working communities created sacred spaces: a tree worshipped as divine; the grave which memorializes a beloved *bhagat* (faith-healer/shaman/elder) or union leader; the notion that machines are possessed by spirits; and the ways in which women will speak about the tea bushes' "life-force."

All of these narratives of the sacred speak to another kind of understanding about work. They suggest an epistemology of labor which embraces, in one weave, the worlds of ritual, orality, and memory. In that light, this essay seeks to disrupt a functional analysis that is predicated on the division between structure and superstructure, material over symbolic. Rather, in placing bodily and affective stories at the center of its analysis, the essay seeks a parallel understanding of how the "political" and the "religious" work together to define other terms of labor. These are the codes of a ritual political economy.

In another more obvious way, the principal narrators of these forms of ritual/spiritual labor are women whose daily lives are bound within the deeply unequal and feudal system of plantation patriarchies. As the most subordinated and marginalized of plantation workers, their stories, and claims, of the feminized divine suggests an alterity which challenges the gendered, religious, classed, and ethno-racial domination of the plantation system. Furthermore, their claim about divine embodiment is as much a laboring act as it is anything else. Propitiation, discipleship, and the daily economic maintenance are all necessary acts of will and power. They require the energy, force, and intelligence—creative action upon the world—which are all at the core of the most basic understandings of what constitutes "labor."

Thirdly, the feminized divine works through the conditions of excess and mystery. Her power, and the power of narratives about Her, are enigmatic. As She dances with an apparent madness, filled with the Goddess, our anthropological lens might catch her within a functionalist frame: She gains legitimacy as a marginalized woman; she taps into an ancient folkgeist of what constitutes divinity within the Indian subcontinent. Certainly, this is the case. Yet, her power also rests in a riddle deep within the body. It is sacred, perhaps, because the body's passion and suffering spin into excess. She cannot be fully grasped by the discourses of the "rational." She spills over the edge of analysis—into the realms of an affective economy which is "unspeakable"—inscribed into a terrain in which the body, and silence, escapes conventional forms of representation.

Meeting Durga Mata. Munnu Kujoor, an Oraon woman worker at Sarah's Hope Tea Estate, tells me of a Durga Mata who lives in Chamurchi, on the border between India and Bhutan. It is in July 1993. I have spent some fruitless months trying to befriend Durga Mata I, an elderly Nepali woman with the face of an aristocratic and beautiful duena, who lives in the Factory Line of Sarah's Hope where I am staying. Durga Mata I allows me to sit in on some consultations with plantation women, but it is seems clear that she is uncomfortable with my interest in her work. I live in the plantation, in an empty bungalow, and everyone knows that I am from the plantocracy, a strange *memsahib*. My presence is intrusive and so I stop going.

But my curiosity is piqued, because it is clear that women rarely make claim to spiritual mastery in the dazzlingly diverse religious worlds of the plantation. Plantation patriarchies are buttressed by various ritual legitimations of masculine authority: wandering Bihari *bahman* priests earning their livelihood from conducting various marriages and pujas, to Oraon bhagats presiding over *jhar-phuk* (exorcisms).

When Munnu Kujoor tells me about Chamurchi's Durga Mata, who lives in a village not connected to Sarah's Hope, I am eager to meet her. She is a young woman and is friendly, willing to speak about her special gifts. We have numerous conversations over the next few months, and she tells me about her gift of possession. We meet in her small house in the village. Her husband is a jeep driver, who ferries people in a local "maxi taxi" between Banarhat and Chamurchi. She was born in a neighboring plantation and had married into this village.

"I am nothing without Her," she says. "She started coming to me when I was very young, and at first I did not understand what was happening. I was very frightened. Now I realize that this is a gift. But it might stop tomorrow. Just like that. She might stop coming to me. So I try to help people though many say bad things—that I make money from people. But I take what is given. I ask for nothing. I wanted to build a small temple outside my house but others in the village threatened to take the cement. I wanted to make the temple outside, because I did not want my family to benefit from the donations. When it is Her birthday, there is big feasting, and I pay for it through selling my betel nut for around

12,000Rs. ($286). But donations are given. I try and help people but there are these misunderstandings."[10]

Durga Mata is economically successful, because she has built a steady coterie of disciples around her. Significantly, these are Marwari women, daughters and wives of the small prosperous business community of conservative caste-Hindus who live in Chamurchi and Banarhat, the neighboring small town. Because of their economic standing and surplus, they donate enough money for her to buy an impressively ornate image of the goddess, and add a *pucca* (cement) room to her house. I understand that there is a campaign to build a small temple for her but as she notes, her village neighbors—all Nepali—are not happy with this turn of events.

I saw Durga Mata's propitiation once. She schedules this every Tuesday morning, though she does tell me that the Goddess comes "whenever she wants." I notice that the small group of ten women—and only women—come to her are both Marwari and Bengali. Except for Bhagirathi Mahato and Munnu Kujoor, who have brought me, I don't see other Nepali or *adivasi* women from the plantation.

Durga Mata's body begins to shake imperceptibly. She begins to undulate slightly. She throws her head back and forth. It moves in a circle, faster and faster. She utters sounds I cannot understand. The language she speaks sounds like something beyond language. But I am told later that it is Nepali. As she becomes, in this strange spinning, the Goddess Durga, women start to ask for her advice around a range of problems. A Bengali woman, clearly distressed, throws herself at the feet of Durga Mata, weeping. She is constantly dizzy, and her only daughter is suffering in her marriage. What should she do? Durga Mata responds in her rapid-fire Nepali. In this moment of cross-linguistic connection between disciple and Goddess, I lose meaning, because I have lost linguistic comprehension. Perhaps all I need to understand is the strange spinning, the undulations. Isn't this beyond language? All I know is that a prescription of flower, seeds, and prayer are given as a possible antidote to her family problems. The woman looks relieved.

Durga Mata tells me later that most of the women who come to her want to talk to her about their domestic issues. Many of these "family problems" have to do with trouble conceiving a child. More specifically, trouble conceiving a male child. All want sons. I ask her whether women

[10] I have used this very specific dialogue/narrative in my book, *A Time For Tea*, but have expanded greatly on the analysis (and narrative) of feminized divinity in this particular essay. For a very detailed rendering of religious practices and power, and ritual political economy, in the plantation, *see A Time for Tea*, pp. 263-274.

come to meet her outside the propitiation ceremony. I am not surprised to hear that they do. Durga Mata is seen as wise, a space for counsel and some solace, even when she is not the Goddess. The paradoxes of patriarchy should be clear in this instance: a woman garners social legitimacy by invoking feminized divinity. This is an invocation which should, for her women disciples, help them birth sons.

At the session where I witnessed the propitiation, Munnu Kujoor—an Oraon woman worker and close interlocutor—had accompanied me. Like everyone in the room, she is trilingual, and as she was translating the scene, she noted: "Did you hear what she said when she was in possession? She kept saying that there is a 'black person' in the room who is unclean. I know she was speaking about me." I told her that I did not understand most of what she said so I missed this referent. It is an important gesture on Munnu's part.

Why? These are the terms of ethno-racial difference in the plantation. A Nepali woman-Goddess is surrounded by Marwari and Bengali women-disciples who are caste-Hindus. The anthropologist is an upper-caste Hindu, Brahmin no less. Munnu is the only person in the room who is *adivasi.* She should be outside, on the other side of this sacred ambit. Her own sense of "blackness" marks her own unease in this space of women and the feminized divine. I am not surprised by her quick marking of exclusionary difference.

Such are the terms of intersectional otherness. The Goddess is feudal, too. She is aware of her constituency—the terms of feminized patronage and capital. Her disciples might not appreciate being in the same room with one who is marked as the Other. Her temple might not be built. She is canny even in possession. Her many-arms must discriminate. They dance the code of millennial distinctions, calibrated on such fine cruelties, across language.

Yet, let's look at other simultaneous axes of difference and power in the Durga Mata's attempt to gain legitimacy across these vectors of social identity. Durga Mata tells me about gendered contests to her attempt at wider public acceptance. There is a wandering guru from the north, whose large public meetings suggest considerable economic and organizational power. She was invited to a dinner where he was a guest of honor. Other guests were calling her *Ma*, or Mother, and he asked her, "in a *neech* (condescending) way" why she was called that. She said, "I did not like the way he was asking me this. I told him that my in-laws lived here and my house is here. I am bou-*ma* (daughter-in-law). I stay here. My children call me *ma*. My mother-in-law calls me *ma* (mother). I am not like you. I cannot move around meeting my devotees. If I make a mistake, my family suffers. If I kill myself because I have dishonored my family, will my son be able to hold his head up?"

Durga Mata's commentary offers a sharp critique of the patriarchal terms by which a ubiquitous guru can mobilize his constituency. It begins with his ability to be mobile—to wander. His travels create material access to a "public" world—a movement through space which is peopled by potential disciples. A woman of her background is unable to do this. She does not have the mobility. The terms of patriarchal family honor—mobility in one instance—severely constrain her ability to garner wider discipleship, and social legitimacy. Her role as a daughter-in-law clearly restrains her ambitions to "break" out of her domestic—and domesticated—circle of influence. She is acutely aware that at some level she is a Domestic Goddess.

She tells me that after she has vehemently defended her status of divine *Ma-ness*, the guru challenged her around textual history—and her insignificance within it: "He asked me where I was in the *itihas* (history), and I told him that "just because you read and write does not mean you know. I do not read but what I know is within me. She tells me all." Her brief but sharply contesting claim to sacred knowledges, and indeed to a certain understanding of history, presents a gendered analysis about ritual power and legitimacy. It is also an important gesture to the gendered politics around literacy and textual mastery in religious claims to knowledge.

Durga Mata knows this well when she admonishes the guru for patronizing her. Her direct access to the sacred bypasses his textual monopoly and asserts another modality of "knowing." In "becoming" the Goddess, she challenges the very modality of mediation. He must act, move toward. She is.

In this rendering of an encounter between a Durga Mata and a powerful wandering *guru*, we catch glimpse of the gendered complexities inhered with heterodox and folks traditions of religious belief—and the politics of literacy and faith. It gestures to the ways in which gendered differences create the fault lines even within "heterodox" and "folk" religious practices. These also constitute the patriarchies of the sacred.

The Nepali Durga Mata embodies a challenge to not only the patriarchal codes of the "Little Traditions," she also poses a challenge to the "orthodox" practices of Goddess worship in Bengal. Certainly, she pulls from her own lexicon of Nepali Hindu-ness to shape herself into this particular rendering of shakti and feminine power, but she also operates within a cultural context in West Bengal which Durga is viewed as an iconically *Bengali* goddess. Thus, when the grand spectacle of the Durga puja occurs in North Bengal, across the towns and into the plantations, every aspect of worship is controlled by Bengalis. Indeed, each plantation sponsors a pandal and the patronage of Bengali managers and staff dominates these spectacles. Durga Mata conducts her own feasts but she is marginalized from these larger ritual performances around the Goddess.

Durga Mata won't take this lightly. As the festivities of the Durga Puja come to their climax, she comments on a priest's ritual work in a neighboring plantation's large pandal. On the Tuesday of the Durga Puja, she says, "Yesterday, I had a dream. I dreamt of fire. I dreamt that fire would consume me. Today, I find out that the pandal is half burned because the pandit (priest) was careless with matches. This is what happens when you are sinful." Sure enough, the roof of the tent is singed. Ontology is not merely functional. This is a convenient dream. Perhaps. Perhaps, she does dream. Perhaps, she celebrates a direct flame.[11]

The Goddess and The Witch: Dangerous Illegitimacies. Durga Mata is Nepali, she lives in the hinterlands where her ethnicity, rural working-class status, and claims to the Goddess are legitimate (in their invocation of an ancient lexicon of the feminized divine) but also marginalized. This is a complex marginality, marked by her ethno-racial position *vis-à-vis* the dominant ethnic elite in the region, the Bengalis, and their hegemonic performances around the Goddess. She does claim a spectacular power, but it is a smaller spectacle when viewed against the dominant rituals of claim especially in the puja season.

Yet, as her heterodox performance challenges the Bengali spectacle, and troubles the dominance of a wandering guru, she still spins within the socially sanctioned belief system of Hindu-ness. Durga Mata chafes at the boundaries of family honor but such are the terms of power: the Goddess can be domesticated, she must spin within the demarcated private. But as I have suggested, through Munnu's comment about the Goddess' remark about her "blackness," the Goddess is also located with other recognitions of feminized sacred power. These are embodiments which refuse the terms of domesticity. They are viewed as dangerous because their otherness cannot be revealed. These are understandings that bank on secrecy and even out-casteness. They are most commonly found across a range of *adivasi* practices.

What explains a strange death, a freak birth? It might be a spirit, jealousy, the evil eye. The borders between human and supernatural are

[11] As I have noted earlier, this aspect of the analysis is rendered in *A Time for Tea,* pp. 272-273.

straddled by acts considered deviant because they cause harm. Such acts are subterranean, and if humanly willed, they must be apprehended. The bhagat's divination may pinpoint not only an evil spirit, but a human one who has set it to its terrible task. The sacred wrestles with its own negation.

Enter the *daini*, the witch. Evil enters a woman. She has no shadow. A man might be a witch, but in the plantation, this is rare. A *daini's* mastery of the sacred threatens the bhagat, the ritual master of many *adivasi* religious practices. Says Mongra Bhagat, "A real bhagat can make a *daini* dance, beg for mercy. A *daini* has two and half gun (mantra/power), an ojha has one and half, but a real bhagat has five gun, which is why a bhagat can make a *daini* dance." A mathematics of ritual mastery is thus plotted.

Where might a *daini* learn her tricks? All is secret, I am told, but be careful of those who envy you. Mongra Bhagat adds, "They come out only during the Kali Puja, when there is no moon. They dance around the tree that sits on the border, near the Umesh Kholla. They dance naked. My grandfather who was a great bhagat caught them once, made them unconscious while they were dancing. In the morning, the villagers found them there. Then everyone knew."[12]

Stories of witchcraft capture the moral economies of gender and power in striking ways. Women might seize the sacred but they must do so under the cover of night. How many can claim to be Durga Mata? For one who dares, she might be stigmatized as a witch. The sacred is not legitimate in this case. Because it is gendered, there is a certain negation. Such negation wears a gendered and *adivasi* body: a woman who dances madly.

But I hear other whispers. An old woman is beaten to death by her own sons, accused by them of being a witch. She was a retired worker and a widow. She was living in her own labor quarter, refusing to leave. Three cows died one day and she was accused of killing them. They killed her in front of the village. This was not a secret killing. It was socially sanctioned. Some women I speak to shrug their shoulders when I suggest that struggles over property, widowhood, and isolation caused her death. The political economy of her death resides in the catacombs of cruel rationalizations. The secret and the sacred encompasses a space where value is coded through the ephemeral. This is no simple place of mystification. The sacred contains a political economy. Political economy implicates the patriarchies of the sacred.

---

[12] Ibid, p.272-273.

The Goddess cannot be understood without the Witch. Within the moral economies of the plantation, the social sanctions of feminized divinity are premised on complex modes of othering and control. How many human embodiments of the Goddess are there, actually? Can they rise to the public claim of a wandering guru, even if their ritual performances speak to the ancient pulsing of *shakti*? Most women faith-healers who claim this form of divinity gain local recognition but often cannot go beyond a small coterie of followers. Their cultural and symbolic capital is constrained by the terms of patriarchy.

Shakti, when manifested, must be controlled by male priests—enshrined in an inert idol. As symbol and icon, the Goddess Durga gestures to the possibilities of women's power within the context of daily patriarchy—but she, too, is domesticated. She, too, will weep as she is sent to the river after days of worship.

It is more common, actually, to hear about witches in the plantation, and this suggests another set of alterities around the sacred—and the dangerous power of women if they are perceived as laying claim to the sacred, without the social sanction of ritual masters such as priests and bhagats. Indeed, such a claim might cost a woman her life.

A complicated set of performances creates the landscape of intersectional otherness. The Goddess must be understood within plural social manifestations which traffic across overlapping axes of power. These constitute simultaneous alterities. Sometimes these create important contradictions. Durga Mata challenges patriarchal authority with the wandering guru. She also challenges ethnic hegemonies around ritual performance and claim. Yet, simultaneously, she marks her superiority against "blackness." Her claim to divinity still marks the terms of ethno-racial and religious dominance in the plantation. But those "black" practices—such as witchcraft—also throw into relief the constraints of her own legitimacy in claiming such extraordinary power. Indeed, the Witch—in all her illegitimacies—unmasks and makes more transparent the moral economies of patriarchy and the language of the sacred which makes both her and the Goddess possible.

CHAPTER NINE

THE POLITICIZATION OF AN ICON: DURGA/KALI/BHARAT MATA AND HER TRANSFORMATIONS

MARY-ANN MILFORD-LUTZKER

Over fifty years ago, at midnight on August 14/15, 1947, ninety years after the first war of independence, also known as the Indian Mutiny, India finally achieved independence from the British. The battles had been fought doggedly, courageously and with great endurance. The motivating figurehead for the freedom fighters was Bharat Mata, Mother India, who was a manifestation of Mahadevi, the great goddess. Bharat Mata, as an idea and also as a spiritual icon, inspired the people of India to assert themselves against colonial suzerainty. *Bande Mataram,* Hail to the Mother, became the rallying cry for the revolutionaries. It was a refrain that was initially secular in nature and universal in its inclusiveness.[1]

As an icon, Bharat Mata conveyed strength through the mystical experience of *darshan,* the act of seeing and being seen by a sacred image that is imbued with the power of a deity, an act that permeates the Hindu religious experience. The principal gods Siva and Visnu, together with the goddess Devi, in their multiple manifestations, penetrate the imagination of the faithful with their hypnotic stares. The wrathful Durga and the terrifying Kali, both of whom are manifestations of Devi, were called forth to rid the universe of demonic *asuras,* evil forces, and were the inspiration for Bharat Mata to be worshipped as a leader and savior of the idea of

---

[1] Lise McKean discusses in depth the rise of Bharat Mata worship and the founding of the eight-storey Bharat Mata temple in the pilgrimage town of Hardwar, in her chapter entitled "Bharat Mata: Mother India and Her Militant Matriots," *Devi: Goddesses of India,* ed. John Stratton Hawley and Donna Marie Wulff (Berkeley and Los Angeles: University of California Press, 1996), 250-280.

India. Over the aeons India has been invaded and ruled by outsiders—Greeks, Turks, Persians, Afghanis, Mughals, British. All to a certain extent have been absorbed into India's culture and all have been perplexed by the bewildering number of deities and their extraordinary forms. Durga and Kali were among the most perplexing deities, due to their wrathful and bloodthirsty natures which seemed at such odds with the Hindu patriarchal system that insisted upon a strict code of female behavior. Yet it was these goddesses who were to provide the iconic touchstone for the nationalist movement that emerged in the nineteenth century.

The year 1857 marks the beginning of the modern era in India. The seminal event was the eruption of fighting between Indian sepoys and British military forces at Meerut on May 9, 1857, which gave birth to the First War of Independence in India that was known by the colonial British powers as the Great Indian Mutiny. With protests spreading throughout the Gangetic Plains, the Punjab, the Deccan, the Thar Desert and the eastern regions of Bengal, it was realized that a figurehead or symbol was needed, that would be instantly recognizable to all Indians regardless of caste, religious or regional differences. *Sakti,* the female principle of the universe, and of whom Mahadevi (Devi) is its deified expression, was the fundamental source of power for Bharat Mata as Mother India who would nurture, support and inspire the revolutionary spirit of the new India. Bharat Mata is an abstract concept that brings to mind ideas of autochthonous powers, not readily recognized in palpable form. Devi, on the other hand, takes on multiple personae in her various incarnations. She was and is loved, respected and feared. Therefore, it was through the desire and need for a strong and unifying icon that Devi manifested herself as Bharat Mata, who in turn absorbed the powers of Durga and ultimately those of Kali.

Both Durga and Kali were called into being at times of crises, at times when the great Hindu gods were unable to fight off powerful demons who threatened the stability of order in the universe. It was fitting, therefore, that they should be called upon at this great hour of need in the nineteenth century. What is singularly significant is that both Durga and Kali had proven themselves as efficient and successful warriors who were victorious in all their battles. As inspiring and determined warriors, they became the most appropriate icons for the Swadeshi independent movement that was forming towards the end of the century.

Over time deities have emerged through mythologization of an idea, largely in recognition of the powers of Nature and the perceived need to appease her in order to bring rain, or stem the flow of monsoon floods, to use the rays of the sun for growth and warmth, or to end the sun's power during times of deadly droughts, to steady the force of gales or to bring refreshing breezes. A certain inherent duality resided within all the powers of Nature. Such ambiguity can also be traced in the emergence of Devi, the Goddess, as she manifests herself as Durga and then as Kali, for she exhibits both benevolent and malevolent characteristics, and therefore is both adored and feared.

Durga

An early representation of Durga was carved in relief in a granite cave in Mamallapuram, Tamil Nadu, during the reign of the Pallava king, Mamalla I (r. ca. 630-674 CE) (Figure 1). In this large narrative sculpture that stretches across the entire north wall of the cave, the youthful and beautiful Durga rides her lion vehicle, the same lion that is the heraldic animal of the Pallava Dynasty. In each of her multiple hands she holds weapons bestowed upon her by Siva and Visnu, and all the Hindu deities, in order to overpower and slay Mahisasura, the demon buffalo king who had vanquished the armies of Indra to become the ruler of the heavens. It was a time of extreme crisis for the gods, just as it was for the Indian people in the nineteenth century. Born out of this time of great trial was Durga. The myth is described in the *Devi Mahatmyam* wherein all the gods led by Siva and Visnu came together and a blinding light issued forth from their bodies.[2] This brilliant light revealed a blazing mountain that filled the universe from which emerged the beautiful female form of Durga. All the gods bestowed upon her their wealth, their jewels, and their weapons. And, so equipped, Durga rode out on her lion vehicle to battle Mahisasura who approached her accompanied by millions of armies of *asuras* (demons), battle chariots, elephants, and horses. Single-handedly Durga slays every one of her opponents including all the great demon's generals. Ultimately she faced the greatest threat of all, Mahisasura. In the relief the demon has taken on the form of a buffalo-headed giant. He balances a weighty club in his hands as if considering whether or not to lash out at the nymph-like Durga. Each time Durga, the formidable one, slays Mahisasura he transforms himself into another demonic being. The battle is incessant as waves of incarnations of the great demon replace those Durga slays until she drinks a potent brew

---

[2] The myth of Durga's creation is told in the *Markandeya Purana,* cantos 81-93, which form the text known as the *Devi Mahatmyam.* Swami Jagadiswarananda, trans. *Devi Mahatmyam (Glory of the Divine Mother) 700 Mantras on Sri Durga* (Mylapore, Madras: Sri Ramakrishna Math, 1977), chapters 2 and 3, pp. 22-51.

given to her by the gods, and in her intoxicated state she leaps on his neck and finally slays him. In the relief the battle is reaching a crisis. Slain incarnations are strewn around. There is an air of tense suspense as the two well-matched warriors pause before the final onslaught. The viewers know the outcome, yet the sense of frozen energy that is about to explode keeps them spellbound. Devi, the Goddess as Durga, is the great savior in times of crisis. With little physical effort she can restore calm and peace–—but not always!

An endearing feature of Indian mythology is the almost human sense of vulnerability that embraces the personalities of the gods—they can do great things; however, in moments of weakness they tend towards generous gestures to kings who empowered by their divine gifts become monstrous demons that have to be disposed of. So Durga is called upon to clean up essentially the (mis)deeds of the gods. But, even the valorous Durga has her limits.

Kali

A tenth century carving from Rajasthan of the awful, yet awe-inspiring goddess Kali, who is also known as Chamunda, depicts her as a hideous cadaverous figure dancing in a cremation ground (Figure 2).[3] Her rib cage is punctuated by two flaccid breasts that hang over the cavernous area where her stomach should be. The muscles of her arms and legs are reduced to flat, ribbon-like strips. Endowed with twelve arms she grasps a corpse above her head with her back hands, and in her other hands she holds the weapons bestowed upon her by the gods including Siva's trident and *khatvanga* (a skull-topped staff made of human bone). She is truly a frightening and gruesome creature to behold, as her protruding eyeballs and lolling tongue transfix the devotee. Like the figure of Durga at Mamallapuram, Kali is shown in a dynamic mode, which intensifies her ferocity. Often Kali/Chamunda squats on her haunches as she gorges her insatiable appetite on her prey of human bodies. In the early images her emaciated body exhibits similar characteristics to the Rajasthani image, with sunken eyes, exposed rib cage, lolling tongue and skeletal body that is barely covered by thin wisps of skin. Her multiple arms wield her donated weapons; she wears a crown of skulls, and a garland of freshly

[3] *Goddess Chamunda*. Ca. 9th-10th century CE. Rajasthan. Pink sandstone. H. 23 in., W. 15 in. Avery Brundage Collection, Asian Art Museum, San Francisco (B62 S39+).

severed heads around her neck that cascade down between her legs. Such images of the dark goddess exude a sense of deathly fear.

This dreadful creature that can inspire a nation in its revolt, is herself the product of extreme anger for she was born of Durga's rage. Durga with her great powers was instructed to dispose of numerous enemies of the gods, all of which she deftly accomplished, until faced with two *asuras,* Canda and Munda. This tale also appears in the *Devi Mahatmyam,* where we are told that Durga's face became as dark as ink, until out of her forehead sprang Kali, the black goddess, the most terrifying manifestation of Devi.[4] Kali was armed with a sword, a noose, and a skull-topped staff; she was wearing a garland of skulls, and was clad in a tiger's skin; her emaciated flesh dripped from her skeletal frame; her long tongue protruded from her gaping mouth; her deep-sunk blood-shot eyes glared out at the world as she filled the regions of the sky with her roars. She immediately grabbed demon elephants, horses and warriors and devoured them all. She then destroyed all the armies of the *asuras,* and ultimately seized and decapitated the demon generals, Canda and Munda, after which she became known as Camunda.

In the early extant images of Kali she personifies death. She destroys all that she touches in order to satiate her appetite. Her destructive powers became so uncontrollable that finally Siva, her spouse, his body covered in ashes from the cremation grounds, lies down on the ground so that she may dance upon him in her frenzy, exhaust herself and be calmed. Later images dating from the eighteenth century, especially those of Daksinakali, begin to reveal a latent sexual force from which Tantric ritual uses have evolved, and a certain seductive ambiguity enters into visual renderings of her (Figure 3). She remains the black goddess with lolling extended red tongue, wreathed in severed heads, but her body is no longer skeletal in form. It has muscle and firm flesh. Kali becomes the black Durga sporting a disquieting sensuality. This form of Kali became the patroness of subversive groups such as the Thuggees and also of dacoits and robbers, all of whom became the *bêtes noires* of the British. With little understanding of whom either Durga or Kali were the British perceived them as being demonic entities, reflections of the paganism that they believed prevailed in India. In an ironic twist this interpretation played into the hands of the independence movement activists who were growing in strength towards the end of the nineteenth century, and who were seeking an appropriate and inspiring icon that would be identified with their nationalist ideals. Such an icon needed to be strong,

---

4 *Devi Mahatmyam,* chapter 7, pp. 94-99.

courageous, and a warrior. It was essential that it have popular recognition and also be secular in nature. This latter requirement was in recognition of the diversity of India's population—it also led to the development of a hybrid form of Bharat Mata.

The transformation of Kali may have its roots in the growing Vaisnava movement which began when Krsna, the ninth *avatar,* descent, of the great god Visnu and beloved protagonist of the tenth century *Bhagavata Purana,* became the most popular of all the Hindu deities. Kali's terrifying aspect and insatiable bloodthirsty appetite probably held little appeal for daily interaction between herself and devotees. By the eighteenth century, well before the serious altercations with the British occurred, Kali was in a state of metamorphosis.[5] Her capricious temperament was never questioned; she would remain the most powerful of all the deities with an extraordinary temper that could quell all who crossed her, yet she was gradually transformed from a cadaverous hag into a seductive and sensual figure which resulted in a highly equivocal form of this formerly repellent female deity. Her blue-black arms and legs have a smooth, inflated appearance. Her full youthful face is usually depicted smiling as she sticks out her tongue in a somewhat coquettish manner. She still brandishes multiple weapons in her arms, and is adorned with garlands of skulls and belts of severed hands. The ghoulish aspects, however, have been diminished and become almost decorative in nature. If the color blue can be described as radiant, then this is how Kali is now presented, dancing over the body of Siva who appears to writhe beneath her feet in ecstasy. The style of such images was popularized by Raja Ravi Varma (1848-1906), the court painter from Travancore, who had set up a printing press in Bombay to produce oleographic prints for the public to use and enjoy.

Kali for the British represented all that was negative and terrifying about Indian culture. It was beyond their abilities to control her or her devotees whom they saw as subversive agents intent on undermining their colonial powers. In Bengal the sacrificial "white goats" favored by the bloodthirsty Kali, who could only be appeased through ritual sacrifices, became veiled references to the British. By the latter part of the nineteenth century, following the mutiny at Meerut in 1857, subversive activities

---

[5] Sanjukta Gupta, "Domestication of a Goddess: Carana-tirtha Kalighat, the Mahapitha of Kali." Rachel Fell McDermott and Jeffrey J. Kripal, Editors, *Encountering Kali: In the Margins, at the Center, in the West.* Berkeley: University of California Press, 2003, pp. 60-79.

spread throughout the land like wildfire.[6] Many of the secret organizations proclaimed Kali as their deity. They were encouraged in their revolutionary tactics by inflammatory writings in newspapers and broadsides, such as the following excerpt which appeared in *Yugantar* (1905):

> Rise up, O sons of India, arm yourselves with bombs, despatch the white Asuras to Yama's abode. Invoke the mother Kali....The Mother asks for sacrificial offerings. What does the Mother want?...She wants many white Asuras. The Mother is thirsting after the blood of the Feringhees [foreigners] who have bled her profusely. ...[C]hant this verse while slaying the Feringhee white goat...: With the close of a long era, the Feringhee Empire draws to an end, for behold! Kali rises in the East.[7]

By the turn of the twentieth century the lines of battle between the Indian nationalists and the British colonialists were clearly drawn, despite the British government's pretensions of empire and overlordship. The British, as foreigners, were suspicious to the point of paranoia. For them Kali represented all that was reprehensible. She was powerful, she had an insatiable appetite for bloodshed, and exuded a strange, magnetic sexuality.

Bharat Mata

In 1882, Bankim Chandra Chatterjee (1838-94), the Bengali author, wrote *Ananda Math,* a novel in which Kali is "...the symbol of the Indian nation, the Motherland, who is both glorious in her original splendor and terrible in her present oppressed condition: 'Kali was at once a symbol of the degradation of the society under alien rule and a reservoir of unlimited power.'" [8] As the dark, enraged, yet subtly sensual goddess, Kali provided her devotees and followers with a powerful image that they recognized and followed, yet a curious development occurred that was stimulated by the philosophy of secularism followed by the *bhadralok* and intellectual elite of Bengal. Bankim Chandra Chatterjee believed fervently in Bharat

---

[6] Hugh B. Urban discusses Kali worship in Bengal and colonial attitudes in "Sacrificing White Goats to the Goddess: The Appropriation of the Image of Kali in the Bengal Nationalist Movement," in Rachel Fell McDermott and Jeffrey J. Kripal, Editors—*Encountering Kali,* pp. 182-188.

[7] This text from the magazine *Yugantar* (1905) is quoted by Urban, p. 182.

[8] *The Abbey of Bliss (Anandamath),* trans. Nares Chandra Sen-Gupta (Calcutta: Cherry Press, n.d.), pp. 40-41, quoted in Urban, p. 185, and fn. 65.

Mata, the goddess as Mother India. Bharat Mata personified the sacred earth that was India, and in the 1890s he composed and dedicated India's national anthem to her entitled, *Bande Mataram* (Hail Mother) for which Rabindranath Tagore (1861-1941) wrote the music.[9] In this song the beautiful nature of Bharat Mata is extolled. None of the grim qualities of Kali remain evident. The revolutionary fervor aroused by visions of Kali's strength has completely disappeared. This gently nuanced goddess required a different visible presence, which was provided by Abanindranath Tagore (1871-1951) who painted an image of the goddess in a highly romantic vein (Figure 4). Bharat Mata floats like a vision of the Virgin Mary above darkened waters and white lotuses. Her body is modestly covered with a saffron *sari* that is drawn over her head. In each of her four hands she brings gifts to her devotees, instead of the customary weapons of Durga and Kali. She holds out sheathes of rice, a cloth, a book, and a rosary of beads—these are gifts needed to sustain life physically, intellectually and spiritually.

Abanindranath's painting of Bharat Mata underscores the ambiguous nature of the role of the Goddess, and also the conflicting tensions between the aggressive policies of the Swadeshi freedom fighters and the more tempered approach of the *bhadralok*. As Geeti Sen has pointed out, she lacks the passion and furor of Kali.[10] She looks off to her right, avoiding the gaze of her devotees, and also avoiding the mystical

---

[9] *Bande Mataram*

Hail to thee, Mother!
Rich with thy hurrying streams,
Bright with thy orchard gleams,
Cool with thy winds of delight,
Dark fields waving,
Mother of might, Mother free.
Glory of moonlight dreams,
Over thy branches and lordly streams—
Clad in by blossoming trees,
Mother, giver of ease,
Laughing low and sweet!
Mother, I kiss thy feet,
Speaker, sweet and low!
Mother, to thee I bow!

[10] Geeti Sen has written on the changing identity of Bharat Mata as the symbol of the nationalist independence movement, in "Iconising the Nation: Political Agendas," in *India a National Culture?* Editor, Geeti Sen (New Delhi: India International Centre, Sage Publications India Pt. Ltd., 2003), 154-175.

empowerment that she could endow through the ritual of *darshan.* Such an image does not have the power to incite a nation to revolt.[11]

The tensions between the nationalist Swadeshi movement and the British exploded in 1905 with the partition of Bengal by the British into West Bengal and East Bengal. The gentle, docile figure of Bharat Mata was overshadowed by the militant need for a far more powerful symbol. Sakti in her most terrifying form as Kali became the goddess to whom revolutionary groups such as the Calcutta Anusilan Samiti and the Dacca Anusilan paid tribute and offered blood sacrifices.[12] Rabindranath Tagore responded to the British arrogance through his writings that won him the Nobel Prize for literature in 1911. In his novel *Home and the World,* he writes of the need for a powerful visual symbol:

> True patriotism will never be roused in our countrymen unless they can visualize the motherland—We must make a goddess of her! ... 'Let us devise an appropriate image,' they exclaimed. 'It will not do if you devise it,' I admonished them. 'We must get one of the current images accepted as representing the country—the worship of the people must flow towards it along the deep-cut grooves of custom.'" [13]

Rabindranath's protagonist Bimala resolves the issue of which "current image" can represent India, by exclaiming:

> "I am only human. I am covetous. I have anger. I would be angry for my country's sake...(we) must have some visible symbol casting its spell upon (our) minds. I would make my country a Person and call her *Mata, Devi, Durga*—Mother, Goddess, Durga—for whom I would redden the earth with sacrificial offerings. I am human, not divine."[14]

India was to become personified as the primordial goddess Shakti, Mata, Devi, Durga, Kali, Laksmi, et al. She was to be a secular goddess, yet Rabindranath and Abanindranath perceived her very differently. Rabindranath recognized Devi's powerful qualities: her rage, her invincible strength and her insatiable hunger for the enemies of Bharat (India) to be brought to her as sacrificial offerings. Abanindranath, on the other hand, represented her tranquil nature and nurturing qualities. It is,

---

[11] Mitter, Partha. *Art and Nationalism in Colonial India: 1850-1922:Occidental Orientations* (Cambridge: Cambridge University Press, 1994), 295.

[12] Urban, p. 184.

[13] Rabindranath Tagore, *The Home and the World,* trans. Surendranath Tagore (Madras: Macmillan India Limited, 1919, reprinted 1992), 90-91.

[14] Tagore, 92.

however, the dynamic image of Kali that explodes upon the consciousness first of Bengal and then the rest of the country. Her image depicted by local artisans, begins to appear on posters, calendars and broadsides.[15] In 1913 in the March edition of *Bande Mataram,* a magazine published in Geneva, Switzerland, and edited by Madame Bhikaji Cama, an Indian nationalist who lived in Paris, Bharat Mata is shown drawing a long, curved sword from its scabbard with the map of India behind her. This is significant because Mme. Cama was described by the Indian Government as "the recognized leader of the revolutionary movement and was said to be regarded by the people as a reincarnation of the goddess Kali."[16] She, in fact, endorsed political assassinations and armed revolts, and encouraged women to take up exercise and physical training while they were living in the West, because they were forbidden to do so in India. She exhorted them to learn to use rifles, as the time would be coming soon when they would need to join with the Swadeshi freedom fighters in driving the British out of India.

By the 1930s Bharat Mata had absorbed Kali's powers. She had become the patron deity of Swaraj and subversive groups that under the Nationalist Party were aiding the independence movement. Posters, magazines and broadsides were painted and printed showing her receiving human sacrifices. A popular revolutionary hero was Bhagat Singh, the nationalist activist who was executed by the British in 1931. He is depicted in posters offering his head to Bharat Mata as the ultimate sacrifice for his country. Texts on these posters were often printed in both Hindi and English and declare that he is offering his life for the freedom of Bharat Mata. These words leave no doubt that revolutionary activists were fighting for their motherland in the name of the Goddess, which underscores the role of *Sakti,* as the primordial source of power, as the creator, as the destroyer, and as the nurturer. The transformation of Durga/Kali/Bharat Mata occurred almost seamlessly in response to the nationalist agenda.

---

[15] For discussion of poster art, see Patricia Uberoi, *From Goddess to Pin-up: Icons of Femininity in Indian Calendar Art* (Fukuoka: Fukuoka Asian Art Museum, 2000).

[16] Geeti Sen discusses Mme. Cama's writings for *Bande Mataram: Monthly Organ of Indian Independence,* a journal published in Geneva, Switzerland, in Geeti Sen, "New Agenda for Women in Prohibited Posters," in *Feminine Fables: Imaging the Indian Woman in Painting, Photography and Cinema* (Ahmedabad: Mapin Publishing, 2002), 30-36.

After Independence was achieved in 1947 and the departure of the British, communal unrest erupted ignited by the partition of India and Pakistan. During the years of violence that followed Bharat Mata continued to inspire leaders of revolts. However, she was no longer conceived of as a secular entity supporting all the peoples and faiths of India. Increasingly, she was recognized as the icon of the Hindutva, the movement that proclaimed that Bharat (India) was the land of the Hindus. In 1957 the film, *Bharat Mata, Mother India,* was produced and directed by Mehboob.[17] The starring role was played by the popular and beautiful Bollywood actress Nargis. She transformed the heroine, Radha, a young village woman into the personification of Bharat Mata as she fought for social justice by absorbing the frustration of the Hindu nation. Radha was enraged by what had befallen her land. She became a superwoman who breathed life into the faltering revolutionary spirit that was being stifled by the policies of the Congress Party. The sheer physicality of Nagis's performance gave life to the iconic presence of the goddess who was present everywhere to support the vision of a united land against all perceived foreigners. Through Nargis's portrayal of Radha—the beloved of Krishna, and the mirror of Sita—Bharat Mata was deemed to be present in every woman of India.[18]

The transformative role of the goddess has not followed a straight trajectory. As the primordial *Sakti,* as the mother who is both malevolent and benevolent, and as the warrior and slayer of demons, her iconic image has risen above sectarian politics, and has still remained engaged and relevant. In 1994 Arpita Singh (b. 1939), an artist who lives in Delhi, was invited to design the front cover of the Durga Puja issue of *Desh,* a Bengali magazine.[19] She painted an image of Durga which appeared on the cover of the magazine (Figure 6). It caused an immediate outcry amongst local politicians who demanded that all copies be destroyed. Of all the images of Durga/Bharat Mata, it resembles most closely that of Abanindranath Tagore's early twentieth century painting of the goddess. The figure is modestly clothed in a white sari. She looks off to the left avoiding the viewer's gaze. The similarities end here because she brandishes a revolver in one of her hands, a modern substitute for the ancient and indigenous weapons bestowed upon her by the gods. Beneath her feet is the prostrate image of a local politician, again a modern

[17] *Bharat Mata: Mother India,* film produced and directed by Mehboob, staring Nargis, 1957.

[18] Geeti Sen discusses the role of the goddess and early cinema in India in "Bharat Mata: Woman or Goddess?" in *Feminine Fables,* 41-53.

[19] Arpita Singh, *Durga.* Cover of the 1994 Durga Puja issue of *Desh,* Calcutta.

substitution for the demons that Durga overwhelmed in the *Devimahatmyam Purana.* In this painting Singh has produced an image of the goddess who is clearly present to help rectify the corrupt reality of Bengali politics. That those in power interpreted it as being subversive raises the question regarding the meaning of freedom of expression in the world's largest democracy. The disturbing fact remains that the goddess Durga/Kali/Bharat Mata is not the provenance of a secular nation—she is claimed as the figurehead and deity of Hindu India.

Nalini Malani (b. 1946), an activist artist who has infused her artwork with social and political commentary, drew attention to the continuing communal unrest in her video installation for the Indian Pavilion at the 2005 Venice Biennale entitled, *Mother India: Transactions in the Construction of Pain.* Using multiple video projections of film footage of the Gujerati genocide of 2002, overlaid with images taken during the Partition of 1947 when India was divided into two separate nations—India and Pakistan—she underscores the consequences of a nation torn apart. A compelling video projection of a young woman with a large *bindi* containing an image of the Devi as Laxmi, the goddess of wealth and good fortune, on her forehead is a haunting reminder of how religious fanaticism can destroy the values of a land.[20] A reading of Malani's work underscores the innate power of women, particularly when drawing upon faith in the Goddess, yet she also shows how this power can be skewed and distorted for political exigencies.

Bharat Mata, as the Mother Goddess of India, in her multivalent manifestations has protected and nourished the soul of India. The people of India, Bharat Mata's children, have skirmished between themselves over 'rightful' access to her, yet she has remained a constant source of inspiration, courage and valor for all. At times her gaze has faltered, as the gods like the demons, display human traits. But it is the *dharma* of the goddess that ultimately prevails.

References

Caldwell, Sarah. "Bhagavati: Ball of Fire." *Devi: Goddesses of India,* edited by John Stratton Hawley and Dona Marie Wulff. Berkeley and Los Angeles: University of California Press, 1996.

—. *Oh Terrifying Mother: Sexuality, Violence and Worship of the Goddess Kali.* New Delhi: Oxford University Press, 1999.

---

[20] An interview of Nalini Malani by Johan Pijnappel appears in *iCon: India Contemporary*. La Biennale di Venezia 2005 (EIH Press, Delhi, 2005), 38-47.

Dehejia, Vidya. *Devi: The Great Goddess: Female Divinity in South Asian Art.* Washington, D.C. Arthur M. Sackler Gallery, Smithsonian Institution, 1999.

Devi-Mahatmyam: The Glorification of the Great Goddess. Edited and translated by Vasudeva S. Agrawala. Ramnagar: All India Kashiraj Trust, 1963.

Fell McDermott, Rachel and Jeffrey J. Kripal, Editors. *Encountering Kali in the Margins, at the Center, in the West.* Berkeley and Los Angeles: University of California Press, 2003.

Gadon, Elinor. *The Once and Future Goddess: A Symbol for Our Time.* New York: Harper and Row, 1989.

Hawley, John Stratton and Donna Marie Wulff. *Devi: Goddesses of India.* Berkeley, Los Angeles: University of California Press, 1996.

Kinsley, David R. *The Goddesses' Mirror: Visions of the Divine Feminine from East and West.* Albany: State University of New York Press, 1989.

—. *Hindu Goddesses: Visions of the Divine Feminine in the Hindu Religious Tradition.* Berkeley and Los Angeles: University of California Press, 1986.

—. "Kali: Blood and Death Out of Place." *Devi: Goddesses of India,* edited by John Stratton Hawley and Donna Marie Wulff, pp. 77-86. Berkeley and Los Angeles: University of California Press, 1996.

—. *The Sword and the Flute: Kali and Krsna: Visions of the Terrible and the Sublime in Hindu Mythology.* Berkeley and Los Angeles: University of California Press, 1975, 2000.

Pinney, Christopher. *Photos of the Gods: The Printed Image and Political Struggle in India.* London: Reaktion Books Ltd., 2004.

Sen, Geeti. *Feminine Fables: Imaging the Indian Woman in Painting, Photography and Cinema.* Ahmedabad: Mapin Publishing, 2002.

—. Editor. *India a National Culture?* New Delhi: India International Centre, Sage Publications India Pvt. Ltd., 2003.

Singh, Amrit and Rabindra Kaur Singh. *Images of Freedom.* New Delhi: Indialog Publications Pvt. Ltd., 2003.

Tagore, Rabanindranath. *The Home and The World.* Madras: Macmillan India Ltd., 1919, 1992.

Wolpert, Stanley. *A New History of India.* Oxford: Oxford University Press, 1993.

Illustrations

Figure 1. *Durga Mahisasuramardini,* mid-seventh century CE. Mahabalipuram, Tamil Nadu, Granite Carving. (Photo Mary-Ann Milford-Lutzker)

Figure 2. *Goddess Chamunda.* Ca. 9th-10th century CE. Rajasthan. Pink sandstone. H. 23 in., W. 15 in. Avery Brundage Collection, Asian Art Museum, San Francisco. B62 S39+

Figure 3. *Kali,* 20th century CE. Calcutta. Postcard.

Figure 4. Abanindranath Tagore, *Bharat Mata,* ca. 1902-05. Water color and wash on paper. Rabindra Bharati, Calcutta.

Figure 5. Arpita Singh. *Durga,* 1992. Cover of *Desh Magazine,* Calcutta. (Sen 188)

CHAPTER TEN

COME ONE, COME ALL, TO THE FAIR OF THE MOTHER'S TRANSFORMATIONS! SOME GLIMPSES OF KALI AND HER TEMPLES IN WEST BENGAL

JUNE MCDANIEL

Goddesses come in many forms. They may be seen in visionary experiences or *darsan*, they may be ritually placed in statues, they may spontaneously appear in rocks and springs, and pervade the atmosphere of sacred sites. They may enter the minds of human beings, and take them over fully or partially. There may be one goddess with many manifestations, and many goddesses who are really the same goddess. A goddess may also benefit her devotees and priests in many ways. These benefits are almost as diverse as her forms.

In West Bengal, the male deity most famous for having many forms is Vishnu, in his ten avatar forms. However, the goddesses also come in many varieties. In the *Devi Mahatmaya* or *Candi Saptasati*, the story of Durga's appearances from the *Markandeya Purana,* the goddess Durga takes on many forms to fight demons and protect the world. Durga is often shown in nine forms for the nine nights of her festival, Durga Puja (and on one of these nights, in the Sakambhari or plant goddess form, her statue is composed of nine types of plants).

The goddess Kali is also understood to have a variety of *rupas* or forms. She is a wild child and a passionate woman, a goddess of death and destruction, and a nurturing mother who guides the soul into its next life. While in many areas of India Kali is frightening because of her moodiness and association with death, in West Bengal she is often a charming, appealing goddess, whose black skin is sky-blue, or even white, and who smiles at her devotees. On Kali Puja, her annual festival of worship, people dress in their best clothes to go from shrine to shrine, looking at the statues of Kali made for the occasion. The figures of Kali are located in temporary shrines or *pandals*, and show her in elaborate clothing and with complex backgrounds. People examine the statues for her *bhavas* or moods. Sometimes she is majestic and absolute, sometimes stern and angry. She shows protective love towards her worshippers and punishes her enemies (as shown in her raised sword). As a woman, she is believed to love beauty and ornament. Her shrines are full of light and color, and she wears elaborate jewelry and crowns of gold tinsel or white *solapith*. She is sensitive to neglect, and to lack of artistry—she inspires poets like Ramprasad Sen and Kamalakanta Bhattacharya to create beautiful songs. As Mother she watches over her devotees, and evokes willing obedience from them. For the devotees, the benefits are both social, as families join together to visit the goddess shrines, and aesthetic where the forms are admired for their artistry.

Kali may be found in nature, in her temples and shrines, in the ritual centers or *sakti-pithas*, and within the *pandals* for her yearly festival of Kali Puja. This paper describes several portrayals of the goddess Kali and the benefits given to her devotees and an exploration of her temples in West Bengal, their rituals and festivals, Kali *pithas* and their background stories, and an identification of categories that shed light on the goddess' diversity of form.

In most rural areas, Kali is a goddess associated with the Adivasis or tribal people. Though they are not exactly Hindu, they often incorporate worship of Hindu deities. Among the Santals, we see the worship of the goddess Kali Bonga, who is understood as one of the local deities or *bongas*, and is offered goats as her sacrifice. There is also Bankali, who is goddess of the forest. Among Oraon black magicians, the goddess becomes Kali Mai, and she is worshipped at altars made of mud and asked to fulfill the goals of the practitioners.

More broadly, Kali is worshipped in the villages as Kali Budi, the great ancestress of the village people. *Budi* literally means old woman, and the goddess is worshipped as an old woman who is wise because she was there in ancient times. This is a different view of the goddess than we see in more urban Hinduism, where the goddess tends to be young and beautiful. In villages, she is often represented in the form of a black, rounded rock, which is understood to be empowered. As an example, we may look at the Kali Budi who was installed in the Midnapore village of Ranjana, in an old temple to the god Dharma. This Kali came to the village as the result of a dream command or *svapnadesa* sent by the goddess, which ordered a man of the Sadgopa clan to find the stone and offer it worship. Though this Kali was ill-tempered, it was nevertheless understood to be alive and grant boons, and an improvement over the previous deity of the temple, who was even more grouchy.[1]

Kali sleeps in the goddess stone until she is awakened and decides that she wants worship. She may then send out a dream command to some chosen, receptive person. Thus empowered, goddess stones are associated with miracles: they may change in size, from large to small, and they can move on their own, if they find an environment that they prefer. The goddess in the stone can bless or curse, depending on her mood, so people need to find out her preferences. Some Kalis prefer to stay out in the open air, at the foot of a large tree or at the mouth of a cave, while others prefer a temple and a full-time priest. While village Kalis may be stones or statues, they sometimes take other forms.

Another example of a form of a folk Kali temple is the Dangali Kalitala in the town of Bolpur. It is unusual in that the form of the goddess worshipped is a large pair of tree roots which strongly resemble a woman's body from the waist down. These leg-like roots are understood to be the lower half of Dangali Kali, who appeared to Raja Surat during the Satya Yuga and told him to build the temple. The story was told to me by the temple priest, as older women in red and white saris sitting nearby chanted the names of the goddess: "Ma Jagatmata, (O Mother of the Universe), He Ma Devarani (O Queen of the Gods), Jaya Jaya".

According to the priest, Raja Surat made a vow to the goddess that he would sacrifice one hundred thousand animals to her if she would fulfill his desires. She did so, and in turn he sacrificed a *lakh* of goats on Durga Puja. The current name of the town, Bolpur, is derived from "*bali-pur*," or place of sacrifice. Surat had an intuition that Kali was living in the tree, and then had a dream which affirmed this. He began the temple right on the tree roots, but soon died, and the temple was completed by his followers. While the foundation was being laid, three stones were found, in which Kali, Shiva and Durga were believed to dwell. The Kali stone is currently between the goddess' legs (at the base of the tree root), with Shiva off to the side. The priest said that they had lost Durga, but she is probably around somewhere—people care more about Kali anyway.[2]

According to another story, Raja Surat offered the hundred thousand goats to the goddess due to his own fear and guilt. In his youth he had been cruel and vicious, but he had a dream in which he met the ghosts of all those he had caused to suffer. He met men he had killed and virgins he

---

[1] This temple is described in Gouranga Chattopadhyaya, *Ranjana: A Village in West Bengal* (Calcutta: Bookland, 1963), pp. 203-204. Ranjana is a fictitious name for the village studied by this anthropologist.

[2] Interview, Shakta priest, Bolpur, 1994.

had raped, and they pursued him. He fled in terror. Then the goddess appeared in his dream, and told him that the only way he could atone for his crimes was by leading a virtuous life. When he awoke, he vowed to give her one hundred thousand sacrifices and improve his life. When he died, the ghosts of his victims beheaded his ghost, and he was then able to enter into the heaven worlds.[3]

The deity area of the temple is a small, nearly square room. The tree roots are painted red, one with glossy vermilion, which resembles wet blood; (this is given as prasad and put onto the foreheads of devotees). The 'legs' are draped with garlands of red hibiscus flowers and decorations, and built into a wall which has been covered with pink tile. The whole room is full of tree roots—there are at least four major trees, with various other roots coming in along the side wall, and on the trees are photos and paintings of Kali and Tara (who is understood as another form of Kali). For blessings, visitors are given bags of red hibiscus flowers and small amounts of food.

Raja Surat believed that Kali lived in the tree, and since that time, others have also had this firm belief. According to the priest, they do not have visions or direct encounters with the goddess, but they have faith in her. Dangali Kali can benefit her devotees by answering their prayers, and calming their fears. He said that very few people want visions or liberation when they visit—only the silent sadhus, and they don't talk about it. Most people want the boons of folk religion: good marriages, houses, and victory over enemies. He said that the women who came here to chant the prayers to the goddess and sing her hymns did so to gain benefits for themselves and their families.

The priest was himself a Shakta devotee, initiated into the worship of Kali by his guru, who lived in a distant village. He said that for a while people stopped worshipping, when communism first came into power, but they have come back now. This is a very small temple, but it has grown popular in recent years.

Folk worship may also occur in a less formal style. Sometimes Kali is said to appear in human form, and later become a stone statue to be worshipped. In the village of Kaiti, there is annual worship of a Kali statue which was believed to have originally been a low-caste girl. According to the story, a high-caste villager was returning to the village from a long pilgrimage, and encountered an orphaned Santal tribal girl. Out of compassion, he took her back to the village and gave her a job as a cow-keeper in his brother's house. One day, one of the cows escaped her

[3] L. S. S. O'Malley, ed. *Bengal District Gazetteer, Birbhum, 1910*, p. 127.

care and trampled a neighbor's rice plants. The neighbors chased the Santal girl to punish her. The frightened girl found refuge in an oil-grinder at a nearby oilman's house. They searched for her everywhere, but she disappeared from the village. A few days later, the brahmin who had brought her to the village learned in a dream that she was really the goddess Kali in human form, who had chosen to stay in his house. The goddess told him in the dream to search the oil-grinder, and he would find a deity carved of stone within it. He did so, and told the villagers about it, and a temple was built in that oil-grinding room and daily worship was arranged. Over time, a larger statue of the goddess was created and installed. The old statue from the oil-grinder is still used today for worship.[4] This Kali is understood by villagers of the area to be especially alive or conscious, and large crowds come to worship her during the *puja* festivals. A goat is sacrificed on every new moon, and many people offer her special vows (*manat*), in which they agree to do something for the goddess if she will do something for them.

The 'folk' forms of Kali tend to be found in nature and natural objects. However, another approach to Kali is to understand her as the major deity of yogic and tantric practices, who represents infinity and who acts as the spiritual guide of the practitioner. In this second approach, when Kali is viewed as a yogic/tantric deity, there is more room for human choice and contemplation. The tantric Kali is abstract, a principle of wisdom or power or creativity, and human yogis and sadhus may invoke her presence during rituals in temples and cremation grounds. She may be Kali of primordial power, Adya Shakti Kali, or Mahakali of the Mahavidya goddesses. These different manifestations may be specialized, as they are at the astrology temple of the Mother.

At Matrimandir Asrama, in Kalimpong in the mountainous region of northern West Bengal, there is an astrology temple dedicated to the goddess' Mahavidya or Great Wisdom forms. This temple was founded by the Shakta Tantric renunciant Jnanananda, and has images of the Mahavidya goddesses, which are here associated with astrology. The goddesses are believed to control the planets, and possess specific planetary associations. The temple priest explained the correspondences between the Mahavidya goddesses and the planets and stars followed by this temple:

1. Tara- Sun
2. Kamala- Moon

---

[4] Mitra, Asok. *Pascimbangera puja-parban o mela* (Delhi: Controller of Publications, 1992), vol 4, Bardhaman Diustrict, p. 121.

3. Bagala-	Mangala (Mars)
4. Tripura-	Budha (Mercury)
5. Matangi-	Brihaspati (Jupiter)
6. Bhuvaneshvari-	Sukra (Venus)
7. Dakshinakali-	Sani (Saturn)
8. Chinnamasta-	Rahu
9. Dhumavati-	Ketu
10. Durga-	Shakti (as universal power)

At the front of the temple, the smiling black Kali statue in the center area was adorned with heavy silver jewelry: she wore necklaces, bracelets, an ornate silver crown with red jewels, and a belt of large, shiny silver hands. She carried a silver sword with a large eye on it, and there was a silver lamp over her head. Behind her was a sky-blue halo made of wood, with painted images of the Mahavidya goddesses in the perimeter. The Mahavidyas are understood to be Kali's ten major forms or emanations.

According to the priest, Shiva is the joint husband of all of these Mahavidya wives. The goddess assumes different shapes for different functions. If a person has problems with Budha, there is no energy for work; with Mangala, he loses his business and has political problems; with Sukra, he has too much desire. Bagala helps with legal problems, both civil and criminal.

When people come to the temple with problems, the priest looks at their palms to find out which planet is the cause of the trouble. He finds out the date of birth, and consults the almanac (*panjika*), and does calculations. Once he has decided upon the planet which is causing problems, the person can then worship and give offerings to the goddess who controls that planet, and thus take care of the problem. The priest finds out which planet is causing the trouble by means of palmistry or horoscope, and then that goddess is consulted. Astrology has come to be a specialization of tantrikas, and here astrological insight is associated with the tantric knowledge gained through worship of the Mahavidyas. While many wandering tantrikas make their living doing astrological predictions and selling astrological gems informally, here we have a temple dedicated to the practice.

Of his own experience of the goddess, the priest said:

> I am myself a devotee of the goddess, and my form of the goddess was chosen by my guru. Kali appears in my dreams, looking like her statue, and she gives me suggestions and instructs me. One may do Vedic *puja* [ritual worship] or tantric *puja*—here we do tantric *puja*. During tantric

> *puja* I am the son of the Mother, and I cling to her. We do not sacrifice many goats to her, for the goat is only the symbol of lust [*kama]*, which must be sacrificed to have spiritual love [*prema*].
>
> Kali is like a fire under a kettle, but you cannot put her out. People are like matches- if you go too close to her, you too will catch fire. But she is also a person, and she has a personality. This is shown by the fact that she gives boons and she listens to devotees when they call. But she is invisible, and people have to sense her presence without seeing her.
>
> Kali is a good goddess. Ma cannot be dangerous to her children, for she loves them, and she only punishes wrong actions, according to karma. She can change karma, but only to the good. She only destroys attachments *[ripus]*, not her devotees.[5]

Tantric worship uses different mantras than does Vedic worship, and the devotee seeks a more personal relationship with the goddess. According to the priest, the major goal of Kali worship is the destruction of worldly attachments, which is a boon given by the goddess. She destroys the bonds which bind the devotees, and brings liberation to those who seek it. As most people seek only favors, she gives gifts and suggestions to devotees through dreams and visions. She primarily gives moral instruction in dreams. Of the temple's founder he states:

> Usually, the role of guru is handed down from father to son, but sages and sannyasis learn from other gurus. The founder of this temple, Jnanananda, was a wandering sadhu who spent much time in Bengal and Assam. He did tantric ritual meditation at burning grounds, with *pancamunda asanas* and many skulls. We do not do Tantric ritual meditation here, only tantric *puja*. But we remember Jnanananda, and hope that one day we may be like him.

Here, the goddess' multiple forms represent a specialization of labor. Kali's *rupas* have control over the powers of the various planets, and each form benefits the devotee in a different aspect of life. However, the Mahavidya goddesses may not be inclined to influence the planetary energies without prayers and assurances by the devotees.

There are many stories of sadhus who have seen the goddess in all of these forms (the most famous is probably Sarvananda, whose vision occurred on a new-moon night while he practiced the *sava-sadhana* or corpse ritual). However, specifically Tantric temples are few in West Bengal. Most temples combine Tantric imagery with folk and bhakti traditions.

---

[5] Interview, Shakta priest, Kalimpong, 1994.

The third approach to Kali, that of devotional love or *bhakt*i, may be the major urban approach to the goddess, as seen in the annual festival of Kali Puja, and her temples.

Kali Puja night is a time for magic shows and theater, for fireworks and celebrations, but also for animal sacrifice to the goddess and contemplation of her importance in this world and in the universe. For most devotees, she is not merely Shiva's wife, but rather the origin of the universe, and her night reminds devotees of the fragility of their lives and their dependence upon a goddess who is alternately ruthless and compassionate. Many informants emphasized how careful one must be in worshipping Kali, for an error in worship could incur her wrath. As she is a goddess of both creation and destruction, her anger could mean anything from the loss of a job to a death in the family.

During the festival, Kali's images are varied in the different street-corner shrines which are set up to celebrate Kali Puja. Some shrines are the size of small walk-in camping-tents, made of rattan or bamboo, with Kalis like voluptuous dolls or withered old women, with white ornaments made of *solapith* and bright crepe-paper streamers. Large shrines may have beautiful Kalis standing on pale Shivas, dressed in silk, gold lamé, or imitation tiger skins. In recent years I have not seen the politicized style from 1983, when Kali and Shiva represented different cultural values. I vividly remember one set of statues, a tribal-style Kali with dark skin wearing animal skins and a fierce expression stepping on a blond crew-cut Shiva dressed in a three-piece grey Western business suit, holding a briefcase. Next to him was a jackal, who stood beneath the severed head which Kali was holding, drinking its dripping blood. However, there were some Kalis at the 1993 Kali Puja with dark skin, large noses and kinky hair, 'politically-correct' Kalis resembling the Adivasis or tribals of West Bengal rather than Aryan invaders or Western imperialists.[6] Some Kalis were bright blue, voluptuous, and smiling happily, looking mature for a sixteen-year-old. In the larger and more well-funded community *pandals* were giant statues, fifteen feet high or more, with piles of offerings all around.

Most temples involve *bhakti*, but one temple shows an interesting move from a folk tradition to a devotional one. At the Dhanvantari Kalibari (or temple) at Jayanagar-Majilpur, in the district of South 24 Parganas, there is a statue of Kali-Dhanvantari. This form of Kali has an unusual title, as Dhanvantari was the ancient physician of the Vedic gods.

[6] India has problems with affirmative action and prejudice, as does the West. In the case of the Kali with non-Aryan features, the statue shows respect for the Adivasi or tribal people who wish representation and concern for their cultures.

This is a healing temple, specializing in rheumatism, and its title translates out loosely as the temple of 'Doctor Kali.' People ordinarily come for evening worship (*arati*) by the priest, listen to the music of drums, cymbals, and conches, and pray to the goddess for healing.

People come here from many miles away to be cured of rheumatism. The patient bathes, and comes in directly in wet clothes. The medicine is given to him or her inside a betel leaf, and the person then takes a vow. He or she will not eat rice on the days of the new moon or full moon, or will give up certain bananas and parched rice until cured. The person may also vow to perform *dandi kata* (prostration before the deity in which the person falls forward like a stick of wood), offer a sacrifice (usually a black goat), or fast before the goddess for three or four days. The patient may also collect hard pieces of clay and tie them up with strings. These are hung around the temple as signs of the vows, which can remind the goddess in case she forgets.

Some people perform more ascetic practices: they carry three earthen pots (*malsa*) full of burning coals, one on the head, and one in each hand. A fire is lit with the twig of a wood apple (*bel*) tree, and powdered resin is sprinkled onto the burning coal. The devotee must carry it as long as the fire lasts, and the priest continues to chant mantras throughout. The priest conducts the ritual, and the devotee may stand or dance carrying these pots. Once the fire dies, the pots are thrown into the lake.

According to one group of informants at the temple, the sacred stone of Kali in her role as Dhanvantari was installed in 1783. It is said to have been found in a local pond called the Kalikunda. Land for a temple was granted from the zamindar family of Savarna Chaudhuri in the name of the goddess Kali. The stone was initially placed in a thatched hut (*than*) which served as a temporary temple, and then moved to the permanent temple.[7]

According to another set of local informants, when the area was still forested, the sadhu Rajendu Chakravarti was an Ayurvedic doctor who lived nearby. He knew herbal medicine, and many patients came to him to be cured. However, one patient was not cured by his efforts. The goddess Kali appeared in a dream, saying that he was prescribing the wrong medicine for the patient. However, he ignored the dream, insisting that he was right. Still the patient was not cured, and Kali came again in a dream. Then he decided to follow her advice, and the patient was cured (the same curing technique is used today). After this, Kali gave him a dream command. She said that she was hidden in the bottom of a lake, in the

---

7 Interview, Temple sevayats, Jayanagar, 1994.

form of a black stone, and he must find her. Chakravarti found the stone, which was carved with a bas-relief of a four-armed goddess, and took it from the lake and installed it in a hut near his house. He named her Kali Dhanvantari, or doctor, saying that she was the true healer, and he was not. Many years later, the stone was transported to the temple complex.[8]

The current Kali form at the temple is a double one: the black stone sits amid a bed of flowers and ritual objects, and above it is a statue carved of neem wood of a large black Kali with staring eyes, golden tongue, and four raised arms. Her feet rest on the stone, and Kali is understood as dwelling in both the stone and the statue. Her guardian, Banadevata, stands nearby, with a golden head and a large curled moustache. Around the corner is a niche with a statue of Shani, god of bad luck, on his vulture. They accompany Kali, who is here understood as a sociable goddess who likes to be around other deities. Kali can benefit both the doctors who learn from her, and the patients who are cured by her.

Healing temples are traditional in Bengal, especially for Kali temples, but this one had added an interesting twist. Their statue of Kali each year goes through a set of transformations in which she takes on the forms of other goddesses, and is dressed differently for each transformation by the priests. Being a modern goddess, she takes on modern fashions (such as the goddess Santoshi Ma, who has only become popular over the past decade, with the release of a movie in which she had a starring role). This festival was said to have been started by a tantric sadhu named Swami Bhairavananda, and he called it the "Mayarupavesa" festival (the festival when the goddess takes on or is taken over by illusory forms). I translate it below:

***

> At the Dhanvantari temple at Jayanagar-Majilpur, South 24 Parganas [come see] Sri Sri Queen Mother Kali's auspicious appearance, extending on this occasion for over two weeks. It is the "Celebration and Great Fair of Mother's Bodily Transformation"! (*Mayarupavesa Mahamela*). Once you have seen these fascinating forms of the Mother, your life will be blessed! [It is] Remarkable! Extraordinary! Come and see it. Far in the past, at an auspicious time, a great tantric sadhu had a vision of the Mother. Each year, following his vision, it happens again in the same way. From the bright first lunar day of Baisakh until the full moon day, on each evening, Sri Sri Goddess Mother Kali will appear adorned with various attractive roles (*bhavas*) and forms (*rupas*). This is truly Mahamaya's transformation of form, and Mahashakti's revelation of various [types of]

[8] Interview, Devotees, Jayanagar, 1994.

beauty. It is said that those who come to her for shelter, saying prayers inwardly [to her] and seeing these various forms, will have their wishes fulfilled, and will gain their hearts' desires.

***

The forms of the goddess include:

Santoshi Ma
Ganeshjanani
Bipattarini
Narasinghi
Adyavidya
Jahnavi
Kaliyadman
Sorashi
Matrisadhana
Kumari
Krishnakali
Sankatkali
Jagaddhatri
Annapurna
Dakshinakali

***

As one of the devotees at the temple phrased it, for Kali a bodily form (*rupa*) is like a new set of clothes: She gets tired of having the same bodily manifestation, and wants to have new ones:

> You see, many girls now wear modern dress, they wear blue jeans and skirts. Even ten years ago they did not do this. Ma Kali, too, wants to wear new fashions. So she has put on Santoshi Ma as one of her forms. In this way, she is fashionable, she is wearing something new.[9]

This yearly transformation has been very popular, and attracted a large number of visitors to the temple, who hope to have *darsan* of a living 'fashionista' deity.

Here we see the various *bhavas* (moods) and *rupas* (forms) of the goddess as a sort of show. The festival is not devoted to healing, as one might think because of the temple at which it occurs, instead, it is a celebration (*mela*) dedicated to the goddess' transformations which occur during different incarnations. Its focus is divine creativity and beauty, and the rise of devotional love as a response to the goddess' beauty. The focus of the temple moves from the more practical goals of folk religion to the devotional love desired for bhakti. When a goddess is loving and beautiful and creative, admiration is the expected human response. The goddess's role as a healer is not diminished even when she undergoes a complete makeover as a fashionable deity.

---

9. Interview, Teacher, Jayanagar, 1993.

Most goddess temples include all of these aspects, and perhaps the most famous set of goddess temples is known as the *sakti-pithas*. There are many temples and shrines dedicated to Kali which arise from the story of the *sakti-pithas*. These are centers of power which extend over India, and represent the goddess' identity in a variety of locales. These sacred sites of the goddess are based on a myth—the destruction of the sacrifice of Daksha Prajapati by the god Shiva, also called Rudra. The story is found in many sources, the earliest probably being the *Mahabharata* (XII, 282-283), though it is also found in several puranas (including the Matsya, Padma, Kurma, and Brahmanda puranas). The most well-known variant was in Kalidasa's *Kumarasambhava* (I.21), in which Sati was the wife of the god Shiva and the daughter of Daksha. When Daksha created a great sacrifice to which neither Shiva nor Sati was invited, Sati decided to attend anyway, and was insulted there by Daksha. Sati died of this insult, and Kalidasa says that she threw herself into the fire and perished. When Shiva found out about this, he angrily came with his attendants and destroyed the sacrifice. Three of the Shakta puranas, the *Kalika, Mahabhagavata,* and *Devibhagavata* puranas, also have versions of this story.

In the *Kalika Purana*, Daksha did not invite his daughter Sati and her husband Shiva to his sacrifice, When Sati learned of this, she generated yogic power which burned her body with yogic fire. Shiva took her corpse on his shoulders and began to dance madly. To shake Shiva out of his frenzy, the gods Brahma, Vishnu and Sanaiscara entered the corpse and cut it into six pieces, which fell to earth and formed the six *sakti pithas.* The area where Shiva had danced, "the eastern part of the earth," came to be called "the sacrificial land."[10]

In the *Mahabhagavata Purana*, Daksha decided to have a sacrifice, but would not invite Shiva. Narada suggested that they attend the sacrifice anyway, and Sati agreed, but Shiva refused. At this Sati became furious, took on a wrathful expression and generated ten forms of herself, the ten *mahavidya* goddesses. Sati predicted that these forms would be worshipped in the future by Shaktas in tantric rituals. Shiva was very frightened by her terrible forms, and praised her, telling her he would obey her. Sati later split into two forms, one of which stayed hidden, and the other, which was a shadow or *chaya* form, committed suicide. Thus, Sati was able to survive her suicide. Shiva was angry at Sati's apparent death, and generated out the form of the warlike Virabhadra, who went to destroy

[10] *Kalika Purana*, chapters 17 and 18, cited in Usha Dev, *The Concept of Sakti in the Puranas* (Delhi: Nag Publishers, 1987), p. 146.

Daksha's sacrifice. This is a popular variant of the story.

Brahma and Vishnu told Shiva that the real Sati was alive and invisible, and that it was the Chaya Sati who had apparently died in the fire. All three gods praised Sati, who then appeared before them in the form of Kali. She told Shiva to create the *pithas* by carrying Chaya Sati's body on his shoulders, and letting her limbs fall in different places. Then Shiva chose to live in the fifty-one *pithas* in the form of rocks (*lingas*).[11]

In the *Devibhagavata Purana* story, Daksha ignored a gift from his daughter Sati, thus insulting her, and she became angry and burned herself to ashes in a yogic fire generated by her rage. Shiva roamed the world with Sati's corpse on his shoulders, and Vishnu severed her limbs with his arrows. These limbs fell to earth in 108 pieces, creating the 108 *sakti pithas*.[12]

As we can see, there are a variety of origin stories for these sacred sites and their temples. There are also several different lists of *pithas* in various puranic and tantric texts, and the numbers range from four to one hundred and eight.

There are different forms of the goddess at the different *pithas*. This gives the originating goddess Sati the role of Shakti or mother goddess generally, for her body parts are places where other goddesses dwell. For instance, Sati's tongue rests at Jvalamukhi, and the goddess Ambika dwells there with her consort Unmatta (the mad one), while Sati's right ankle lies at Kurukshetra, and the goddess dwells there as Savitri with her consort Sthanu. In Calcutta, the goddess' toes are at Kalighat, and she dwells there as Kali with her consort Nakulisha.[13]

The *pithas* are a network of sacred places throughout India, the places where the goddess' power and blessings are most accessible. Often the *pithas* are located in unusual natural stone formations (which resembled some aspect of the goddess), as well as springs and hills. They grew up as pilgrimage sites, and different forms of Hindu belief clustered around them.

Sati was a martyr to dharma, responding to her own dishonor and the conflict between her husband and father by suicide. As a martyr, her relics were split up among communities rather quickly (when the gods decided that it was time to divide her body), and the shrines or *pithas* grew up at those sites. Some of the shrines became specialized for certain benefits—

11. *Mahabhagavata Purana*, chaps. 7-11, cited in Dev, Ibid, pp. 147-150.

12 *Devibhagavata purana*, VII, chap. 30, cited in Dev, Ibid, p. 151.

13 This is the dominant view. However, some sources list the deities at Kalipitha as Jayadurga and Krodhisa, and say that Kali's skull is at Kalighat. Others say that there are two Kalighats or Kalipithas, with two different body parts.

people could gain liberation at the *siddha pithas*, while power or merit was gained at the *sakti pithas*. Most of the *pithas* motivated priests to come, and Shakta devotees have donated money for temples and shrines. They have become religious sites for folk Shaktas, tantrikas, and urban devotees. We see in the mythic stories of the goddesses and the temple origin stories a combination of the three approaches that run through Bengali Shaktism.

While such temples emphasize traditional theology and ritual, some of them have developed in other ways. One of the most famous of the *sakta-pithas* is Kalighat, a relatively late addition to the *pithas*, probably coming to prominence after the founding of Calcutta in 1690.[14] There is mention of Kalikshetra and Kalighat in two sixteenth-century texts, Bipradas Papalai's *Manasa Mangal* and Mukundaram Chakrabarti's *Chandikavya,* but references become more prominent in the eighteenth century.[15] The seventeenth or eighteenth century text *Pithanirnaya* lists several *pithas* in rural areas of Bengal, with both the goddess and her consort (*bhairava*) dwelling there, and it includes Kalighat in the text.

At this temple, Kali has become the goddess of options-trading. Various economic approaches are found in many temples, but Kalighat's system has become particularly well-known due to its court cases. As we are looking at Kali through her temples, this gives a slightly different view to the proceedings. Here Kali's benefits go to the owners and priests who run the temple.

The Kalighat temple is the oldest temple in the Calcutta area, begun in the 1700s and completed in 1809. Before it was built, Kali was worshipped in that area in a small hut, and in the sixteenth century it was enlarged into a small temple by King Mansingha. Later, the landowner Santosh Kumar Roy Chowdhury built the present temple, in the Atchala (eight-roof) pattern, based on the style of thatched roof huts in West Bengal. The ground is considered to be sacred because it is believed that a body part of the goddess Sati (*sati-anga*) rests there. According to temple lore, this part is preserved in the temple-room and bathed once a year, though there is some uncertainly as to the exact locale of the relic (one author suggests that it is in an iron box below the image).[16]

---

14 There are some fifteenth century references to Kalighat, but it is not known if these are later additions to the texts. See Sircar, p. 24.

15 Surajit Sinha, "Kali Temple at Kalighat and the City of Calcutta" in Surajit Sinha, ed. *Cultural Profile of Calcutta* (Calcutta: Indian Anthropological Society, 1970), p. 62.

16. Indrani Basu Roy, *Kalighat: Its Impact of Socio-Cultural Life of Hindus* (New Delhi: Gyan Publishing, 1993) , p. 4.

The temple statue of Kali is a face made out of dark stone with four golden arms. The rest is normally covered with garlands and invisible to onlookers, and a new sari is added each night. When the load of saris becomes too great, and they start to decay from the various offerings of milk, fruit juice and sweets, they are privately changed by the priests.

One story links the beginning of Kalighat temple with a devotee named Brahmananda Giri, who was meditating alone in South India, on Nilgiri Hill. As Kali would not appear to him, he decided to commit suicide, at which point she appeared. She told him that she would never leave him, unless he asked her to leave. Later another devotee visited him, and Kali decided to take them to the site of her future temple. She gave them a stone to hold and told them to close their eyes, and in a moment they were in Kalikshetra.

Following the goddess' instructions, they travelled north and installed that stone and began to worship her. Soon they discovered the stones of Shiva and Sasthi in a nearby lake. A woman named Padmavati, an ancestress of the current caretakers of the temple, saw a light on the water and brought her husband and the devotees to see it. The light radiated from a floating rock, which was really Sati's toes shining on the water. They worshipped the toes, which were in the form of a large stone. However, the stone was broken years later, when caretakers were fighting over possession of the toes, and the rock was dropped and broken.[17]

After the death of the original devotees (and after Brahmananda had lost Kali's presence because he did not recognize her in her disguise as a crazy girl and told her to go away) various tantrikas and skull-bearing *kapalikas* took up residence at the *pitha* and practiced their rituals. Kali decided that she wanted a married priest who was a bit more stable. A passing salesman who sold conch-bangles later married the daughter of the acting caretaker, and this marriage began a lineage of temple caretakers at the *pitha*. These Kalighat ancestors were Uma, the daughter of Bhubaneswar Brahmachari (a Dasanami sadhu), and Bhabanidas Chakravarty. Their descendants were given the title "Haldar" in the eighteenth century, by leaders of the Maratha invasion of Bengal. They are Rarhi Shreni lineage brahmins, and today there are five major lineages which claim descent from the five grandsons of Bhabanidas.

Much infighting was involved in gaining the title Haldar, and in later debates about access to the temple, between brothers and members of the extended family. This was the beginning of the fighting over distributions of shares in the temple and division of income which have marked the

---

17. Roy, Ibid, p. 18.

Kalighat temple's history. Because of the large income, and the large number of "*sevayats*" (literally servants, but more accurately caretakers or owners), a system of organizing income had to be developed.

After much litigation, a 1949 decision by the Calcutta High Court declared that the religious endowment of the goddess Kali at Kalighat was a public one, and the Haldar caretakers could not claim hereditary rights as trustees of Kali's large amount of land in the Calcutta area. The caretakers were only entitled to "turns" (*palas*) doing service for the goddess, as ritual worship of Kali and the associated deities.[18]

A *pala* is a period of time during which temple earnings are calculated—it is usually a day. A caretaker "owns" one or more days, and the earnings from that period of time. Half of the day's earnings go directly to him, and (since the 1965 decision of the Calcutta High Court) half goes to the Kalighat Temple Committee for temple upkeep and expenses. Temple expenses are also covered by outside donations, interest on investments, and rent of temple land to shopkeepers and others (selling ritual objects, flowers, sweets, pictures and statues of deities, books, bangles, toys, and other objects).

The *pala* rotates through the various caretakers on the basis of day. Since it is a large source of income, it is treated as property, and those who get *pala*-days more frequently are more fortunate. Major shareholders may get more than one *pala*-day per month, while minor shareholders may only get one in thirty-five years, or one day in fifty years.[19]

The owner of a *pala* is called a *paladar*. He is supposed to be an official caretaker or *sevayat*, and one of the descendents of the Haldar family, but this is not always the case. *Palas* are often transferred to people who are not official caretakers or members of the Haldar family. There are several reasons for this. Some *sevayats* leave the town, or the state, and would not be able to take their turns. Some do not have any children, and may gift or sell their hereditary turn to somebody else. Some people rent out their *pala* times for profit, or to avoid the calculations and organization needed for temple work (the *paladar* must hire other people to collect offerings at the various altars and at the smaller temples, to direct animal sacrifices and collect taxes for it, and to supervise the various collections). As Roy states,

> In fact there are some people who have been professional in *pala* manipulation. They buy *pala* from the original party at a low price and then deal personally to make large profit. Again, a *pala* can also be sold

[18] Sinha, Ibid, p. 64.
[19] Roy, Ibid, p. 25.

> several times in a day from man to man in a low margin. Generally all such re-sales occur within the group. Professional persons of this type are plenty in number and most of them belong to *dauhitra* or *bhagne-dauhitra* group, whose original shares are too little.[20]

Thus, the *paladars* own nothing substantial, but only the right to collect income on one or more days. However, if the monsoons come early and the temple is empty on the chosen day he may receive no income at all.

Because of the large numbers of pilgrims and devotees who visit Kalighat temple, some days are especially valuable, like the first day of the month of Baisakh and Akshaya Tritiya day that can command more money than other days. In general, Saturdays, Sundays and Tuesdays are also more valuable days with higher numbers of visitors. As Surajit Sinha states,

> If an average is worked out, Kalighat may perhaps occupy the foremost position among all the places of pilgrimage in India so far as the visitors are concerned. The large number of pilgrims visiting Kalighat may be accounted for two reasons. Firstly, it is one of the 51 Shakta Pithas, and secondly, it is located in the largest city of India. All our old respondents confirmed that the volume of pilgrims has increased substantially during the last 50 years.[21]

In his study of pilgrimage at Kalighat temple, Sinha notes the major reasons that people visit the temple: to fulfill a vow, to gain merit (*punya*), to have peace of mind, to perform specific rituals, for safety in a long journey, to gain a job or promotion, to win a law case. While many visitors came to have the sight of the goddess, others wished for very secular ends: cure of disease, employment, wealth, children, gaining a good spouse. Many people also come to the temple for ceremonies such as name-giving, initiation, and marriage, for Kalighat has a reputation for simplified performances of elaborate Hindu rituals and rites of passage.[22] Temple priests there are also willing to perform marriage ceremonies

---

20. Roy, Ibid, p. 25,

21. Sinha, Ibid, p. 67.

22 Sinha, Ibid, p. 68. Kalighat is also quite popular with many Westernized children of traditional Hindu parents for this reason. Often such modern children wish to spend as little time as possible on traditional ceremonies, but do not wish to offend their aging parents by ignoring the rituals entirely. Kalighat provides a good middle ground with its "condensed" rituals, which cut out mantras, mudras and offerings which are determined by the priests to be of secondary importance.

which other temples are unwilling to perform, especially mixed marriages which violate traditional rules of dharma.[23]

As with Indian temples, economics is an extremely important factor, and this is especially so at the Kalighat temple. It is quite famous locally for its guides, or *pandas*, many of whom demand money from visitors on sight. While the idea of graded admissions charges was voted down, informal admission charges abound—often running into demands for hundreds of rupees.

The concern with money makes visiting the site difficult. A Bengali friend told me of his own experience at the temple. He was taking a guest from out-of-town to see the temple, and a temple guide (*panda*) took him off alone to see the goddess.[24] The *panda* then gripped his hands, and demanded that he contribute a large amount of money to the temple. When he refused, the *panda* would not let him go, and he was unable to break the *panda's* grip. Finally he agreed to contribute money, and he was allowed to get up. When the *panda* held out his hand for the money, he refused to give it to him, saying that he only promised it under duress. The *panda* was furious, and screamed that my friend was now cursed by the goddess, because he had lied before her image. However, this did not worry my friend, who was a dedicated atheist. His great concern was being able to leave.

Part of the reason for this monetary emphasis is that temples are often some of the major economic institutions in the town. While the smaller shrines and temples may only have one priest, as they grow larger, more and more people get involved. One older writer described the temple situation as a sparrow which must be divided between an ever-growing number of people as their dinner. The situation of dividing the same profit between more and more people has caused a great deal of anxiety, and during my time in Calcutta there was a scandal about a woman who was attacked by *pandas* for not offering enough money to the temple. The situation was resolved by the Temple Committee saying that they would write up a set of ethical guidelines for the temple.[25]

---

[23] Sinha, Ibid, p. 68.

[24] The *panda* acts as a guide, but is also a caretaker of the goddess and a keeper of genealogical records.

[25] The Calcutta papers wrote in 1984 of a scandal involving the temple, in which a woman refused the pandas' demands for money and ended up in a fight with them. It turned out that the woman's parents were politically important, and the resulting political pressures ended up in the Kalighat temple agreeing to write up a code of ethics for its priests and pandas. I left India before this document was written.

It is perhaps ironic that such concerns for money and capitalist values show up in communist West Bengal. This approach has led to less emphasis on Kali's transcendent aspects, and more on ritual and exchange. One way that the temple is making more money is by abbreviating rituals and compressing mantras, making ritual faster and more efficient, if less contemplative and traditional.

While the *sakti pitha* myth divided the goddess spatially, the *pala* myth divides the goddess temporally—different days of her year go to different people (as do the proceeds from those days). Thus the goddess is spread at this *pitha* over time and space. Yet like a hologram, she exists fully and equally in all of her fragments.

Kalighat is the largest *sakti pitha* in West Bengal, and has the most ritual activity. Most *pithas*, however, are quiet and deserted (unless the Government of India Shakta Pilgrimage Bus is taking people to visit the sites during *puja* time). Some have priests who are Vaishnava rather than Shakta; as one priest of a rural *sakti pitha* told me, "This is just a job. When I go home I worship Krishna." Sacred sites may be visited on pilgrimages, but most Shakta worship is private, and many sites are fairly quiet on most days. This may well be because of the rise of universalist Shakta bhakti, where all deities are ultimately the same, and no sacred space or time is necessary.

Goddesses do not always require temples, and sometimes goddesses are worshipped in unexpected places. In the Calcutta High Court building is a rock worshipped as Highcourteshwari, or High Court Goddess, who is said to bless litigants and bring court decisions favorable to her devotees. An anthropologist friend in Calcutta had a grandfather who was a judge in the court, and told the people before him not to be so superstitious as to worship a rock in the building. However, most would not listen to him, saying that they would be at a disadvantage if the goddess blessed their opponents and not themselves. There is also a Highwayishwari, or highway goddess, existing in the form of a rock beneath the Howrah bridge.[26] Goddesses are not prejudiced in favor of tradition in their decisions as to where to manifest.

But what if we were to ask: Who is the goddess behind the changing faces, and what benefits does she bring? This depends on the philosophy involved. In the Bengali tradition of Shaktism, there are three major outlooks or types: folk, tantric/yogic and bhakti. Each of these understands the goddess in different ways.

---

26 Khushwant Singh, *Kalighat to Calcutta: 1690-1990* (New Delhi: Lustre Press LTD, 1993), p. 59.

According to folk understandings, the form of the goddess who helps you is the true form of the goddess. If indeed she is a manifestation of some more distant goddess, this is fine, but not terribly relevant. It is immediate experience that is important: the goddess who sends you dream commands, heals your parents, makes your son win his lawsuit, and gives your daughter a good husband. The Kali of your village is different than the Kali of the next village, and probably superior (there is much rivalry between local goddesses, especially Kalis). Indeed, some villages have competitions to show which form is most powerful. Kali is specific, and indeed semi-material: she may be trapped in a rock or statue and unable to leave. She may also represent the power of the local hill or stone formation. The understanding is pragmatic: the Kali behind the changing faces is the one who can do things for you. She can give comfort and material success.

From the tantric/yogic perspective, the goddess represents the universe, and may be known by esoteric ritual. Kali may exist as Shakti or Prakriti, the active female essence of the universe, or she may use her rajasic aspect to exist in mandalas, *bija* mantras, even hand positions or *mudras*. Kali may be found in ritual locales, in temples associated with meditation and supernatural insight, in burning grounds, or more abstractly as an aspect of universal consciousness. The understanding is metaphysical: the Kali behind the changing faces is universal awareness which manifests in centers of power, in ritual action (*sadhana*), and in supernatural ability (*siddhi*). The yogic/tantric Kali gives supernatural benefits, and helps practitioners though spiritual realizations.

From the devotional or bhakti perspective, Kali is a loving presence, guarding the soul at birth and at death. She is its escort through the realms of reincarnation, and she brings it to good rebirth, or to her heaven (known variously as Manidvipa and Kailash). If the soul attains her heaven, it may spend eternity in the lap of the Mother (or sometimes in her arms as her child), or it may be older and devoted to her, as the *gopi* milkmaids are devoted to Krishna in his eternal paradise of Vrindavana (according to the *Devi Bhagavata Purana*, all souls in her heaven are female, and even the gods must be transformed into goddesses in order to enter). Kali may be the playful little girl, the wild dancer, the passionate woman, the all-powerful goddess, the Mother who protects and helps. The understanding is emotional: Kali brings love, joy, and salvation, she is a divine Person who cares about her devotees. She benefits her devotees through love and caring.

In each sacred form, in each sacred place, Kali benefits her devotees, priests, yogis, and temple owners in a variety of ways.

CHAPTER ELEVEN

STATUS OF WOMEN IN AN AGRARIAN ECONOMY: DECONSTRUCTION OF ORIYA LAKSMI VRAT-KATHA

BIDYUT MOHANTY

> "From thy propitious gaze, oh mighty goddess, men obtain wives, children, dwellings, friends, harvests, wealth. Health, strength, power, victory, happiness are easy of attainment to those upon whom thou smilest ...Oh thou who purifiest all things, foresake not our treasures, our granaries, our dwellings, our dependents, our persons, our wives." Hymn to Lakshmi.
> —*Vishnu Purana*

> "She has no temples, but being the goddess of abundance and fortune, she continues to be assiduously courted and is not likely to fall into neglect."
> —John Dowson, "Lakshmi" in a classical Dictionary of Hindu Mythology.[1]

The Context

Rudolph and Rudolph quoted the above sentences to show how the power and wealth in the form of Lakshmi go hand-in-hand in the Indian culture particularly in so far as the electoral process is concerned. They were analyzing the results of the 1957 election as well as other features of development in India. In this essay however, it is to be shown that how a myth related to goddess Lakshmi—the goddess of rice—has helped to shape the consciousness of the Oriya men in general and women in particular. The myth relating to Laksmi not only gives high status to the goddess but also acknowledges the contributions of women in household

[1] Both these quotes are from Rudolph and Rudolph *In Pursuit of Lakshmi The Political Economy of the Indian State.* Chicago: University of Chicago Press, 1987.

economics. This has been made possible by several factors. First of all, women are involved significantly in different stages of rice cultivation and in the management of post harvest crops. Secondly, the contributions of women's labor were never realized fully in a patriarchal society like India, particularly in Orissa, till a social reformer called Balaram Das, living in the sixteenth century, rewrote the text of the Oriya Lakshmi Vrat-katha acknowledging the contributions of women and equating them with the goddess of Lakshmi–the goddess of rice and fertility. This Vrat-katha is recited in each and every household of rural Orissa on the occasion of Laksmi puja every year in the months of late October and early November. Since the sixteenth century, Lakshmi is worshipped in peasant households with much fanfare. The text rewritten in the sixteenth century under the influence of the Bhakti movement is marked by the second wave of the Bhakti movement that posed a challenge to the existing caste order and to some extent patriarchy. Many social reformers like Balaram Das and Jagannath Das translated Sanskrit texts into Oriya and made those texts accessible on a popular level. For example, Jagannatha Das translated the Bhagavad Gita into Oriya and read it aloud in the precinct of Lord Jagnnatha to illiterate women who used to come there every day. Another contributing factor for reinterpreting the text of Laksmi Vrat-katha has been a relatively egalitarian tradition of Lord Jagannatha which tolerates the presence of all castes and all religions in the temple in certain occasions.[2] And Lakshmi Vrat-katha was linked with Lord Jagannatha since she has been depicted as the wife of lord Jagannatha.

In this essay, however, the focus would be on the linkage between the agrarian economy, role of women and a content analysis of the Oriya Lakshmi Vrat-katha particularly in a rice growing economy, to show how the Vrat-katha has shaped societal notions about women. In order to proceed the following steps will be followed. The first section will discuss the role of women in a rice growing economy and status of women in Orissa, one of the eastern states of India. After that a discussion on the rice and culture in rice growing areas will be highlighted. An analysis of the text of the Oriya Vrat-katha will be presented to show in what ways it has

[2] Marglin F.A. (1985) *The Wives of God -King: The Rituals of the Devdasies of Puri (*Delhi, OUP) pp.171-184. Marglin for example writes that even though the members of Scheduled castes, and Muslims are not allowed to enter the temple of Lord Jagannatha, people of all castes and religions can share the offerings (cooked food) from the same container outside the temple. The principles of purity and pollution are not observed while taking the offerings. Similarly people from all castes participate in pulling the ropes of chariots carrying all three idols namely, Lord Jagannatha, Balabhadra and Subhadra, during the annual car festival in Puri.

gaged in that trade far exceeded that of men.[7] Similarly Sen observed at paddy husking is a marginal occupation that many rural families pass rough on the way to total destitution particularly during famine. Entry to is occupation is extremely easy, it is low-paid and is done exclusively by omen.[8] He was discussing the Bengal famine of 1943. Paddy is edominantly cultivated in Eastern and South India. In contrast, almost the agricultural activities of the wheat growing area are done by the n workers. In spite of existing evidence Bardhan didn't substantiate the pothesis by using hard data. In addition, women take a main role in ganizing rice related festivals as well as other social festivals which quire raw rice which is not parboiled and is husked at home.

Taking a cue from Bardhan, Leela Gulati[9] examined the association ween the sex ratios of the Eastern and South Indian states and female rk participation rates. She took the statistics of female work ticipation rates of the 1971 Census and correlated those with the area ler rice cultivation and sex ratios. If Bardhan's hypothesis is true then areas which grow rice would have higher sex ratio and higher female k participation. But she noticed that though Orissa devoted 91 percent s total cultivated area to rice in 1971-2, female work participation rates e only eight percent particularly in rural areas. Compared to the all-a average (952), however, the sex ratio in rural area was very high ely, 1003 in 1971. Incidentally, Orissa continues to be a rice growing iomy even now. More than 80 percent of the cultivated land is devoted inter rice[10]. The sex ratio was higher than that of most of the wheat ving states in 2001. For example, Orissa has 972 females to 1000 s. In contrast Punjab has 876 women per 1000 men. Haryana which is qually prosperous state has a lower sex ratio than that of Punjab. At ll-India level, the sex ratio is only 933. Orissa is considered to be a le- surplus state leading unfortunately thereby to the export of brides ther female deficit areas of India.[11] In some of the communities ding the tribes the practice of bride price still continues.[12] Thus

ır and Orissa Census Report, 192,1 Vol.1.

, A. K. *Poverty and Famines: An Essay on Entitlement and Deprivation.* d, Clarendon Press, 1981, p.72.

ati, Leela. "Female Work participation: A Study of Inter-state Differences". Vol. X, 1975, Nos.1-2 pp. 35-42.

://dacnet.nic.in/rice/PA-Table-18-Orissa.htm

ya newspaper reports are full of such stories though extensive research has en carried out.

course things are changing rapidly as the Oriya middle class gets integrated e rest of India. Instances of female infanticide and bride burning are being ed recently.

acknowledged the contributions of women and in what w images of women in their own eyes as well as in the e discussion on different approaches to the relation bet goddesses will complete the chapter.

Role of Women in Rice Econom

In rice growing areas of Asia, women play a very only in the process of production but also in the post ha They also take active part in rice related commercial a refers to women's role in the time of weeding and sel seed of rice in those areas. For instance, anthropolog the weeding is predominantly done by women. In fact in maintaining the paddy field well. Moreover, your large number of children take charge of extracti beginning of the planting time in Vietnam. These w Rice Mothers.[4]

In India, Pranab Bardhan[5] pointed out that femal lower in a rice growing economy than in a whea because rice cultivation requires female labor more th area. Thus women are valued more highly in the fo examined the death rate differentials across the Indi the conclusion that the ratio of female deaths to r significantly lower in rice growing areas than that i which are predominantly wheat growing areas.

He further pointed out that paddy cultivation re of female workers during the time of transplanting and threshing, etc. It is also interesting to note th harvest paddy rice extensively. The dietary habi requires paddy to be processed before it is milled a in that process exclusively.[6] The Census Report produced statistics on the rice trade in Orissa and

---

[3] Ammayao, Aurora and Hamilton, Roy W. *The Art of R in Asia.* Los Angeles: University of California-Los Ange

[4] Ibid.

[5] Bardhan, Pranab, "On life and Death Questions" *Econ (EPW)* Special No. 1974, p. 1304.

[6] Orissa and Bengal people eat parboiled rice which r paddy and dry it and send for milling or husk it at ho women's Self Help Groups (SHGs) are engaged in the particularly in the rice belt.

Gulati concluded that the variations in work participation rates in India may be due to some non-economic factors such as culture and not due to favorable sex ratios and economic requirement of the region as observed by Bardhan. The author also referred to the work participation rates of different countries like Catholic, Muslim and non-Muslim countries to establish some kind of linkage between the two. It was noticed that certain non-Muslim countries in Africa show a very high rate of female work participation which is due to strong farming tradition among the women. Similarly the female work participation rates in the Southeast Asian countries are between 20-30 percent reported in 1971 and women have been active workers in the field. Gulati was right in tracing the linkage between the cropping pattern, work participation rates and sex ratios but she used the census data of 1971 which defined worker in a much stricter way than the earlier or later censuses. She is aware of this weakness though she didn't try to rectify that. For example, according to the 1971 Census, if a woman pounds rice at home and her husband takes that for selling in the market she will not be considered as a worker, for the husband will be considered as the worker. Secondly, the data collectors, the informers at the household level as well as at the village level, are predominantly males and being a patriarchal society there is a tendency to underestimate the economic contributions of the women. Apart from these weaknesses Gulati has rightly pointed out that the tradition or culture determines the female work participation in an economy. This is where Bardhan's hypothesis can be linked with certain types of culture that are associated with rice cultivation and that will be taken up next.

Rice Culture

Jacqueline M. Piper's study of rice cultivation in South-East Asia observed that the stages of production and its place in the minds of the local people reveal the cultural tenets of that area.[13] The same thing can be said regarding the other parts of Asia which grow rice. It is also interesting to note that many common threads weave together in comparing rice growing areas. Hamilton, for example, observed that many in Asia believe that rice is a sacred food, divinely given, and integrally linked to the life of human beings. It is a common belief that symbolically human body and soul are made up of rice only.[14] Since the cereal has been the staple food for centuries, it is regarded as a symbol of spirituality. Each stage of rice

[13] Piper, Jacquiline M. *Rice in South-East Asia, Cultures and Landscape*. OUP: Kuala Lumpur, 1993.

[14] Similar sayings are also prevalent in Orissa.

production is done on an auspicious day and some rituals are performed. To substantiate, Hamilton[15] quoted Lansing on the interchangeability of the calendar of agricultural rites and the master calendar of social life. Almost all the major festivals of Asia are linked to agricultural cycles. From plowing to transplanting, harvesting and storing the paddy are marked by different rituals. Rice itself is seen as female in gender.[16] Barnes points out that in Asia, explicit fertility rituals and symbols are recurring motifs throughout the rice belt. In other words rice cultivation is interwoven with female fertility. The tradition of royal plowing ceremonies is still practiced in Japan, Thailand and Nepal.[17] These festivals also take place in Nepal and Thailand. In Japan, on the other hand, seedling festival is a communal festival in which young women take active part in transplanting the seedlings while young men help them organizing. In the harvesting festival held in Vietnam, the rice Mother is worshipped before the rice is harvested. Before it is cut a young woman cuts the first stalk of the rice. Similar rituals are observed when the rice is stored in the granary[18].

Rice in Rituals

In India in general and Orissa in particular, the tradition of rice culture is very strong particularly in comparing rice growing areas to wheat growing ones. In Orissa, people observe Raja festival to welcome the onset of monsoon.[19] On that occasion it is believed that mother earth or

---

[15] Ammayao, Aurora and Hamilton, Roy W. *Art of Rice, op. cit.,* 'Introduction.'

[16] Barnes, Cynthia (2003) "The Art of Rice" *Humanities* vol.24, no.5, (Sept-October)

[17] Ibid.

[18] Ibid.

[19] In Orissa the onset of monsoon coincides with the onset of a festival meant only for women in general and young women in particular and the belief is that the mother earth is ready for rice cultivation which is the main livelihood for the local people. The festival is known as Raja and the women are not supposed to touch earth on bare foot for those days of the ritual. The ritual lasts for four days. On those days mother earth or the goddess Lakshmi menstruates. On the fourth day the mother earth gets purified with water mixed with turmeric and raw cow dung. Since the women symbolize mother earth they are not allowed to take part in any household activities. (Marglin (1999) succinctly describes the festival as the articulation between cycles of natural regeneration and cycles of human regeneration. She has taken up a particular place in Orissa in which men of all the villages stay together in a sacred Grove known as Har Candi Grove and women stay in the villages on the occasion of Raja. .All forms of agricultural activities are

Bhudevi/Lakshmi becomes fertile. So women who represent mother earth celebrate it with much fanfare. It is observed at the community level. The first plowing in the field takes place on *askhi-trutiya* day. This day is an auspicious day throughout India and several thousands of children get married in some parts of northern India. But in Orissa, the farmer takes the plow to the field for the first time.

On *Gahma Poornima* (certain full moon day) the bullocks which plow the rice field are worshipped and given a bath, and offered special food, etc. Similarly, when the grains begin to form and swell a special ritual takes place. That day is known as *garvana sankranti.* Special offerings are made to the rice field on that day. Again, the selection of rice seeds is held on an auspicious day. Finally, the goddess of wealth is worshipped by the agricultural community to thank her for the bountiful harvest. All these days are noted in the Oriya *panjika* (calendar) as auspicious days. So almost all people who are engaged in agriculture observe those festivals. Agricultural laborers having no land or bullock have no special incentive to observe those festivals, but on those occasions they are given special food by the agricultural communities. In addition, the members of Scheduled Caste (untouchables) try to observe those festivals once they acquire land. The stages of rice cultivation are very well demarcated and each stage is welcomed by the agricultural communities—both Hindus and Muslims.

Hamilton points out that since the 1960s Asiatic societies have undergone tremendous changes in terms of green revolution. The mono–crop replaced multi-crops, etc, so some of those rituals would have become defunct. In Orissa, also the green revolution has brought summer rice but that rice is never considered as sacred as the winter rice, which has been cultivated, from the very beginning of the settled cultivation. The cycles of the cultivation are not the same winter rice and summer rice. Summer rice is never used in the temple of Lord Jagannatha and summer

barred for the above four days. People from all religions and from all castes (except Brahmin) take part in this festival. Marglin of course, concludes that "—unicity is lethal to diversity and that secular nation states have everywhere adopted science as both a strengthening and legitimizing tool, thus endangering diversity." Marglin, F. A.(1999) "Secularism, unicity, and diversity: The Case of Harcandi Grove" in Das Veena, Gupta D, and Uberoi, P., (eds) *Tradition, Pluralism, and Identity in Honour of T N Madan* (New Delhi, Sage publication). In other words there are sacred events which can be treated as secular since people of all religions participate in that. In addition since the festival marks the onset of agricultural activities it indicates the importance of women in the realm of rice cultivation.

rice is not used in any important rituals. Winter rice is sacred and its culture sets the patterns for Oriya life and cuisine.

Piper talks about the multiple uses of rice in different rituals of South-east Asia. People offer cooked food to the friends as well as to the gods. As a paste it is used in many purification ceremonies. In India also rice is used as a purifying medium in major ceremonies relating to birth, death and marriage. Similarly, in Orissa the use of rice is taken for granted in almost all the social and religious rituals. It is used as a medium of gift, and exchange. Cooked food is offered to the departing soul for a period of thirteen days coinciding with the purification period. The ancestral remembrance is always made after offering rice to the priests and immersing a portion of the same in the holy river. A gift of rice is considered to be the best gift. Further, the bride and groom are welcomed with sprinkling of puffed rice. The priest blesses the newly-wed couple with yellow rice. Finally, as mentioned earlier, the offerings of cooked food offered to Lord Jagannatha is shared by the members of all castes and religions without getting polluted. As mentioned earlier, in all these occasions the winter rice is considered pure, but not the early rice of summer season. On a fasting day women take winter rice to observe the fast. Interestingly, only winter rice is considered a symbol of Lakshmi, hence sacred grain. The culture of rice is deeply rooted in the culture of Oriya people.

Goddess Lakshmi

Almost all the cereal growing societies believe in the existence of many female and male goddesses and gods.[20] Piper for example talks about those rice goddesses who taught mankind how to cultivate, harvest and store rice. In different countries the names and the functions of the gods and goddesses change.[21] She refers to the rice goddess of Thailand and Bali which perform similar functions. They are known as Mae Posop

---

[20] Piper Jacqueline (1993) *Rice in South-East Asia Cultures and Landscapes.* (Oxford University Press, Kuala Lumpur). The author has given names of those goddesses prevalent in those societies.

[21] Pattanaik, Devdutt (2002) *Lakshmi: The Goddess of Wealth and Fortune, An Introduction.* (Mumbai, Vakils, Feffer and Simons Private Ltd.) "The practice of personifying the beauty and bounty of earth as a goddess was prevalent in all ancient cultures. The Greeks had Core, the corn goddess, who was known to Romans as Demeter. The Egyptians had Isis, Sumerians had Innana, Babylonians had Ishtar, Persians had Anahita, and Vikings had Freia. Sri Lakshmi is the Hindu form of the timeless mother goddess who nurtures and nourishes all lives." p.3.

and Dewi Sri respectively. Both of them play a protective role in providing sustenance to the human beings. As mentioned earlier, Thai farmers designate certain heads of rice as the Rice Mother. In the same vein, Hamilton writes that one underlying belief of Asian people is that they believe in the existence of spirit or spirits of rice. In other words the rice plant possesses a living spirit that lives from year to year in the form of rice spirit, sometimes visualized as the rice mother or rice deity.[22] Similar practices exist in rice growing areas of India. David Kinsley reported that those agricultural motifs are visible in the worshipping of Lakshmi in certain areas of India.[23] The corn goddess for example is known as Laksmi or Annapurna in areas where rice is the principal crop.[24]

Kinsley observes that Laksmi or Sri is a pre-Buddhist goddess who has been associated with prosperity, well-being, royal power, and illustriousness. She has always been associated with the royal power. In some myths she has been depicted as being associated with Lord Indra or the god who controls rain. Along with him she is represented in helping to bring good rain to the earth and abundant crops and thereby ensuring prosperity to people. But in certain other myths she is the consort of Lord Vishnu representing prosperity herself.

In Bengal, people worship Lakshmi on three occasions coinciding with sowing of the paddy, appearance of the ears of corn and after reaping the harvest of the main rice crop.[25] The main festival for goddess Lakshmi takes place after the harvest is over. In Bengal, Maity observes that a distinction is made between Alakshmi and Laksmi. According to him, the former one was being worshipped by the tribal people as the goddess of corn. Later on the Brahmins invented the goddess of wealth and prosperity and tried to discard the original one. So on the main festival of Laksmi, Alakshmi is worshipped first at the door and then driven away by the men of the households. Kinsley agrees with Maity to the extent that Laksmi represents good luck and Alakshmi represents ill-luck so she has to be disfigured and driven out by beating drums and lighting lamps. It is important to note that the main hero of the Vrat-katha is the king who buys Alakshmi to honor his *dharma.* In the process the goddess Lakshmi leaves

---

[22] Hamilton, *op. cit.* p.11.

[23] Kinsley, David (2003) *Hindu Goddesses: Vision of Devine Feminine in the Hindu Religious Tradition.(*Delhi,, Motilal, Banrasidass Publishers) p.33.

[24] She is worshipped all by herself in rice growing area. In contrast she is worshipped along with lord Ganesh in the wheat growing area. Diwali is celebrated to remember both Ganesh and Lakshmi.

[25] Maity, P.K. (1988) *Folk Rituals of Eastern India.*(Delhi, Avinav Publication), p.15.

him but later on comes back since Alakshmi leaves his house on her own accord. Thus the tradition of Laksmi is attached to royal power in Bengal. The writers of Bengali Vrat-katha have described various types of Laksmi such as Rajlaksmi, Bhagyalaksmi, Jasolaksmi and Kullaksmi.

In order to welcome the goddess various scenes depicting the stages of cultivation are drawn on the floor and walls. Rice powder mixed with water is used to draw those scenes.[26] It is important to note that women themselves think of rice as Laksmi. This kind of thinking is also prevalent even among migrant women living in the USA.[27] In addition, Indian women identify themselves with Lakshmi. They worship Lakshmi on every Thursday. During the Lakshmi puja raw paddy is symbolized as Laksmi. As in Bengal, Lakshmi is also associated with food and rice in Orissa. So much so that children are socialized to show respect to rice and not to indulge in wasting the same. The saying in Oriya goes that if one wastes one morsel of grain a large amount of food grains would vanish from the cooking pot. This shows that rice cultivation has passed through the period of scarcity. The saying exhorts cultivators to save every morsel of rice as a valuable commodity. Similarly nobody is allowed to drop even a single food grain on the floor while eating. Severe social strictures are expressed by the elders if somebody drops rice by mistake. He or she is branded as a person who would have incurred anger of the goddess Laksmi. Sometimes the saying is also invoked in the name of goddess Laksmi. In contrast to Bengal however, there is no distinction between Laksmi and Alakshmi in Orissa. Other characteristics of Lakshmi are that she is the wife of lord Jagannatha–another *avatar* of lord Vishnu and she is born out of the ocean.[28] Balaram Das who wrote the Vrat-katha in the sixteenth century painted her as the goddess of corn. The most important thing to note about the goddess is that she respects the egalitarian and tolerant societal order of lord Jagannatha tradition.[29] Laksmi is worshipped

---

[26] Those depictions are known as Alapana in Bengali or Chita in Oriya. To draw good Chita is a good qualification of a potential bride.

[27] Ray, Shohini (2003) 'Lakshmi of the House: Rituals, Realities, and Representation of the Women-hood in the Modern Bengal.'in Roy, Hamilton (Ed.) p. 309.

[28] The temple of lord Jagannatha is situated on the shore of Bay of Bengal.

[29] Before Balaram Das wrote the Vrat Katha, of Lakshmi, the earlier version depicted Lakshmi coming to the rescue of an old Brahmin woman. Since Balaram Das was a Vaisnavaite and believed in challenging the existing caste order he painted Lakshmi as a rebel wife who observes the just principles of lord Jagannatha even if He forgets to abide by. Balaram Das also wrote Ramayana making it more relevant to Oriya people .The characters of Ramayana looked as if they belonged to Orissa only. Incidentally the sixteenth century was characterized

thrice in a year but the main festival comes in the month of Margsira just after the harvest of the winter rice.[30] All the four or five Thursdays of that month are devoted to worshipping Lakshmi. It is indeed a private affair and priests are not needed to perform the *puja.* Married women and unmarried daughters take part in the *puja.*[31] Newly harvested raw paddy is filled up in two cane baskets in the form of a goddess. These baskets are used as the measures of paddy and rice in Orissa. On the top of those baskets a piece of red cloth is placed to decorate the paddy. It gives an appearance of a newly married woman. Along with that a coconut and some betel nuts are also kept.[32] Like the 'Rice Mother' of Vietnam[33] the children are asked to maintain silence when the *man basa* is in progress lest it would incur the wrath of goddess Laksmi. The entire household gets purified with raw cow dung mixed with water. Thursdays are vegetarian days particularly for women and on those days fish markets give a deserted look even in the towns and cities. On other Thursdays of the year

---

by an upsurge of Oriya literature. This era is welcomed by many because of the literary up surge. But this era is also criticized by many because the king didn't pay much attention to the welfare of the kingdom. So Orissa's progress suffered a great deal.

[30] The other Lakshmi *puja* is celebrated as Gaj-Lakshmi in certain parts of Orissa with much fan fare on *kaumudi poornima* day. The combination of elephants and Lakshmi show that the elephants imbuing the very qualities with which Lakshmi is characterized with. It is also associated with royal power depicting *rajavishek.* It is celebrated in public and the priests are required to perform *puja.* Again Lakshmi is also worshipped in the households if three things coincide namely, Thursday, lunar cycle leading towards full moon and tenth day of that fortnight. It is again a private affair but on a smaller scale than that of Lakshmi *puja.*

[31] It is important to note that married daughters are excluded from taking part in the *puja* indicating the fact that the quantity of grain can't be stretched in the time of scarcity. They are even not allowed to have access to the offerings of Lakshmi. The married daughters are not even allowed to leave their parental houses on Thursdays lest the goddess Lakshmi would leave with the daughters. This practice still continues even today in Orissa. In contrast the married daughters pitched in worshipping Lakshmi along with mother and sisters in law in North India. Does it mean that Lakshmi is attached to business and the network helps in expanding the same. It is also to be noted that the Vrat-katha is being generally recited by the unmarried girls or young married women. This practice has encouraged Oriya women of high caste to read and write.

[32] Margilin (1985) has used the same terminology as is used by the Oriya people and has described the above *puja as man basa.*

[33] 'Rice spirit doesn't like any noise so the 'Rice Mothers' walk silently to the field to select the seeds.

also women of the rural households purify their houses with cow dung mixed with water.

The women of the agricultural community and members of other high castes perform Laksmi *puja*. As mentioned earlier, traditionally members of the Scheduled Caste and Tribe do not take part in this. As we have already seen, if the goddess Lakshmi bestows riches on an untouchable woman because of her restless nature and, if she favors members of any caste and community can become rich. So nowadays the rich section of the Scheduled Caste does perform the *puja* which allows them to be part of the Sanskritisation process.

Oriya Laksmi Vrat-katha: A Deconstruction

As mentioned above, the Vrat-katha is recited on the occasion of Laksmi *puja*. The text of this Katha had been influenced by the Bhakti movement. The abridged version of the Katha is given in appendix 1. Interestingly the Katha is recited by the women of the households and the same booklet or palm leave *potha* is preserved along with the *man* as sacred articles for the years together. So the chances of changing the text become less likely. In a nutshell the text of the story is as follows:

Goddess Lakshmi visits a household of an untouchable woman named Sriya Candalini who was worshipping her early in the morning on Thursday of Margshira. Being satisfied with her cleanliness and devotion she grants her many boons and returns to the Jagannatha temple in Puri. Since she had visited the house of an untouchable woman the elder brother Balaram gets very angry and both the brothers decide to throw her out of the temple. She leaves the temple but curses the brothers saying that because they have neglected her they will not get any food for twelve years until and unless she offers them food. Interestingly Balaram Das made the goddess Laksmi say if Jagannatha would fail to understand the importance of Laksmi, the men of *kali yug* will also fail to understand the women's role in managing the household affairs! It is important to note that the above couplet is being cited quite frequently by women if they get neglected by their husbands even nowadays. Lakshmi, however, doesn't go to her parent's place (the ocean) but takes the help of the heavenly bodies and builds a palace near the ocean. It is important to note that there is a temple called Laksmi-Nrishingh temple which has been described as the palace in the story that Lakshmi had built for herself when she left

Lord Jagannatha's abode. This temple is situated near the sea.[34] The story of Laksmi is being recited by the priests of the temple on the occasion of *man basa.* She also takes away all the movable and immovable assets of the temple without the knowledge of both the brothers. Since they are devoid of Laksmi they don't get a morsel of rice until Laksmi herself gives them cooked food and extracts a promise that she has to take a tour of the universe on the days designated for her. In addition, the cooked food of the temple will be shared by members of all castes without getting polluted.

Several things become clear from the above story. First, Balaram Das has depicted the goddess Lakshmi as an ordinary Oriya woman. She feels cheated by her husband when her husband asks her to leave and reminds him of his commitments to forgive her for ten times as a part of the marriage deal. Like an Oriya woman she takes off all the ornaments to be kept by the Lord Jagannatha for his second wife.[35] But unlike ordinary Oriya woman she doesn't end up in her parents' house. Instead she tries to teach them a lesson and succeeds also. In this Vrat-katha she propounds the value of cleanliness, frugality, industriousness and maximum utilization of food grains. For example she tells the trader's wife whom she meets first en route to her tour, she never visits them who do not wear clean dress, do not keep houses clean and waste food grains by throwing them away. She also says that if women and men don't get up early in the morning and keep on quarreling with each other she shuns those houses. The women of rural Orissa have internalized such values. They also try not to quarrel at least on Thursdays. But so far as the wastage of food grain is concerned women particularly older women are conscious of that. They even try not to throw away a single particle of rice.[36] They become more conscious of that on Thursdays–the days of goddess Laksmi. Perhaps Balram Das knew the Oriya society well and was aware of the wife beating even though he himself didn't get married. Laksmi tells the trader's wife that those who beat their wives come under the angry spell of the goddess. Of course, it has not prevented wife beating completely but

[34] Marglin (1985) *op. cit.,* p. 175.

[35] The description of jewelries is really fantastic in the Vrat-katha. It gives a vivid description of the various types of ornaments worn by the women of Orissa in the sixteenth century.

[36] This attitude towards rice shows the nature of uncertainties faced by the local people and their efforts to save as much as possible. If somebody is found wasting food grain, the social sanction operates in the name of Lakshmi. Interestingly enough only rice and no other food grain are considered to be as valuable as wealth. Similar kind of saving attitude is noticed in other agrarian societies like China.

there exists a social sanction and people describe those who beat their wives as *Laksmi-chada* or shunned by goddess Laksmi.

In the same vein the Vrat-katha states that if women don't listen to their husbands and don't show them respect, Laksmi will leave them forever. Balaram Das obviously didn't want a breakdown of the existing social order, while conceding some grounds to women. Again on the one hand the goddess Laksmi challenges the male principle of hierarchy in terms of purity and pollution but on the other hand washes the feet of her husband when he visits her to get some food. Certainly women of Orissa get the proper message that one can challenge the patriarchy to some extent but not to rupture the social fabric. Similarly by accepting Laksmi on her own terms, the male social order recognizes the importance of women's role in the management of food and cooking.[37] Marglin narrates this point beautifully.[38] It also becomes clear that goddess Lakshmi as well as women are sole providers of food and sustenance.

It is also important to note that when Laksmi leaves the temple the two brothers starve and nobody recognizes them. Thus without Laksmi or Sri the sovereignty leaves lord Jagannatha. Marglin quotes Hiltebeitel[39] to show how Sri and Laksmi are one and the same and Sri is repository for those virtues which are connected with sovereignty. So when Lakshmi leaves somebody he loses the sovereignty.[40] It is also worthwhile to note that Bhakti movement challenged the caste order. The writers of that period emphasized this point again and again. Balaram Das was no exception. But interestingly he chose women as the medium of change and not men. In reality however, women are the upholders of religious purity and pollution. However, by getting a waiver of purity and pollution with regard to *Mahaprasd,* Lakshmi as well Balaram Das has achieved one important concession. They could challenge the existing caste order. To that extent this Vrat-katha can be used as a source of 'critical traditionalism' or a 'non-exclusionary reading of the native legacies.'

---

[37] It is important to note that the role of women in management of food is recognized by the women themselves as well as the society. But the principle of purity and pollution in so far as the cooked food is concerned is strictly adhered by them though the exception is made with regards to the *Mahaprasad*- the offerings of Lord Jagannatha.

[38] Marglin(1985) *op. cit.,* pp. 180-181.

[39] Hiltebeitel, Alf (1976) *The Ritual of Battle: Krishna in Mahabharata.* Cornell University press, Ithaka, London) p.149, p.152, and p.153.

[40] Expressions like *Sriheen, Hatasri* meaning devoid of Sri are very common in Oriya language.

According to Dallmayr[41] the Bhakti poetry provides an insight to the existence of a 'liberating transformative spirit' in which everybody is a part.

Gender and the Goddess

The question of raising the status of women by equating women with goddess has been debated again and again in the context of the Nationalist Movement of India. In order to oppose colonialism, the nationalists reinterpreted the sources of tradition and described women as a part of Sakti, the source of energy. But after independence women were relegated to the domestic sphere in the name of Shakti again. In other words, equating women with goddesses didn't improve their status at all—even after independence.

It required the women's movement to make women's needs visible. For example Chatterjee[42] commented on the absence of addressing women's questions by the nationalists in the following way. They produced the notion of the 'modern woman' who is 'embodiment of the spiritual superiority' of the nation. The modern woman was conceived as that kind whose emancipation and education were tied to the spiritual qualities of self-sacrifice, benevolence, devotion and religiosity. So she couldn't get any space for herself in the public space. Sarkar[43] raised similar concerns. She pointed out that the grounding of public political action of women was formulated in language which was full of traditional and religious images. The modern woman was depicted as the self-conscious alternative to the Western norm. However, John[44] argues that within the same framework it was possible to find prominent women leaders who drew the 'potent ingredients of the cultural nationalism' and were given a chance to grow.

---

[41] Dallmayr Fred (1992) 'Modernization and post-modernization: Whither India' *Alternative*, vol. 17, pp. 421-452.

[42] Chatterjee (1993), Partha *The Nation and its Fragments: Colonial and postcolonial Histories.* (OUP. Delhi), pp.131-33.

[43] Sarkar, Tanika (1989) 'Politics, and Women in Bengal-The Conditions and Meaning of Participation' in J Krishnmurthy (Ed)*Women in Colonial India: Essays on Survival, Work and the State* (OUP, Delhi) p.241 quoted in John, Mary (2000) 'Alternate Modernity? Reservations and Women's Movement in 20th Century India. *EPW*, p. 3823.

[44] John (2000) Idem.

Now coming to the more specific relationship between women and goddesses, Tracy Pintchman,[45] who has examined the rise of great goddesses, says that it is very complex. She has examined the goddesses like Durga, Saraswati and Kali and has come to the conclusion that 'despite the rich tradition of goddess reverence, the human female has been and continues to be tremendously undervalued.' At the same time she also points out that the Brahmanical Hindu tradition has supported a rich tradition of mythology in which the feminine principle finds an important place. In other words it offers a possibility to Indian women to sieze the opportunity and feel empowered. In this context it will be interesting to note the feelings of the women who participate publicly in the festivals meant for female goddesses. The festivals are Holi, Sitala Mata, Dasamata and Gangaur which are celebrated in Rajasthan. Gold[46] has shown that 'women in rituals celebrating female power, demonic or divine, make claims for female worth and community that run counter the male-authored devaluation and fragmentation.'

In the case of Laksmi Vrat-katha in a rice growing area the relationship is slightly different. First of all the Vrat-katha was written by a person who was trying to challenge the Brahmanical tradition of caste order and patriarchy through Lakshmi, a female goddess who upheld the just principle of her husband. She gets identified with an ordinary woman who could be considered as Lakshmi if and only if she keeps her house clean, does not waste food grains, and obeys her husband and observes Laksmi *puja* on Thursdays. The society also recognizes the essential role of women in the management of food economy once the rice is harvested. This role of a manager was accorded to her because the agrarian society had undergone the period of scarcity and prosperity when it was important to save each and every grain for the hard time. Since women of the household take charge of those activities society recognized the contributions of the women. At the same time being a part of the Sanskritization, in the words of Pintchman, the patriarchy undervalues women. Still it is relatively more tolerant towards the women in general and baby girls in particular compared to the wheat growing areas. In other words as discussed above, the rice related culture carves out a niche for women within the patriarchal social structure. Interestingly, the Bengali

---

[45] Pinchman, Tracy (1994) *The Rise of the Goddess in the Hindu Tradition* (State University of New York Press, NY) pp. 213-4.

[46] Gold, Ann. Grodzins (2000) 'From Demonic Aunt to Gorgeous Bride: Women Portray Female Power in North Indian Festivals', in Leslie, Julia and Mary McGee(eds.) *Invented Identities, The Interplay of Gender Religion and Politics in India* (OUP, Delhi), p.213.

Vrat-katha doesn't accord the same type of status to ordinary women though Laksmi is an important goddess and is being worshipped alone. As in Oriya society, the girl child is not treated badly. Maybe goddess Durga plays an important role in addition to rice culture. Similarly the status of women is relatively better in South India than in North India. Goddess Laksmi is worshipped alone but the Vrat-kathas don't acknowledge the essential role of women. Other local traditions may explain the above phenomenon.[47]

Conclusion

Thus it is noticed that the status of women in a rice-cultivated economy of India is relatively better in comparison to the wheat growing economy. The sex ratios in rice growing areas are higher than that of the wheat growing areas. Similarly the survival of female children is much better in the former economy than that of the latter. The explanations are being offered in terms of the labor requirement of each crop. However, research shows that even though the area under rice is more than 80 percent the female work participation rate does not cross 20 percent. So it was felt that the culture plays a major role in determining the status of women.

An analysis of rice-related culture showed that rice plays an important role in the lives of the inhabitants of the rice growing areas. Among all the food grains only rice has been treated as sacred. Rice is used in almost all the important social and religious functions of an agrarian economy. Each stage of its production is marked by a ritual. Rice symbolizes the presence of a goddess. Each region has a different name for the deities but they represent prosperity and well-being and fertility. One such goddess is Laksmi who is worshipped in the rice growing areas of India namely, Orissa and Bengal. Goddess Laksmi has been an important goddess in India in general and in the rice growing areas in particular. She is worshipped alone and she has a particular day to herself. But in wheat growing areas she is worshipped along with lord Ganesh. Vrat-kathas relating to Laksmi are full of the praises of her power. For instance,

Bengal has three Vrat-kathas for goddess Laksmi which are recited in different Laksmi *pujas*. In each story it is shown how people have benefited by worshipping her. Orissa also has a Vrat-katha which is recited by the women of the household on the occasion of the *puja*. This Vrat-katha, however, was rewritten in the sixteenth century by a social

---

[47] All the Vrat-kathas have been collected and will be published in the form of a book.

reformer, Balaram Das, who was influenced by the bhakti movement. This story not only challenged the caste order through purity and pollution in relation to cooked food but also allowed untouchables to enter the houses and questioned the patriarchy to some extent. In addition, the Vrat-katha unlike other stories of Laksmi, captures the contributions of the women as the managers of the food grains. In other words, the myth in the form of Laksmi Vrat-katha has become legitimized in the society because it was taken up by a social reformer consciously for making people aware of the contributions of women.

PART IV

ONE AND MANY: MULTIPLICITY AND MANIFESTATIONS OF THE GODDESS

CHAPTER TWELVE

THE GODDESS AND ECOLOGICAL SENSITIVITY: THE CULTIVATION OF EARTH KNOWLEDGE

CHRISTOPHER KEY CHAPPLE

Ecological sensitivities and sensibilities can be seen woven throughout classical Sanskrit literature that pertains to the goddess and in ancient and continuing rituals that honor the Devi. In this chapter, we will explore Vedic references to the Earth and to the river goddess Sarasvati as well as key passages venerating the earth goddess in the *Prthivi Sukta* of the *Atharva Veda.* We will then turn to a discussion of Prakrti within Samkhya philosophy, the feminine principle of worldly creation. We will examine the story of the World within the Rock from the *Yogavasistha*, which narrates how Kali dances forth the creation of the world. The chapter will close with a brief survey of contemporary work by women scholars and activists in creating dance dramas, artwork, and rituals in honor of the earth.

The Vedic Tradition

In the *Rig Veda*, heaven and earth cooperate to create the bounty needed to support humankind:

> May Heaven and Earth make food swell plenteously for us,
> All-knowing Father, Mother, wondrous in their works.
> Pouring out bounties, may, in union, both the Worlds,
> All beneficial, send us gain, and power, and wealth.
> —*Rig Veda* VI: 70, 6[1]

[1] Ralph T.H. Griffith, *The Hymns of the Rigveda: Translated with a Popular Commentary* (Delhi: Motilal Banarsidass, 1973), p. 329.

Other verses of the *Rig Veda* discuss specific elements:

> The waters in the sky, the waters of rivers,
> the waters in wells whose source is the ocean,
> may all these sacred waters protect me.
> —*Rig Veda* VII: 49, 2[2] (Dwivedi, p. 181)

> May plants, the waters, and sky preserve us,
> And woods and mountains with their trees for tresses…
> May the swift wanderer, Lord of refreshments,
> List our songs, who speeds through cloudy heaven.
> And may the waters, bright like castles, hear us,
> As they blow onward from the cloven mountain.
> —*Rig Veda* V:41,11-12 (Dwivedi, p. 59)

The praise hymns of the *Rig Veda* extol the elements (*mahabhutas*), giving recognition to earth, to water, to fire, and to air.

Sarasvati appears several times in the *Rig Veda.* In one hymn to the Asvin twin solar deities, the poet (*rishi*) proclaims that Sarasvati accepts sacrificial offerings, regards her to be a "mighty flood" that "with her light illuminates [and] brightens every pious thought" (*Rig Veda* I:5.12, Griffith, p. 3). She was regarded simultaneously as a naturally occurring river and a goddess, a common conflation of supernatural deity as manifested through a physical reality. Her name appears more than four dozen times in the *Rig Veda*, indicating her importance both as a living river and as a symbol for erudition, abundance, culture, and knowledge. Sarasvati can be seen as a harbinger of ecological insight, combining the physical reality of a river with the symbolic importance of intellect, purity, and refinement.

At a later period in Indian history, perhaps as recent as the fifth century B.C.E., another collection of Vedic hymns was compiled. This document, known as the *Atharva Veda*, compiled a host of medical literature and helped instruct Brahman priests who served as physicians about how to ply their trade for those who needed healing. This lengthy text includes one section in praise of the earth: the *Prthivi Sukta*, or stanzas pertaining to the Earth. It comprises the first 63 verses of the twelfth book of this important work. Because of its extended length and its thematic consistency, it provides a ready window into the earth-consciousness of later Vedic India. Lynn White, Jr., found fault with the early Judeo-Christian biblical material of Western religious traditions, suggesting that

---

[2] As translated by O.P. Dwivedi, *Environmental Crisis and Hindu Religion,* (New Delhi: Gitanjali Publishing House, 1987).

it paved the way for the rape of nature. In reading the *Prthivi Sukta*, one gets an opposite impression. The rishi-poet does not urge his or her listener to ravage the earth, does not provide advice on how to obtain food, nor lauds the human as superior to the earth in any way. Instead, the *Prthivi Sukta* describes the abundance of the earth and asks that she protect humans.

The *Prthivi Sukta* includes verses that praise the earth, petition the earth for protection, and provide admonition that the earth must be protected.[3] Two major terms are used to refer to the earth, both of which come to be associated with names of goddesses: Prthivi and Bhumi, with variations yielding the terms Prthivima and Bhu Devi. The Earth is always referred to in the feminine gender. The text acknowledges that all works and all religious endeavors rely upon the earth, and that medicines arise from the earth. It includes two stanzas that seem to speak directly to our current environmental situation, one referring to water pollution (30) and the other to the development of roads (47).

The praise verses of the *Prthivi Sukta* provide rich imagery. The author lists many attributes, noting that the Earth is "adorned with many hills, plains, and slopes" (2). The physical landscape is described in some detail, with the author proclaiming that "Upon the earth lie the oceans, many rivers, and other bodies of water" (3), that "On her body food is grown everywhere and on her the farmer toils" (4), and that "The earth is the home of cows, horses, and of birds" (5). The text continues with additional details on the grandeur of the earth: "Sacred are your hills, snowy mountains, and deep forests" (11). Verse 56 praises a variety of earth's places:

> Irrespective of the place and region where we are,
> whether in a rural area, in the woods,
> in the battleground, or in a public place,
> may we always sing your praises.

The earth is seen as the "wish fulfilling cow (*kamadhenu*)" (45, 61) and lauded for her expansiveness and generosity: "You are borderless, you are the world-mother of all things, you are the provider of all things in life" (61). Acknowledgement can be found of human reliance on the earth in several verses, such as "My mother is this earth, and I am her son" (12), "You are the world for us and we are your children" (16), with reference

[3] The translations from the *Prthivi Sukta* have been rendered by O.P. Dwivedi and edited by the author as part of a forthcoming book project.

to her support for the many races and nations found on earth (11) and "The five races of human beings [that] live here" (42).

While these verses typologize the various functions and forms of earth, the *Prthivi Sukta* also carries a clearly anthropocentric message. In verse after verse, the author petitions the earth to render protection and succour to human beings: "May the world Mother provide us with a wide and limitless domain for our livelihood" (1), "may she spread prosperity for us all around" (2), "May the Earth confer on us all riches" (3), "May that Earth replenish us in plenty with cattle and food" (4), "May that Earth protect us, grant us prosperity, and bestow upon us vigor" (5), "May you give us wealth and good fortune!" (6), "May She make our nation strong, powerful, and studded with splendour" (8), and so forth. Nearly every verse ends with a request for enhanced well-being. An extended set of verses also discusses interpersonal relationships, with the author asking that the Earth spare one from hatred and gird one in battle against enemies (18, 24, 25, 32, 37, 41). Additionally, several verses ask for protection from the harm and danger to be found in the natural world:

> Keep away from us venomous reptiles
> such as snakes and scorpions which cause thirst when they sting;
> keep away those poisonous insects which cause fever,
> and let all those terrible crawling creatures
> which are born in the rainy season keep away from us.. (46)
> Keep all menacing animals away from harming us,
> such as the lion, the tiger, the wolf, the jackal.. (49).

The *Prthivi Sukta* does not only extol nature but sees a need to profit from nature and to be wary of nature's dark side.

In a metaphysical sense, the text reflects the Samkhya philosophy of the great elements (*mahabhuta*s) and their relationship to the subtle elements (*tanmatra*s) and the sense orgrans (*buddhindriya*s). The *Samkhya Karika* associates the earth, also referred to as *prthivi*, with the sense of smell and fragrance, a theme found in several verses of the *Prthivi Sukta*:

> O Mother Earth!
> Instill in me with abundance that fragrance which emanates from you
> and from your herbs and other vegetation, as well as waters.
> This fragrance is sought by all celestial beings. (23)
> O Mother Earth!
> May that perfume come to us in abundance,
> the perfume that is in the lotus,
> the fragrance worn by gods when the sun marries the dawn.. (24)

O Mother Earth!
The fragrance that you have granted to men and women
and which is also present in horses, deer, and elephants,
shines like the radiance in maidens.
May that radiance come to us.. (25)
Bless us with… fragrance…
Grant us peace, tranquillity,
fragrant air and other worldly riches (59).

Several other verses also refer to the great elements, particularly fire (*agni*) and water (*ap*). Alluding to earlier texts of the *Rg Veda* and the *Upanisads*, the *Prthivi Sukta* asserts that the earth arose from the water of the ocean (8). For a series of verses it extols the power of fire, claiming that fire energizes the earths's herbs and medicinal plants, as well as the clouds that give rain to the earth (19-21).

The gods are spoken of in relationship to the earth. Agni, the aniconic god of fire, has been mentioned above. Two anthropomorphized gods find special mention: Indra and Vishnu. In the *Rg Veda*, Indra conquers the dragon (*Vrtra*) of drought, frees the monsoon, and allows structure to emerge on earth (*RV* X:125). Verse 37 echoes this episode, which states that the Earth chose "Indra as her companion rather than Vrtra." The text refers to Indra as the consort of the Earth (6), states that she is "protected by the great strength of Indra" (18). It also states that she provides the place where "Indra is invoked to drink Soma," the substance used for religious inspiration (38). Verse 10 alludes to the famous stanza in the *Rg Veda* that describes how Vishnu created the earth in three great strides.

The Earth supports religious ritual and sacrifice and ensures social stability. She yields the medicine used in healing practices (17, 19, 20, 62). She houses the "sacred universal fire" (6), the "ever-vigilant and all-caring gods" (7), and serves as the site for sacrifices:

Events for the welfare of all
are consecrated by performing sacrifices on this Earth.
Good and virtuous people assemble here to perform such functions.
Strong sacrificial posts are erected here for making offerings.
Here is where spirituality gets imparted.. (13).
Oblations and sacrifices are duly performed for Mother Earth.. (22).
Places for oblations can be found on this Earth.
Here can be found the poles for the sacrifice.
This is where the sacrificial post is situated.
This is where Brahmans well-versed in the Vedas recite hymns.. (38).
It is upon this Earth
where the Seven Sages, the creators of worlds,
performed sacrifices and austerities,

chanted hymns, and carried out sacred rites (39).

In both an expansive, cosmic sense, the Earth contains all things. The Earth also provides the specific ground upon which human beings may acknowledge their dependence on the Earth through religious activities.

The *Prthivi Suka* also proclaims that, even in light of her magnitude and magnificence, humans need to do their best to not harm or injure the Earth. Along with petitioning the Earth for her blessings, the author of the text puts forth an admonition that the Earth must be guarded from human interference in the following passages: "May no person oppress her" (2), "May we never harm your vital parts" (35), "Please do not become outraged by our destructive tendencies" (45), and "May I have the strength to subjugate those who poison our Mother Earth" (54). Toward the end of the text, the author's vehemence increases: "If anyone tries to harm you, destroy them with the same ease as when a horse shakes off the dust on it" (57) and "May I have the ability of swiftness and strength so that I am able to vanquish those who exploit you" (58). These verses seem to anticipate a misuse of the earth and perhaps reflect some of the rapid changes inflicted by human interference during the settling of the Gangetic Plains.

Two verses in particular indicate that human impact was being felt upon the earth. In verse 30, a specific warning is given in regard to water pollution.

> O Mother Earth!
> May our bodies enjoy only the clean water.
> May you keep away from us that which is polluted
> and may we do only the good deeds.

Though pollution can arise from many sources, this verse indicates an awareness that unclean water can lead to disease and death. Verse 47 acknowledges that human expansion and road building have altered the face of the earth. In the following verse, the author states that has been freely given by the earth, but asks for protection on these roads:

> O Mother Earth!
> You have given people many roads
> where both the chariots move and bullock-carts with grains ply,
> where both the virtuous and wicked people travel.
> Protect these networks of transportation from robbers and thugs.
> May we be victorious and may we receive
> the auspicious and benevolent things in life.

The first verse asks for wholesome resources; the second verse acknowledges that trouble can arise where human beings congregate. If we extend the metaphor from this juxtaposition, human beings need clean resources to flourish. If these become endangered, then stability can founder. In an expression of proto-environmentalism, and in a sense responding to the problem articulated above, verse 27 makes an appeal for venerating the Earth, both for her sake, and for the sake of human welfare:

> We venerate Mother Earth,
> the sustainer and preserver of forests, vegetation,
> and all things that are held together firmly.
> She is the source of a stable environment.
> Without remembering Mother Earth, forests disappear, water becomes foul, and the air becomes unbreatheable.

Samkhya Philosophy: Earth and Nature as Prakrti

In the articulation of Samkhya philosophy during the classical era (ca. 200 C.E.), the feminine principle, known as Prakrti, lies at the root of all manifest existence.[4] From her creative, dancing powers the building blocks of experience arise. Prakrti's field serves as the repository for all karmic impressions (*samskaras*) and inclinations toward particular states of being in the world (*bhava*). From this constellation of forces arises a fixed identity (*ahamkara*) and the operations of the thinking mind (*manas*). The sensory organs and the action organs coalesce to bring the subtle body into contact with the external world of the five great elements. Reality and experience make themselves manifest (*vyakta*) through the operations of this matrix clearly designated with the marker of the feminine. Prakrti serves two purposes. She provides experience for the enjoyment and perhaps amusement of consciousness. She also, when her dance comes to an end, allows consciousness to reside in its own nature of nonjudgmental awareness, referred to as a state of liberation (*moksha*). Without the feminine creative principle, life would be impossible. Some have argued that the Samkhya system and its Vedantic successors remain skeptical and critical of the manifest world.[5] I have argued that the

---

[4] See Gerald J. Larson, *Classical Samkhya: An Interpretation of Its History and Meaning* (New Delhi: Motilal Banarsidass, 1969) and Frank R. Podgoski, *Ego, Revealer-Concealor: A Key to Yoga* (Lanham, Maryland: University Press of America, 1984) and recent studies by Knut Jacobsen.

[5] See Rita DasGupta Sherma, "Sacred Immanence: Reflections of Ecofeminism in Hindu Tantra" in Lance Nelson, editor, *Purifying the Earthly Body of God:*

reciprocity between the feminine, creative realm of manifestation and the male-gendered 'aloof' state of pure awareness, indicates a recognition of the importance of enjoying the bodily and sensory realms as a key feature of Indian philosophy. This celebration of the manifest world is expressed in aesthetic theory and abundantly in evidence in India's rich traditions of color, flavor, movement, and an overall appreciation of beauty.[6]

In Samkhya and Tantra, the five great elements (*mahabhutas*) appear when in proximity to the five subtle elements within the human body (*tanmatras*). The world is experienced through the five great senses or gods of perception (*buddhindriya*). The earth (*prthivi*) reveals itself through the sense of smell (*gandha*) linked to the human nose (*nasa*). Water (*jal/ap*) reveals itself through taste (*rasa*) found in the mouth (*mukha*). Fire (*agni/tejas*) reveals form (*rupa*) experienced through the eyes (*aksa*). Wind (*vayu*) unveils touch (*sparsha*) known through the human organ of the skin (*tvak*). Space (*akasha*) contains all sound (*sabda*) which is perceived through the ears (*karna*). The outer world only emerges when the sense organs are directed by the mind to identify as such. The particulars of physical reality obtain fruition only on contingency. They only take shape in the context of human presence. Without the basic orientation and directionality and intentionality of the mind, no world can be known. The world and consciousness exist in reciprocity.

In the tenth century, the Kashmiri philosopher Abhinavagupta took the seemingly dualistic ideas of the Samkhya system and transformed them into an expression of a near-Sufi like celebration of spiritualized consciousness, in which all phenomena provide an occasion for an experience of bliss.[7] This ascetic suggests that all interaction between awareness and objectivity contains the potential of revealing "non-dual

---

Religion and Ecology in Hindu India (Albany: State University of New York Press, 1998), p. 102-103.

[6] See my articles "India's Earth Consciousness" in *The Soul of Nature: Celebrating the Spirit of the Earth* edited by Michael Tobias and Georgianne Cowan (New York: Plume, 1994), pp. 145-150) and "Hinduism and Deep Ecology" in *Deep Ecology and World Religions: New Essays on Sacred Grounds*, edited by David Landis Barnhill and Roger S. Gottlieb (State University of New York Press, 2001), pp. 60-75.

[7] See Paul E. Murphy, *Triadic Mysticism: The Mystical Theology of the Saivism of Kashmir* (Delhi: Motilal Banarsidass, 1986), John Hughes, *Self-Realization in Kashmir Shaivism: The Oral Teachings of Swami Lakshmanjoo* (Albany: State University of New York Press, 1994), and Paul Mueller-Ortega. *The Triadic Heart of Siva: Kaula Tantricism of Abhinavagupta in the Non-Dual Shaivism of Kashmir* (Albany: State University of New York Press, 1989.

Ultimate Reality." [8] Notably, unlike Advaita Vedanta, which refers to the world as illusory, the Sakta philosophy associated with Tantra, building on the principles of Samkhya, "posits the world of plurality as real."[9] This affirms the importance of knowing the nature of the world as key to the discovery of consciousness and hence liberation.

The *Yogavasistha*, which appeared in its current form almost a millenia ago, helps to demonstrate the importance of feminine creativity in Indian tradition. As noted by Karen Pechilis, this text provides a prototype for the emergence of Hindu female gurus in the story of Queen Chudala, the young woman who achieves highest spiritual knowledge and then becomes the teacher of her husband.[10] Stories of female spiritual prowess and creativity can be found laced through this epic-sized tale,[11] indicating that the affirmation of the reality of the world results in the espousal of a reverent attitude toward the role of the feminine, the emblem and expression of manifest reality. One particular story sequence extoling the power of the feminine can be found in the second section of the *Nirvana Prakarana*, the last book of the *Yogavasistha*. In this tale, "The World Within the Rock," Vasistha narrates his own vision of how the goddess Kalaratri or Bhagavati created and held under her power the world of cities, forests, and mountains. Vasistha then describes discovering these creative abilities within himself as he performs progressive concentration (*dharana*) on the elements and senses within his own body.

Elements and Consciousness in the *Yogavasistha*

In the sixth book of the *Yogavasistha*, the sage Vasistha narrates how a celestial woman, identified as Kalaratri or Kali, brought him into a great rock (one can visualize perhaps the great sculptures of Mahabalipuram), where she showed him her husband, a sleeping "creator," identified as Rudra or Siva. In proximity to her husband, the goddess begins to dance, emitting from her body the entire world.

---

[8] Grace E. Cairns, *Man as Microcosm in Tantric Hinduism* (New Delhi: Manohar, 1992), p. 45.

[9] Ibid.

[10] Karen Pechilis, ed., *The Graceful Guru: Hindu Female Gurus in India and the United States* (New York: Oxford University Press, 2004), pp. 16-17, 19, 26-27.

[11] Another tale that highlights the elevated status of womanhood is the story of Lila, who through her worship of the goddess Sarasvati, both attains *samadhi* and releases her husband, King Padma, from the clutches of death. See "The Story of Lila" in *Vasistha's Yoga*, translated by Swami Venkatesananda (Albany: State University of New York Press, 1993), pp. 55-91.

The goddess—Prakrti or Kali—who takes Vasistha on this remarkable journey comes by many names in this narrative.

> She is called by the names Jaya and Siddha
> because she is accompanied by victory and prosperity at all time.
> She is also designated as Aparajita or the invincible,
> Virya the mighty, Durga the inaccessible,
> and is likewise renowned as Uma,
> composed of the powers of the three syllable om.
> She is called the Gayatri from being chanted by everybody
> and Savitri from being the matrix of all things.
> She is named Sarasvati for giving us insight
> into what appears before our sight.
> (NPII:84:10-12) (Mitra & Arya 1998: 283).

She is not portrayed here as unconscious or inert or carrying any negative connotation. To the contrary, Vasistha states that

> All cities and continents, mountains and islands,
> Hang on her agency as a string of gems around her neck.
> She holds together all parts of the world
> and influences her force as vibration (*spanda*) in them all ...
> (NPII:84:20) (Mitra & Arya 1998: 284).
> She is the one great body of the cosmos.
> It is this power which supports the earth, with all its seas
> and islands, and its forests, deserts, and mountains
> (NPII:84:22) (Mitra & Arya 1998: 284).

With elegant phrases, Vasistha describes the creation and maintenance of the world through the dance of Kali:

> Dancing with her outstretched arms which looked like a forest of tall pines... arrayed with all kinds of weapons….
>
> She contains the world in the vibration of her mind (*cit-spanda*) (NPII:85:1-4) (Mitra & Arya 1998: 286-87).

This vision of the goddess caused Vasistha to observe that "the world was seated in his own heart" (NPII:87:2) (Mitra & Arya 1998: 294). He saw that his spiritual part was purely *akasha* or space (NPII:87:9) (Mitra & Arya 1998: 294); from this space came the movement of the intellect (*buddhi*), the sense of self, then the mind; from this emerges the five senses and five organs, and then, from the subtle elements (*tanmatras*), the world (NPII:87:12) (Mitra & Arya 1998: 295).

At first, Vasistha watched Kali generate the world through her body and senses. He then saw the world emerge from his own body. He saw that whatever arose in the world was not different from his own body (NPII:87:44) (Mitra & Arya 1998: 297). On the one hand, he declared the world to be empty (*sunya*), an epithet for space or *akasha*; on the other hand, he saw himself fill the world (NPII:87:45-47) (Mitra & Arya 1998: 298).

Vasistha first observed Kali's creation of the world as external to himself. He then saw himself manifest in his own body the creative powers he had seen in the goddess. He became the goddess, playing with the creation of the world:

> Thinking myself the master of the earth, I became amalgamated with the earth... I thought myself as the sovereign of the whole...I became changed into the earth's forests and woods, which grew as hairs on my body... I was full of villages and valleys, of hills and dales, and of infernal regions and caverns; I was the great mountain chain and connected the seas and their islands (NPII:87:58-61) (Mitra & Arya 1998: 299).

Vasistha's descriptions rejoice in the beauties of nature and lament with the suffering and sorrow of warfare and tornadoes and drought. At the end of chapter 88 he states,

> I smile with the smiling lotuses, when they are slightly shaken in their beds by the gentle winds of heaven, and I parade with the gliding of rivers, to the ocean of eternity for final extinction (NPII:88:23) (Mitra & Arya 1998: 301-302).

Vasistha repeats again and again that ultimately all things are empty (*sunya*) and that all things are constructed by the mind. But with wild exuberance and clear, pure enjoyment he revels in describing the results of the creative process. He proclaims he is united with valleys and forests of the earth, and then, in the next chapter, turns to watery forms of creation:

> I saw the waters ascending and riding on the back of the clouds,
> and there joining with the lightning as their hidden consorts
> (NPII:90:20-21) (Mitra & Arya 1998: 305).

Following the progression of elements as found in Samkhya, he describes the forms and manifestations of fire:

> It discloses the field to day-light and ripens the grain by dispelling darkness from the face of the earth. It washes also the glassy bowl of

heaven, and glitters in the dewey waters upon its face (NPII:91:12) (Mitra & Arya 1998: 307).

Having ascended from earth through water and fire,
he then sees himself as air:

Then blew the winds, with the soft breath of the shepherds horns, and drove away the clouds like cattle, and blasted the showering raindrops that served to set down the dust of the earth (NPII:92:16) (Mitra & Arya 1998: 313).

In one beautiful passage pertaining to wind (*vayu*), Vasistha recounts:

I became the breeze with a desire to view the beauty
of the lovely plants all about me,
and to smell the sweetness of the fragrant blossoms of Jasmine,
and I taught the grass, leaves, creepers, and the straw the art of dancing.
(Venkatesanda 1984: 408).

Having gone beyond the airy realm into space, he witnessed a perfect being. This Siddha had descended to the earth and shared with Vasistha his own insights into the transitory nature of life. This personification of space took the form of a saint and shared his story:

I wandered on the tops of hills and roved in the airy regions on the summits of the Meru Mountains. I traveled to the cities of many a ruler of men, and met with nothing of any real good to me anywhere. I saw the woody trees, the same land of earth cities, and the same sort of fleshy animal bodies everywhere; I found them all frail and transitory. I saw that no riches, no friends, no relatives nor enjoyments of life were able to preserve any one from the clutches of death. (NPII:93:56-58) (Mitra & Arya 1998: 321).

As the story of the World within the Rock draws to a close, Vasistha announces that he sees things as none other than a dream, and exhorts Rama likewise to grow into this wisdom so that his delusion might also disappear.

The story of the World within the Rock carries a fascinating account of how Samkhya categories came to be employed within the larger stories of the Saiva tradition. Siva is depicted as a remote, meditating figure, like a king who has lost interest in his domain. The goddess Kali, in ghostly form, emits the world as a shadow when she comes close (*samyoga*) to her beloved. In poetic detail, Vasistha articulates the relationship between the senses (*buddhidriyas*) and the subtle elements (*tanmatras*) and the gross elements (*mahabhutas*) of earth, water, fire, air, and space. He sees the entire manifest world within his own body. He receives wisdom from a sage and then returns to the court, taking up his task of offering instruction to Rama.

This particular story is noteworthy because Vasistha is not telling a story about someone else. He is telling Rama about his own meditation experiences, and in the process instructing Rama how to meditate in succession on the different *tattvas* of the Samkhya system. By gaining intimacy with the fundamental functions of nature in the form of the five elements, Vasistha describes in detail how to experience meditation by concentrating upon and appreciating the beauties of nature.

In this story, Kali shows the processes through which the world emerges and demonstrates the dynamic, living relationship between the material of the world and the processes of sense perception, all of which are in service of consciousness (*cit*). The story of the World within the Rock tells of a repeated return to the world of manifestation and creativity, followed with yet another ascent into a state of abeyance and removal from worldly entanglements. In each instance of creative engagement, the world of the senses and elements is described in loving detail, with a constant reminder of its beautiful yet chimerical and fleeting quality.

This story takes the reader into space, leading one to a state of purified, powerful awareness (*cit-shakti*, IV:34). It provides an interpretation of how the elements of Samkhya fit with the Kashmir Saivaite teaching of Spanda. By having the dance of the goddess reveal the power of consciousness itself, the *Yogavasistha* revises Samkhya and brings it into a world of its own special form of nondualism. It affirms and celebrates the story of the world by spinning a beautiful tale about the process of its emergence. While affirming, almost reluctantly, the importance of the solitary, aloof, detached meditating yogi, it simultaneously delights in the wondrous beauty of the goddess and the elemental world she creates. It draws the reader into sense of immediacy and rapport with the elements. The poetic exuberance of this narrative underlines the unwillingness of the *Yogavasistha* to denigrate and reject the lessons to be learned by a close observance of and intimacy with the natural world. The telling of the *Yogavasistha* stories themselves can perhaps be sufficient to establish one in an imaginative space sufficient to effect subtle transformation, into a state appreciative of beauty and the creative powers of the goddess.

Contemporary Environmentalism and the Goddess

I would like to highlight some of the connections between the representations of nature as the manifestation of the goddess, and the role of contemporary women in the environmental movement in India, as well as the emergence of Green Yoga in the United States. First, the passages we have encountered from the Vedas and the *Yogavasistha* underscore the sanctified role of the feminine in understanding nature. The trope of "Mother Earth" is carried out in exquisite detail from Samkhya through Tantra and Puranic cosmology. These traditions refer to the manifest world as an emanation of Prakrti, the creative principle and matrix of all things apart from consciousness. Even in Jainism, the cosmos, consisting of hell realms, the earth (Jambudvipa), and the heavens, is depicted in the form of a woman.[12] The body of the mother provides the context for all experience, from the smell of the earth to the power of human memory. Consequently, women logically can be seen as having a primal connection with the earth, and hence a deep responsibility for her well-being.

Vandana Shiva is perhaps India's most well-known environmental activist. She has championed the remembrance of the Bishnoi movement three hundred years ago, led by Amrita Devi, a woman who inspired a movement of three hundred people, some of whom "sacrificed their lives to save their sacred *khejri* trees by clinging to them."[13] Vandana Shiva has brought attention to the Chipko Movement that has worked at forestation projects in the Himalayas, and herself is an international spokeswoman on the topic of seed preservation.

Vijaya Nagarajan of the University of San Francisco, in addition to founding a non-profit organization for the promotion of nature awareness through backpacking, has documented the role of women's domestic art in giving praise and acknowledgement to beauty and nature's evanescence. Each morning throughout Tamil Nadu, women adorn their thresholds with intricate designs crafted of rice flour. These designs are inspired by the Yantra patterns that celebrate the intersection of the Yoni (symbolized by the downward triangle) with the Lingam (symbolized by the upward triangle). The Yoni represents the manifest, visible aspects of the earth and of Prakrti; the Lingam stands for consciousness or Purusa. By bending toward the earth before the glimmer of dawn, these women humble themselves, making an offering to be consumed throughout the day by ants, keeping the house pestilence-free while inviting all guests to cross over a sacred threshold to enter the home. In describing their work, one woman commented on the connection between the decline of the

---

[12] Pratapaditya Pal, *The Peaceful Liberators: Jain Art from* India (Los Angeles: Los Angeles County Museum of Art, 1995), pp. 220-221.

[13] Vandana Shiva, "Women in the Forest." In *Ethical Perspectives on Environmental Issues in India*, edited by George A. James (New Delhi: A.P.H. Publishing Corporation, 1999), p. 84.

ozone layer and the increasing neglect of the Kolam due to the pressures of modern life: "We are losing the ability to give to each other and to give to God. We are forgetting that we need to practice giving constantly... We used to give to each other. We used to give to the gods goddesses.... We have to learn to give again."[14] The women of Tamil Nadu see the earth as Bhu Devi. Nagarajan comments that "Bhu Devi acts as a reminder of the fragility of the soils and the earth; she is a mnemonic device serving to shape the conceptualization of the natural world." Another of her informants states that "Bhumi Devi is our mother. She is everyone's source of existence. Nothing would exist without her. The entire world depends on her for sustenance and life. So, we draw the Kolam first to remind ourselves of her."[15]

Commenting on the adaptation of traditional nature-based rituals to modern life, Madhu Khanna of the Indira Gandhi National Centre for the Arts in New Delhi, sees Durga Puja, widely practiced throughout Bengal, a way to invite seasonal agricultural festivals into the city. She notes that "the ritual, as it exists today, has the potential to inspire urban dewellers to use symbols rooted in the earth for ecological activism."[16] Similarly, Vasudha Narayanan of the University of Florida writes about the use of the performing arts to convey an environmental message, "communicating the tragedy of ecological disasters using such art forms as Bharata Natyam."[17] She cites in particular Mallika Sarabhai's dance drama about the Chipko Movement performed in "Shakti: The Power of Women" and Sujatha Vijyaranghavan's work, choreographed by Radha in Chennai, that condemns pollution by dramatizing the rescue of a poisoned world by Lord Shiva, whose throat turns blue as a consequence.

Laura Cornell, founder of the Green Yoga Association, has advanced a Green Yoga Values Statement that notes "Yoga developed in the context

---

[14] Vijaya Nagarajan, "Rituals of Embedded Ecologies: Drawing Kolams, Marrying Trees, and Generating Auspiciousness." In Christopher Key Chapple and Mary Evelyn Tucker, eds., *Hinduism and Ecology: The Intersection of Earth, Sky, and Water* (Cambridge, Massachusetts: Center for the Study of World Religions, Harvard Divinity School), pp. 453-454.

[15] Vijaya Nagarajan. "The Earth as Goddess Bhu Devi: Toward a Theory of 'Embedded Ecologies' in Folk Hinduism." In *Purifying the Earthly Body of God: Religion and Ecology in Hindu India* ed. by Lance Nelson (Albany: State University of New York Press, 1998), pp. 272-273.

[16] Madhu Khanna, "The Ritual Capsule of Durga Puja: An Ecological Perspective." In Chapple and Tucker (above), p. 491.

[17] Vasudha Narayanan, "Water, Wood and Wisdom: Ecological Perspectives from the Hindu Traditions" in Richard C. Foltz, ed., *Worldviews, Religion and the Environment* (Belmont, California: Wadsworth Press, 2003), p. 137.

of a close relationship with the earth," and that "the viability of the earth's life systems is in danger." This Values Statement includes a five point action plan for use by practitioners of Yoga worldwide, including to "cultivate an appreciation for and conscious connection with the natural environments in which we live" and to "include care for the environment in our discussion of Yogic ethical practices."[18]

Each of these women has brought to public awareness ways in which the contemporary issue of environmental degradation is being addressed through making a connection between the earth goddess and the current state of the world. From the Himalayas to the north, Rajasthan to the west, Tamil Nadu to the south, and Bengal in the east, women in all corners of India are drawing upon the imagery of the goddess to communicate a modern message. According to traditional Indian philosophy and cosmology, the world is a gendered, feminine place. Throughout the Indian story tradition, women have embodied the power symbolized by numerous goddesses. By giving honor to the earth, women give honor to the goddess and recognize the power of the goddess who resides in themselves. Just as the dancing Bhagavati Kali brings forth the world and stirs the sage Vasistha into deeper awareness and appreciation, so also devotion to the goddess, in both traditional and contemporary forms, can stir the world to an increased sense of urgency in regard to the plight of Mother Earth.

[18] See www.GreenYoga.org.

CHAPTER THIRTEEN

GOMĀ: AN EMBODIMENT OF THE GODDESS

DEEPAK SHIMKHADA

In this paper I propose to examine Gomā, the protagonist of the *Swasthāni Brata Kathā.*[1] Although in the text Gomā is portrayed as an ordinary woman, the extraordinary circumstances in which she was born and the challenges she faced clearly place her in the category of a goddess. If viewed in this way, Gomā is a goddess incarnate. I will demonstrate that Gomā is indeed a goddess in mortal form who, like her counterparts Śati and Pārvati, overcame the obstacles hurled at her by Śiva in order to please him with surrender.

The Swasthāni Brata Kathā, written in the style of a *Pūrāṇa*, allegedly originates in the Kathmandu Valley of Nepal. Although there is no one single author that the Swasthani text can be ascribed to, names of scribes frequently appear in the manuscript colophons with both Buddhist and Hindu origins. The earliest manuscript of the *Swasthāni Kathā* is dated 1573 CE. Its language is Sanskrit, but is written in Newari script. There are over nine hundred manuscripts of the *Swasthāni Kathā* currently preserved in the National Archives in Kathmandu, Nepal.[2]

After narrating the creation story that occurs almost halfway through the text, the *Swasthāni Kathā* suddenly switches to the story of a poor but pious Brahmin couple named Śiva Bhatta and Sati. After many years of devotion to Siddhi Gaṇeśa, the Brahman couple becomes rich and is able to perform even more pious acts of charity as a result. Since they were

---

[1] *Swasthāni Brata Kathā* in Nepali translated by Pundit Viswaraj Sharma, Sarva Hiteisi Company, Varanasi, 1990.

[2] Linda Iltis, *Swastāani Brata Kathā and Newar Women and Ritual in Nepal.* University of Wisconsin, Madison, Wisconsin, 1985, unpublished Ph.D. dissertation.

childless, they prayed again to Siddhi Gaṇeśa, their patron deity, for a child.[3]

As instructed by Gaṇeśa, Śiva Bhatta and Sati went to the temple and waited there for a cow to appear. Cows figure prominently in Hindu mythological texts such as the *Bhāgavatam*, where cow is Krishna's companion and hence he is the protector of the cow.[4] As the cow dropped her dung, Śiva Bhatta caught it in his hands and took it home, where he placed it in a *tasalā* (a rounded cooking vessel in the form of womb) and covered it with another *tasalā* on top. When the old couple opened the container after four days, to their surprise the cow dung had turned into a beautiful baby girl. Since the child was born of cow dung, the parents appropriately named the child Gomā—"Go" means cow and "ma" means mother. Combined the word literally means "cow mother" or "mother cow."

After dropping the dung, the cow disappeared, suggesting the miraculous nature of the cow and Gomā's birth. The cow that appeared just for the purpose of giving birth to Gomā must thus be none other than *Kāmadhenu*, the cow that fulfills one's every desire, as I will discuss later.

Gomā grew rapidly and developed thirty-two *lakshaṇās* (auspicious physical signs). She had a pleasant disposition, her complexion was as bright as pure gold, and her beauty could be compared with the moon.[5] Although everything seemed to be going well, a twist in the story occurs. The throne in Amaravati of Indra, the king of the gods, begins shaking as a result of the intense religious practices and acts of charity performed by Gomā's parents. Frightened, Indra goes to Śiva to request that Śiva Bhatta and Sati do not perform any more religious practices. Śiva agrees.

---

[3] The story begins in chapter nineteen and continues through chapter 31 where the story of Goma ends with a happy ending. Slight variations in story appear in earlier versions. However, my reading of the story is based on the newer version of the text translated by Pundit Viswaraj Sharma.

[4] In Hinduism the cow is held sacred due to the fact that it is very dear to Krishna. This is explained in the Hindu scriptures as follows: *namo brahmaṇya-devāya go-brāhmaṇa-hitāya ca, jagad-dhitāya kṛsnāyagovindāya namo namah.* [*Vishṇu Pūrāṇa* 1.19.65] "I offer repeated obeisances unto Lord Krishna, who is the protector and well-wisher of the cows and the brahmanas. He is also the protector of the entire society. Unto that Lord, who is always satisfying the senses of the cows, I offer my obeisances again and again."

[5] SBK, chapter 30.

It is from this point that Gomā's hardships begin—an odyssey of misfortunes and her total surrender to the goddess Swasthāni.

To please Indra, Śiva comes down to earth while Gomā's parents are performing daily rituals in a nearby river. Disguised as an ascetic, Śiva asks Gomā for alms but Gomā, who is preparing for daily puja inside the house, does not hear his begging. When she finally does hear him she comes running out with alms, but Śiva is already angry, having been provided with the excuse he was looking for. He refuses to accept the alms on the pretext that he had to wait longer than necessary, and curses Gomā for her inattentiveness. The curse compels Gomā to marry a seventy-year-old man when she is barely seven years old—a cruel curse, indeed!

When Gomā turns six, her father secures the help of a matchmaker to find a suitor for her. As fate would have it, the matchmaker cannot find a suitable match. Śiva Bhatta takes on the task himself and looks for a suitor for Gomā. In the meantime, Gomā turns seven. One day as Śiva Bhatta returns home from the failed mission, he meets an old man by the riverbank. His name is Śiva Sharma, a Brahmin who has been looking for a wife since the age of sixteen. Fulfilling Śiva's curse, Śiva Bhatta is compelled to give Gomā to this seventy-year-old man in marriage, who the text clearly states is Śiva in disguise.

Śiva tricks Gomā again, this time into marrying him. After spending some ten years at Gomā's parents' home, Śiva Sharma and Gomā go to a neighboring city where Gomā becomes pregnant. Śiva Sharma leaves Gomā alone on the pretext of finding employment to support her and the infant who would soon be arriving. Instead, he never returns because he is killed by accidentally falling out of a tree. The real Śiva is, of course, immediately transported to Mt. Kailaśa where his wife Pārvati waited for him.

Now Gomā's real struggles begin. Several chapters in the text are devoted to describing her hardships while raising a son. When Pārvati finally notices the injustice done to Gomā, she demands that Śiva free Gomā from her miseries. At Pārvati's insistence, Śiva promises to transport Gomā from her present situation. This is where the *pūjā* and recitation of the *Swasthāni Brata Kathā* come in, but we cannot spend time on the goddess Swasthāni to whom the book is dedicated. It is worth focusing on Gomā's character instead because of her complexity and her association with Śiva.

I now examine the divine nature of Gomā and her place in the text. If Śiva Sharma is Śiva, as is the case here, then Gomā is Śiva's wife. As a wife of Śiva the god, Gomā thus becomes a goddess. She may not be the supreme goddess like Pārvati, but she is nonetheless a goddess in a mortal body. She certainly displays supernatural attributes. For example, she was born of cow dung under supernatural circumstances; she is described as very beautiful, one of the defining characteristics of a goddess, especially Pārvati; and she is also said to have all thirty-two physical signs of auspiciousness.

Even at just seven years old, Gomā was able to understand the principle of karma and in fact soothes her grieving mother when her father decides to marry her to a seventy-year-old Brahmin. A mortal girl would not agree to such a marriage under any circumstances, but Gomā did because she understood divine intervention and perhaps felt a connection with Śiva. In other words, Gomā was not an ordinary human being.

Although there are references to Śiva and the cow in Purāṇic texts, there is no one specific reference linking Śiva with the cow in the same way that Parvati is connected to Śiva. For example, in the *Anusāsana Parva* of the *Mahābhārata*, cows on earth were born from Surabhi, the divine cow obtained as a result of the *Samudra Mathana* (the Churning of the Ocean of Milk), and the foam of milk that flowed like a sea and rose and fell into Śivaloka (the land of Śiva). Śiva did not like this, and when he opened his third eye the flames of his energy caused spots on the cows. The frightened cows took refuge with Chandra, but Śiva's rays followed them there as well. When Prajāpati presented Śiva with a bull for his vehicle, he was pacified.[6] However, the *Drona Parva* of the same text mentions that Śiva appeared as a calf when gods made the earth into a cow and milked her.[7]

Although images of bulls and cows come from the Indus Valley culture, the lack of written documents makes it difficult to connect them as husband and wife the way we do with Śiva and Pārvati. However, the

---

[6] *Pūrānic Encyclopedia, A Comprehensive Work with Special Reference to the Epic and Pūrānic Literature* by Vettem Mani, Delhi: Motilal Banarsidass Publishers Private Limited, 1996, p. 730.

[7] Ibid.

Vedic literature that flourished in the Indus Valley region is full of pastoral symbolism. Lodrick states that "Dyaus, the great father of the Indo Aryan pantheon, the starry Heaven, the bull with the thousand horns, fertilizes *Prithivi,* the Earth Cow, and from this union spring the gods and all creatures."[8] He further states, "The Divine Bull, as Indra, is the seeder who impregnates the cows with his warm *retas* (semen); and as the Sun he is sacrificed for the gain of his warm sap that could nourish vegetation by promoting rain."[9] It should be noted that Parjanya, Soma, Agni, and Rudra are all Vedic gods who are represented as bull gods.[10] Rudra is transformed into Śiva in later Hinduism; hence there should be no difficulty in associating him with a bull, Nandi, as his vehicle. Although Nandi is represented as Śiva's vehicle, most of the bull's characteristics, such as sexuality demonstrated by lust, virility, brute force, and anger are found in Śiva himself. The fact that Śiva is depicted in *urdhalinga* posture (erect penis) is a direct reference to the bull's state of arousal. No Hindu god other than Śiva is symbolized by a phallus. These aspects do tend to superimpose Śiva's qualities on the bull (Nandi), or vice versa. Although we have a preponderance of textual references to connect Śiva with the bull, there is very little to connect him with the cow. However, there is an interesting story that points to Gomā's connection with the cow. After Surabhi, the divine cow, came out of the *Samudra Mathana*, she gave all gods a place to reside in her body except the goddess Lakshmi. Unable to find room in Surabhi's body, Lakshmi settled in the cow's dung.[11] According to this myth, cow dung can thus be considered as the goddess Lakshmi herself. This is borne out by the Hindu ritual of wiping the floor with cow dung on Lakshmi puja day.

When the *Swasthāni Brata Kathā* was composed in the sixteenth century, many symbols were available to represent the character of a young girl called Gomā. However, the author chose a cow. The question is why? The cow is a symbol of prosperity since she gives milk that humans drink for health, and calves that are used for tilling land. In addition, both her dung and urine are used in religious rituals since they have curative properties. Her dried dung is also used as fuel. Because of

---

8 Derrick O. Lodrick, *Sacred Cows, Sacred Places: Origin and Survivals of Animal Homes in India*, Berkeley, California: University of California Press, 1981, p. 51.

9 Ibid.

10 Op. cit, *Pūrānic Encyclopedia*, p. 730.

11 Deryck O. Lodrick, *Sacred Cows, Sacred Places: Origin and Survivals of Animal Homes in India*, Berkeley, California: University of California Press, 1981, p. 4.

this utility, the cow stood for economic value in ancient India and hence was considered as a symbol of Lakshmi, who brought prosperity to humanity. The choice of the cow for the character of Gomā therefore seemed natural, and is more than an accidental choice in the text of the *Swasthāni Brata Kathā*.

Since Gomā played the role of a mortal who lived on earth, she fulfilled the role of cow as giver. The popular Hindu proverb to "give like a cow," which implies being generous without any expectations in return, attests to the view of the cow as a giver. As a giver, Gomā did not expect a great deal from her parents. She gave them companionship, love, and happiness by performing chores around the house. When a seventy-year-old man requested her hand in marriage, she gladly accepted it as her fate and comforted her grieving parents, telling them it was her karma that placed her in that circumstance. Since one of the major qualities of the goddess is to give and love, in the *Swasthāni Brata Kathā* Gomā is associated with the cow.

The most treasured gift in the Vedic period and also in later Hinduism is the cow—the giving away of a milk cow as *dakshinā* has been mentioned in the Rig Veda.[12] When the childless Brahman couple stood in front of the temple of begging for a child, Gaṇeśa gave Gomā to the couple as a gift in a fashion similar to when a *yajamāna* (patron) gives a cow to the officiating Brahman as *dakshinā*. While money given to a priest as *dakshina* could be lost, robbed, or spent in a matter of moments, a milk cow can live much longer, bringing pleasure and happiness to the receiver. Hence the gift of a cow was considered a highly prized gift.

Since Gomā was a gift from Gaṇeśa to Śiva Bhatta and Śati, she can be viewed as a prized *dakshinā,* like the gift of a milk cow to a priest. However, Gomā's connection to the cow and her symbolism in the context of modern Hinduism has not been seriously analyzed. This may change in the future since a number of Western scholars are now taking an interest in the *Swasthāni Brata Kathā* text, as is evident from a number of students from American universities pursuing research in Kathmandu. My own theory is based on evidence whose origins go back to the Vedic times, when the Aryans were supposed to have arrived in India with Vedas and

[12] Doris Srinivasan, *Concept of Cow in the Rigveda*, Delhi: Motilal Banarsidass, 1979, pp. 116-117.

cows, and the cow came to be identified with the mother goddess.[13] Arthur Anthony Macdonell in *Vedic Mythology* cites a rather obscure source about the cow that I find relevant to this essay. He links cows with the clouds because like clouds, cows drip, move, and roar, and their milk is rain. Rain, which is water, is the lifeline of India or any place else for that matter; without it living beings cannot survive. It is not surprising, then, that in the Indian context the cow has been considered the divine mother and her milk is the life-giving source. Macdonell elaborates this concept in a literary context as follows:

> "The atmosphere is often called a sea (*samudra*) as the abode of celestial waters. [I might add that the abode of god Vishnu is the Milky Ocean, which is also in heaven, where he sleeps on the coils of the Śeṣa Nāga, the cosmic serpent of colossal scale.] It is also assimilated to the earth, inasmuch as it has mountains and seven streams which flow there, when the conflict with the demon of drought takes place. Owing to the obvious resemblance the term "mountain" (*parvata*) thus very often in the Rig Veda refers to clouds, the figurative sense being generally clear enough. The word "rock" (*adri*) is further regularly used in a mythological sense for "clouds" as enclosing the cows released by Indra and other gods. The rain clouds as containing the waters, as dripping, moving and roaring, are particularly liable to therimorphism as cows, whose milk is rain."[14]

Attributing everything in nature to the goddess is also attested by a verse in the *Saundarya Lahari* composed by Sri Ādi Śankarāchārya himself where he says of the goddess "Thou art the mind, *ākāsa* (sky) and fire. Thou art water and earth too." (90). Cow thus fits the archetype of the divine mother for a role Gomā performs in the *Swasthāni Brata Kathā* text.

We know from the story that Gomā was born of cow dung, and as it was a miraculous birth, we can assume that the composer of the *Swasthāni Kathā* intended to make Gomā a divine being. Clearly she was a goddess. Now the question arises, which one? Although one could argue philosophically that all gods and goddess are the same because they are simply various forms of one ultimate reality called Brahman, Lakshmi is assigned to Vishnu and hence cannot be the wife of Śiva. We saw earlier

---

13 W. Norman Brown, *Man in the Universe*, Calcutta: Oxford and IBH Publishing Company, 1966, p. 43.

14 Arthur Anthony Macdonell, "Vedic Mythologies" in *Gundries der Indo-Arischen Philologie und Alterunskunde*, ed. G. Buhler, Strassburg: Karl J. Trubner, 1897, p.2.

that Śiva through his vehicle of the bull is connected to the cow. Most significantly, if we follow the story it is implicit that Śiva took the mortal shape of an old man, Śiva Sharma, and married Gomā. Regardless of whether or not her birth is divine, Gomā takes Śiva as her husband. By virtue of being the wife of a great god, Gomā is thus automatically elevated to the status of goddess.

A short bibliography

Jha, D.N., *The Myth of the Holy Cow*, London: Verso, 2004.

Lodrick, Deryck O., *Sacred Cows, Sacred Places: Origins and Survivals of Animal Homes in India*, Berkeley, California: 1981.

Mani, Vettem, *Puranic Encyclopedia, A Comprehensive Work with Special Reference to the Epic and Puranic Literature*, Delhi: Motilal Banarsidass Publishers Private Limited, 1996.

Pal, Pratapaditya and Seid, Betty, *The Holy Cow and Other Animals: A Selection of Indian Paintings from the Art Institute of Chicago* (exhibition catalog), Chicago: The Art Institute of Chicago, 2002.

Prime, Ranchor, *Hinduism and Ecology: Seeds of Truth*, New York: Cassell Publishers Limited, 1992.

Sharma,Viswaraj (translator), *Swasthani Brata Katha* (in Nepali), Varanasi: Sarva Hiteisi Company, 1990.

Srinivasan, Doris, *Concept of Cow in the Rigveda*, Delhi: Motilal Banarsidass, 1979.

CHAPTER FOURTEEN

SARASVATI: GODDESS OF NO HUSBAND, NO CHILD

MAŁGORZATA (MARGARET) KRUSZEWSKA

Resisting Patriarchy

Much of current literature on Hindu goddesses perpetuates a patriarchal interpretation of their roles in mythology and cosmology which reduces them to female "consorts" of the great male divinities Brahma, Visnu and Siva. Feminist methodologies can provide a reconsideration of the pre-Vedic origins of brahmanized goddesses to reveal a multitude of independent goddesses who were not tied to maternal or wifely duties. In particular, Sarasvati, a goddess of no husband and no child, can be reread to show female resistance to the Aryan patriarchal systems of marriage which controlled female sexuality. In *Women in the Vedic Age*, Shakuntala Rao Sastri observes that textual evidence proves that gender tensions existed during Vedic times because of the large numbers of references "in the earlier books, prayers and incantations for restoring concord between a man and his wife."[1]

My research runs contrary to prevalent statements that most Hindu goddesses were blissfully united (and historically assimilated) with male deities. In fact, I believe that the origins of most Indic goddesses, including the later Brahmanical goddesses, show them to have been happily **unattached** to husbands or children. This premise challenges literature describing goddesses as either mother figures or as merely drawing their powers from the male gods. Madhu Khanna, in a recent AAR conference presentation, reiterated this distinction between the independent non-Vedic goddesses and Brahmanical goddesses who

---

[1] Shakuntala Rao Sastri, *Women in the Vedic Age* (Bombay: Bharatiya Vidya Bhavan, 1952), 53.

"derive power from their relationship with the husband."[2] David Kinsley, summarizes the significance of the unmarried village goddesses in his book, *Hindu Goddesses*.

> It has been argued that goddesses in Hindu mythology are generally portrayed as dangerous, violent, and aggressive if they are unmarried and as docile, obedient, and calm if they are married. This reinforces social norms by suggesting that it is necessary for women to marry and express their sexuality in 'safe' ways and under male supervision and authority. In the human realm marriage is assumed not only to complete a woman but to tame her, channeling her dangerous sexual energy in acceptable ways. The god or the male is a civilizing, calming, ordering presence. Alone, goddesses and women are perceived as powerful and dangerous.[3]

Sarasvati, as independent goddess, and the stories of her rejection of both wife and mother roles will be the focus of this paper as central to the discussion of female resistance stories in Hindu mythology. In fact, Sarasvati, unlike even the fiercest goddess Durga, does not acquire her force and power from the gods.

Hopefully, such reconsideration will open the field to fresh research on the Hindu goddesses' unique functions, roles and cosmological significance in origin stories and mythologies of the Indic civilization that have been co-opted and reconfigured to support male hierarchies in current Vedic and non-Vedic practices.

Calling into question an assumption that female=mother=power is necessary to dislodge a belief embraced by both feminist and patriarchal agendas. How is motherhood upheld in patriarchy that is similar to current statements within the women's spirituality movement? Are all females, including goddesses, to be judged primarily in their capacities as mothers and wives? Sarasvati's transformation from powerful river energy to the serene symbol of high civilization occurs at the same time she is assigned the social role of wife and mother. Stories of her reluctance to become either are central to this discussion. I will be focusing on three Puranic tales of her rebellious disassociation from motherhood to wifehood.

My own positioning as a feminist scholar of religion living in the U.S. frames this discussion in reexamining the significance of Sarasvati as goddess of no husband, no child. (I hesitate to identify myself as a "Western" feminist because I was born in Eastern Europe where deeply

---

[2] Madhu Khanna, AAR Annual conference, Philadelphia, Pennsylvania, November 2005.

[3] David R. Kinsley, *Hindu Goddesses: Visions of the Divine Feminine in the Hindu Religious Tradition* (Berkeley: University of California Press, 1988), 203.

embedded matrifocal traditions have always existed). Reading within a hermeneutics of suspicion such as that utilized by feminist Biblical scholar Elisabeth Schussler Fiorenza allows for a fuller, more complex interpretation of the Hindu goddess Sarasvati.[4]

Much criticism has been directed at non-Indian scholars interpreting non-Western traditions.[5] However, I believe that it is precisely because of my position as a non-Indian Devi devotee (and therefore not obliged to fulfill what is still perceived to be the ultimate role for every woman in India) that I am able to reconsider the myths and iconography of Sarasvati as offering another history, one of resistance to patriarchy and as a role model for female *sakti* powers not tied to domesticity and motherhood. As a feminist, and especially as a feminist scholar and practitioner of women's spirituality, my goal is to counter the patriarchal construction of the Mother in religious traditions. The origins of Sarasvati do not support later patriarchal constructs of Her as the nurturing Mother, a role that is often emphasized in times of intensified nation-building.[6]

For women's spirituality scholars working within a feminist hermeneutics, going beyond patriarchal readings of female mother seems a necessary inquiry, even for women who have embraced this traditional role. I am proposing that by acknowledging Sarasvati as She who has no husband, no child, we can begin to redefine for ourselves the female principle in goddesses. One option may be to consider Her as Thought Woman or Thinking Woman, a female role prominent in American Indian cosmogyny on which author Paula Gunn Allen writes extensively in her book *The Sacred Hoop: Recovering the Feminine in American Indian Traditions*. Paula Gunn Allen begins her scholarly collections of creatrix tales with the words, "In the beginning was thought, and her name was Woman."[7] Likewise, feminist scholar Mary Daly also proposes naming Her, The Thinking One.[8] The creation aspect in Sarasvati can then be defined as knowledge Herself, which includes: memory, ancestral wisdom,

---

[4] A hermeneutics of suspicion, as used in feminist methodologies, includes strategies of exposing text ideologies and looking for omitted truths about the "Other."

[5] See Chandra Talpade Mohanty, "Under Western Eyes: Feminist Scholarship and Colonial Discourses," Feminist Review No. 30, Autumn 1988.

[6] For example, in Poland Our Lady of Częstohowa became the political symbol for the Solidarnośc movement.

[7] Paula Gunn Allen, *The Sacred Hoop: Recovering the Feminine in American Indian Traditions* (Boston: Beacon Press, 1986), 11.

[8] Mary Daly, author's notes from presentation at Whittier College, Whittier, California, April, 2005.

expression of sounds, stories, visions, arts, scientific techniques and formulas, healing medicine.

If there is an essence associated with Sarasvati in all her manifestations, it is the power of her flow. She is thunderous river, She is poetic inspiration, She is eloquence of words, She is the creation from sound. The origins of Sarasvati, as forceful river, can then be viewed as a site of rebellion against the historical transition into the patriarchal Aryan rule, when Her powers came to be appropriated, manipulated and, to use a popular scientific term when speaking of water's power, "harnessed" to construct civilization.

Sarasvati's origins and forms are indeed as fluid as water and as ever-changing as fire, two elements she is associated with throughout Vedic texts. Iconographically, Sarasvati sits on or near rushing waterfalls.[9] The transition of Sarasvati the river to Sarasvati the goddess of knowledge, arts and sound remains a puzzle in literature and in the history and evolution of Sarasvati in text and iconography.

In fact, a closer examination of textual references to Sarasvati in early Rig Veda points to a human essence already ascribed. Although not completely in the anthropomorphic form that appears in later Puranic literature, Her attributes already include human-like qualities such as strength, protection and beauty as described in passages from the Rig Veda VII.95.

In statues and paintings Sarasvati is most frequently described as being four-armed, dressed in white or of white complexion (although descriptions do exist of Her being a coral color), holding a *vina*, *mala*, book or manuscript and sometimes a water pot. These implements connect her with sound, the arts, music, knowledge, education, Sanskrit, and the wisdom of science, technology and medicine. Conspicuously missing are any symbols suggesting a maternal or wifely role such as holding a child or offering food. Stories of Sarasvati intentionally dodging, disobeying and punishing her assigned male "husband" (most frequently Brahma but also Vishnu) create a clear picture of her desires to remain independent and childless and not married, pregnant or attached to male gods.

A feminist hermeneutics includes a reconsideration of those socio-religious agendas that transformed Her from an indigenous fierce water deity into a symbol of Vedic civilization. If we begin with the premise that Sarasvati, as the mighty river, existed well before Aryan presence,

---

[9]Although early Vedic references do associate her with the sacrificial fire, I have not found any visual depictions of Sarasvati near or with fire.

then we must also accept that she would not have necessarily been an Aryan goddess. In fact, she may have been revered by the Aryans precisely because of her potential to destroy them. Raganath Airi in his book *Concept of Sarasvati*, discusses the prominence of the Sarasvati River in Aryan mythology, in which Sarasvati was described as "a fortress of iron' (*ayasi puh*) and "the sure defence (*dharnam*)."[10]

Descriptions of Her water movement suggests strength and tremendous force as She rushes down from the Himalayas as a river that is "limitless (*ananta*), unimpaired (*ahruta*), swift-moving (*tresa*), agile (*carinu*), mighty and goes ahead with a roaring sound."[11] Airi further states that historically the area of the Sarasvati river was inhabited by the "Sunahatras, the Purus and the Vasisthas [who] lived on the banks of Sarasvati and it seems that in their steady progress east-wards, the Aryan tribes were stopped for a time in the regions of the Sarasvati and were unable to find their way through the masses of the aboriginals holding the great gateway of India."[12] Sarasvati was then claimed by the Aryans as their own partly because of her significance to the pre-Aryan tribes.

Furthermore, as proven by numerous scholars of ancient India, pre-Aryan cultures were, in general, matriarchal with female-centered practices.[13] Sarasvati's powers would have already been honored by pre-Aryan societies. The historical origins of the arrival of the Aryans remains a highly contested theory, escalated by nationalistic claims by Hindu fundamentalists who dispute the invasion theory.[14] Whether Aryan presence occurred by invasion, migration or as regional geographical movements of internal cult groups is insignificant to the key argument of this paper which places the origins of Sarasvati, who later became the symbol of the Aryan civilization, in pre-Aryan times. Stories of her resistance to marrying Vedic gods and being forced to procreate with them can therefore be read as resistance stories to the oppressions by Aryan patriarchal systems. Donna Jordan's work on the fierce *sakti* element in indigenous cultures emphasizes this socio-historical shift as seen through a subaltern lens.

---

[10] Raghunath Airi, *Concept of Saraswati in Vedic Literature* (New Delhi: Rohtak Co-operative Print and Publishing Society, 1977), 16.
[11] Airi, 16.
[12] Airi, 16.
[13] See the works of N.N. Bhattacharyya, Savithri de Tourreil and Heide Goettner-Aberndoth.
[14] See Arvind Sharma, "Dr. B. R. Ambedkar on the Aryan Invasions and the Emergence of the Caste System in India," Journal of the American Academy of Religion, September, 2005, 843-870.

> The brahmanic synthesis of tribal, ethnic, and village deities into a unified pantheon in which ancient Mother Goddesses were brahmanized as spouses or other property of brahmanic gods, is, therefore, a metaphor of both the imposition of the caste system on the indigenous and the stringent marriage and inheritance constraints that would be placed on upper-caste wives.[15]

Historically the Manu Laws institutionalized the social oppression of women during Vedic times. Although Shakuntala Rao Sastri argues that both married and unmarried women participated in Vedic rituals, there is an undeniable shift favoring male preference in matters of inheritance, education and spiritual authority. Matters of knowledge transmission and ritual acts were claimed as male activities despite a continued worship to the female goddess Sarasvati for guidance in these domains.

Furthermore, contrary to brahmanized depictions of Sarasvati as a serene and gentle goddess, many stories exist describing her temper, disobedience and punitive attributes. In fact, in later Puranic tales she is closely aligned with Durga/Kali where she is said to have "slayed the demons Sumbha and Nisumbha."[16]

Sarasvati is often categorized as opposite to the fierce, wild goddesses thus upholding a prevalent polarization in patriarchal systems. Patriarchal assumptions by both Indian and Western scholars have perpetuated this "nice goddess/crazy goddess" paradigm. I believe that this is largely due to male unease with fully engaging the powerful goddesses of India who can embody a full gamut of attributes. Women, and female goddesses, can indeed be both benevolent and wild—and everything in between—and all at once! Female scholars need not continue this male behavioral encoding when interpreting the goddesses.[17] This is especially true for contemporary women of non-Indian heritage who are embracing Indian goddess-centered practices partly because these goddesses offer an embodied integration of destructive and constructive energies not offered in Judeo-Christian traditions.

My feminist hermeneutics includes what male scholars may not see in research on Sarasvati. My spiritual name is Sarasvati. I received this energy during my initiation ceremony in 1990 with the Sivananda

---

[15] Donna Jordan, "A Post-Orientalist History of the Fierce Sakti of the Subaltern Domain" (Ph.D. diss., California Institute of Integral Studies, 1999.

[16] Mackenzie C. Brown, *The Triumph of the Goddess: The Canonical Models and Theological Visions of the Devi-Bhagavata Purana* (Albany: State University of New York Press, 1990), 140.

[17] One of the "wild goddess'" signifiers is wild hair. In fact, there also exist images of even the perfectly coifed Sarasvati having a wild-hair day!

organization of Kerala. When I received this name I did not know of Sarasvati. Receiving a spiritual name is like receiving a clue to an inner essence you may not be aware of at that particular time. So when I speak of a feminist hermeneutics, I include how I as researcher and practitioner, arrived at my knowledge. In addition to extensive research into the origins, iconography and literary references on Sarasvati, my methodology included other ways of knowing. I have sung the Sarasvati mantra thousands of times since receiving it. I have learned to play the *vina*, her sacred instrument. I have carried her image constantly with me. In a sense, I have tried to embody her. I am also by choice: "no-husband, no child." In embodying Sarasvati energy through my spiritual practice, my process and insights differ from male scholars or even male devotees, who view Sarasvati as the gendered "other," and who may project onto her the superiority of "civilization" that domesticates natural forces, frequently also imagined as the wild female.

Sarasvati as River

Earliest Vedic hymns identify Sarasvati as a great river. This river flowed from the Himalayas into the northwestern area of India and present day Pakistan. The mysterious disappearance of the river by 800 BC is variously attributed to climate changes, geological shifts, possible earthquakes and drought.[18] In myths, the disappearance of the Sarasvati River is attributed to Sarasvati's punishment of the gods who manipulated Her powers.

Identifying the source of her powers as glacial or terrestrial remains a popular point of scholarly debate. Kinsley points out that Sarasvati is specifically "associated with moving water such as clouds, thunder and rain."[19] If Sarasvati originates from a celestial source then her powers differ from those of the more earthly mother goddesses. This question frames later interpretations of her divine powers associated with falling water rather than those associated with the fertility of the earth.

---

[18] The historical disappearance of the Sarasvati River may have occurred as early as 1900 BC with evidence of it still existing as a narrow river bed till 800 BC. Dates of the Sarasvati Civilization range from 10,000 BC to 3000 BC.

[19] Kinsley, *Hindu Goddesses*, 58

Sarasvati of the Rig Veda

References to Sarasvati in the Rig Veda number about 70-80 (in some Vac, who is later aligned with Sarasvati, is specifically invoked); in the Atharvaveda and Yajurveda Sarasvati is mentioned in all sacrifices. In the Brahmanas, Sarasvati appears in two types of myths (relating to the creator of animate and inanimate beings and relating to the origins of the different *yajnas*).[20] A sampling of the Rig Vedic hymns to Sarasvati shows her clearly as a river, but also already becoming a deity form. Rig Veda 1.3.11-12 sings:

> Sarasvati, the mighty follow,--she with her light illuminates,
> She brightens every pious thought.

Rig Veda 7.95 portrays her double abilities as forceful river and as keeper of wealth and blessings.

> This stream Sarasvati with fostering current comes forth, our sure defense, our fort of iron.
>
> The flood flows on, surpassing in majesty and might all other waters.
>
> Pure in her course from mountains to the ocean, alone of streams Sarasvati hath listened.
>
> Thinking of wealth and the great world of creatures, she poured for Nahusa her milk and fatness.

The Sarasvati River is all-important in Vedic literature. The River existed before the Aryan settlement and would have already been sacred to the Purus and Vaisisthas. Sarasvati's importance in Vedic literature may be attributed to early territorial clashes between these groups. It has even been postulated that the Aryans considered Sarasvati a mighty river because historically the Aryans were stopped by her tremendous powers.

A few references connect Sarasvati with the power of fire. She is called *Agni-jihva Sarasvati* and considered the tongue of fire that communicates with the gods.[21] In Shristikhanda of the Padma Purana, Vishnu entreats Sarasvati "to carry fire (*anala*) from Puskara and to drop it

---

[20] Airi, 1-3.
[21] Airi, 77

into the sea (*lavana sagara*)."[22] In the Vedas, fire comes out of water and early cosmogony presents the notion of fire as a primordial reality. This may be a remnant of pre-existing beliefs in fire being associated with female powers as elaborated by Tracy Pintchman.

> Both heat or fire and speech are portrayed in a general way as sources of creative power that produce or evolve into the cosmic waters. This motif of a principle of creative energy or power giving rise to a principle of primordial materiality also has parallels in later Puranic literature where, as we shall see, sakti gives rise to prakrti."[23]

Sarasvati Iconography

Dwight A. Tkatschow identifies Sarasvati's early iconography as originating from the *gandharva* and *yaksa* tradition, both pre-Vedic female images. The first representation of Sarasvati may be from the Sunga period (185-72 BC) on a railing from Bharhut.

> The Bharhut relief depicts a partially nude female figure clad in a knotted loin cloth with a heavy yoke-like necklace around her neck. Under her left arm she is holding a six-stringed lyre. She is standing on top of a full-blown lotus in the casual stance, of sālabhañjikā 'kicking the sāla tree.' [24]

Several features identify goddess iconography as being Sarasvati. She is usually four-armed, holding a musical instrument sometimes called a lyre or vina; mala beads (*aksamālā*), and a book or manuscript (*pustaka*). Her most common vehicle is the swan but she is also sometimes with a goose or, in non-Brahmanical text, she appears with a peacock. She is most frequently seated in the one-legged *lalitāsana* pose, wears earrings, necklaces, and a conical crown and is rarely with a male consort or child. Kanailal Bhattacharyya's extensive study of Sarasvati iconography also mentions these less frequently occurring but significant features: she wears a sacred thread (*yajnopavita*)[25] in sculptures found in Karnataka, her other vehicles include a lion, ram and even a bull, she holds additional

---

[22] N.N. Bhattacharyya, *Sarasvati: A Study in Her Concept and Iconography* (Calcutta: Saraswat Library, 1983), 53.

[23] Tracy Pintchman, *The Rise of the Goddess in the Hindu Tradition* (Albany: State University of New York Press, 1994) , 66-67.

[24] Dwight A. Tkatschow, "Sarasvati: Observations on the Iconography of an Ancient Indian Goddess," in *Mother Goddess and Other Goddesses*, ed. V. Subramanian (Delhi: Ajanta Publications, 1993), 78.

[25] The sacred thread is usually reserved for "twice-born" men.

implements such as a water pot, goad and noose. There also exist standing and dancing Sarasvatis whom Bhattacharyya associates with Siva. These additional aspects form a more dynamic picture of Sarasvati's powers as including not only serenity and refined culture but also a dynamic *sakti* that manifests in many forms.

The implements give clues to her true attributes. Brahmanical interpretations define her as the goddess of knowledge, further confining her to the power of the Vedic teachings which ushered in and validated Aryan supremacy. A closer examination of "knowledge" might include not just the written word but memory, intelligence, insight, skill, ingenuity, ideas, and the ability to perform rituals and sing mantras.

Sarasvati's association with the arts includes storytelling, music, science and technology, medicine and most importantly a metaphysical realization of the universe as sound. Sarasvati always holds the vina which is the knowledge of the vibrations of the body and the universe itself. Her earliest powers were associated exclusively with the arts of medicine as she is said to have cured even Indra. She embodies the knowledge of the healing powers of sound, water, herbs and minerals.

Tales of Disobedience and Subversive Acts

The Vamana Purana describes yet another episode of Sarasvati's cleverness and independence in response to the controlling demands of Brahmin priests. Known as the tale of Vishwamitra's Curse in chapter 40; Sarasvati is ordered to use her waters to transport Vishwamitra to Vasista in order to kill him. Instead, Sarasvati immerses Vasista in her waters, preventing a killing and angering Vishwamitra who curses her by changing her water into blood that nourishes the demons.[26] If any tale begs a feminist interpretation, it is Vishwamitra's Curse! The definition of Sarasvati's "flow" being restored to menstruation flow would align with women's spirituality scholar Judy Grahn's metaformic theory that considers all of civilization to be built on symbols of menstrual rituals.[27] An often overlooked but obvious biological fact is that menstrual blood indicates non-pregnancy. Hence, the interpretative leap that many male scholars have imposed by labeling these as fertility stories, needs to be reconsidered.

---

[26] Chitralekha Singh and Prem Nath, *Saraswati: (Gayatri, Savitri, Bag Devi)* New Delhi: Crest Publishing House, 1999), 18.
[27] Judy Grahn, *Blood, Bread and Roses*, (Boston: Beacon Press, 1993).

Sarasvati as Evasive Wife

C. Mackenzie Brown's detailed analysis of Devi manifestations in the Bhagavata Purana offers at least three separate incidents of Sarasvati dodging marriage. Her unmarried state is of great concern as Mahisa tries proposing to her and is rejected because "the Devi declares that she desires no man but the supreme Purusa and in any case she has come to the world to protect the righteous."[28] In the older Varaha Purana, she laughs at the proposal "as she is under a vow of perpetual virginity."[29] Here, "virginity" is also redefined by feminist scholars as a female's ability to transform her sexual energy for healing herself and community.

Perhaps one of the most fascinating observations about contemporary worship of Sarasvati is by N.N. Bhattacharyya in a footnote of his book, *Indian Mother Goddess.* In West Bengal, Sarasvati is worshipped by the prostitutes, "not because she is the goddess of learning but because, in popular belief, she is unmarried and of doubtful moral character."[30]

Two additional tales challenge the scholars' assertion that Sarasvati "rarely possesses fearsome qualities."[31] Both stories illustrate the feisty nature of Sarasvati and also show Sarasvati's considerable power over Brahma. The first story addresses how Brahma came to possess five heads and the second is why Brahma is rarely worshiped.

The popular tale of Brahma's multi heads centers on his obsession with the lovely Sarasvati whom he tries to catch glimpses of as she evades him with her swift movements in all directions.[32] Certainly, any female would recognize this behavior as intentionally dodging an unwanted suitor! The second story, found in the Skanda Purana, involves Sarasvati (as Savitri) taking her time in dressing for a ritual to take place with Brahma on Mount Pushkara. Brahma, impatient with her delay, asks Indra to find him another suitable female for the ritual. Indra obliges and chooses a local milkmaid, Gayatri, whom Vishnu and Rudra approve for the task. When Savitri enters the hall and sees her replacement, she curses all the male divinities including Indra, Rudra and Vishnu, who have sanctioned such an insulting act. Her punishment for Brahma includes that "thereafter Brahma would never be worshipped in temples and sacred places, except

---

[28] Brown, 99-100.
[29] Brown, 99.
[30] N.N. Bhattacharyya, 39.
[31] Kinsley, *Hindu Goddesses*, 62.
[32] Singh, 9.

one day in each year."[33] Certainly Sarasvati proves her strength of character in repeated tales of standing up to the controlling gods.

Sarasvati as Reluctant Procreator

Perhaps most disturbing for feminist practitioners and scholars is the tale of Sarasvati's forced copulation with Brahma. In reading different summaries of the Matsya Purana 3.30, I noticed how male authors avoided the obvious assessment that a female might experience in hearing of Brahma's willful "desire to mate" -as an act of **rape**. Kinsley comes closest to acknowledging the transgression in his essay in *Mother Goddess and Other Goddesses.*

> In the Hindu goddess Sarasvati we have another goddess who is only weakly associated with motherhood, and who is strongly associated with culture. Sarasvati, to be sure, is sometimes said to give birth (as in the story of the birth of Manu) but she is, like Amaterasu and Athena, a reluctant mother. In this case, her father, the god Brahma, forces her sexually and the result is the birth of Manu, the first human being.[34]

Kinsley's language comes closest to describing what "forces her sexually" may mean to a female reader. Even more striking is that this tale involves father-daughter incest, a taboo that is sometimes said to have been one of the causes of Brahma's demise. Despite Kinsley's efforts to articulate the obvious violation in this story he creates an even graver disservice by upholding the patriarchal categorizing of mother/nature vs. spiritualization in his analysis of Sarasvati's lack of maternal signifiers. This prevalent dichotomy in Western thought disassociates women from the arenas of "civilization". She can be either "mother" (and therefore not part of civilizing forces) or "non-mother" when she participates in nation-building, education or the arts.

Sarasvati offers us another possibility. She is Creatrix of the universe but not necessarily based on a model of maternity. She is MA- originator of the universe through sound – a profound esoteric concept that seems to be deemphasized in current commentaries. How do we conceptualize a female creatrix without relying on the metaphor of the female birthing body? Once again, I am re-inspired by Paula Gunn Allen and Mary Daly's concepts of Her as "The Thinking One" in an expanded sense that includes all knowledge and not in the limited definition arising from Greek

[33] Kanailal Bhattacharyya, 54-58.
[34] Kinsley, *Mother Goddesses and other Goddesses*, 71.

philosophies. If in fact Sarasvati became known as Knowledge, might not this quality also have been the creation principle? In this sense, Sarasvati is then the embodiment of both thought and sound.

Nila-Sarasvat

Finally although masculinist interpretations categorize Sarasvati as sattvic, pure, benevolent, non-threatening and gentle, her multi-forms include many dynamic and volatile forms including the tantric goddess, Nila-Sarasvati, who takes on fierce qualities usually associated with Kali or Tara. According to the Tantric text, *Brhat Nila Tantra* as described by Acharya Dina Nath Shastri, Nila-Sarasvati is a blue goddess who is worshiped in cremation grounds and "for the acquisition of poetic power."[35] Kinsley considers Nila-Sarasvati a form of Tara as described in the *Tantrasara*:

> I bow to you mother, Nilasarasvati. You give well-being and auspiciousness. You are situated on the heart of a corpse and are advancing aggressively. You have three fearful, bright eyes. You carry a skull bowl, scissors, and a sword. Your form shines like a blazing fire. Give me refuge. Give me golden speech. Please let your gracious nectar drench my heart, remover of pride. You are decorated with snakes as ornaments, you wear a tiger skin as a skirt, you ring a bell loudly, and wear a garland of chopped off heads. You are frightening and remove fear.

Sarasvati therefore encompasses a range of aspects and qualities, including rejecting, disobeying and punishing Brahma and manifesting in versions associated with negative aspects.

Current Significance of Sarasvati for National Bharati Identity

A recently published seven volume compilation on the archeological and geographical evidence of the Sarasvati River by Dr. Kalyanaraman may prove to be a significant contribution to understanding the historical identity of the "Sarasvati Civilization."[36] Although the extensive series is

[35] Acharya Dina Nath Shastri, "Tantricism in Kashmir" http://www.kplink.com/gallery/details.php?image_id=1189&sessionid=a3b96cc5bc0c3cb9da2986d2e3f44056 (October 2005).

[36] Dr. Kalyanaraman repeatedly proposes that "the civilization should be called Sarasvati Civilization, the foundation of Bharatiya Culture." (Volume 1, 15).

motivated by nationalistic agendas, Dr. Kalyanaraman's study attempts to trace the legends of Sarasvati by scientific light. The course of the Sarasvati River is mapped out, artifacts from 2,000 archaeological sites are reviewed, including detailed chapters on beads, coins and tablets. Of course, such a theory rejects the Aryan invasions theories. He states that "this civilization was an indigenous evolution from earlier than 10000 BCE and can be said to be one of the oldest civilizations in the world, heralding the Vedic heritage."[37]

Dr. Kalyanaraman's volume on Language claims that early glyphs can be deciphered and point to a common "substratum language [which] was mleccha.[38] This statement serves to connect the Indo-Aryan dialects with pre-Sanskrit languages such as Dravidian and Munda. Once again, although the nationalistic purpose of such sweeping statements may be didactic, Kalyanaraman's cross-disciplinary approaches may generate more research and analysis of these materials. Another possible benefit of the Sarasvati River revival project advocated by Kalyanaraman is the integration of water management concerns for the Northwest areas of India. Included in this proposal will be an attempt to identify existing groundwater sanctuaries along the Sarasvati route to create drainage systems for those areas.[39]

Sarasvati in non-Hindu traditions

Sarasvati's continued presence in later Buddhism, Jainism and Sikhism attests to the importance of Her powers and Her clearly defined attributes. She continues being associated with the arts and inspiration, pictured with a swan (or for the Digambra sect of Jainism, with a peacock) and holding a musical instrument.

In Buddhist iconography she is "surrounded by four goddesses who are apparently facets of herself: Insight (*prajna*) in front, cleverness (*medha*) to her right, memory (*smrti*) to her left and behind her is intelligence (*mati*). In the Tibetan Buddhist "Compendium of Contemplative Practices" she is described more often as being independent than with Manjughosa as her consort.

Sarasvati is especially popular in Jainism precisely because she is known for rejecting Brahma and therefore also braminical Hinduism. My

---

[37] Dr. S. Kalyanaraman, *Sarasvati: Volume 1: Civilization*, (Bangalore: Babasaheb (Umakanta Keshav) Apte Smarak Samiti, 2003) 277.

[38] Dr. S. Kalyanaraman, *Sarasvati:Vol. 6: Language*, 15.

[39] Kalyanaraman, *Sarasvati: Vol. 3: River*, 6.

own experience visiting a Jain temple in Rajasthan, where I introduced myself by my spiritual name of Sarasvati confirmed the great respect Jain practitioners have for her. It was also one of the few places in India where my unmarried status was not probed.

Sarasvati with Other Goddesses

Several stories describe a sometimes tempestuous Sarasvati when she is forced to share her "husband" with another goddess. She is described as being jealous of Gayatri when she is paired with Brahma at Mount Pushara; jealous of Lakshmi when she is paired with Vishnu; and jealous of Ganga when she is paired with Siva. A feminist reading of these stories considers that (1) patriarchy creates stories of female animosity toward each other to strengthen male status and (2) she once again clearly expresses her disagreement with any of these arrangements. Furthermore, she resolves the situation by either identifying herself as an ascetic and therefore not interested in any compromising marriage arrangements or she gets her way resulting in the "other wife" appeasing and apologizing to her. In all situations, she places curses on the male gods to punish their hubris and for creating rivalry.

In the later Tantric Puranas, she is said to have been born from either Lakshmi or Radha. In the early Rig Veda, she is often mentioned in a trio of female names along with Bharati and Ila. One of the more interesting gender-bending iconographies of Sarasvati is that when Siva worshiped Her, he "installed her in the form of linga at the Sthanutirtha."[40] Throughout her evolution, she is more likely to be affiliated in groups of female divinities or alone, rather than with male deities.

Conclusion

Research on Sarasvati has been filtered through patriarchal agendas that dismiss the power of her independence and non-maternal attributes and reduce her to a female consort and symbol of Aryan culture. As a feminist scholar and Sarasvati devotee, I wish to reconsider the significance of her pre-Aryan origins and how she was shaped by brahmanical systems. A key reconsideration is her status as creatrix energy, a form that must be read beyond essentialist and patriarchal constructions of motherhood. Perhaps then Sarasvati will be reclaimed by women as another aspect of the sacred feminine, and become a viable

[40] Kinsley, 82.

alternative to goddesses being defined mainly in their duties as mothers and wives.

Bibliography

Airi, Raghunath. *Concept of Saraswati in Vedic Literature* New Delhi: Rohtak Co-operative Print and Pub. Society, 1977.

Allen, Paula Gunn. *The Sacred Hoop: Recovering the Feminine in American Indian Traditions* Boston: Beacon Press, 1986.

Bailey, Greg. *The Mythology of Brahma*. Delhi: Oxford University Press, 1983.

Bhattacharyya, Kanailal. *Sarasvati: A Study in Her Concept and Iconography*. Calcutta: Saraswat Library, 1983.

Bhattacharyya, N.N. *Indian Mother Goddess*. Calcutta: Indian Studies, 1971.

Brown, C. Mackenzie. *The Triumph of the Goddess: The Canonical Models and Theological Visions of the Devi-Bhagavata Purana.* Albany: State University of New York Press, 1990.

Daly, Mary. "Amazon Grace: Recalling the Courage to Sin Big" Lecture at Whittier College, April 15, 2005.

Fiorenza, Elisabeth Schussler. *In Memory of Her: A Feminist Theological Reconstruction of Christian Origins*. New York: Crossroads, 1992.

Goettner-Abendroth, Heide. *Matriarchal Mythology in Former Times and Today*. California: The Crossing Press, 1987.

Grahn, Judy. *Blood, Bread and Roses*. Boston: Beacon Press, 1993.

Griffith, Ralph T. H., *The Hymns of the RgVeda: Translated With A Popular Commentry*.Delhi: Motilal Banarsidass, 1973.

Jordan, Donna, S. A Post-Orientalist History of the Fierce Sakti of the Subaltern Domain. dissertation CIIS, 1999.

Kalyanaraman, Dr. S., *Sarasvati: Volume 1: Civilization*. Bangalore: Babasaheb (Umakanta Keshav) Apte Smarak Samiti, 2003.

—. *Sarasvati: Volume 2: R.gveda*. Bangalore: Babasaheb (Umakanta Keshav) Apte Smarak Samiti, 2003.

—. *Sarasvati: Volume 3:River*. Bangalore: Babasaheb (Umakanta Keshav) Apte Smarak Samiti, 2003.

—. *Sarasvati: Volume 4:Bharati*. Bangalore: Babasaheb (Umakanta Keshav) Apte Smarak Samiti, 2003.

—. *Sarasvati: Volume 5:Technology*. Bangalore: Babasaheb (Umakanta Keshav) Apte Smarak Samiti, 2003.

—. *Sarasvati: Volume 6: Language* Bangalore: Babasaheb (Umakanta Keshav) Apte Smarak Samiti, 2003.

—. *Sarasvati: Volume 7: Epigraphs*. Bangalore: Babasaheb (Umakanta Keshav) Apte Smarak Samiti, 2003.

Khanna, Madhu. "Visual Metaphysics and Representations in Hindu Shakta Tantra: Some Methodological Explorations." Lecture at American Academy of Religion, Philadelphia, PA, November 2005.

Kinsley, David R. *Hindu Goddesses: Visions of the Divine Feminine in the Hindu Religious Tradition*. Berkeley: University of California Press, 1988.

—. " 'Mother Goddesses' and 'Culture Godddesses' " in *Mother Goddess and Other Goddesses.* Delhi: Ajanta Publications, 1993.

—. *Tantric Visions of the Divine Feminine: The Ten Mahavidyas:* Berkeley: University of California Press, 1997.

Mohanty, Chandra: "Under Western Eyes: Feminist Scholarship and Colonial Discourses". In: *Feminist Review*, no. 30, autumn 1988.

Pintchman, Tracy. *The Rise of the Goddess in the Hindu Tradition* Albany: State University of New York Press, 1994.

Rocher, Ludo. *The Puranas: A History of Indian Literature*. Ed. Jan Gonda. Vol. II Wiesbaden: Harrassowitz, 1986.

Sastri, Shakuntala Rao, *Women in the Vedic Age*, Bombay: Bharatiya Vidya Bhavan, 1952.

Savithr, de Tourrel, "Nayars: matrilineal or matriarchal or a bit of both?: How do they fit into a South Indian Matrix?" 2nd Women's Congress on Matriarchal Studies, San Marcos, Texas, 30 September 2005.

Sharma, Arvind, "Dr. B.R. Ambedkar on the Aryan Invasion and the Emergence of the Caste System in India. Journal of the American Academy of Religion. September, 2005. Vol. 73, No. 3, p843-870.

Shastri, Acharya Dina Nath. "Tantricism in Kashmir" http://www.kplink.com/gallery/details.php?image_id=1189&sessionid =a3b96cc5bc0c3cb9da2986d2e3f44056

Singh, Chitralekha and Prem Nath. *Saraswati: (Gayatri, Savitri, Bag Devi).* New Delhi: Crest Publishing House, 1999.

Subramaniam, V.. *Mother Goddess and Other Goddesses*. Delhi: Ajanta Publications, 1993.

Tkatschow, Dwight A. "Sarasvati: Observations on the Iconography of an Ancient Indian Goddess" in. *Mother Goddess and Other Goddesses*. Delhi: Ajanta Publications, 1993.

PART V

MYTH MAKING AND SERVING THE GODDESS TODAY

CHAPTER FIFTEEN

THE MODERN LEGEND OF MIAOSHAN THE DEVELOPMENT OF THE *SANGHA* OF VEGETARIAN NUNS IN CHINA

CHIA-LAN CHANG

Zaigu or *caigu* (vegetarian nuns) and the establishment of *zaitang* or *caitang* (vegetarian houses or convents) appear mainly in Quanzhou, Xiamen, and Zhangzhou of Fujian province. However, for this study my subjects come from contemporary Quanzhou city and Huian County, which were affiliated with Quanzhou prefecture in the late imperial period and are still considered a self-contained cultural sphere. Buddhism in the Quanzhou area experienced prosperity during the Tang and Song periods and saw a demise in the Ming and Qing eras. However, local *yinci* (profane shrines), such as those worshipping female deities, and *zhai jiao* (vegetarian cults, including several sects whose practice includes taking vegetarian meals and accumulating religious merits by conforming to Confucian familial systems) maintained prosperous status by borrowing from Buddhism concepts such as reincarnation and retributions. The appearance of vegetarian nuns serving as abbesses in convents and temples from the late nineteenth century is thus a result of the interaction of orthodox Buddhism and local cults. The noteworthy phenomenon of the vegetarian nuns in late imperial Quanzhou area attracted respect, in part, through their incorporation of orthodox Buddhism, which enjoyed a revival in the early twentieth century.

Vegetarian nuns are not *bhiksuni*s (fully ordained Buddhist nuns), because they receive neither *bhiksuni* precepts nor tonsure according to *Vinaya Pitaka* rules. Similar to the unshaven laywoman image of Bodhisattva Avalokitesvara in the legend of Miaoshan (the indigenous manifestation of Bodhisattva Avalokitesvara or Guanyin in China), vegetarian nuns do not express their religious piety in the form of receiving tonsure or Buddhist ordination rites, but rather in their religious consciousness and daily practice. Vegetarian nuns leave their families, practice *pancasila* (Five Precepts) or *Bodhisattva-samvara* (Bodhisattva Precepts), and live in convents under a vow of celibacy. They subjectively identify themselves as orthodox Buddhist nuns and obtain recognition as such from both Buddhists and the public in Quanzhou. Vegetarian nuns thus embody the legend of Miaoshan and constitute a special female *sangha* (monastic order) between fully ordained Buddhist nuns and *upasika*s (female lay devotees).[1]

Though vegetarian nuns do not receive the tonsure, in the Quanzhou area they are easily distinguishable from non-Buddhist laywomen by their hairstyle and dress. They always wear traditional Han-style white, gray, or black blouses, black trousers, and *luohan xie* (Buddhist shoes). In addition, many old vegetarian nuns gather their hair in a bun on the back of their heads, which is called *caigu tou* (vegetarian nun hairstyle). Today's young vegetarian nuns, however, are accustomed to short, ear-length hair. Unmarried, elderly vegetarian nuns or *qinggu* (clean maidens) are called *gunian* (maidens) to show respect by novices and local people. Married women before entering the convents are called *laogu* (old maidens) or *gupo* (grand-maidens). Whether previously married or not, only women who remain chaste are qualified to be called vegetarian nuns.

Studies on vegetarian nuns usually ascribe socioeconomic contexts as the principal reasons these women reject marriage and opt to become vegetarian nuns. Many scholars pay attention to the connection between resistance to marriage and the emergence of vegetarian nuns. Marjorie Topley, Andrea Sankar, Janice Stockard, and Cao Xuansi have all

[1] Some scholars categorize vegetarian nuns as laywomen (*upsikas*). See Jiang Canteng江燦騰. "Cong zaigu dao biqiuni: Taiwan fojiao nuxing chujia de bainian cangsang" 從齋姑到比丘尼：台灣佛教女性出家的百年滄桑 (From Vegetarian Nuns to Fully Ordained Buddhist Nuns: The Century-Old Vicissitudes of Home-Leaving Experiences of Buddhist Women in Taiwan), *Lishi yuekan* 歷史月刊 105 (1996): 23-32. Wu Youxiong吳幼雄. *Quanzhou congjiao wenhua* 泉州宗教文化 (The Religious Culture in Quanzhou). Quanzhou: Lujiang chubanshe, 1993, 162. Others build a branch from *upsikas* (laywomen) and call these vegetarian nuns "*chujia upsika*s" (home-leaving laywomen). Faqing法清. "Minnan caigu de qiyuan han diwei" 閩南菜姑的起源和地位 (The Origin and Status of Vegetarian Nuns in Southeast Fujian], *Minnan foxiuyuan xiubao*閩南佛學院學報 7 (1992): 98. Ven. Hongyi 弘一called vegetarian nuns "*fanxing qingxin nu* (laywomen who practice Buddhist doctrines), that is, "*Brahmacarya upsikas*". See Faqing, 97.

published socioeconomic studies on *zishu nu* (spinsters or "self-combers") and vegetarian houses in Shunde, Guangdong.[2] Economic independence and freedom from marriage or any other such strictly institutionalized organization, they contend, were the two motivating features of Guangdong spinsters. These studies are enriched and complemented by more studies on the spread and lineages of sectarian (Buddhist) cults in Chinese history. For instance, Chikusa Masaaki's study on Song vegetarian cults argues that sectarian cults in Quanzhou could be spread via sea routes and through the influence of Manichaeism.[3] Ma Xisha and

---

[2] Both Sankar and Stockard illustrate the causation between the demand of the labor force and anti-marriage practices. Economic factors, such as the silk industry in the early twentieth century, gave spinsters the economic independence to resist marriage by moving into Spinster Houses or Vegetarian houses of the Great Way of Former Heaven (*Xiantian dadao*), a Buddhist sect, or allowed bride daughters more independence from their husbands and in-laws through the option of staying in natal families. In addition to economic factors, Topley points out that the incentive for most women joining in the Great Way of Former Heaven was to acquire freedom from institutional bonds and emotional attachment. Cao highlights the religious features of the custom of "self-combing." He finds that spinsters in vegetarian houses of the Great Way of Former Heaven rely on sworn spinsterhood and the worship of Guanyin to justify their resistance to marriage, to leave male domination behind, and to be cleansed by mimicking Guanyin's exemplary behavior. See Andrea P. Sankar, "Spinster Sisterhoods: Jing Yih Sifu: Spinster-Domestic-Nun," in *Lives: Chinese Working Women*, eds. Mary Sheridan and Janet W. Salaff (Bloomington: Indiana University Press, 1984), 51-70; idem, *Sister and Brothers, Lovers and Enemies: Marriage Resistance in Southern Kwangtung Anthropology and Homosexual Behaviour* (The Haworth Press, Inc, 1986); Janice E. Stockard, *Daughters of the Canton Delta: Marriage Patterns and Economic Strategies in South China, 1860-1930* (Stanford: Stanford University Press, 1989); Marjerie Topley, "Chinese Women's Vegetarian Houses in Singapore," *Journal Malayan Branch of the Royal Asiatic Society* 27.1 (1954): 51-67; idem, "Marriage Resistance in Rural Kwangtung," in *Women in Chinese Society*, eds. Margery Wolf and Roxane Witke (Berkeley: University of California Press, 1991): 67-88; Cao Xuansi曹玄思, "Xiantian dao de zishunu" 先天道的自梳女(Spinsters in the Way of Former Heaven), in *Huanan hunyin zhidu yu funu diwei*華南婚姻制度與婦女地位(The Marriage System and Women's Status in Southeast China), eds. Ma Jianzhao馬建釗, Qiao Jian喬健, and Du Ruile杜瑞樂 (Guangxi minzu chubanshe廣西民族出版社, 1994): 124-140.

[3] Chikusa Masaaki筑沙雅章, "Guanyu 'chicai shimo'"關於喫菜事魔 (On "Vegetarians Who Served the Evil"), in vol. 7, *Riben xuezhe yanjiu zhongguoshi lunzhu xuanyi*日本學者研究中國史論著選譯 (Selected Translations of Studies on Chinese History by Japanese Scholars) (Beijing: Zhonghua shuju, 1982), 361-385.

Han Bingfang's, and Tan Songlin's edited works on Chinese secret societies separately discuss the lineages and spread of sectarian cults and point out women's active participation and leadership in the cults.[4] Jiang Canteng bridges these two aspects of studies on vegetarian cults and vegetarian nuns by exploring the development of Taiwanese vegetarian cults and their three main sects in Fujian and Taiwan—Longhua, Jinchuang, and Xiantian sects—in order to discuss the state's involvement in vegetarian nuns' incorporation of Buddhism during the period under Japanese rule.[5]

In all the aforementioned studies, vegetarian nuns' self-identity and voice are either overlooked or presented as "the Other," alienated from the local society, the familial system, and orthodox Buddhist society. Rarely do any vegetarian nuns speak for themselves. In Quanzhou, however, this custom of becoming vegetarian nuns is still preserved and locally appreciated even as it undergoes numerous changes. Faqing's article in 1992 is the first systematic introduction about the origin and status of vegetarian nuns in Southeast Fujian (mainly within the Quanzhou area) and represents the orthodox Buddhists' emphasis on strict doctrinal qualifications for vegetarian nuns.[6] Zhou Minghui's anthropological research details the power relations among vegetarian nuns and reflects well their voice in the late 1990s.[7] Chen Zhenzhen, a female Quanzhou Buddhist leader who (re)established in Quanzhou the first and only Buddhist Academy especially for vegetarian nuns in 1948 and 1987,

---

[4] Ma Xisha馬西沙, and Han Bingfang韓秉方, *Zhongguo minjian congjiao shi*中國民間宗教史(The Popular Religious History in China) (Shanghai: Shanghai renming chubanshe上海人民出版社, 1992); Tan Songlin譚松林 ed., *Zhongguo mimi shehui* 中國祕密社會(Chinese Secrete Societies), (Fuzhou福州: Fujian renming chubanshe福建人民出版社, 2002).

[5] Jiang Canteng, "Cong zaigu dao biqiuni: Taiwan fojiao nuxing chujia de bainian cangsang," 23-32; Jiang Canteng, and Wang Jianchuan 王見川eds., *Taiwan zhaijiao de lishi guancha yu zhanwang: shoujie Taiwan zhaijiao xueshu yantao hui lunwenji* 台灣齋教的歷史觀察與展望: 首屆台灣齋教學術研討會論文集(Historical Observation and the Prospect: Essays from the First Conference on Taiwanese Vegetarian Sects), (Taipei: Xinwenfeng chuban gongsi 新文豐出版公司, 1994).

[6] Faqing, "Minnan caigu de qiyuan han diwei," 93-99.

[7] Zhou Minghui周明慧, "Yicun yu jiuge: Huian Chongwu de caigu yu caitang, " 依存與糾葛：惠安崇武的菜姑與菜堂 (Reliance and Entanglement: Vegetarian Nuns and Vegetarian Houses in Chongwu, Huian), (MA thesis. Taiwan: Qinghua University, 1999).

introduces the proliferation of vegetarian nuns *sangha* in the twentieth century.[8] She stresses that she is not a vegetarian nun herself, because the opposition of her parents prevented her from leaving her family (she lives with her brother's family), but she follows a vegetarian diet, observes rigorous Buddhist practice, and retains the celibate lifestyle of a vegetarian nun. Given that her life is devoted to preserving the tradition of vegetarian nuns, I consider Chen Zhenzhen a representative of vegetarian nuns in Quanzhou and her essay as a reflection of their self-identity. Developing from these studies and based on my own fieldwork, this essay thus focuses on the identity formation of vegetarian nuns and how they are perceived by orthodox Buddhism and the local community.

The Emergence of Vegetarian Nuns

Faqing attributes the origins of vegetarian nuns in Quanzhou to three sources—they were worshippers of the Xiantian sect, worshippers of other sectarian cults, and laywomen who moved into and managed neighborhood temples and convents without abbesses. According to Jiang Canteng's research on vegetarian cults, these three sources should be reduced to two—worshippers of vegetarian cults who converted to Buddhism, and lay orthodox Buddhists. Some wealthy families built small *jingshe* (refined residences) for widows or unmarried daughters who were willing to "keep a vegetarian diet and chant the name of Buddha" in order to preserve chastity. It was not unusual that this type of refined residence was transformed into vegetarian houses (of either orthodox Buddhism or other sectarian Buddhist cults) or large convents by inviting in more vegetarian nuns as companions. Shijia si (Sakya Monastery), according to the temple records, was originally built by Ming official Li Wenjie in the sixteenth century for his daughter who vowed to remain chaste for her deceased fiancé.[9] On the other hand, Chen Zhenzhen traces the origin of vegetarian nuns back to the Song dynasty, arguing that unshaven nuns, who could be *sikasamana*s (female probationers who receive two years of training) or *sramanerika*s (female novices), were vegetarian nuns.[10] I

[8] Chen Zhenzhen, "Tan Fujian de 'Fangxing qingxin nu'" 談福建的「梵行清信女」 (About Laywomen Who Practice Buddhist Doctrines in Fujian), *Fayin yuekan*法音月刊 1 (January 2000): 63-68.

[9] Shijia si釋迦寺, *Quanzhou Shijia si gaikuang* 泉州釋迦寺概況 (A General Introduction to Sijian Monastery in Quanzhou) (Quanzhou, China): 1, 38.

[10] Chen Zhenzhen, "Tan Fujian de 'Fangxing qingxin nu,'" 64.

suspect that Chen Zhenzhen's ignorance of vegetarian sects' conversion to Buddhism and search for historical origins underlie her effort to justify the existence and preserve the tradition of vegetarian nuns in today's Buddhist society.

The question of origins aside, Faqing, Zhou Minghui, and Chen Zhenzhen all note that the goals of vegetarian nuns are to seek purity and assurance of a favorable reincarnation through celibacy. Resistance to marriage and influence of family members are the most common motives for vegetarian nuns' participation in the monastic order. Many vegetarian nuns leave their families due to fear, frustration with unhappy marriages, being widowed at a young age, or because they obtain no financial support from either their natal or marital families.

Case 1. Suyan si (Swallow-Residing Convent)

Suyan si is one of the six largest convents for vegetarian nuns in the urban area of contemporary Quanzhou. According to legend, the founder Yang Jiagu was widowed in her twenties and her in-laws could not support her, so she gave up her two daughters for adoption as *tongyangxi* (little daughters-in-law) and retreated to a cave in a mountain outside Quanzhou city to worship Guanyin. Her chastity and religious piety attracted the attention and respect of local people. Both gentry and common people donated money to help her establish Suyan si. After being widowed, Yang Jiagu's daughter, Lin Yinggu, entered the Suyan si with her three-year-old daughter Zhang Wenlian. Raised in this religious setting, Zhang Wenlian vowed to be a vegetarian nun while still a young child. Yang Jiagu died in 1937 and Lin Yinggu took over the abbacy but died two years later; Zhang Wenlian thus carried on this monastic tradition with the help of another vegetarian nun, her cousin Huang Jigu, who is also Yang Jiagu's granddaughter. Later, Zhang Wenlian and Huang Jigu successfully established a new branch of the Suyan si as well as a charitable clinic in the Philippines.[11]

[11] Feilubin suyan si菲律賓宿燕寺, *Feilubin suyan si wenlian shizhen suo jinian kan*菲律賓宿燕寺文蓮施診所紀念刊 (*Record in Memory of Wenlian Free Clinic and the Philippine Swallow-Residing Convent*), (Philippine: Suyan si, 1983).

The High Valuation of Chastity in Quanzhou Society

Suyan si, if we overlook its monastic characteristics, was established and expanded by three generations of a matriliny, the maternal line of Yang Jiagu, Lin Yinggu, Zhang Wenlian, and Huang Jigu. The first and second generations are widows, and the third generation includes two unmarried granddaughters who took vows as vegetarian nuns. In fact, on a proclamation posted outside the convent in 1906, the Jinjiang magistrate responded to the appeal of local literati to protect this convent:

> You (people) should know that the fund-raising for renovating Suyan si is for the sake of preserving Yang's and Lin's chastity. All chaste and martyred women can be allowed to reside there. Willingness to do charitable work is indeed a local philanthropic act. All nearby residents in that area must not look for excuses or go into the convent, make noise or disturbances, or steal materials such as wood, stone and tile. If anyone purposely disobeys this rule, I will arrest him immediately without exception and sentence him to the maximum punishment. I will never be lenient. I hope you will all seriously follow this proclamation without violation. This is a special notification.[12]

In the eyes of local officials and gentries, Suyan si was more like a *qingjie tang* (Widow's Home). Its purpose of housing chaste women is closely linked to the local valuation of chastity and kinship, particularly when the convent founders formed a family tradition of chastity. This proclamation was also a representation of this Confucian chastity-production system. In the late imperial period Quanzhou prefecture had a reputation for stressing chastity. As discussed by T'ien Ju-k'ang, the strict requirement for women to preserve chastity even encouraged them to practice the notorious ritual of *datai* (putting up a platform) to hang themselves in public or to die of starvation.[13] However, we find no mention of the establishment of Widows' Homes in any Ming-Qing gazetteers from the Quanzhou area. In addition, Ming and Qing legal codes forbid people from establishing convents in private without approval or registration.[14] One of the best places for chaste women to settle down

---

[12] Ibid., 97.

[13] T'ien Ju-k'ang, *Male Anxiety and Female Chastity: A Comparative Study of Chinese Ethical Values in Ming-Ch'ing Times* (Leiden: E. J. Brill,1988), 48-66.

[14] Shen Zhiqi沈之奇, *The Great Qing Code*, Part III, (Laws Relating To The Board of Revenue, Chapter 1, Households and Services [Corvee Labor], Article 77. "Privately Establishing a Buddhist or Taoist Convent and Ordaining Taoist or

was thus a convent donated and built by local officials and gentries, as was Suyan si.

Nevertheless, today's temple record retains this Miaoshan (Guanyin)-like religious feature and makes Yang Jiagu similar to a reincarnation of Guanyin. The preservation of this religious trait of Suyan si is a result of the revival of Buddhism in the early twentieth century. In response to the decline of Ming-Qing Buddhism and the conscription of temple property by the late Qing government, many monks, such as Taixu, Huiquan, Zhuanfeng, and Yuanying, encouraged the establishment of Buddhist associations and charitable works, supported Buddhist education, and revised the regulations of Buddhist institutions.[15] Worshipping Guanyin was truly de-emphasized in the proclamation of Suyan si but became an expedience to support their resolution of celibacy in Widow's Home-like secluded convents; the religious motive of establishing convents was then ignored. The religious characteristic of vegetarian houses started to become a part of local culture from around the 1930s. In 1928 Ven. Hongyi recorded the hard-working Buddhist practices, self-sufficient lifestyles, engagement in agriculture and handicrafts, and valuation on chastity of vegetarian nuns. He renamed them *fanxin qingxin nu* (laywomen who practice Buddhist doctrines), that is, *Brahmacarya upsikas*,[16] recognizing vegetarian nuns and incorporating them into Quanzhou Buddhist society for the first time. Then, in 1948 Ven. Xingyuan held an ordination ceremony to transmit the *Bodhisattva-samvara* to vegetarian nuns, thereby endowing them with more religious legitimacy.[17] A special account in *The Record in Memory of Wenlian Free Clinic and the Philippine Suyan Si* offers evidence that prior to the 1940s,

---

Buddhist." This statue succeeds *The Great Ming Code*. See *The Great Qing Code*, trans. William C. Jones (Oxford: Oxford University Press, 1994), 105-106; Huai Xiaofeng 懷效鋒ed., *Daming lu*大明律(The Great Ming Code), (Beijing: Falu chubanshe法律出版社, 1999), 46-47; Shen Zhiqi, *Daqinglu jizhu*, vol. 1大清律輯註 (Compilation of the Great Qing Code), ed. Huai Xiaofeng懷效鋒 (Beijing北京: Falu chubanshe法律出版社, 2000), 194-195; Xue Yunsheng薛允升, *Duli cunyi*讀例存疑 (Doubts Remaining after Pursuing the Substatutes), ed. Huang Qingjia黃靜嘉 (Taipei: Chinese Materials and Research Aids Service Center中文研究資料中心, 1970), 243-246.

[15] Wang Rongguo, *Fujian fojiao shi* 福建佛教史 (The History of Fujian Buddhism), (Xiamen: Xiamen University, 1997), 340-406.

[16] Faqing, "Minnan caigu de qiyuan han diwei," 98.

[17] Chen Zhenzhen, "Tan Fujian de 'Fangxing qingxin nu,'" 63.

most vegetarian nuns were not formally recognized as Buddhist nuns by organized Buddhists. According to Zhang Wenlian's biography, Zhang never received a fully valid ordination; after years of managing Suyan si, she only received *Bodhisattva-samvara* for a *upasika* from her instructor Ven. Xingyuan in the Philippines.[18] In other words, before these records and ordination ceremonies were proposed by famous monks, vegetarian nuns were respected by Quanzhou society for their celibacy but not yet accepted as real Buddhist nuns. Only after the 1930s did the Buddhists' efforts successfully incorporate followers of various religious practices and vegetarian cults into a revived Buddhist society and replace the value once given to nuns' chastity with the value of Buddhist piety.

The Resistance of Marriage and the Self-Identity of Vegetarian Nuns

The phenomenon of women resisting marriage and living in groups of isolated residences is neither unheard of nor unstudied by scholars. Two significant cases of this long-standing tradition of marriage resistance are spinsters' "self-combing" practice in Shunde, Guangdong and "extended natal residence marriage" in Huian, Fujian. These Guangdong Spinster Houses and vegetarian houses lacked any engagement with local societies or Buddhist institutions compared to those in Quanzhou such as Suyan si, in spite of the fact that Guangdong spinsters were equally devoted to the worship of Guanyin and Amita Buddha. Becoming a vegetarian nun for Guangdong spinsters meant losing their freedom of movement for it entailed a lifelong commitment to the monastic tradition. Their objective was to find a refuge where they could obtain "care while alive and a funeral after death." In contrast, Quanzhou vegetarian nuns from the late nineteenth century (except during the Cultural Revolution) have received all kinds of encouragement, support, and involvement from local gentry, families, government, and Buddhist associations. Without economic factors such as the demand of labor in the industry of sericulture, Quanzhou women's best alternative to obtaining freedom from marriage was entering convents.

The Huian custom of "extended natal residence marriage" will shed light on the socio-cultural background for vegetarian nuns' entrance into convents. Until the late nineteenth century Huian women returned to and

---

[18] Feilubin suyan si, *Feilubin suyan si wenlian shizhen suo jinian kan*, 95-96.

worked for natal families three days after their weddings; they were called "bride daughters." In the years following the wedding Huian bride daughters had to avoid any sexual contact with their husbands even when they visited their marital families. According to Chen Guoqiang, Qiao Jian, and Sara Friedman, the valuation of chastity combined with the discriminatory practices of female infanticide and heavy labor in fields and construction sites demonstrate Huian women's inferior status in marriage and in local society. Yet Huian bride daughters banded with other women to build a collective identity in sisterhood founded on the common predestination of suffering from marriage. This constituted a mutual surveillance mechanism to prevent any member from physical interaction with her husband.[19] Seventy folk songs and slogans collected by Sara Friedman confirm the anxiety and plight of Huian women.[20]

Quanzhou and Huian women's subordination in socioeconomic and ideological realms is a significant reason for their search for an emotional outlet within monastic order, a practice explained well by deprivation theory. All of my informants relate the custom of "extended natal residence marriage" to the appearance of many vegetarian nuns in Huian and Quanzhou areas. They conclude that it is a justified and honored alternative for women to move into Buddhist nunneries or local shrines and take vows as vegetarian nuns. Studies on Buddhist nuns in contemporary Taiwan demonstrate that the nuns witnessing the growth of Buddhist society voluntarily enter the monastic order to search for the meaning of their lives and construct their self-identity within modern Buddhist education and institutions.[21] Unlike these modern Buddhist nuns,

---

[19] Chen Guoqiang, "How Marriage Customs Differ within and without Chongwu Town, Huian County," in *Urban Anthropology in China,* eds. Greg Guild & Aidan Southall (Studies in Human Society, E. J. Brill, 1993), 381-386; QiaoJian喬健, Chen Guqiang陳國強, Zhou Lifang周立方 eds., "Huidongren yanjiu"惠東人研究 (*Studies on Eastern Huian People*) (Fujian jiaoyu chubanshe福建教育出版社, 1992); Sara Lizbeth Friedman, "Reluctant Brides and Prosperity's Daughters: Marriage, Labor, and Cultural Change in Southeastern China's Hui'an County" (Ph.D. diss., Cornell University, 2000).

[20] Sara Lizbeth Friedman, "Reluctant Brides and Prosperity's Daughters: Marriage, Labor, and Cultural Change in Southeastern China's Hui'an County," 361-369. One extreme manifestation of resistance to marriage is the phenomenon of women's group suicides in the first half of the twentieth century. Although the incidences of women's suicide has decreased in the past two decades, women's disadvantageous position in society has not significantly changed.

[21] Hillary Crane, "Resisting Marriage and Renouncing Womanhood: The Choice of

Quanzhou vegetarian nuns, mostly illiterate or semi-literate, do not benefit from higher education or feminist thought but struggle with their predicament within a patriarchal society. As Susan Starr Sered reminds us, a woman could be both deprived and autonomous.[22] In light of the examples of Shunde's spinsters, Huian's bride daughters, and Quanzhou's vegetarian nuns, their independence and agency in religious and socioeconomic activities are especially noteworthy.

Transformation from Neighborhood Temples to Buddhist Convents

Case 2. Erlang qingtong an (Erlang Rejoiced Union Convent)

Erlang qingtong an is a complex consisting of Qingtong an and Erlang miao. According to a temple inscription written in 2000 and based on oral history passed down through its abbesses, this convent devoted to the worship of Guanyin was first built in the late Ming period by a Buddhist nun named Wuzhu.[23] When the Erlang miao was razed, the local people built a hall for Erlang deity and asked for Wuzhu and her succeeding abbesses to perform incense-offering. After the Cultural Revolution, people in Erlang *jing* (territory)[24] asked CQB,[25] an unmarried disciple of the deceased abbess Ding Chengfa (a fully ordained Buddhist nun), to take charge of this convent/temple. According to CQB and her disciple HG, all four vegetarian nuns here offer incense to the Erlang deity but only pay basic respect to him; they direct their religious piety mainly toward Guanyin and other *Buddha*s in the back hall where they recite their daily sutra.

Erlang qingtong an represents both features of a Buddhist convent and a neighborhood temple, and its history reflects the close interaction

---

Taiwanese Buddhist Nuns," *Critical Asian Studies* 36.2 (2004): 265-284.

22 Susan Starr Sered, *Priestess, Mother, Sacred Sister: Religious Dominated by Women* (Oxford: Oxford University Press, 1994), 64.

23 Once again, the mention of worshiping Guanyin here highlights the value of chastity. This temple inscription indicates that "women who want to remain chaste and practice the Way, either unmarried or widowed, can come to perform the hair-shaving ritual and reach enlightenment via self-cultivation." Erlang qingtong an also played the function of Widow's Home after its establishment.

24 "*Jing*" was a smallest administrative unit of Quanzhou city in the Ming-Qing periods.

25 All vegetarian nuns I interviewed will be referred to by initials only.

between local society and vegetarian houses. Neighborhood temples are especially common in the Quanzhou area. In each lowest administrative unit of Quanzhou prefecture from the Qing dynasty onward, such as the village in the countryside or *jing* inside the city, local people worship certain tutelary gods and thereby formed their local identities. Local people thus need and actively invite vegetarian nuns to tend the temples. The original reason for establishing this temple was not only for encouraging female chastity but also for preserving the centripetal force of a local folk belief, even though the temple was gradually transformed into a Buddhist convent. From the inscription we learn that most deceased abbesses were fully ordained Buddhist nuns while only vegetarian nuns live there today, indicating that the demarcation line between Buddhist nuns and vegetarian nuns seems to be blurred in terms of chastity. Both CQB and her disciple HG are "clean maidens"; they entered Erlang qingtong an unmarried at an early age and soon vowed to be vegetarian nuns. This isolated lifestyle prevents them from extensive social interaction with other convents. The only income for this convent/temple comes from rent money on part of its property and the donations offered in exchange for the services nuns provide interpreting fortunes for worshippers. The frequent visits of local people have little influence on the monastic quietude; on the contrary, they show that Erlang qingtong an and the vegetarian nuns constitute an inevitable part of local religious life.[26] The Quanzhou and Huian Buddhist Associations allow vegetarian nuns to pay basic respect to local deities and to offer local people all kinds of religious services, provided that they register as Buddhist convents instead of Daoist temples. This phenomenon in Southeast Fujian reflects the dynamics of religious beliefs, moral concerns, and the interaction between the government and local societies in the past century.

Case 3. Lingan zunwang gong (Palace for the Honorable Lord of Efficacy and Peace) or Jingxin tang (Pure Mind Convent)

Lingan zunwang gong is a neighborhood temple in Huian County where people from three generations live, including one senior clean maiden, another three clean maidens in their thirties (two are sisters), two vegetarian nuns in their early twenties, and three teenagers. They run this temple with the donations from local people by explaining the verses on

[26] CQB and HG, interview by author, 23 January 2005, discussion, Quanzhou, China.

temple tallies and writing prayers. They also identify themselves as Buddhist nuns by arranging a hall to worship *Buddha* and Guanyin and by registering this convent (Pure Mind Convent) in the Huian Buddhist Association.

The local identity of and emotional bonds among vegetarian nuns are the main factors governing young vegetarian nuns' decisions about their Buddhist career. My main informant, YMH, a twenty-three-year-old "novice-nun" in this convent, was sent by her natal family at the age of three. The serene life in the convent and the strong sisterhood among girls attracted YMH's elementary schoolmate GMH to join her and to become a "novice-nun" when she was about ten years old. Before GMH left her family, her parents felt honored but warned her not to return to secular life. Now both young women want to leave the convent. GMH feels regretful about her childish decision to become a vegetarian nun.[27] YMH, who is teaching Chinese literature in Quanzhou Buddhist Academy, expresses her intention to pursue a graduate degree and to share a romantic love with a man.[28] But they dare not return to laity now for two reasons. The first is pressure from local society. YMH told me that girls or women who once lived in convents are always treated by local people as vegetarian nuns, whether or not they have ever received any precepts or ordination. Having once lived in convents, their return to laity would be a great shame to the convent and their natal families. People who pass up ordination could hardly reside in their natal neighborhood. A few cases of renouncing nunhood in Huian years ago deeply damaged the image of vegetarian nuns in local society.[29] YMH's instructor nun thus said to her: "If you do not come back after finishing education, you will set a negative example for the next generation and the neighborhood."[30]

For women living in neighborhood temples like Erlang qingtong an and Lingan zunwang gong, their self-identity as vegetarian nuns becomes a sub-category of local identity and is formed and continually informed by the public gaze. On the other hand, the neighborhood identity is strengthened by local pride in these chaste women who do not live on the confirmation of religious tonsure and ordination ceremonies but rather on their own religious and moral resolution. Ordinary Quanzhou people categorize all women who subsist on a vegetarian diet, remain chaste, and

[27] YMH, interview by author, 1 May 2005, discussion, Huian, China.
[28] YMH, interview by author, 28 April 2005, discussion, Quanzhou, China.
[29] YMH, interview by author, 1 May 2005, discussion, Huian, China.
[30] YMH, interview by author, 21 April 2005, discussion, Quanzhou, China.

live in convents as vegetarian nuns. "There were almost no Quanzhou nuns who received tonsure from the late nineteenth century to the 1980s," writes Chen Zhenzhen.[31] Her statement completely reflects this pride pervading Quanzhou Buddhist society and local people. However, Chen's self-reference as a lay devotee rather than a vegetarian nun illuminates the strict definition of the *sangha* of vegetarian nuns in the mind of Quanzhou Buddhists. Clearly a gap exists between the public recognition and the Buddhist qualification of vegetarian nuns, while both Buddhists and ordinary people place the same high valuation on vegetarian nuns' celibacy. Therefore, Chen's statement, overstated or not, does reflect the formation process of vegetarian nuns' self-identity and consensus among local neighborhoods.

The retroactive gratitude of novices to their instructor-nuns is the very bond that sustains these lineages of vegetarian nuns. YMH frequently visits her family, running between the convent and her natal family whenever she is in town, but she reports that her relationship with her parents is polite and distant and cannot be compared to her strong love for the vegetarian nuns. She implies that her distant relationship with her natal family results from her feeling of abandonment. Love from her instructor-nun helped YMH to endure local pressure and become the first vegetarian nun in town to complete a college education. YMH often claimed to have been spoiled by her instructor-nuns. On the other hand, although GMH is YMH's closest friend, she concurrently feels jealous of the love and support that YMH receives. GMH only received a junior high school degree and stays behind to help the senior vegetarian nuns manage temple affairs. In fact, YMH's instructor-nun expects that YMH and GMH will cooperate with each other in order to fulfill Lingan zunwang gong's expectation that GMH stay behind to manage the daily rituals and YMH receive a higher education and socialize with more Buddhist institutions in order to promote the temple.[32]

---

[31] Chen Zhenzhen, "Tan Fujian de 'Fangxing qingxin nu,'" 63. Urged by Ven. Xinyuan, Chen Zhenzhen founded Quanzhou Buddhist Academy, which was first established under the name of Juehua Buddhist Academy in 1948. It operated until 1955. All trainees were vegetarian nuns.

[32] YMH, interview by author, 1 May 2005, discussion, Huian, China.

Case 4. Baohai an (Treasure Sea Convent)

It is said that Baohai an was first built by an Indian monk in 987 C.E., but vegetarian nuns moved into this convent during the late Qing period. The incumbent abbess, LXZ, who is currently in her seventies, followed her mother in keeping a vegetarian diet early in life and received *Bodhisattva-samvara* in 1948. She fought against great adversity and refused to return to laity during the Cultural Revolution instead supporting herself by working in factories. However, another vegetarian nun named YH gave in to the pressure; she married during the Cultural Revolution but returned to Baohai an after her children had grown up. The last two teenaged adopted girls are attending now elementary school and call LXZ "Mother" (*A-nian*) instead of "Maiden" (*A-gu*).

Family-Styled Organizations and the Mother-Daughter Bond in Convents

Although there are no blood connections between the instructor-nuns and novices in either cases of Lingan zunwang gong or Baohai an, their ties and responsibilities between them are no less distant than those in kinship relationships. According to my observations from these case studies, Quanzhou vegetarian nuns nurture a motherly love for their novices and derive satisfaction from this childrearing. In the case of Baohai an the appellation "Mother" reveals love and intimacy between the instructor-nun LXZ and the two novice girls and suggests a relationship similar to the close tie between mother and daughter. This could be an exception. However, vegetarian nuns, especially in Huian, enjoy the cultural privilege of "adopting" one niece from their brothers' family to carry on the lineages of vegetarian nuns. These are rarely legal adoptions; most nieces still register in their natal households. In other cases a daughter following in her mother's footsteps by entering a convent is not unusual, for it is believed that one family member who becomes a vegetarian nun will grow "seeds," that is, may accumulate merits for family members' good fortune in their present lives as well as in future reincarnations. As for the cases of legal adoption, each vegetarian nun can adopt a girl in accordance with the one-child policy; the children come from either distant poor families or from the discriminatory practice of abandoning baby girls in front of the gates of convents.[33] Senior vegetarian nuns hope that these novices will assist them during their old age and that they will succeed into the abbacy and inherit the monastic property. This process of lineage-building by adoption and use of kinship terms does turn the convents into family-styled organizations of instructor-nuns and novice-nuns.

As is well known, this family-like organization of convents is a negotiated reaction to the Confucian and Buddhist family value systems. Buddhism's family value defers to Confucianism in terms of filial piety, which is clear in the legends of Miaoshan and of Mulian's Saving Mothers, as Chun-fang Yu and Alan Cole indicate.[34] In the legend of Miaoshan, Yu argues:

> By refusing to get married and produce an heir, Miao-shan committed the most unfilial action imaginable in Confucian society. The breach in familial and cosmic harmony could only be mended by having herself reincorporated by her father through the latter's eating of her flesh. This is an act of redemption. Her rebellion did not lead to a real separation, but ended with her 'reincorporation,' into the family.[35]

Although Confucianism is no more a state ideology, its family value system still dominates the minds and daily lives of most Chinese. The infanticide of baby girls and the revival of recovering/writing family genealogies since the 1980s echo two of the three factors which guarantee the continuation of a Chinese family/lineage: the transmission of the patrilineal descent line, and men's loyalty to a common ancestor. Tani Barlow asserts of women in imperial China that "acting within the boundaries of ethical-practical kin relations makes a person recognizably female."[36] Few women could escape the mothering responsibility or bypass the definition of femininity through the function of reproduction. Nancy Chodorow states, "The reproduction of women's mothering is the basis for the reproduction of women's location and responsibilities in the

---

[33] In a legal sense, vegetarian nuns can adopt children.

[34] Chun-fang Yu, *Kuan-yin: The Chinese Transformation of Avalokitesvara* (New York: Columbia University, 2001); Alan Cole, *Mothers and Sons in Chinese Buddhism* (Stanford: Stanford University Press, 1998).

[35] Chun-fang Yu, *Kuan-yin: The Chinese Transformation of Avalokitesvara*, 341.

[36] Tani E Barlow, "Theorizing Woman: *Funu Guojia, Jiating* (Chinese Woman, Chinese State, Chinese Family)," in *Body, Subject and Power in China*, eds. Angela Zito and Tani E. Barlow (Chicago: University of Chicago, 1994), 256.

domestic sphere."[37] After the revolutions in 1911 and 1949, did this social pressure lessen in China? In mid-sized cities like Quanzhou or small towns in Huian, where Confucian familialism has been challenged less than in other places, no such change was discernable by the 1990s. Following Miaoshan, vegetarian nuns forsake marriage and vow to be chaste; they thus lose the chance to be biological mothers and commit the greatest sin in patriarchal familism—being unfilial to ancestors and discontinuing the line of patrilineal descent. However, they obtain emotional relief and support from a group of "childless" or "childfree" women[38] as they demonstrate their autonomy and recuperate their identity in the eyes of local society. Due to the valuation of chastity and religious beliefs in Quanzhou culture, vegetarian nuns are not alienated from secular society; their sense of filial impiety is also less than that of other Buddhist nuns. If hair symbolizes sexual attractiveness and head shaving signifies a "renunciation of family life and willingness to assume a new orientation,"[39] vegetarian nuns' not receiving the tonsure not only requires a stronger resolution to remain celibate, but it also symbolizes a link between vegetarian nuns and Confucian family ideology. Therefore, vegetarian nuns construct an exemplary paradigm for women. Two different practices missing in Miaoshan's legend—adopting orphans and encouraging nieces and daughters to enter a monastery—afford these nuns respect and allow them to become reincorporated into the scope of traditional familism. They are not "the Other" to ordinary women or Quanzhou Buddhists; rather, they insist on controlling their desire while searching for spiritual freedom in the form of ordinary women in the secular world. A convent is like a Widow's Home, an orphanage, and a "family surrogate" for women to live peacefully. Chen Zhenzhen and Wu Songbo, the Secretary-General of the Quanzhou Buddhist Association, both leaders in Quanzhou Buddhist society, proudly call these convents

---

[37] Nancy Chodorow, "The Psychodynamics of the Family," in *The Second Wave: A Reader in Feminist Theory*, ed. Linda Nicholson (New York: Routledge, 1997), 195.

[38] I borrow the concepts of "childless" and "childfree" women from Mardy S. Ireland in order to discuss how female identity is formulated and separated from motherhood. See Mardy S. Ireland, *Reconceiving Women: Separating Motherhood from Female Identity* (New York: The Guilford Press, 1993).

[39] Karen Lang, "Shaven Heads and Loose Hair: Buddhist Attitudes toward Hair and Sexuality," in *Off with Her Head! The Denial of Women's Identity in Myth, Religion, and Culture*, ed. Howard Eilerg-Schwartz and Wendy Doniger (Berkeley: University of California Press, 1995), 34-35, 46.

jiazushi antang (family-styled convents).[40] A convent functions as more than housing for extra-family groups; it is a self-constructed "family," a product of the mercy and agency of vegetarian nuns.

The mother-daughter bond in convents is pivotal to preserving this surrogate family. A recurrent theme in late imperial Chinese Buddhist literature is the acquisition of merit in order to repay the burdens of mothering, and ultimately to transcend emotional attachment. On the one hand, the surrogate-family of the convent creates a sense of motherhood for vegetarian nuns. Vegetarian nuns restore their deprived social roles as mothers and elevate their social status in their matrifocal "families" and in the matrilineal system. Margery Wolf uses the concept of "uterine family" to examine kinship relationships in patriarchal society and redefine "family" for women: "*Their* [sci] family is the one they create themselves out of their own flesh, that is, their children and grandchildren, or their mother's family."[41] Vegetarian nuns leave out the flesh and blood factors but focus on the emotional ties with their novices to reach a compromise between chastity and motherhood. They feel safe and no longer need to feel like a daughter who fears the dislocation from their "family" when they marry out, or like a mother-in-law who worries about a potentially disruptive threat to her uterine family from her incoming daughter-in-law. This mother-daughter bond, formed through the rejection of marriage, is sustained through an emotional tie to religious lineage.

On the other hand, it is exactly the same intense bond that creates tension among vegetarian nuns, which is similar to sibling conflict. Novices compete for the love of instructor-nuns and the abbacy. Determining which young nuns can most increase the temple's fame and property is the primary concern for senior nuns as they select an heir and one that gradually dominates the nature of their family-convent. A convent is not built only on familial dyadic relationships; it takes a more corporate organization. Each vegetarian nun must devote herself to the convent, to

---

[40] The unspoken reason to allow the existence of these family-styled convents, I assume, is to demonstrate the historical continuity and uniqueness of Quanzhou Buddhism by legitimizing the existence of vegetarian nuns and combining the lineages of fully ordained Buddhist nuns and vegetarian nuns.

[41] Margery Wolf. "Beyond the Patrilineal Self: Constructing Gender in China" in *Self as Person in Asian Theory and Practice*, eds. Roger T. Ames, Wimal Dissanayake, and Thomas P. Kasulis (Albany, NY: State University of New York Press, 1994), 259-260. Wolf has more discussion about "uterine family" in her other book. Please see Margery Wolf, *Women and the Family in Rural Taiwan* (Stanford, CA: Stanford University Press, 1972).

farming, or to rituals in order to earn a livelihood and expanding the convent's "religious sphere." Any imbalance between the love and expectation, or any prejudice against or preference for a certain novice would generate tension and cause the dissolution of the "family-surrogate."

The Decline of the Phenomenon of Vegetarian Nuns at the Turn of the 21st Century

For years the Quanzhou Buddhist Association, which supervises the renovation of all local convents, has devoted itself to legitimizing vegetarian Buddhism. This effort blurs the difference in *Vinaya Pitaka* between a female lay devotee and a fully ordained Buddhist nun and provides vegetarian nuns with more confidence. However, it reveals objections to and pressures on the practice of vegetarian nuns by Buddhist societies outside Quanzhou area.

Case 5. Huiren si (Mercy and Humanity Convent)

Huiren si was renovated in 1996 with funding from a family named Li in Huian. The incumbent abbess is a fully ordained Buddhist nun named CR, who was "adopted" at age seven by her aunt LXL (now in her seventies), also a vegetarian nun. CR finished her high school education in 1981 and went to Fuzhou Buddhist College for higher education until 1987, when she returned to Quanzhou to teach in Quanzhou Buddhist Academy. She received her tonsure in the late 1990s. CR usually spends three or four days in the academy and on weekends returns to Huiren si, where she raises another adopted novice who is attending junior high school. In terms of her relationship with the instructor-nun LXL, CR remains respectful to her seniority while taking on responsibilities for managing convent affairs. As for educating the young girl, she sends her to the best private high school and helps with her homework whenever she can. CR's expectation for this novice is very high, but she says she would never push her to take vows: it will be up to the young girl when she reaches the age of twenty years.[42]

As interregional interaction became more frequent and restrictions on religious activities gradually loosened after 1979, more orthodox

[42] CR, interview by author, 21 April 2005, discussion, Quanzhou, China.

Buddhists visiting the Southeast Fujian area felt surprised to see the unshaven, laywoman-like (*upasika-like*) appearance of the vegetarian nuns. The National Buddhist Association started to urge Quanzhou society to universalize the image of Buddhist nuns, asserting that vegetarian nuns should receive the tonsure and *bhikusuni* vows if they want to retain their identity as Buddhist nuns. Vegetarian nuns who went to Buddhist colleges outside Quanzhou area were also urged to receive the tonsure. How vegetarian nuns should respond to this pressure, acquire recognition from Buddhists nationwide, and pursue higher education in Buddhist colleges of other areas have become the greatest worries for the Quanzhou and Huian Buddhist Associations in terms of the continuity of vegetarian nun lineages. First, the Associations continue helping vegetarian nuns renovate ruined convents. Second, the Quanzhou Buddhist Association assisted Chen Zhenzhen in reviving Quanzhou Buddhist Academy in 1987 with the view of elevating the level of vegetarian nuns' literacy. Though this academy accepted exclusively vegetarian nuns in the last three years of the 1980s, in 1990 a Buddhist nun from northern China was hired as the provost who accepted fully ordained Buddhist nuns as students. This created a long-term negative impact on the continuity of vegetarian nun lineages. Young vegetarian nuns gradually came to feel inferior to Buddhist nuns because their Buddhist nun classmates convinced them that to shave their hair would demonstrate more religious piety.[43] In addition, some "vegetarian nun" teachers in this academy, such as the abbess CR of Huiren si, overthrew the old identity of vegetarian nuns by receiving the tonsure in order to be included in the national Buddhist society and to serve important positions in Buddhist Associations. Chen Zhenzhen told me that CR's decision irked her instructor monk in *Kaiyuan si* (the most famous temple and the leading Buddhist society in Quanzhou) and many other Quanzhou Buddhists. They thought that CR disturbed the lineage of vegetarian nuns and deviated from the Quanzhou Buddhist tradition.[44] However, in the greater Quanzhou area, the trend of receiving the tonsure has all but disappeared.

This change in self-identity of vegetarian nuns inevitably poses a great threat to maintaining the family-surrogate feature of convents. In CR's case, her instructor-nun LXL lives a leisurely retired life and allows CR to make all the decisions as long as CR often returns to Huiren si. Given this

[43] SZ, interview by author, 19-20 April 2005, discussion, Quanzhou, China; Banyan, interview by author, 22-23 April 2005, discussion, Quanzhou, China.

[44] Chen Zhenzhen, interview by author, 6 May 2005, discussion, Quanzhou, China.

aunt/instructor-nun's love for CR, there is no obvious conflict over authority between the two. In fact, many novices shave off their hair and then wish to start their own monastic practice by joining large convents or renovating ruined convents. A fully ordained Buddhist nun SY serves as another example. In 1999 SY secretly took the entrance examination to Fuzhou Buddhist Academy in order to force her instructor-nun to allow her departure. SY now teaches in Quanzhou Buddhist Academy. Although the Quanzhou Buddhist Academy is close to her instructor's convent, she rarely goes back to visit.[45] CR's and SY's examples illustrate the fact that the number of young vegetarian nuns is decreasing and many convents are facing difficulties continuing the lineages of vegetarian nuns.

In addition, not all convents can experience such a peaceful reverse of power as in CR's case when facing the shift of authority or a hierarchical inversion between instructor-nuns and novice-nuns. Young Buddhist nuns now possess more religious authority than the old instructor-nuns: they no longer bow to instructor-nuns even though they return to their small convents, and they stand in front of their instructor-nuns during morning and afternoon services. Some young Buddhist nuns even refuse to participate in any of the convent's agricultural and cleaning activities. Unable to bear this shame, some vegetarian nuns in their seventies or eighties also ask to perform hair-shaving rituals.[46] In short, other than giving up nunhood,[47] the deepest worry for senior vegetarian nuns is that the novices will take a *bhiksuni* vow as well as receive the tonsure, but refuse to return to the convents. Many old vegetarian nuns thus prohibit their novice-nuns from leaving the convents and their hometowns to pursue higher education; some ask the novices to drop out of schools and return to the convents to take care of the aged nuns and monastic affairs. Interaction with outside Buddhists disrupted this tradition and altered the self-identity of vegetarian nuns. As an increasing number of vegetarian nuns are influenced by their peers to shave their hair and receive *bhikusuni* vows, the decline of the vegetarian nun phenomenon seems irreversible.

---

[45] SY, interview by author, 23 April 2005, discussion, Quanzhou, China.

[46] Chen Zhenzhen, "Tan Fujian de 'Fangxing qingxin nu,'" 65.

[47] The number of vegetarian nuns returning to laity is increasing, as I was told in Quanzhou Buddhist Academy by teenage vegetarian nuns themselves.

Conclusion

This essay centers on how Quanzhou people in the past century have localized Confucianism and Buddhism to fit their social needs and preserved the historical development of the phenomenon of vegetarian nuns. I identify two aspects of this localization process. First, how the high valuation of chastity, familism, and strong local cults in Quanzhou society encouraged the establishment of convents; and second, how vegetarian nuns developed a special mother-daughter bond which created and strengthened vegetarian nuns' self-identity and continuation.

First, the emergence of convents results from three value systems—Confucian familism (including high valuation of chastity), Buddhist precepts, and folk beliefs—which are embedded in Quanzhou local culture. Buddhism in late imperial and Republican Quanzhou compromised and was reinterpreted within the scope of local religious practices. These cases highlight the functional transformation of convents during the past century. As implied in Chen Zhenzhen's essay, today's Quanzhou Buddhists see the appearance of vegetarian nuns as an honorable feature of Quanzhou Buddhist culture, though they ignore the contributions of local cults to this phenomenon. I stress that the growth of the *sangha* of vegetarian nuns reflects the engagement of local societies. Under the public gaze, the virtue of chastity in Neo-Confucian familism contributed to the emergence of vegetarian nuns and the formation of their self-identity. Vegetarian nuns are always under the scrutiny of Buddhists and local communities. Maintaining a balance between an ideal Buddhist nunhood and Confucian family ethics such as filial piety and chastity once won them local support. In the 1930s, however, Buddhist monks endeavored to convert vegetarian nuns and recognize them as Buddhist nuns. Their effort to incorporate vegetarian nuns into a broader religious society, however, elicited a decline in this phenomenon which started in the 1990s and continues to the present day. It was the localization process, in other words, that had distinguished vegetarian nuns from other Buddhist nuns or laywomen.

Second, the last three case studies (Lingan zunwang gong, Baohai an, and Huiren si) have demonstrated how aunt-niece and instructor-novice relationships are transformed into a mother-daughter bond. Originally based on family ties and the authority of kinship hierarchy, these bonds sustain the lineage of vegetarian nuns and help build a link between the Buddhist home-leaving tradition and Confucian family values. Their pessimistic view of married life allows vegetarian nuns to retain their agency and self-determination, while their family-surrogates and mother-daughter bonds overthrow the belief that traditional or illiterate women fled to convents as refugees. These practices prove that vegetarian nuns have no less resolution and agency than fully ordained Buddhist nuns and account for the continuity and development of their *sangha* in the twentieth century.

Works cited

Banyan, Buddhist nun and student of Quanzhou Buddhist Academy. Interview by author, 22-23 April 2005, Quanzhou. Discussion. Quanzhou Buddhist Academy, Quanzhou, China.

Barlow, Tani E. "Theorizing Woman: *Funu Guojia*, *Jiating* (Chinese Woman, Chinese State, Chinese Family." In *Body, Subject and Power in China*, eds. Angela Zito and Tani E. Barlow, 253-289. Chicago: The University of Chicago Press, 1994.

Cao Xuansi曹玄思. "Xiantian dao de zishunu." 先天道的自梳女(Spinsters in the Way of Former Heaven). In *Huanan hunyin zhidu yu funu diwei*華南婚姻制度與婦女地位(The Marriage System and Women's Status in Southeast China), eds. Ma Jianzhao馬建釗, Qiao Jian喬健, and Du Ruile杜瑞樂, 124-140. Guangxi minzu chubanshe廣西民族出版社, 1994.

Chen Guoqiang 陳國強. "How Marriage Customs Differ within and without Chongwu Town, Huian County." In *Urban Anthropology in China*, eds. Greg Guild and Aidan Southall, 381-386. Studies in Human Society, E. J. Brill, 1993.

Chen Zhenzhen 陳珍珍. "Tan Fujian de 'Fangxing qingxin nu'" 談福建的「梵行清信女」 (About Laywomen Who Practice Buddhist Doctrines in Fujian), *Fayin yuekan*法音月刊 1 (January 2000): 63-68.

—. female lay devotee. Interview by author, 6 May 2005. Discussion. Quanzhou, China.

Chikusa Masaaki筑沙雅章. Guanyu 'chicai shimo關於喫菜事魔 (On "Vegetarians Who Served the Evil"). In *Sixiang Congjiao*思想宗教(*Thoughts and Religions*) . Translated by Xu Yangzhu許洋主. Riben xuezhe yanjiu zhongguoshi lunzhu xuanyi日本學者研究中國史論著選譯 (Selected Translations of Studies on Chinese History by Japanese Scholars), ed. by Liu Junwen劉俊文, Vol. 7, 361-385. Beijing: Zhonghua shuju中華書局, 1982.

Chodorow, Nancy. "The Psychodynamics of the Family." In *The Second Wave: A Reader in Feminist Theory*, ed. Linda Nicholson, 181-197. New York: Routledge, 1997.

Cole, Alan. *Mothers and Sons in Chinese Buddhism*. Stanford: Stanford University Press, 1998.

CQB, vegetarian nuns of Quanzhou. Interview by author, 23 January 2005, Quanzhou. Discussion. Erlang qingtong an, Quanzhou, China.

CR, vegetarian nun of Quanzhou. Interview by author, 21 April 2005, Quanzhou. Discussion. Huiren xi, Quanzhou, China.

Faqing 法清. "Minnan caigu de qiyuan han diwei" 閩南菜姑的起源和地位 (The Origin and Status of Vegetarian Nuns in Southeast Fujian), *Minnan foxiuyuan xiubao*閩南佛學院學報 7 (1992): 93-99.

Feilubin suyan si菲律賓宿燕寺. *Feilubin suyan si wenlian shizhen suo jinian kan*菲律賓宿燕寺文蓮施診所紀念刊 (*Record in Memory of Wenlian Free Clinic and the Philippine Swallow-Residing Convent*) . Philippine: Suyan si, 1983.

Friedman, Sara Lizbeth. "Reluctant Brides and Prosperity's Daughters: Marriage, Labor, and Cultural Change in Southeastern China's Hui'an County." Ph.D. diss., Cornell University, 2000.

HG, vegetarian nuns of Quanzhou. Interview by author, 23 January 2005, Quanzhou. Discussion. Erlang qingtong an, Quanzhou, China.

Huai Xiaofeng 懷效鋒ed. *Daming lu*大明律(The Great Ming Code). Beijing: Falu chubanshe法律出版社, 1999.

Ireland, Mardy S. *Reconceiving Women: Separating Motherhood from Female Identity*. New York: The Guilford Press, 1993.

Jiang Canteng江燦騰. "Cong zaigu dao biqiuni: Taiwan fojiao nuxing chujia de bainian cangsang" 從齋姑到比丘尼:台灣佛教女性出家的百年滄桑 (From Vegetarian Nuns to Fully Ordained Buddhist Nuns: The Century-old Vicissitudes of Home-leaving Experiences of Buddhist Women in Taiwan). *Lishi yuekan* 歷史月刊 105 (1996): 22-32.

Lang, Karen. "Shaven Heads and Loose Hair: Buddhist Attitudes toward Hair and Sexuality." In *Off with Her Head! The Denial of Women's Identity in Myth, Religion, and Culture*, ed. Howard Eilerg-Schwartz and Wendy Doniger, 32-52. Berkeley, Los Angeles, London: University of California Press, 1995.

QiaoJian喬健, Chen Guqiang陳國強, Zhou Lifang周立方 eds. "Huidongren yanjiu"惠東人研究 (*Studies on Eastern Huian People*). Fuzhou福州: Fujian jiaoyu chubanshe福建教育出版社, 1992.

Sankar, Andrea P. “Spinster Sisterhoods: Jing Yih Sifu: Spinster-Domestic-Nun.” In *Lives: Chinese Working Women*, eds. by Mary Sheridan and Janet W. Salaff, 51-70. Bloomington: Indiana University Press, 1984.

—. *Sister and Brothers, Lovers and Enemies: Marriage Resistance in Southern Kwangtung Anthropology and Homosexual Behaviour*. The Haworth Press, Inc, 1986.

Sered, Susan Starr. *Priestess, Mother, Sacred Sister: Religions Dominated by Women*. Oxford: Oxford University Press, 1994.

Shen Zhiqi沈之奇. *The Great Qing Code*. Translated by William C. Jones. Oxford: Oxford University Press, 1994.

—. *Daqinglu jizhu “shang”*大清律輯註（上）(Compilation of the Great Qing Code Vol. 1), ed. Huai Xiaofeng 懷效鋒. Beijing北京: Falu chubanshe法律出版社, 2000.

Shijia si釋迦寺. n.d. *Quanzhou Shijian si gaikuang* 泉州釋迦寺概況 (A General Introduction to Sijian Monastery in Quanzhou). Quanzhou, China.

Stockard, Janice E. *Daughters of the Canton Delta: Marriage Patterns and Economic Strategies in South China, 1860-1930*. Stanford: Stanford University Press, 1989.

SY, Buddhist nun of Quanzhou. Interview by author, 23 April 2005, Quanzhou. Discussion. Quanzhou Buddhist Academy, Quanzhou, China.

SZ, vegetarian nun and student of Quanzhou Buddhist Academy. Interview by author, 19-20 April 2005, Quanzhou. Discussion. Quanzhou Buddhist Academy, Quanzhou, China.

T’ien Ju-k’ang. *Male Anxiety and Female Chastity: A Comparative Study of Chinese Ethical Values in Ming-Ch’ing Times*. Leiden: E. J. Brill, 1988.

Topley, Marjerie. “Chinese Women’s Vegetarian Houses in Singapore.” *Journal Malayan Branch of the Royal Asiatic Society* 27, no. 1 (1954): 51-67.

—. 1991. “Marriage Resistance in Rural Kwangtung.” In *Women in Chinese Society*, eds. Margery Wolf and Roxane Witke, 67-88. Berkeley: University of California Press.

Wang Rongguo. *Fujian fojiao shi* 福建佛教史 (The History of Fujian Buddhism). Xiamen University, 1997.

Wolf, Margery. 1972. *Women and the Family in Rural Taiwan*. Stanford: Stanford University Press.

—. "Beyond the Patrilineal Self: Constructing Gender in China." In *Self as Person in Asian Theory and Practice*, eds. Roger T. Ames, Wimal Dissanayake, and Thomas P., 251-268. Kasulis. Albany, NY: State University of New York Press, 1994.

Wu Youxiong吳幼雄. *Quanzhou congjiao wenhua* 泉州宗教文化 (The Religious Culture in Quanzhou). Quanzhou泉州: Lujiang chubanshe鷺江出版社, 1993.

Xue Yunsheng薛允升. *Duli cunyi*讀例存疑 (Doubts Remaining after Pursuing the Substatutes), ed. Huang Qingjia黃靜嘉. Taipei: Chinese Materials and Research Aids Service Center中文研究資料中心, 1970.

YMH, vegetarian nun of Quanzhou. Interview by author, 21 April 2005, Quanzhou. Discussion. Quanzhou Buddhist Academy, Quanzhou, China.

YMH, vegetarian nun of Quanzhou. Interview by author, 28 April 2005, Quanzhou. Discussion. Quanzhou Buddhist Academy, Quanzhou, China.

YMH, vegetarian nun of Quanzhou. Interview by author, 1 May 2005, Huian. Discussion. Lingan zunwang gong, Huian, China.

Yu, Chun-fang. *Kuan-yin: The Chinese Transformation of Avalokitesvara*. New York: Columbia University, 2001.

Zhou Minghui周明慧. "Yicun yu jiuge: Huian Chongwu de caigu yu caitang 依存與糾葛： 惠安崇武的菜姑與菜堂 (Reliance and Entanglement: Vegetarian Nuns and Vegetarian Houses in Chongwu, Huian)." MA thesis. Taiwan: Qinghua University, 1999.

Select Bibliography

Cao Xuansi曹玄思. "Xiantian dao de zishunu" 先天道的自梳女(Spinsters in the Way of Former Heaven). In *Huanan hunyin zhidu yu funu diwei*華南婚姻制度與婦女地位(The Marriage System and Women's Status in Southeast China), eds. Ma Jianzhao馬建釗, Qiao Jian喬健, and Du Ruile杜瑞樂, 124-140. Guangxi minzu chubanshe廣西民族出版社, 1994.

Chen Guoqiang 陳國強. "How Marriage Customs Differ within and without Chongwu Town, Huian County." In *Urban Anthropology in China*, eds. Greg Guild and Aidan Southall, 381-386. Studies in Human Society, E. J. Brill, 1993.

Chen Zhenzhen 陳珍珍. "Tan Fujian de 'Fangxing qingxin nu'" 談福建的「梵行清信女」 (About Laywomen Who Practice Buddhist Doctrines in Fujian), *Fayin yuekan*法音月刊 1 (January 2000): 63-68.

Cole, Alan. *Mothers and Sons in Chinese Buddhism*. Stanford: Stanford University Press, 1998.

Crane, Hillary. "Resisting Marriage and Renouncing Womanhood: The Choice of Taiwanese Buddhist Nuns," *Critical Asian Studies* 36.2 (2004): 265-284.

Faqing 法清. "Minnan caigu de qiyuan han diwei" 閩南菜姑的起源和地位 (The Origin and Status of Vegetarian Nuns in Southeast Fujian), *Minnan foxiuyuan xiubao*閩南佛學院學報 7 (1992): 93-99.

Friedman, Sara Lizbeth. "Reluctant Brides and Prosperity's Daughters: Marriage, Labor, and Cultural Change in Southeastern China's Hui'an County." Ph.D. dissertation. Cornell University, 2000.

QiaoJian喬健, Chen Guqiang陳國強, Zhou Lifang周立方 eds. "Huidongren yanjiu"惠東人研究 (*Studies on Eastern Huian People*). Fuzhou福州: Fujian jiaoyu chubanshe福建教育出版社, 1992.

Sankar, Andrea P. "Spinster Sisterhoods: Jing Yih Sifu: Spinster-Domestic-Nun." In *Lives: Chinese Working Women*, eds. by Mary Sheridan and Janet W. Salaff, 51-70. Bloomington: Indiana University Press, 1984.

—. *Sister and Brothers, Lovers and Enemies: Marriage Resistance in Southern Kwangtung Anthropology and Homosexual Behaviour*. The Haworth Press, Inc, 1986.

Stockard, Janice E. *Daughters of the Canton Delta: Marriage Patterns and Economic Strategies in South China, 1860-1930*. Stanford, CA: Stanford University Press, 1989.

T'ien Ju-k'ang. *Male Anxiety and Female Chastity: A Comparative Study of Chinese Ethical Values in Ming-Ch'ing Times*. Leiden: E. J. Brill, 1988.

Topley, Marjerie. "Chinese Women's Vegetarian Houses in Singapore." *Journal Malayan Branch of the Royal Asiatic Society* 27, no. 1 (1954): 51-67.

—. "Marriage Resistance in Rural Kwangtung." In *Women in Chinese Society*, eds. Margery Wolf and Roxane Witke, 67-88. Berkeley: University of California Press, 1991.

Yu, Chun-fang. *Kuan-yin: The Chinese Transformation of Avalokitesvara*. New York: Columbia University, 2001.

Zhou Minghui周明慧. "Yicun yu jiuge: Huian Chongwu de caigu yu caitang 依存與糾葛： 惠安崇武的菜姑與菜堂 (Reliance and Entanglement: Vegetarian Nuns and Vegetarian Houses in Chongwu, Huian)." MA thesis. Taiwan: Qinghua University, 1999.

CHAPTER SIXTEEN

THE BODY OF THE GODDESS, ECO-AWARENESS AND EMBODIMENT IN HINDU MYTH AND ROMANCE

STHANESHWAR TIMALSINA

Introduction

This essay explores select Hindu myths of the goddess found reverberating in romantic literature in light of embodied cosmology and ecological vision. The archetypal myths to be analyzed herein characteristically weave together multiple images and concepts that apply a non-dual understanding of consciousness and the body.[1] The body of the goddess here is a multi-layered placeholder, representing self-sacrifice, the paradoxical character of presence-in-absence, an image of regeneration, mortification, union, food and milk, while simultaneously the suppressed, dark, scary, and wild.[2] The carnal bliss of the goddess in light of these

---

[1] The application of the concept of archetype borrows from Jungian psychology, which itself draws upon the Indian cosmology. Select readings utilized in developing this essay include Jung, Karl Gustav. *Man and His Symbols,* Doubleday and Co., 1964; Jung, Karl Gustav, and Kerenyi, C. *Essays on a Science of Mythology: The Myths of the Divine Child and the Divine Maiden.* Translated by R. F. C. Hull, Revised edition, Harper and Row, 1963; Neumann, Eric, *Amor and Psyche: The Psychic Development of the Feminine: A Commentary on the Tale by Apuleius.* Translated by Ralph Manheim. Pantheon Books, 1956; Neumann, Eric, *The Great Mother: An Analysis of the Archetype.* Translated by Ralph Manheim. Pantheon Books, 1955.

[2] For 'body' as the 'other,' see de Certeau, Michel. *Heterologies: Discourse on the Other.* Trans. Brian Massumi. Vol. 17, *Theory and History of Literature.* Eds. Wald Godzich and Jochen Schulte-Sasse. Minneapolis, 1986; Cooey, Paula M.

myths and romances is that of emptying oneself while also giving birth to cosmic and organic forces through shattering one's own body.[3] The body of the goddess addressed here, therefore, is both the sacrificial object and also the source of immortality.

The approach here of reading myth and romance is not historical. The truth revealed through archetypal narratives woven through myths and romance cannot be confined to a linear time-frame. This, however, does not remove fiction from the realm of reality: the lack of historicity does not displace it from the realm of human experience. The deconstructive method applied here again does not seek the historical context to confine the meaning to India of the past, as these myths and narratives still resonate within the larger, contemporary culture. The mythical, along these lines, outlives the historical, and the 'fictional' that lives in the imaginative realm of human consciousness contributes to shaping collective consciousness with no less impact than the phenomenal. In this reading, the meanings attributed to the plot narratives may not be limited to the original intent. Myths live through civilization and gain their own voice. The reality of this romantic realm is immediately felt and not placed in a distant past: this is after all the tender side of the body of the goddess that is being touched.

Myth is a poetic spontaneity, and to unravel myth is to deconstruct poetry. In order to understand the mythical vision of India as an embodiment of the goddess, we will explore select examples from the enchanting romantic epics of Kālidāsa.[4] By no means exhaustive but as an exemplary survey, this study will demonstrate the harmony existing between humans and nature in classical depictions, providing a ground for the argument of non-dual experience that binds the subjective and objective realms of consciousness.

Invoking myths and romance against this backdrop is of course a type of exorcism. The context deracinates myths' potential powers. Speaking

---

"Experience, Body, and Authority." *Harvard Theological Review,* 82/3 (July 1999): 325-342; Cooey, Paula M. *Religious Imagination and the Body: A Feminist Analysis,* Oxford University Press, 1994. (what is this?)

[3] For the concept of *jouissance* and French feminism, see Irigari, Luce. *This Sex Which Is Not One.* Eds. Catherine Porter and Carolyn Burke. Ithaca, 1985.

[4] Looking at Kālidāsa's writing from an ecological perspective, however, is not unique to this author, as scholars have spelled out similar reflections in their writings. For example, see T. S. Rukmini's "Literary Foundations for an Ecological Aesthetic: Dharma, Ayurveda, the Arts, and Abhijnanasakuntalam," in *Hinduism and Ecology: The Intersections of Earth, Sky, and Water,* eds. Christopher Key Chappel and Mary Evelyn Tucker, pp. 101-125.

through myth now in the wake of the language of commerce can already be found among the wild irrational savages: we are proud to wake up from mythical slumber to industrial reality and technological enhancement. Enchanted by the boons of industrialization, its power to create new circles of marginalized and untouchables by rendering them without dignity has been ignored. Mankind is always living in a dream, whether in the slumber of early civilization or in the blindness of modern awareness. This is what makes invoking an alternative vision of rationality relevant. The purpose of this regeneration of the body of Śakti or reading the myth in a new light is to reconstruct a rationality that does not endanger the very being of human civilization.

Myth 1: The Descent of Gaṅgā

Bhagīratha conducts severe penance so that the Ganges may descend from the heavens and soak the dry land where the bodies of the sons of Sagara were incinerated by the fury of a sage. Śiva agrees to spread his matted hair and hold the Ganges as she descends to earth. Gaṅgā not only liberates the sons of Sagara with her flow, she forever emancipates the people of India.

In Hindu cosmology, goddesses are present everywhere in nature. Gaṅgā is the prototype of all Indian rivers; the 'daughter of the Mountain' manifests in caves, peaks, and slopes, while other goddesses unite with Śiva in the snowy peaks and confluences. She is present in herbs and plants, in rocks, soil, and sand. There is nothing that is devoid of the goddess. This Śākta vision of non-dual experience depicts an embodied cosmology, with consciousness being an integral part of the body. The myth of the presence of the goddess in nature is also the placeholder of her presence in the body. As self-sacrificing Satī, as Gaṅgā, she sustains the life of millions of Indians while dying in the new fire-pit of capitalism, with modern industries poisoning her life fluids. As a repressed subaltern, she is the voiceless one. Her vital energy manifests in 'pouring out,' in being extinguished while giving birth, and in quenching the thirst of her children.[5]

[5] For 'subaltern' and the 'female body,' see Gayatri Chakravorti Spivak, "A Literary Representation of the Subaltern," in *Subaltern Studies* (Vol. V): *Writings on South Asian History and Society*. Ed. Ranjit Guha, Calcutta: Oxford University Press, pp. 91-134.

Myth 2: Satī's Body

Satī is in love with Śiva, a wild wanderer who smears ashes over his body, lives in the cremation ground, walks naked in public, and rides an old bull. What could be more humiliating to the prototypical Indian father Dakṣa who, at the pinnacle of caste and class hierarchy, agrees to wed his most beautiful daughter to this hermit, having successfully arranged the marriages of all other daughters with gods? Although Satī marries Śiva, she remains as a scar, a source of humiliation to the elite Dakṣa family. The betrothed couple does not receive invitations for the events at Dakṣa's house. Despite being ignored, Satī appears, as if revolting against the exclusion. Unable to bear the pain of humiliating words heaped upon her consort, she jumps into the sacrificial fire and immolates herself. Śiva pulls her body from the fire, but Satī is already dead. Śiva, in grief, carries her body as he wanders throughout the Indian sub-continent, with different parts of Satī's body falling at different sites. Each of these sites becomes a power-shrine for worshipping the goddess. Satī is the prototypical Indian daughter. Whether before or after birth, being Satī implies being dead. She is dead to save the dignity of her parents. In this way, she is also the placeholder for those repressed who cannot speak, not only because they are silenced, but also because they have not found their own voice.

The myth of Satī does not end with the immolation of her body. In Hinduism, consciousness precedes the body. Just as the seasons change and new leaves grow, so does the new body manifest on the foundation of consciousness. While Śiva is in deep meditation, Satī is reborn as the daughter of Parvata, mountain. She does not wish to marry anyone but Śiva. Kālidāsa recounts this story, found in several Purāṇas, in his epic *Kumārasaṃbhava* (KS). The myth of Satī speaks of love, self-immolation, regeneration, and union.

As Satī, the goddess is the mother, as Śakti, she is the embodied force, and as Śrī or Pārvatī, she is the divine consort. The power-shrines distributed all over India are considered to have emanated from the dismembered body of Satī. Death, decomposition, and the absence of a single body are preconditions for her effulgent manifestation, as the goddess emerges from death to life. The goddess is also Śakti who is inseparable from Śiva. As Pārvatī, the goddess is rebirth, union, the end of suffering, and the placeholder of liberation. In this way, the goddess-myths are not only myths of power, they are also powerful myths of transformation.

Myth 3: Śakuntalā

Śakuntalā, an abandoned child raised by a hermit, succumbs to the blandishments of a wandering king. Her life changes forever after one small meeting that the king does not even remember. The latter part of this essay endeavors to deconstruct the narrative of Śakuntalā at greater length.

Bhārat Mātā: The Mother-Cow and the Mother-Spider

The most powerful of the nature myths are those that spring from the descent of Gan̊gā, and those that include the presence of Satī's body, which fell to all parts of the Indian sub-continent, the land then empowered by her physical presence. In both depictions, divinity is found in the form of the mother. This image culminates in a single image of Bhārat Mātā, Mother India. The processes of myth-making and demythologizing both play a role in modern-day India. In Indian myth and the cultural past, land is not a property to own, but a conscious, living, and caring mother of her children. Just to demonstrate how the myths mentioned above still speak to the people of the Indian sub-continent, hundreds of millions of people visit one or another of the goddess shrines every year. India is conceptualized as surrounded by the physical parts of the goddess through her shrines from Kāmākhyā to Kanyākumārī to Vaiṣṇodevī. Many more Hindus visit the sacred sites by the Ganges, and dip into her waters. The Kumbha Melā draws one of the largest populations for any religious gathering that occurs around the globe. These myths are woven into the fabric of Indian society and confirm the presence of the goddess in her earthly body, residing in her mountain-caves and sacred sites called *piṭhas*, and in her presence as the Ganges. As land, the goddess provides shelter and food, and as river, she offers nourishing fluid. In an enchanting Śākta vision, a believer is eternally seated in the lap of the mother goddess.

This myth is also enlivened by the independence-day invocation of India as the mother, or Bhārat Mātā. Through the writings of Bankim Chandra or Aurobindo, India again appears living, with her sons fighting for her independence against the colonial forces raping and dismembering her motherly body, the continent itself. In this vision, the milk and blood of India is squeezed out for the industrial benefit of the imperial powers. Any external invasion of India is seen as a rape. This colonial depiction of the subdued mother emerges again, but now with her own children exploiting the resources of the land and waters.

While India is conceptualized as the Mother in its myths and in the political sphere, a new consumerism reverses this myth. With a double-digit GDP and population of over a billion in this triangle-shaped country identified by Tantric vision as the vulva of the goddess, the body of the goddess becomes individual property for consumption and profit. The river Ganges, the earthly presence of the divine mother, turns to literal sewage, carrying tons of organic and chemical waste. The once-green mountains and plains are crowded by eternally hungry sons of "Mother India," with her mines and minerals consumed by giant companies that compete in the global market. As corporations penetrate deeply underground for hidden resources, no part of the body remains untouched. Each new consumer group is ready to literally devour everything the land and water of India can provide.

In mythical slumber, India is the mother. Her physical presence ensures liberation and the fulfillment of worldly desires. In the modern technologically aware and awakened India, the body of the 'mother' is sold and consumed. In colonized India, both Indians and India are the subalterns; neither has their voice. In decolonized India, Indians can speak, but India cannot. This conquered body of nature is now the victim of her own people, not satisfied by her nourishing milk, squeezing the very lifeblood by emptying the natural resources.

Hindu myths depict the earth in the form of a cow. Revered as a sacred animal, the cow as a mother provides milk for her children. This mythical depiction clearly represents that humankind and the earth are interdependent: humans care for the earth just like they do for their cattle, and the earth provides nourishing 'milk.' Humans consume the milk without risking the life of calves, and in the case of the earth, consume natural resources while protecting her innocent and subdued children, the wildlife. However, with the increase of greenhouse gases produced, the nourishing milk of earth is being poisoned and with the temperature increase, the life of the Ganges is at risk. This new way of consumption is not that of milking the cow, but of the spider babies devouring their mother before searching for food outside.

Geologically, India is one of the places on earth most vulnerable to global warming and climate change. Already warm, India will have to cope with rising heat and parts of India already suffering from drought will have to wait longer to see drops of rain. With the rise of temperature, snow peaks will melt, glaciers will flow, and the map of Himalaya will change. Even now, near the Brahmaputra and Koshi Rivers, the northeast of India is hard-hit, with millions displaced and thousands killed by floods. This will be nothing compared to the wrath of the Ganges with the meltdown of snow that sustains the water system of India. If this is ignored, for years there will be floods, and then, a perpetual drought. Mountains once green will become naked and the land once fertile will turn to sand. Using the mother-spider as a metaphor for India, before her babies will be able to crawl out, the body of the mother spider will be drained of its juice.

This is not the picture of a welcoming future. However, it is not possible to avoid it by dwelling in perpetual slumber instead of facing this reality. Yet it has not been on the priority list of the leaders, intellectual masses, or the corporate elites. From the mythical slumber of a resplendent past to the technological slumber of not wanting to face reality, the gap between what is civilized and primitive is marginal. From an ancient rationality of deification to the modern rationality of consumption, the only change that has been made is that the early myth enlivened the earthly body as the mother, only to have it transformed into an object of consumption and profit. In this modern sacrifice of Satī, neo-cons of capitalism are the new Dakṣa. While the ancient myth ensures the presence of the goddess in different parts of India, the modern myth of consumerism elevates the role of pleasure in the process of rationalizing and de-spiritualizing India. The land once sacred is now capital, and the once-liberating Ganges is now merely water, and even a sewer.

Ecological concern, in relationship to these myths, is not merely a 'tree-hugging' vision, but rather, it is the vision of rationality transformed by the assumption that the analytical and emotional are not binary opposites.[6] Following this vision, humans and nature are interdependent, and that awareness is both felt and experienced.[7] The underlying assumption here is that nature and culture are not aspects of two opposites that exist by negating the other, but that it is one integral process of the same reality manifest in different forms. The constructions of the self and

---

6 For ecology and the divine feminine, see, Adams, Carol (ed.). 1994. *Ecofeminism and the Sacred.* New York: Continuum; Birch, Charles, William Eakin, and Jay B. McDaniel. (eds.) 1990. *Liberating Life: Contemporary Approaches to Ecological Theology.* New York: Orbis Books; Shiva, Vandana. 1997. *Bipolarity: The Plunder of Nature and Knowledge.* Toronto: Between the Lines; Warren, Karen. (ed.) 1997. *Ecofeminism: Women, Culture, Nature.* Bloomington: Indiana University Press; Eaton, Heather, and Lorentzen, Lois Ann. 2003. *Ecofeminism and Globalization: Exploring Culture, Context, and Religion.* New York: Rawman and Littlefield Publishers, Inc.

7 For eco-feminism, see Mellor, Mary. "Eco-feminism and Eco-socialism: Dilemmas of Essentialism and Materialism." *Capitalism, Natur, Socialism: A Journal of Socialist Ecology* 3/2 (June 1992), 43-62.

the 'other,' in this perspective, are impositions on the same spontaneous experience shared by all sentient beings. This again is not the eco-vision where humankind is just one small fraction of the process, helpless and bound. Following the metaphor of a cow, the human here enjoys greater freedom and has the choice of co-existence or mutual extinction. The dualistic vision, wherein God gives humankind a soulless nature and authorizes the conquest and exploitation of nature, has not only separated man from the rest of the universe, it has allowed the self-justification of human superiority. The Indian masses, armed with modern Western education, have adopted the external shell of the above-mentioned myths while overlooking their substance, the message where nature and humankind constitute one single consciousness. In the absence of a cultural regeneration, the sleepwalking of India is mistakenly identified as awakening. Often translating domestic accoutrements as domestic happiness, those enraptured by rapid industrialization have ignored cultural and natural sensitivities, including tribal linguistic and cultural existence, ethnic and local governance, and the traditional sciences, including medicine.

The present scenario demands a serious consideration of co-existence and mutual dependence as a model for humankind interacting with nature, as it is the human being who stands atop the food-chain and exercises his mastery over nature. The negative consequences of this mastery have become visible in the ability of the ruling culture to abolish minority cultures, and of mankind to exploit resources and drive plant and animal species to extinction. The suggested model of interdependence confirms that nature, the body, the repressed, and the subaltern are integral to the rational, to culture, consciousness, and the elite. Within this paradigm is sensation, emotion, the irrational, and romantic, undivided by mind and rationality.

The Myth of Re-union

The myth of Śiva and Pārvatī can also confront the separation of the body and the self, the emotional and the intellectual, and nature and humankind. As a primitive awakens in his ignorance of science and technology, modern man awakens in his ignorance of a collective awareness and his interdependence with nature, and his blind arrogance of mastery over natural laws.

This rationalization begins with the demystification of nature and of the myths themselves. The focus on science and technology in academic institutions moves traditional education, religion, and culture to the margin. As culture and religion have always remained a source of fascination to the masses, this old education becomes the source of income for 'self-enlightened' gurus and the subject of organization for political groups through which they can promote intolerance and social imbalance. Based primarily on 'mass' and on the power to influence through charisma that includes both political and economic forces, the modern religious marketplace is not much different from the governing ideology of modern-day socialism and capitalism, where both conceive of nature as inanimate and the site of perpetual human mastery and exploitation. With this ideological gulf, nature, once a source of awe and reverence that demonstrated power beyond human control, stands for mystery for early mankind, and demystified man stands alone, walking towards annihilation. Although the 'religious' still guides the everyday lives of the rural masses, the force it has is insignificant and often perverted by crooks. Reading myths against this background is then a process of invoking the marginalized.

The actualization of this harmony begins with the non-dual vision that binds humanity with the rest of existence. The dualism of body and mind, and of the world and God, has separated humankind from the rest of the nature. It has also split humankind into two genders with subsequent problems, threatening human civilization itself. On one hand, human civilization has reached its highest aspirations while on the other, human brutality over other races, over other species, and over nature and natural resources has reached new lows. Human aspects of sensation and emotion have been repeatedly denied and the religious focus has shifted from the body to intellect, making spiritual experience into merely philosophical discourse. Reading the myths of Pārvatī against this backdrop is not to claim that ecological issues are explicit in these narratives, neither is it to make a claim that ecological problems can only be solved by reading these myths, but as civilization is a composition of different streams, these myths can be the source for inspiration for social welfare through reunion of the self with nature.

Kālidāsa is aware that the mountain is the source of water, being both the origin of Ganges and several other holy rivers that irrigate India, as well as the physical mechanism keeping clouds within the Indian sub-continent. In the epic KS, when he narrates the birth of Parvata's daughter, he eloquently and at great length describes the mountains and their splendor. This glorification helps us to understand that he is not discussing some gods residing in the mountain, but rather, the mountain itself who is giving birth to Pārvatī, the goddess who wants only to be united with lord Śiva. Her penance to draw Śiva as her consort leaves her parents in awe, whereupon they exclaim, 'Oh! No,' giving the goddess another name, Umā.[8]

The myth of the birth of Pārvatī confirms an embodied and immanent vision of divinity: the divine lives through nature and within creation, sustaining through it, not outside of it. This myth also speaks of birth and death as a natural cycle wherein the two are not negating opposites but rather completing the other. The divine consort is born here, and her presence is found on earth through her birth, death, and regeneration.

The reunion of Śiva and Pārvatī is a metaphor of an embodied cosmology. In this myth, Śiva does not remain isolated in his deep meditative slumber but is conscious of the outside world, of his own body and its needs, and of his surroundings. Nonetheless, it is not an easy union. In Śiva's deep meditation, he withdraws his senses from all worldly experiences, freeing himself from the sphere of emotion. Recognizing the difficulty of reunion with Śiva, Pārvatī also undergoes penance, withdrawing from her senses and emotions. However, her goal is different, to bring Śiva to the mundane world and awaken his emotions.

Śiva's separation from the world is troublesome, as the gods are unable to protect their paradise from being defeated by demons. It is only lord Śiva who could support them and be on their side to fight against the demons, but as long as he is in meditation, he himself is not listening to the prayers of the gods pleading for his assistance in the battlefield. In other words, the lord of gods, if dissociated from mundane experience, is not in communication with the world and will not grant protection or boons. The only way the supreme being can grant what is asked of him is when he has the will. The god without desire is no god at all.

Following the myth, Kāma, the god of desire, is appointed to break the vow of lord Śiva and draw him to the realm of passion and aversion. Kāma's effort bears the fruit of Śiva awakening, but Kāma himself is incinerated to ashes by Śiva's rage. This epitomizes the way the god of desire functions, dying in its body and living through another's awakened desire. Overcoming passion revives desire. In this myth of reunion, Pārvatī's vow to marry Śiva is the metaphor of bringing the self to the body and bodily emotions, whereby Śiva can feel love for Pārvatī, be compassionate to the gods, and fight against the demons. If seen only externally, the myth of Pārvatī is the myth of seduction. When the myth is explored again, this seduction brings divinity to protect the earth. Śiva is in absorption, free from his own bodily feelings and unaware of his surroundings; Śiva is worshipped by gods, but is careless about their

[8] KS 1.26.

feelings and emotions. The myth of Pārvatī is a placeholder for salvation: it is through her self-sacrifice that Śiva can first feel pain and finally the bliss of reunion.

Embedded within this main narrative are other instances that allow us to connect the love of Pārvatī with the love for nature. Pārvatī, as a daughter of the mountain, is deeply connected to her parental home and her parents, the mountains, and to the offspring of mountains, the animals and plants. Kālidāsa does not miss the opportunity to elaborate upon Pārvatī's relation with nature, placing Pārvatī as the caring mother of innocent beings. In both KS and also in *Raghuvaṃśa,* Kālidāsa uses the metaphor of the breast as a pitcher, which Pārvatī uses to sprinkle the plants.[9] In one episode, Pārvatī cannot bear the pain caused by an elephant rubbing his neck on a tree, whereupon she appoints the lion to protect her garden. A further implication of this action is that the land is protected from overgrazing. In this myth, king Dilipa ignorantly uses the land to graze the cattle and the lion appointed by Pārvatī threatens to kill the king.

In the narrative of KS, Pārvatī initiates her penance by planting trees that come into bloom before her penance ends and she is united with Śiva.[10] Pārvatī's return to nature and her care for it in order to be united with Śiva identifies a spiritual path in which the divine is found and felt, not through separation of the mind and body, and nature and culture. Pārvatī's control of consumption as a course of purification demonstrates that the pristine and spiritual within the human are polluted by gluttony and over-accumulation. Pārvatī is eager to leave her childhood home in the mountains to be a divine bride, but that does not translate into ignoring the life and environment of her parental home.

At first glance, the love of Pārvatī appears directed towards humankind and the gods, as the waking of lord Śiva from deep meditation and his engagement to Pārvatī is a requirement for the salvation of gods and humanity. However, Pārvatī's loving care for nature and her intimate relationship with plants and animals both demonstrate that this love envelops all that exists, restoring the harmony and peace interrupted by divisive and destructive demons. At the heart of this emancipation myth is the struggle of Pārvatī, the goddess. The Lord often worshipped in his phallic form is isolated from the surroundings and is in deep absorption. The penance of the self-sacrificing goddess is now to awaken Śiva from the realm of isolated consciousness to physical reality.

Unable to dislodge Śiva from his absorption, Pārvatī undertakes severe

---

[9] KS 5.14; *Raghuvaṃśa* 2.36.

[10] KS 5.60.

penance, providing her with another name, Aparṇā, or 'leaf-less,' having restricted her consumption, denying herself even leaves as sustenance. For both Śiva and Pārvatī, their penance of controlling senses and restricting consumption is the same. This reverses the excessive and exploitive lifestyle of the devas, who have lost their glorious independence due to their greed, lust, and arrogance. And again, as are the devas, so are the asuras. The power of Śiva to bring harmony to the cosmos comes through his strength of asceticism and self-control. In modern consumerism, ten percent of the world's population consumes ninety percent of natural resources. In one part of the earth people are dying of starvation and in the other part, from obesity. This over-consumption, particularly of oil hidden deep into the earth, resonates of the gluttony of Tāraka, the demon that threatens the devas' world.

The myth of Pārvatī embodies the social implication of equality and respect for all forms and stages of life. She herself is the daughter of Himalaya, the source of natural resources and all riches. Sanskrit texts, including the epic of Kālidāsa, never tire of describing the wealth of the Himalayas. At the same time, Hindu myths depict lord Śiva as downtrodden and outcaste. In the myth of Pārvatī that completes the myth of Satī, social balance is maintained and the hierarchy dismantled. If examined in the Indian cultural context, this is a revolutionary myth, in which class, caste, and gender roles are reversed. This new balance is not found at the established center, but emerges from the periphery of the wild and outcaste.

The narrative of Pārvatī culminates with the birth of Kumāra, the fruition of divine engagement. This myth ties both Gangā and Pārvatī together, as Kumāra is a single son of both these mothers. As Gaṅgā is also the daughter of the mountain, this is yet another manifestation of the goddess herself. The significance of the birth of Kumāra is the collective process of regeneration and rejuvenation. The myth that the son of lord Śiva able to fight against the demons is not born of single mother invokes the collective effort that gives rise to emancipation.

The Myth of Recognition: The Subaltern Śakuntalā

Kālidāsa, in the same way, narrates the profoundly rich story of the recognition of Śakuntalā in *Abhijñānaśākuntala* (AŚ). Ecological concern in this drama is explicit from the very first verse, the benediction to Śiva. In this, Kālidāsa invokes the eight bodies of God. Water, fire, and the sacrificer, the sun and the moon, and sky, earth, and air, in Kālidāsa's cosmology, constitute the body of the Lord. Explicitly, there are two categories, the self as the sacrificer, and the physical world that sustains life, and both constitute the divine body. In the myth, the loss of identity for Śakuntalā and the loss of awareness that the king displays both need to be understood in light of this embodied cosmological vision that the poet weaves throughout the story. The union of Śakuntalā with the king is therefore not merely the identity of the repressed, the self-recognition of the forgetful one, the birth of a new nation, but it is also the recognition of the harmony of the nature and the self, as both collectively constitute the body of God.

A deconstructive gaze allows penetration into multiple layers of meaning found in the richly fertile narrative of Śakuntalā.[11] The protagonist in Kālidāsa's drama is an abandoned girl Śakuntalā, the illegitimate child born of the union of a nymph and a sage. As her name suggests, she was raised by birds, or brought up by wild creatures in the wilderness. She later finds shelter in the hermitage of Kaṇva, where she befriends deer and takes care of the garden. In the absence of her adopted parents, king Duṣyanta, etymologically 'the spoiler,' seduces her with the dream of becoming a queen, takes advantage of her innocence, and impregnates her. Bharata, the person whose name gives the identity to the country Bhārata, is born of this union. In this class struggle, Śakuntalā is denied her identity and forced to care for the child alone. Like other romantic comedies of Kālidāsa, Śakuntalā regains her identity as the rightful spouse of Duṣyanta and her son Bharata becomes the powerful king.

The opening of the drama gives a powerful message of the contrast between Duṣyanta and Śakuntalā. Duṣyanta hunts innocent wildlife whereas Śakuntalā protects, heals, and cares for them; Duṣyanta crushes the wild plants with the wheels of his chariot and the hooves of the horses, wheras Śakuntalā tenderly sprinkles water on the plants and cares for the garden; Śakuntalā embodies the teachings of the sage Kaṇva and practices non-violence while Duṣyanta, as a ruler always needing to define his power, finds his glory in his ability to shed the blood of innocents. The union of these two opposites suggests the possible co-existence of those who believe in war and those who do not.

In the narrative, Śakuntalā takes the role of daughter, wife, and mother. As a daughter she grows up like the abandoned children found in the streets; as wife she is forgotten and neglected by one imagined as her

---

[11] The narrative of Śakuntalā first appears in the *Mahābhārata*. This story is found also in the *Padmapurāṇa*. For detail, see M. R. Katre, *The Abhijñānaśākuntalam of Kālidāsa.* Delhi: Motilal Banarsidass, 1969, pages cxi-cxxiii.

husband who saw her only as a passing fancy; and as mother, she reverses the legacy of her own absent mother, and through her child she revisits her past and achieves satisfaction through her motherly love for her child. The struggle of Śakuntalā is that of survival, existence, and a life of dignity. The *jouissance* of Śakuntalā lies not in the moment of passion with Duṣyanta but in giving birth to Bharata, whose glory gave the name to the country. Bharata embodies both the might of his father and untamed qualities of his mother: he befriends lions and fights with tigers.

Bharata, the founding father of India, is the result of the relationship between the elite and the subaltern. Without recognizing the power of Bharata, king Duṣyanta cannot rise to greater heights. The dramatic 'recognition of Śakuntalā' (*Abhijñāna-śākuntala*) is the recognition of the suppressed class by the elite; it is the story of interdependence and co-existence. This story still speaks for the future of India, that the real potentiality of the country lives in the streets among the illiterate masses suffering from malnutrition.

This story expresses the stark contrast between two Indian women, Urvaśī and Śakuntalā. Although there are other female characters in the drama, they lack agency; their subjective paradigm is confined. These two women are aware of and exercise their agency. Urvaśī lives to fulfill her lust; she is the temptress. Her daughter, on the contrary, has no place for lust; she is seduced and conceives. While Urbaśī abandons her child, Śakuntalā devotes her life to her son. The poet enlivens these two characters in two different ways. Utterly absent throughout the drama, Urvaśī speaks through silence. Śakuntalā, however, overpowers all the acts of the play; the other characters there simply remind the viewer of the presence of Śakuntalā. Through the presence and absence of these two characters, the poet indicates that the victimized body cannot reverse the lack of agency by simple clitoral emancipation. Śakuntalā lives for greater liberation, the recognition that grants Bharata the kingly throne. This achievement of Śakuntalā compensates for the *jouissance* of Urvaśī. In this, Śakuntalā embodies the entire Indian repressed and brings them to the throne, and unlike the pleasure Urvaśī gains in momentary seduction, Śakuntalā has the greater ability of self-control and of non-violent struggle against the repressor.

The Revival of the Myths

The range of literature addressed in this discussion is primarily mythical and poetic. In the light of a new rationality, these can be seen as subdued voices, with 'truth' reduced to objective facts, turned into data that does not speak to, or of, human awareness the way a pulsating heart does. In this invocation of the peripheral, the myth of Satī carries a truth deeper than mere data, as it speaks in the language of integrity. The liberating myth of Ganges is another example of the suggestibility of myths. The body of Satī found in the form of India is enlivened by the veins and life-juice of the Ganges. These archetypal myths suffuse all other goddess myths with their cognitive and ecological implications. Sacred groves of the goddess are primarily sustained by the myth of Satī, as her limbs of Satī are present in every sacred grove, and in every hill.[12] Likewise, the Ganges is present in every drop of water that flows on Indian sub-continent.

The identification of the goddess with nature can be further demonstrated by another myth, that of Pārvatī. In many respects, this is the continuation of the myth of Satī. Satī is reborn as Pārvatī and marries lord Śiva after he emerges from his solitude in the Himalaya mountains. The marital bond of Gaṅgā and Pārvatī with lord Śiva gives an integral vision of the self and the body and its vitality. Kālidāsa identifies the Himalayas as the soul of the gods (*devatātman).*[13] In the absence of the Himalayas, there is neither the goddess of groves nor of the rivers. The possibility of life on the lower plains relies upon the balanced life of the snowy mountains.

The original message of these myths unites the divine and human, and nature and consciousness. This sacred gaze is not a process of constituting divine objects, as this completely usurps the original intent of the message. While the sacred groves remain and the Ganges is still a center of devotion, worship shifts from the recognition of the sacredness of life and nature to a confinement of the divine within conditioned space. Worshipping one tree and destroying the forest does not correspond to the message. Making *murtis* of Gangā and worshipping Ganges in the temple does not carry the message of the myth, but simply distorts it, turning the original intent into a misappropriated reduction. For an observing Hindu who invokes the Ganges while taking a bath in a pond or in water from a tap, the myth of Ganges remains alive, confirming all waters sustaining life to be divine. The myth of Satī or of Pārvatī is not to identify one tree or one rock as divine, but rather to ensure that the mountains and plains as the body of Satī remain sacred, and the snowy peaks as the origin of both goddesses may continue to sustain the people of the continent.

---

[12] See Frederique Apffel-Marglin and Pramod Parajuli in *Hinduism and Ecology*, pp. 291-316.

[13] KS 1.1.

The myths of both Pārvatī and Ganges are primarily the myths of healing: Śiva unendingly laments the death of Satī in isolation, and the love of Pārvatī reassures; Sagara's sons are dead and the only consolation for Bhagīratha is the liberating touch of the Ganges. As Himalaya is often depicted as the source of medicine in Indian myths, this restoration does not end in healing surface wounds, but also includes healing burning (or broken) hearts. In the cosmic vision of Śiva and Satī, the first one witnesses death and birth and separates from sensation. In the case of Satī, life encompasses both birth and death, and it is the unchanging foundation of momentary events.

Redefining the 'Rational'

The myths of the goddess are not merely the glory of the feminine force that pulsates in the individual and society, in nature and humankind. They suggest integral consciousness that combines both body and mind. The collapse of integral thinking is linked with the way the rational has been defined as a fundamental duality, with the spirit opposing the body, and nature opposing culture. The process of division and subordination has great implications in our lives. Our family values have been shattered and our society splits into working and leisure classes. The greater freedom that individuals preserve now is the choice to be a slave in one or another corporation. The individual cry for social and ecological transformation is marginalized when truths are made, packaged, and sold for the benefit of the few.

In this paradigm, nature is at the bottom of systematized repression, because it cannot move, speak, get outraged, or strike back. Yes it can, in the long run, through cataclysmic change. And this change disproportionately affects the proletariat that has limited or no resources.

An alternative to this is to accept the non-dual argument wherein nature and humankind do not sit next to each other as two strangers or as master and slave, but with the human acknowledgement of the essential being of nature. In this non-dual argument, plants and humans play the game of life in the garden of nature together, acknowledging partnership free from the complex of domination. The myth of Satī speaks for all time, with the sacred felt and experienced in different sites as the limbs of Satī's body. The divinity, Pārvatī, manifests in and through nature, not outside of this world and controlling it.

This new rationale will redefine what is perceived as right action. Following this, one will not have the right over another's human labor. According to this rationale, a human being does not own the land or control the property, but is a caretaker, a steward. A human being, in this vision, is not removed from the land but is part and parcel of the dust from which he comes and to which he returns. This is the myth of Satī, where the earth is the body of the goddess.

Notes on Contributors

E. N. Anderson is professor emeritus of anthropology at the University of California, Riverside, and affiliate professor at the University of Washington. He lives near Seattle. He continues to work on traditional China and on Native American cultures. His publications include *The Food of China* (Yale University Press, 1988), *Ecologies of the Heart* (Oxford University Press, 1996), and *Everyone Eats* (New York University Press, 2005).

Christopher Key Chapple is the Navin and Pratima Doshi Professor of Indic and Comparative Theology at Loyola Marymount University. He served as Assistant Director of the Institute for Advanced Studies of World Religions and taught Sanskrit, Hinduism, Jainism, and Buddhism for five years at the State University of New York at Stony Brook before joining the faculty at LMU. Dr. Chapple's research interests have focused on the renouncer religious traditions of India: Yoga, Jainism, and Buddhism. He has published several books, including *Karma and Creativity* (1986), a co-translation of the *Yoga Sutras* of Patanjali (1991) and *Nonviolence to Animals, Earth, and Self in Asian Traditions* (1993), *Hinduism and Ecology* (2000), a co-edited volume, *Jainism and Ecology: Nonviolence in the Web of Life* (2002) and *Reconciling Yogas* (2003).

Piya Chatterjee is associate professor of women's studies at the University of California-Riverside. She is a historical anthropologist who works on colonialism, labor, and women's politics in the global South. Her first book *A Time for Tea: Women, Labor and Post Colonial Politics on an Indian Plantation* was published by Duke University Press, 2001 and Zubaan Press, New Delhi, 2003. A co-edited volume (with Manali Desai and Parama Roy), *States of Truma: Gender and Violence in South Asia* is forthcoming from Zubaan, New Delhi. She has published journal articles on pedagogy, feminist ethnography, colonialism and labor.

David B. Gray is an Assistant Professor of Religious Studies at Santa Clara University, in Santa Clara, California, where he teaches a wide range of Asian religions courses. His research focuses on the development of Tantric Buddhist traditions in South Asia, and their dissemination in Tibet and East Asia. His publications include numerous journal articles and book chapters, as well as *The Cakrasamvāra Tantra: A Study and Annotated Translation* (New York: American Institute of Buddhist Studies/Columbia University Press, 2007).

Phyllis K. Herman is an Associate Professor of Religious Studies at California State University, Northridge, California. She received her Ph.D. in the History of Religions from the University of California, Los Angeles. She currently serves as chairperson of the religious studies department at CSUN where she teaches courses in Indian religions. She is the author of many journal articles and book chapters. She is currently working on a book using Sita and Rama as mortal and divine couple in the context of the various Hindu dramas that glorify them.

Janet Hoskins is Professor of Anthropology at the University of Southern California, Los Angeles, where she teaches courses on the arts and cultures of Vietnam, religious diversity, ethnographic film, visual studies and post colonial perspectives. She is the author of two books, *The Play of Time* (winner of the 1996 Benda Prize in Southeast Asian Studies, Association of Asian Studies) and *Biographical Objects* (1998), and the editor of three others (*Headhunting and Social Imagination in Southeast Asia, Fragments from Forests and Libraries, A Space Between Oneself and Oneself: Anthropology as the Search for the Self*).

Helen Hye-Sook Hwang Ph.D. has taught in colleges in Southern California including Cal Poly Pomona, Claremont Graduate University, and University of Redlands. She is presently turning her Ph.D. dissertation into a book tentatively entitled, *The Mago Hypothesis: Reinstating Mago, the Great Goddess, and Magoism, a Trans-patriarchal Gynocentric Tradition of East Asia (Korea , China , and Japan)*. Her articles include "Returning Home with Mago, the Great Goddess from East Asia " in *Trivia: Voices of Feminism* (Issue 6, September 2007) and "The Female Principle in the Magoist Cosogomy" in *Ochre Journal of Women's Spirituality* (forthcoming 2007).

Malgorzata (Margaret) Kruszewska is a Ph.D. candidate in the Philosophy and Religion of Asian and Comparative Studies Program at California Institute of Integral Studies, San Francisco. She teaches comparative mythology and religious studies at Santa Rosa Junior College in California. She has written on female centered spiritual practices in yogic traditions, the Black Madonnas of her native Poland and feminist methodologies in religious studies. Her essays have been published in *She Is Everywhere* and in the *Journal of Women's Studies*. She is also a theater playwright; her produced works include "Daddy meets Durga," "MarX' Daughter," and "MotherGhost."

Kenneth D. Lee is an Assistant Professor of Asian Religions, teaching for the Religious Studies Department at California State University, Northridge. He received his Ph.D. at Columbia University ('01), where he specialized in medieval Japanese Buddhism. His book, *The Prince and the Monk*, discusses the importance of Shotoku worship in Shinran's Buddhism during medieval Japan. He is an active member of the American Academy of Religion and is currently the Chair of the Buddhist Studies Group for the AAR Western Regional Section.

June McDaniel is Professor of Religious Studies at the College of Charleston in Charleston, South Carolina, where she teaches courses on world religions, mysticism, religions of India, myth, ritual and symbol, sacred texts of the East, women and religion, and other areas. She has written three books: *The Madness of the Saints: Ecstatic Religion in Bengal* (University of Chicago Press, 1989); *Making Virtuous Daughters and Wives* (SUNY Press, 2003); and *Offering Flowers, Feeding Skulls: Popular Goddess Worship in West Bengal* (Oxford University Press, 2004). She has also published many articles in journals and edited volumes.

Mary-Ann Milford-Lutzker, Professor of Asian Art History, holds the Carver Endowed Chair in East Asian Studies at Mills College, where she is also Provost and Dean of the Faculty. She has written numerous articles on Indian art and curated exhibitions focusing on contemporary Indian women artists. Her current research is on globalization in the contemporary art world, focusing on the art of India. She serves on the Board of Directors of the College Art Association, ASIANetwork, the Society for the Art and Cultural History of India, and the Advisory Committee for the Society for Asian Art, Asian Art Museum, San Francisco.

Bidyut Mohanty, Head of Women's Studies Department, Institute of Social Sciences at Delhi University, is currently a Visiting Professor in the Global and International Studies, University of California, Santa Barbara. She is a specialist on famine, agrarian history and decentralization studies with a focus on gender, culture and development. She combines grassroots activism with participatory research including a continuing program relating to elected women grassroots leaders. Her publications include several research papers and edited books, among them: *Urbanization in Developing Countries: Access to Basic Services and Community Participation* (1993); *Women and Political Empowerment* (Annual volumes from 1995 to 2006).

Deepak Shimkhada received his Ph.D. from Claremont Graduate University. He was in the faculty of Claremont McKenna College in Claremont, California where he taught courses on Asian religions including Hinduism, Buddhism and the Visions of the Divine Feminine. He is currently an Adjunct Professor at California State University, Northridge. His publications include numerous journal papers and three edited books. He is active in academic as well as local communities. He is the founding president of the Foundation for Indic Philosophy and Culture, President of Asian Studies on the Pacific Coast and vice president of South Asian Studies Association.

Gang Song is a Visiting Assistant Professor of Chinese language, literature, and culture at Lafayette College, PA. In addition to earning B.A. and M.A. degrees in Chinese language and literature from Beijing University, he holds a Ph.D. degree from the Department of East Asian Languages and Cultures at the University of Southern California. His doctoral dissertation explores the hybrid Christian-Confucian identity formed and transformed through Christian dialogues in 17th century China. He has presented his research on Sino-Western cultural exchanges at major conferences and published several articles. His most recent article on Jesuit cartography in China will be published in the *China on Paper* (Los Angeles: Getty Research Institute, forthcoming in November 2007).

Sthaneshwar Timalsina is Associate Professor in the Department of Religious Studies, San Diego State University, California. His research interests include Indian philosophy, Tantric traditions, literary theory, and ritual studies. His first book, *Seeing and Appearance*, was published in 2006 by Shaker Verlag, and his second book, *Consciousness in Indian*

Philosophy, was published in 2008 by Routledge. Besides these books, he has published numerous articles in refereed journals